The
Cambridge Lectures

T. Kerzner, E. O'D. Brown, A. L. Julien, R. S. G. Chester, M. R. Beauregard, R. H. Vogel, B. Williams, B. Langille, P. M. Sweeney, M. R. V. Storrow, P. E. Bernier, R. G. Ferguson, J. R. Belleghem, A. C. Hamilton, J. L. Bowles, J. A. Campion, N. Waterman, K. J. Glasner, H. M. Kindred, W. L. Ryan, E. R. A. Edwards, D. M. M. Goldie, D. H. Fricker, D. W. Shaw, B. MacKinnon, E. J. C. Stewart, W. L. Hoyt, S. G. Stratton, R. E. Logan, H. C. McKay, F. C. Munro, B. P. Goodman, B. Gibson, F. S. Weatherston, J. R. H. Kirkpatrick, R. R. McMurtry, D. Mendes da Costa, D. H. Jones, I. M. MacKeigan, J. Blom, M. Skowronska-Binek, L. Bernstein, C. Curtis, S. Tanner, L. Porteous, R. J. Matas, R. A. Mix, M. Krasnick, G. L. Gerrand, L. A. Kitz, P. B. Currie, D. N. Plumley, D. G. Barker, E. A. McFadyen, E. L. Collins, E. Greville, D. Gillis, R. Grondin, D. Matas, R. W. Cosman, D. T. Rogers, J. Polika, L. Cecchetto, A. Gnat, B. Wein, A. E. Charlton, E. G. Hachborn, A. V. Parish, S. K. Gudmundseth, T. A. Dohm, C. B. Cohen, D. L. Haskett, L. J. Lane, G. I. Lang, M. C. Shumiatcher, J. Lessard, G. R. Fournier, G. Beaudoin, L. S. Bohnen, G. Roberge, E. Mitchell Thomas, J. B. Rooney, B. Emes, R. Tasse, A. M. Linden, H. C. B. Maddison, K. J. Gray, G. Gall, S. Oxner, C. Fortin, A. H. Hollingworth, R. W. Thompson, D. R. Morand, H. G. Chappell, J. L. Davies, F. J. E. Jordan, D. R. Neilson, L. F. Cashman C. J. A. Hughes, D. W. Bowett, N. T. Nemetz, D. H. Carruthers, P. Martin, J. Deschenes, R. B. Peterson, G. Ferguson, F. W. Johnson, R. R. Taylor, C. O. D. Branson, P. J. Le Sage, R. C. E. Wilson, J. M. Murphy, L. W. Houlden, D. J. Fleming, D. C. Ross, J. Y. Mercier, R. Noyes-Roberts.

Not Available for Photograph: R. Abella, C. B. Acheson, J. A. Agrios, E. D. Bayda, M. Bessner, M. Bruce, E. M. Culliton, G. M. Eamon, A. Esau, W. Z. Estey, L. Fast, P. C. M. Freeman, G. Henderson, M. D. Howard, T. L. James, J. P. Jorgensen, R. Langlois, L. F. Lindholm, A. Maloney, D. McRae, A. K. Mitchell, P. C. Nason, J. J. Robinette, H. K. Siddall, J. K. Stewart, P. S. Stewart.

The Cambridge Lectures

Selected Papers Based upon Lectures Delivered at the Cambridge Conference of the Canadian Institute for Advanced Legal Studies, 1979

Edited by
Derek Mendes da Costa, Q.C., S.J.D. (Harv.), LL.D. (Lond.),
Chairman, Ontario Law Reform Commission

Canadian Institute for Advanced Legal Studies
Institut canadien d'études juridiques superieures

BUTTERWORTHS
Toronto

The Cambridge Lectures

Printed and bound in Canada

The Butterworth Group of Companies

Canada:
Butterworth & Co. (Canada) Ltd., Toronto and Vancouver

United Kingdom:
Butterworth & Co. (Publishers) Ltd., London

Australia:
Butterworths Pty. Ltd., Sydney

New Zealand:
Butterworths of New Zealand Ltd., Wellington

South Africa:
Butterworth & Co. (South Africa) Ltd., Durban

United States:
Butterworth (Publishers) Inc., Boston
Butterworth (Legal Publishers) Inc., Seattle
Mason Publishing Company, St. Paul

Canadian Cataloguing in Publication Data

Canadian Institute for Advanced Legal Studies. Cambridge Conference (1979)
The Cambridge lectures

Bibliography: p.
ISBN 0-409-84907-3

1. Law — Congresses. I. Mendes da Costa, Derek, 1929-
II. Title.

K175.C36 340 C81-094233-X

Foreword

The Canadian Institute for Advanced Legal Studies was incorporated "for the benefit of the Canadian community and for the advancement of the administration of justice in Canada to foster, encourage and promote education in law, in legal science and in law reform."

As a first step in meeting these objectives the Institute organized a program that was conducted from July 9 to July 20, 1979 at Queens' College, Cambridge, England. During that fortnight, surrounded by academic history dating back to the 12th century, eminent Canadian and English judges, legal scholars and practising lawyers delivered lectures and led seminars on recent developments in the law. These lectures and seminars were attended by Canadians involved at all levels in the administration of justice from virtually every province and territory in Canada. Apart from the new ideas and concepts to which the participants were exposed in the course of the program, by retreating to Queens' College for two intensive weeks of academic study a unique degree of interaction, discussion and exchange of concepts took place between the Canadian participants and their English and European colleagues which can be described as no less than remarkable.

In order to share at least some aspects of the program with those who were not able to attend and hear some of the leading legal lecturers of the day, the Institute, with the co-operation of many of the lecturers and Butterworths, has published this selection of papers given at the conference. I sincerely trust that you will find the ideas and analysis within these pages to be as stimulating and exciting as did those who had the opportunity to attend.

The Hon. Mr. Justice Douglas H. Carruthers, President,
Canadian Institute for Advanced Legal Studies.

Preface

The first Conference of the Canadian Institute for Advanced Legal Studies was held at Queens' College, Cambridge, from July 9 to July 20, 1979. Papers were delivered during the morning sessions of the Conference, and the afternoon sessions were devoted to panel discussions. Eminent Canadian and British judges, legal scholars and practising lawyers participated in the lectures and the panel discussions.

The organization of the Conference was a formidable task that involved many committed people. Without the untiring work and effort of our Cambridge colleagues, the success of the Conference would not have been possible. It would be neither desirable nor feasible to name all those who did so much for the Conference. However, the Board of Governors wish to acknowledge, in particular, the splendid co-operation of Dr. Derek W. Bowett, Q.C., the President of Queens' College, and Dr. Kevin J. Gray, Fellow of Queens' College.

In planning the Conference, although the Board of Governors had in mind the possibility of publication, no arrangements were made for the delivery of manuscripts. It was the quality of the lectures and the panel presentations, and the interest that the papers generated in the audience, that crystallized our decision to publish these Proceedings. In the case of some participants, the task of gathering material was an easy one: the presentation was delivered from a manuscript, and the manuscript was, there and then, ready for publication. In the majority of cases, however, no manuscript was available. Nevertheless, many of the participants have been good enough to prepare for publication manuscripts that are based upon and that reflect, as far as possible, the presentations at the Conference.

Our thanks are due to our publishers, Butterworth & Co. (Canada) Ltd.: in particular, to our editor, Marie Graham, and to Peter M. Horowitz and Kathleen J. Johnson.

The papers contained in this Volume represent a substantial portion of the Proceedings of the Cambridge Conference. We hope that they will be of interest. We hope also that they will enable the reader to capture the flavour of what we believe to have been a most stimulating and worthwhile experience.

Dr. Derek Mendes da Costa, Q.C.
Program Coordinator

Table of Contents

Biographical Notes

P. S. ATIYAH

studied law at Magdalen College, Oxford, and has taught in universities in four continents, including the Australian National University, the Yale Law School, and Oxford, where he currently holds the Professorship of English Law. His published works include *The Sale of Goods, Accidents, Compensation and the Law* and, most recently, *The Rise and Fall of Freedom of Contract.* Professor Atiyah holds the degree of D.C.L. from Oxford University, and is also a Fellow of the British Academy.

GÉRALD A. BEAUDOIN

Professor of constitutional law, at the Faculty of Law, University of Ottawa. B.A., LL.L. and M.A. from the University of Montreal and D.E.S. from the University of Ottawa. Member of the Quebec Bar, 1954; appointed Queen's Counsel, 1969. Practised law with Paul Gérin-Lajoie in 1955. Advisory Counsel in Justice 1956-1965. Assistant Parliamentary Counsel of the House of Commons 1965-69. Civil law dean, University of Ottawa 1969-1979. Author of "Essais sur la Constitution", University of Ottawa Press. Author of several articles in Canadian and foreign legal periodicals and reviews. Member of the Royal Society of Canada 1977. Member of the Pepin-Robarts Commission on National Unity 1977-79. Officer of the Order of Canada 1980. Vice-President for Canada of the Institut international de droit d'expression française. President of the Canadian Law Deans, 1972-73; President of the Constitutional Law Section of the Canadian Bar Association 1971-73.

DOUGLAS McK. BROWN

is a partner in the firm of Russell & DuMoulin. He was admitted to the Bar of British Columbia in 1936. Preparatory Education: University of British Columbia, B.A., 1933. Legal Education: Vancouver Law School and Cambridge University. President of the Vancouver Bar Association, 1957 and appointed Queen's Counsel, 1962. Vice-President for British Columbia, Canadian Bar Association, 1967-1968. Co-author of the Canadian Bar Association Report, *Towards a New Canada*. Fellow, American College of Trial Lawyers. Trustee, Vancouver Art Gallery. Governor, Vancouver Aquarium Association.

THE HONOURABLE JULES DESCHÊNES

Chief Justice of the Superior Court of the Province of Québec. Attended Collège André-Grasset, Collège de Montréal and Séminaire de Philosophie; B.A., m.c.l. (1943); Faculty of Law, University of Montréal; Master of laws m.c.l.; medals of Governor General and Lieutenant-Governor (1946). He was admitted to the Bar of the Province of Québec in 1946, Queen's Counsel (1961). He was lecturer on Private International Law at the Faculty of Law of the University of Montréal (1962-1969). Senior partner of the firm Deschênes, de Grandpré, Colas, Godin & Lapointe (1966-1972). Justice of the Court of Appeal of Québec (March 1st 1972—August 23rd, 1973). Chief Justice of the Superior Court of Québec (August 23rd, 1973—). The author of *L'Université: Son rôle, le rôle de ses composantes, les relations entre ses composantes* (in collaboration, as President, with the other members of the *Commission conjointe* of the University of Montreal), *Les Presses de l'Université de Montréal*, November 3rd, 1969; *The Sword and the Scales*, Butterworth & Co. (Canada) Ltd., Toronto, 1979; *Les plateaux de la balance*, Editions Leméac Inc., Montréal, 1979; and numerous articles in legal periodicals.

THE RIGHT HONOURABLE LORD JUSTICE DONALDSON

called to the Bar, 1946; appointed Queen's Counsel, 1961; appointed Judge of the High Court, Queen's Bench Division, 1966; President National Industrial Relations Court, 1971-4; appointed Lord Justice of Appeal, 1979.

THE HONOURABLE W. Z. ESTEY

was born in Saskatoon, Saskatchewan in 1919. He was educated at the University of Saskatchewan (B.A., 1940; LL.B., 1942) and at Harvard University (LL.M., 1946). He served in the Canadian Army and Royal Canadian Air Force during World War II. Professor, College of Law, University of Saskatchewan 1946-47; Lecturer, Osgoode Hall Law School 1947-51; Member of Bars of Saskatchewan 1942 and Ontario 1947. Practised law in Toronto 1947-72 and was appointed Queen's Counsel, Province of Ontario 1960. He was appointed to the Court of Appeal, Supreme Court of Ontario in January, 1973; Chief Justice of the High Court, Supreme Court of Ontario June, 1975; Chief Justice of Ontario, December 1976; Puisne Judge, Supreme Court of Canada, September 1977; Commissioner, Steel Profits Inquiry May, 1974—Royal Commission of Inquiry; Commissioner, Air Canada Inquiry April, 1975—Royal Commission of Inquiry. He was formerly a Bencher of The Law Society of Upper Canada; President for Ontario, Canadian Bar Association and Chairman of Board and President of Canadian Cablesystems Ltd. At present he is an Honorary Lifetime Member of the Board of Governors, York-Finch General Hospital; Vice-President, Canadian Institute for Advanced Legal Studies; Board of Directors, Canadian Institute for Administration of Justice; Chairman, Hockey Canada; Honourary Chairman, Canadian Judges Conference and Chairman, Foundation for Legal Research.

D. M. M. GOLDIE

is a partner in the firm of Russell & DuMoulin, Barristers and Solicitors, Vancouver, B.C.; Secondary education: University of British Columbia (B. Comm.) and Harvard Law School (LL.B.). He was called to the British Columbia bar in 1950; appointed Queen's Counsel in 1972. General civil litigation with some emphasis on constitutional and administrative law cases.

GORDON F. HENDERSON

is a partner in the firm of Gowling & Henderson, Ottawa, Ontario. Educated at the University of Toronto (B.A. 1934), Osgoode Hall 1937, called to the Bar of Ontario in 1937 and the Bar of Quebec in 1952. Officer, Order of Canada in 1977; Queen's Counsel in 1953; University of Ottawa (LL.D. 1979). Lecturer in Industrial Property, University of Ottawa 1962—present; Public Law, Carleton University 1946-64. A Bencher of the Law Society of Upper Canada; Editor, Canadian Patent Reporter; Fellow, American College of Trial Lawyers; Honorary Vice-Consul for Liberia. Canadian Bar Activities: Past Chairman, Jurimetrics Committee; Member, Judiciary Committee; Chairman, Canadian Bar Association 59th Annual Meeting; Treasurer, 1978; Vice-President, 1979; a Founder and First Chairman of the Board of Governors, Canadian Law Information Council.

J. A. JOLOWICZ

born, London, 11 April 1926; educated, Oundle School; Trinity College, Cambridge. Fellow of Trinity College, Cambridge, since 1952; Barrister-at-Law, 1952 (Inner Temple and Gray's Inn); Bencher, Gray's Inn, 1978; Professor of Comparative Law, University of Cambridge, 1976.

GARETH JONES

Fellow of Trinity College since 1961 and Downing Professor of the Laws of England in the University of Cambridge since 1975; Honorary Bencher of Lincoln's Inn. Visiting Professorships include Harvard, Chicago and Western Ontario. He is the author with Sir Robert Goff of the *Law of Restitution*.

THE HONOURABLE MR. JUSTICE KERR

was born in 1921, and educated on the Continent and at Aldenham School. During the war he was a serving officer in the RAF as a pilot for 4 years. He obtained first-class honours in law at Clare College, Cambridge, in 1947 and was called to the Bar by Lincoln's Inn in 1948. He joined the chambers of Mr. William McNair KC, which specialised in commercial work, and took silk in 1961. He was a member of the Bar Council and later of the Senate from 1968 to 1972 and became a Bencher of his Inn in 1968. From 1961 to 1971 he was a Deputy Chairman of Hampshire Quarter Sessions. In 1972 he was appointed a High Court judge assigned to the Queen's Bench Division and was appointed a judge of the Commercial and Admiralty Courts. He has written a number of articles and lectures on commercial law and practice. In May 1978 he was appointed Chairman of the Law Commission.

KURT LIPSTEIN

Ph.D., LL.D. (Cantab). Emeritus Professor of Comparative Law, in the University of Cambridge, Fellow of Clare College; of the Middle Temple barrister and Hon. Master of the Bench; formerly University lecturer (1946-1962); Reader in Conflict of Laws (1962-1973); Visiting Professor, University of Pennsylvania in Philadelphia (1962); Northwestern University, Chicago (1966, 1968); Professeur Associé, University of Paris I (1977-78).

THE HONOURABLE LORD MACKENZIE STUART

Judge of the Court of Justice of the European Communities since January, 1973. Born 1924, and educated at Fettes College, Edinburgh, and at Cambridge and Edinburgh Universities. Served in Royal Engineers 1942-1947. He practiced at the Scottish bar from 1951 to 1972 when appointed Judge of the Court of Session. He is the author of numerous articles in legal periodicals and of the 1977 Hamlyn lectures published as "The European Communities and the Rule of Law"; Honorary degrees from Stirling, Exeter and Edinburgh Universities. Honorary Bencher of the Middle Temple.

THE HONOURABLE R. ROY McMURTRY

is the Member of the Ontario Legislature for Toronto-Eglinton, and serves as Attorney General and Solicitor General for Ontario. Educated at the University of Toronto and at Osgoode Hall Law School, he was called to the Ontario Bar in 1958 and was appointed Queen's Counsel in 1969. Following sixteen years of private legal practice Mr. McMurtry was first elected to political office as the M.P.P. for the Toronto Riding of Eglinton in September, 1975 and became Attorney General two weeks later. On September 11th, 1978, he was appointed Solicitor General for Ontario. Mr. McMurtry is a Governor of Frontier College, the honorary chairman of the Big Brothers of Metropolitan Toronto and a National Director of the St. Leonard Society of Canada.

BASIL S. MARKESINIS

LL.B., D.IUR. (Athens), M.A., Ph.D. (Cantab), of Gray's Inn, Barrister (England); Advocate to the Supreme Court (Athens); Teaching Assistant to Chair of History of Law, University of Athens 1965-1968; Fellow of Churchill College, Cambridge 1970-73; Fellow of Trinity College, Cambridge and Director of Studies in Law 1975- ; Lecturer in Law of the University of Cambridge 1975- ; Publications: *The Mother's right of Guardianship according to the Greek Civil Code* (1968); *The Theory and Practice of Dissolution of Parliament*, C.U.P. (1972) (Yorke Prize Essay); *The English Law of Torts: A Comparative Introduction* (co-author) (Brussels, 1976); *An Outline of the Law of Agency* (co-author) (Butterworths, 1979); *Delictual Liability for Unintentional Harm in the Common Law and the Civil law* (co-author) to be published by the C.U.P. in 1981. Also many articles and notes in *Parliamentary Affairs, The Law Quarterly Review* and the *Cambridge Law Journal.*

SIR ALAN MARRE

KCB. British Parliamentary Commissioner for Administration from 1971 to 1976. He was also appointed to be the first Health Service Commissioner in 1973, holding that office also until 1976, and was *ex officio* a member of the Commission for Local Administration from 1974 to 1976. His previous career was in the British Civil Service, where his final appointment, before he became Parliamentary Commissioner, was as Second Permanent Secretary in the Department of Health and Social Security. Among his current appointments is the Vice-Chairmanship of a central Committee which advises the Government which medical consultants should receive distinction awards. He also holds various voluntary appointments.

THE RIGHT HONOURABLE LORD MURRAY (Ronald King Murray)

born 1922, Glasgow, Scotland; graduated Edinburgh University; served in H.M. Forces 1941-1946, latterly in S.E.A.C. as Capt., R.E.M.E.; lecturer in law of evidence, Edinburgh University, 1969-74; Member of Parliament for Leith (Lab.) 1970-1979; Queen's Counsel 1967; P.C. 1974; Lord Advocate 1974-1979; appointed Supreme Court judge (Scotland) May 1979.

JOHN CYRIL SMITH

Professor of Law in the University of Nottingham since 1958, and Head of Department of Law 1956-74, and since 1977; Educ: Downing Coll., Cambridge (Hon. Fellow, 1977). Served Royal Artillery, 1942-47 (Captain). B.A. 1949, LL.B. 1950, M.A. 1954, FBA 1973, LL.D. 1975 (Cantab). Called to Bar, Lincoln's Inn, 1950; Hon. Bencher, 1977. Assistant Lecturer in Law, Nottingham University, 1950-52. Commonwealth Fund Fellow, Harvard Law School 1952-53. Lecturer, 1952-56, Reader, 1956-57, Pro-Vice-Chancellor, 1973-77, Nottingham University. Publications: (with Professor J. A. C. Thomas) *A Casebook on Contract,* 1957, (now in 6th edition); (with Brian Hogan) *Criminal Law*, 1965 (now in 4th edition); *Law of Theft*, 1968 (now in 4th edition); *Criminal Law, Cases and Materials,* 1975 (appearing shortly in 2nd edition); articles in legal periodicals. Appointed Queen's Counsel in 1979. Member of the Home Secretary's Policy Advisory Committee.

JEAN-PIERRE FRANK EUGENE WARNER

Advocate-General, Court of Justice of the European Communities, since 1973; Educ: Sainte Croix de Neuilly; Ecole des Roches; Harrow; Trinity College, Cambridge (MA). Served in Rifle Bde, 1943-47, Actg Major, GSO2 (Ops) GHQ Far East. Called to Bar, Lincoln's Inn, 1950 (Cassel Schol.), Bencher 1966; Mem. Gen. Council of Bar, 1969-72; appointed Queen's Counsel 1972. Junior Counsel: to Registrar of Restrictive Trading Agreements, 1961-64; to Treasury (Chancery), 1964-72. Councillor: Royal Borough of Kensington, 1959-65 (Chm., Gen. Purposes Cttee, 1963-65); Royal Borough of Kensington and Chelsea, 1964-68. Dir. Warner & Sons Ltd. and subsids., 1952-70. Vice-Pres., UK Assoc. for European Law, 1975- . Liveryman, Worshipful Co. of Weavers, 1957. Chevalier du Tastevin, 1952, Commandeur 1960.

GLANVILLE WILLIAMS

Queen's Counsel, LL.B., M.A., LL.D., FBA, is an Honorary Fellow of Jesus College, Cambridge, and an Honorary Bencher of the Middle Temple. He was formerly Professor of Public Law and Quain Professor of Jurisprudence in the University of London, and Rouse Ball Professor of English Law in the University of Cambridge. He has been a member of several law reform committees, including the Criminal Law Revision Committee; and is the author of numerous works including his recent *Textbook of Criminal Law* (1978).

1

The Office of The Attorney General

The Honourable R. Roy McMurtry, Q.C.

Today has been an auspicious, even a historic, day. We have inaugurated a unique, and to my mind, a very significant venture of co-operation between the legal communities in our two countries of England and Canada. It is hard to over-estimate the ongoing significance of this conference. It will give us all a greater sense of the current development, and future direction of the law. It will cause us to reflect on the similarities and differences between our two legal systems, and will strengthen our recognition of the common heritage of ordered justice under law which links our two nations.

The office of Attorney General is a unique example of the English genius for developing eminently practical and exportable institutions which are then patched and altered to meet new conditions and new countries. It is an office of great history, with many different facets. The Attorney General has unique responsibilities to the Crown, to the courts, to the legislative and executive branches of government.

I have had the privilege of serving as Ontario's Attorney General for almost four years now. Each day I face new tasks and challenges which cause me to reflect frequently on the role of an Attorney General, and upon the many duties and responsibilities which the law and custom of the constitution have devolved upon the office.

In England the office of Attorney General has over 600 years of historical development behind it. Initially back in the mid thirteenth century, the Attorney's role was to represent the sovereign's interest in any particular litigation, since the King obviously could not appear in his own courts. The name Attorney General was first given to the Crown's principal law officer in 1461 when he was called on to advise the House of Lords on legal matters. This responsibility to give legal advise to the legislature remains part of my role in Ontario even today.

In Canada, the office has existed since 1749. The office has, however, developed differently in our two countries since then. For example, in England the Attorney General does not usually sit in Cabinet, though he may frequently be asked to give advice to Cabinet or its committees on legal matters. But in Canada for over 125 years the Attorney General has been a political officer and a leading member of the Cabinet team. Indeed on three occasions in Ontario the office has been held simultaneously with the premiership. The Canadian view is that it is essential for the Attorney to be a member of Cabinet since he bears administrative responsibility for a department of government and has responsibilities for policy formation.

Because he supervises the machinery of justice, he must as a Minister of the Crown be responsible to the legislature. One of the essential characteristics of the Attorney General's office is its politically accountable nature. Accountable politically, but also aloof from partisan politics. As the Honourable J. C. McRuer reminded us in his Royal Commission Inquiry into Civil Rights, the Attorney General

> . . . must of necessity occupy a different position politically from all other Ministers of the Crown. As a Queen's Attorney, he occupies an office with judicial attributes and in that office he is responsible to the Queen and not responsible to the government. He must decide when to prosecute and when to discontinue a prosecution. In making such decisions he is not under the jurisdiction of the Cabinet nor should such decisions be influenced by political considerations. They are decisions made as the Queen's Attorney, not as a member of the government of the day.

This was not always the case however. One hundred and fifty years ago the Attorney General was indeed one of the most unenviable figures in government. A book published in London in 1819 entitled "Criticisms of the Bar" commented as follows:

> Of all offices in the gift of the Crown, that of Attorney-General is perhaps least to be coveted; for whether the Government be popular or unpopular, the person filling that place can scarcely avoid being the object of general dislike. . . . He is pretty sure to be charged with having ascended by the usual steps of political fawning and judicial servility and after all he is only to be considered as the servant of servant—the curse of the Israelites. . . . The most unpleasant consequence of all appears to be that the nation at large must look upon the Attorney-General as a sort of ministerial spy whose business it is to ferret out and prosecute all who either by their actions or writings are endeavouring to displace the personages to whom he is indebted for his situation, or who are attempting to promote any reform in the system they support.

The re-establishment of the integrity and reputation of the Attorney General's office came about only because of the maintenance of a punctilious independence from partisan politics in the execution of the unique quasi-judicial responsibilities of the Attorney General. The ideal has been well described by the American political columnist Joseph Kraft:

The ideal Attorney General is an upright man, learned in the law, and with the most delicate sense of fairness, who acts less as a player on the Government team than as an umpire exerting a legal check on arbitrary action of the executive.

Abraham Lincoln's Attorney General, Edward Bates had been a politician, a Congressman, even a Presidential Candidate, but he gave a classic definition of the proper role of the Attorney General:

The office I hold is not properly political, but strictly legal and it is my duty, above all other Ministers of State, to uphold the law and to resist all encroachments from whatever quarter, of mere will and power.

Thus while the Attorney General must remain aware of the political considerations that contribute to a thorough assessment of the public interest, he can never let partisan politics weigh as a factor in any of his quasi-judicial functions, particularly in relation to the conduct of criminal proceedings. Lord MacDermott put it well when he said:

The days are gone when a subservient Attorney could be told whom to lay by the heels or whom to spare. He must now maintain a complete independence in this difficult and sometimes delicate sphere, and if he fails to do so, the remedy lies in his dismissal or that of the Administration.

The cardinal principle of political independence does not mean, however, that the Attorney General must act as a sort of unworldly legal monk, acting from some remote cloister. The Attorney General must always take account of the public interest in his many decisions. I had to weigh many factors in deciding that it would not be in the public interest to lay criminal charges against the former Solicitor General of Canada, Mr. Francis Fox. The special circumstances of the Fox case, the difficulty of ever achieving a conviction, the fact that Fox had already undergone a great deal, and the likelihood that a minimal sanction would have been imposed on conviction, led me to the conclusion that no prosecution should be launched. I gave my views at length to the legislature and I think the position I took was not merely understood, but accepted without criticism. This is perhaps the most difficult and delicate part of the job, the decision in borderline cases whether to prosecute or not. Weight must be given to many factors. Yet I do think that the comparatively small amount of public criticism that surrounds such decisions is indirect testimony to the skill and judgment of those who must help me make them. It also signifies a basic public confidence in the administration of justice.

Recently events in England have combined to focus public attention on the role of the Attorney General. Two years ago, the House of Lords handed down their decision in the case of *Gouriet* v. *The Union of Post Office Workers,*[1] a case which is a landmark in the development of judicial thought about the responsibilities of an Attorney General. In *Gouriet,* a private citizen sought an injunction against a postal union because of its proposed ban on the handling of mail to South Africa. The Attorney General had refused to consent to the action. The courts were faced with the important constitutional question of whether or not they can compel the Attorney General to give reasons for exercising his discretionary powers. Are the courts able to override the Attorney General's decision to consent to a relator action or not?

Lord Denning thought they could. In the fierce rhetoric for which he is so justly famed, he thought that the Attorney General's powers were a fundamental threat to the rule of law. Lord Denning granted an individual citizen, Mr. John Gouriet, an interim injunction and hinted that the maintenance of the British system of justice rested on the courts reserving to themselves the right to review the decisions of the law officers of the Crown.

Thus rebuked by Lord Denning and his colleagues, the Attorney General appealed to the Lords. Not having been in the courtroom I cannot guess whether the progress of *Gouriet's* case through the courts gives any support for the maxim attributed to Lord Asquith of Bishopstone that

> A trial judge should be quick, courteous and wrong. That is not to say that the Court of Appeal should be slow, rude, and right, for that would be usurping the function of the House of Lords.

In any event the Lords reversed the Court of Appeal in a manner described by a former English Attorney General as magisterial, categoric and severe. They said, in a unanimous decision, that the private citizen cannot, under any circumstances, invoke the aid of the civil courts to prevent a threatened breach of the criminal law, other than to protect his personal rights. If the criminal law is actually breached, every citizen retains the residual constitutional right to bring a private prosecution against the offender. But the Attorney General is the only person recognized by the public law as being entitled to represent the public interest in a court of justice; the civil courts may declare public rights only at his insistence. Public rights are constitutionally vested in the Crown, and the Attorney General enforces them as chief law officer of the Crown.

The significance of this case for me is not that it confirmed at the highest level the responsibilities which the Attorney General bears, but rather that it focused public attention for a while on the pivotal nature of the office of the Attorney General, and his constitutional role as guardian of the public interest. The dramatic clash of views between the Court of Appeal and the House of Lords graphically illustrated the unique role of the Attorney General and the pivotal influence of the powers and restrictions that must constantly engage him in making decisions that lie at the very heart of the administration of justice. As Professor John Edwards has so eloquently put it, "the Attorney General must constantly walk the narrow tight rope between the adjacent fields of mainstream politics and independent non-partisan judgments".

The case reaffirms the unique quasi-judicial role of the Attorney General. It reminds all who hold the office, of Harold MacMillan's statement that the obligations of the Attorney General were first to the Crown, second to the House, and only then to the government.

That was not how it seemed to be to the disgruntled litigant, Mr. John Gouriet, who said after the case: "It now seems that the law is no longer above the Attorney General. Recollecting the powerful words of Thomas Fuller 300 years ago, 'Be you ever so high, the law is above you'; the Attorney General has now, by this judgment, been confirmed as being unanswerable to the courts and has taken upon himself a certain divinity."

I think that we are likely to see increasingly in the next few years, the courts return to the issues raised in the *Gouriet* case. The Attorney General obviously must have a primary responsibility for protecting the public interest but the question is more frequently being asked: should this role be an exclusive one? The general question then becomes: whether the Attorney General or the court is best equipped to make a decision about the public interest. Lord Shawcross, a former Attorney General wrote to *The Times* expressing "grave concern" at the implications of *Gouriet*.

> The fact is that we have moved away from Dicey's age of reasoned democracy into the age of power. Responsibility to Parliament means in practice at the most responsibility to the party commanding the majority there, which is the party to which the Attorney General of the day must belong. One has only to remember the so-called Shrewsbury "martyrs" and the Clay Cross affair to realize that that party will obviously not criticize the Attorney General of the day for not taking action which, if taken, might cause embarrassment to their political supporters. . . .
>
> It is naive to observe, as was done in the *Gouriet* case, that the Attorney General may have regard to political considerations but "not of course acting for party political reasons". It is "of course" exactly the present appearance and the future possibility that he might so act which endangers both existing respect for and the future effectiveness of the rule of law, already sadly eroded in many fields.

In Canada, both the Ontario and British Columbia Law Reform Commissions, are currently embarked on research studies with a view to reforming the law of standing. A number of groups claiming to represent the public interest in environmental or other areas, have claimed that our law is far too restrictive in denying access to the courts to protect public rights except through the intervention of the Attorney General. Serious constitutional questions on standing are increasingly being raised in the courts. I am sure they will be discussed at length by the two law reform commissions, and I look forward keenly to reading their reports.

The office of Attorney General is steeped in history and tradition. That history, those traditions, are not merely of academic or scholarly interest. The traditions of the office of Attorney General boil down in their essence to a set of very clear and very high standards of independence and objectivity, against which every holder of the office, whether in England or elsewhere in the Commonwealth, must daily measure his conduct in the matters which come before him for decision. The politically nonpartisan nature of the legal decisions the Attorney General must make, and the strong tradition of legislative accountability of the office, constitute one of the most important bulwarks of the rule of law.

Far from representing the dead hand of historical precedent, the traditions of the office of Attorney General represent a living standard of conduct which constantly and urgently commands the attention of everyone who is privileged to fill that office.

The office can be a demanding and, at times, a lonely one. Many of the Attorney General's tasks simply cannot be delegated, since the accountability for the decisions rests personally on his shoulders. One of the most famous English Attorneys, Francis Bacon once said that the office of Attorney General was "the painfullest task in the realm". It fell to another Attorney General, Sir Patrick Hastings, a few centuries later to say that being an Attorney General was his view of hell. Sir Patrick graphically described his misery in his Autobiography:

> My day began at seven o'clock in the morning and I rarely got to bed before five the next morning. The day was spent in one long rush between the Law Courts, Government departments, and the House of Commons. The night, or rather the early morning was needed in order to get ready for the next day. Nothing that I began was I ever allowed to finish; and nothing was ever finished until something else was begun. Being an Attorney-General as it was in those days is my idea of hell. The only person who enjoyed my exalted position was my chauffeur. As I was in possession of a Cabinet pass I was authorized to drive through the streets without any regard to ordinary police regulations. He invariably elected to cross Trafalgar Square on the wrong side.
>
> I was unpopular with everyone; the policemen in the House of Commons came to me in a body to protest against being kept up so late. I had no idea that because I stayed there all night they were obliged to stay there too. Although I lived only a mile away it was too far, and I was obliged to take rooms in Queen Anne's Mansions in order to have time for any sleep at all. Life was made no easier by bright young Conservatives who devised a pleasant scheme whereby to cause additional annoyance; they made a habit of complaining that the Government were discourteous to the House by not having one of the law officers present during the debates in order to answer wholly unnecessary legal queries. As they knew that I was the only law officer available, and that I was probably far away, their jibe was much appreciated. Anyhow, they made my life unbearable. By the end of the summer I had enjoyed about as much as I could stand.

There are times when I wholeheartedly sympathize with Sir Patrick Hastings' experience.

Attorneys General are above all servants of the law, responsibile for protecting and enhancing the fair and impartial administration of justice, for safeguarding civil rights and maintaining the rule of law. One of the central responsibilities of the office today, as I see it, is to ensure that the law is kept in step with contemporary needs and conditions. Law reform has been one of my major concerns since taking office in 1975. Although it has required an exceptional amount of time in policy-making, in Cabinet, and the House, I am proud to have introduced 63 separate bills in the last four years. I think that major measures such as family law reform, succession law reform and reform of our provincial offences procedure will be of incalculable benefit to the public whom we serve.

Law Reform is a time-consuming and absorbing task. The principles of reform can only become a concrete reality when they have undergone a lengthy process of detailed and searching examination in the legislature. In this process of painstaking attention to detail, absorbing though it may be, one can never lose sight of the central goals of law reform in the classic sense that was expressed so many years ago by Lord Brougham in his famous speech:

> It was the boast of Augustus . . . that he found Rome of brick, and left it of marble; a praise not unworthy of a great prince, and to which the present reign also has its claims. But how much nobler will be the Sovereign's boast, when he shall have it to say, that he found law dear, and left it cheap; found it a sealed book—left it a living letter; found it the patrimony of the rich—left it the inheritance of the poor; found it the two-edged sword of craft and oppression—left it the staff of honesty and the shield of innocence.

I can think of no better precept with which to leave these thoughts on the Office of Attorney General. Lord Brougham's rubric quite properly emphasizes the paramount importance of the administration of justice serving every member of the public. Those of us who are privileged to serve in this office cannot help but be humbled by the sense of historical tradition and duty which has from the earliest day infused the work of the Attorney General.

The office of Attorney General is central to our system of justice, as it is in England, Australia, the United States and all other common law countries. It is sustained by the great traditions shared by our profession, of commitment to ordered liberty under law, to freedom, justice and the rule of law.

NOTES

1. [1978] A.C. 435 (H.L.); revg. [1977] Q.B. 729 (C.A.).

2

Recent Judicial Developments in Private Law

P. S. Atiyah

Until a few years ago I think there can be no doubt that a lecturer called upon to talk of recent judicial developments in private law would have begun by dividing up his material into the traditional compartments— recent developments in contract, in tort, in restitution and so on. My own view is that the most significant development of recent years in the area of private law has been the gradual disintegration of these dividing lines between the traditional categories. It would, of course, remain possible, and, indeed, it would be simpler, to review recent case law under the usual headings. But I think it is much more rewarding to attempt the more ambitious, if more difficult, task of trying to catch a sense of the kaleidoscope actually in motion. We are, I imagine, all aware in a vague sort of way of the fact that contract and tort appear to be merging in a grey area in certain particular areas of law, most notably perhaps in the law of misrepresentation. But I want to suggest here that the process of disintegration and reintegration is more profound and more widespread than this.

Let me begin by suggesting that the key to an understanding of the deeper significance of many recent and current developments in private law lies in re-assessing the central elements of contractual liability. For as long as it matters, contractual liability has been based on an amalgam of three basic ideas—(1) that liabilities can be created by promises or agreements, (2) that benefits should be recompensed, and (3) that detrimental reliance should be protected or guarded against. In classical contract theory, of course, the promise is the central element, and the other two factors, benefit and detriment, are reduced to the relatively minor role of being supportive factors in the doctrine of consideration. What I want to suggest is that many recent developments in private law can best be understood in terms of the changing relative importance of promise or consent on the one hand, and of benefits and detrimental reliance, on the other hand. I will suggest that there is a considerable body of evidence to support the idea that restitutionary and reliance ideas are today gaining in strength at the expense of promissory or consensual liability ideas. We are thus faced with the paradox that, at the very time when the doctrine of consideration in its traditional form seems to have become of less and less practical importance, in another and broader sense, the whole movement of the law of obligations today can be seen as a revival of the importance of the twin ideas in consideration, and the decline in the role of the promise itself. It is, I think, this paradox that led Grant Gilmore to say in his thought provoking book, *The Death of Contract,* that perhaps "the most urgent question we can put to ourselves and our students is: Whatever happened to the doctrine of consideration?" If contract is dead, the message of my lecture will be that consideration is still very much alive and kicking.

My brief is to talk of recent developments, and this is certainly not the time or place for an historical excursus, especially as I have dealt very fully with these questions in my forthcoming book, *The Rise and Fall of Freedom of Contract.* But I would like to spend just a moment or two on the version of legal history which I have offered in that book, because I believe it will make my lecture more intelligible. What I have suggested in my new book is that much of the law of obligations prior to the late eighteenth century can be best understood if we think of the idea of recompense for detriment, or making good losses resulting from detrimental reliance, as independent sources of legal liability. The doctrine of consideration, I have suggested, was not in its origin a mere incident to the law of promises and contracts. It reflected the powerful idea that, promise or no promise, reasonable reliance is often worthy of protection, and benefits are often deserving of recompense. In that sort of ideological world, I have argued, promises often perform a sort of evidentiary function. They do not so much create liabilities, as amount to more or less conclusive admissions of the existence of liabilities. In the nineteenth century, the ideology of free choice and consent became, as we all know, dominant, and under the influence of that ideology promises came to be the centre piece of the law of obligations, consideration and non-consensual liabilities were downgraded into subordinate postions. My lecture will attempt to show that what is happening today is, in some respects, a reversion to an older tradition, to a pre-nineteenth century set of values, a world in which promises are, once again, often—though not always—seen as evidentiary rather than conclusive, and in which the protection of reliance and restitutionary interests is once again becoming the dominant idea of much of the law.

The Declining Importance of Consent

Every contract lawyer is aware of the unreality of attributing many contractual obligations to the consent of the parties. The growth of standard form contracts, with small print exclusion clauses and so forth, is a well worn theme. I do not propose to enlarge on this familiar ground. But I must call attention to a number of recent cases which show increasing awareness of these questions in the courts. We have, first, a series of decisions and dicta which have begun, if slowly and cautiously, to develop a doctrine of unconscionability, or of unfair bargaining power. Outstanding here are the judgments of Lord Denning in *Lloyd's Bank* v. *Bundy,*[1] and of Lord Diplock in *Schroeder (A.) Music Publishing Co.* v. *Macaulay.*[2] In the former case the Court of Appeal set aside a guarantee given to a bank on the ground that the guarantor, himself a customer of the bank, was owed fiduciary duties by the bank. It is clear that the court felt the guarantee was simply an unfair and unreasonable bargain, having regard to the fact that the business being guaranteed was already tottering into insolvency and the guarantee procured only a minimal respite from certain doom. In *Schroeder* v. *Macaulay,* the House of Lords struck down an agreement by a young pop singer with a music publisher on the ground that it was in unreasonable restraint of trade, as the singer tied himself to the publisher for ten years. But Lord Diplock stressed that in reality the argument was being struck down because it was unfair. Professor Trebilcock has argued in an article in the University of Toronto Law Journal that there was nothing unfair about the contract, as it was essentially of a speculative character; and on this point the decision may be open to criticism. But that is almost a minor point. The important point is that, to Lord Diplock at least, the fairness of the bargain was more important than the fact that Macaulay had consented to it. Or, to put it in another way, his consent to the contract was not treated as conclusive evidence that the contract was fair.

The notion that promise, or consent, can be useful evidence of the fairness of a bargain, but should not be treated as conclusive, is also one which is beginning to appear in a variety of other contexts. Indeed, whenever Parliament removes the absolutely binding nature of a contract, it is possible for the courts to treat the consent of the parties as at least *prima facie* evidence of the fairness of the bargain. There is old law to this effect in the case of contracts unenforceable under the Statute of Frauds, or under the Moneylenders Acts (see, *e.g.*, *Way* v. *Latilla*).[3] Recently the same sort of idea has surfaced in connection with agreements between husband and wife who are negotiating as to maintenance and property division pending a divorce. In *Backhouse* v. *Backhouse,*[4] and again in *Dean* v. *Dean,*[5] judges of the High Court held that agreements of this kind did not displace the jurisdiction of the court to make appropriate orders under the Matrimonial Causes Act; but the agreements were treated as evidence—and not conclusive—of what would be reasonable provision for the court to make.

Of course these decisions depend ultimately on some statutory provision enabling the court to reject the absolutely binding character of a contract. And it is true that there are limits to what the courts can do with a contract in the absence of such statutory power. In *Liverpool City Council*

v. *Irwin*,[6] the House of Lords denied that it was possible for the court to read implied terms into a contract just because they seemed reasonable, and insisted that this can only be done where the term is strictly necessary. But the distinction between a necessary term and a reasonable one is almost impossible to sustain. The facts of the case itself illustrate this point, because the case involved the implied duty of a landlord to maintain in working order the lifts in a block of high rise flats. It was clearly accepted on all hands that the landlords were under *some* duty with respect to the lifts, even if it was not an absolute duty to keep them working at all times. But it is impossible to distinguish between what is strictly necessary and what is reasonably necessary with regard to the provision of lifts in a block of flats. How high does a building have to be before a lift becomes necessary? It is strange that the courts are so reluctant to acknowledge the power to read reasonable terms into contracts when one considers how mightily they wield the standard of reasonableness in a tort action. As usual, Lord Denning has refused to hide the creative nature of the judicial decision, and in the *Irwin* case, sitting in the Court of Appeal, he insisted on the power to make reasonable implications in a contract. In the House of Lords this was, in theory, repudiated, but, in practice, as Lord Wilberforce seemed to suggest, the substance can always be achieved, even if the power is overtly rejected.

Another illustration of the courts' ability to arrive at a just result in a contract by a different technique, even where they cannot read in reasonable terms, is provided by *Shell U.K. Ltd.* v. *Lostock Garage Ltd.*[7] In this case the defendant, who ran a tied garage and was bound to take his petrol supply from Shell, found that they were selling petrol at discriminatory prices, so that it was commercially impossible for him to resell the petrol at the prices laid down by Shell, in view of the fact that rival garages close by were selling at much lower prices. He told Shell that he would have to buy petrol elsewhere if they could not lower their prices to him, and, when Shell sued him, he pleaded that there was an implied term in the contract that Shell would not supply competitors at prices so low that he could not compete. The Court of Appeal had some difficulty with this implied term, but in the result they arrived at the desired result through a different route. It was held that it was inequitable to grant Shell the discretionary remedy of injunction, and that Shell's only remedy therefore lay in damages. In fact, there was no evidence of any loss, since the defendant simply could not sell Shell petrol at the prices they demanded, so that for practical purposes the decision once again amounted to a rewriting of the contract so as to make it accord with the court's view of what was fair and reasonable.

The declining role of consent—or at least of the absolutely binding nature of a consent—can also be illustrated from many other legal decisions in recent years. For example, there is the important pronouncement of the House of Lords in *Johnson* v. *Moreton*,[8] concerning the agricultural tenancy legislation. Although the Act, giving security of tenure to agricultural tenants, did not specifically provide that there should be no contracting out, the House of Lords here held that "it can no longer be treated as axiomatic that, in the absence of explicit language, the courts will permit contracting out of the provisions of an Act of Parliament". But it is worth noting the distinction drawn here by Lord Hailsham between an executory and an executed contract. It may well be perfectly permissible for an agricultural tenant to actually give up his tenancy in return for an agreed payment, and, if he does give it up, the agreement, being now executed, is binding on the landlord. The point is important to my thesis; because it shows how the mere element of consent—bare future consent—is not absolutely binding, while the agreement if part executed becomes binding. Once executed, of course, reliance and benefit are present, and the case for enforcement becomes that much stronger.

Another recent decision limiting the absolutely binding character of consent is the case of *North Ocean Shipping Co. Ltd.* v. *Hyundai Construction Co. Ltd.,*[9] where, for the first time in English law, it has been clearly held that a defence of economic duress may be available, at least to a contracting party who is compelled to agree to some concession—here an increased price—by the threat of a totally unjustifiable cancellation by the other party. But it is also interesting to note that the judge held that the plaintiffs here had held their peace too long, after submitting to the duress; although they may not have intended to affirm the amended agreement by their actions, yet completion of the remainder of the contract without further protest on their part had led the other parties to believe that no further complaint was to be made. The element of detrimental reliance as a ground for inferring affirmation is thus made clear: here too, therefore, rights and duties are being altered, not through consent, but through detrimental (or even assumed) reliance.

Another group of important cases concerned with the effect of a breach of contract may also be thought to reflect the declining role being attributed to consent in the law of obligations. I refer here to a whole series of recent decisions which have gradually undermined the traditional condition/warranty dichotomy in the law of contract. Taken together, these decisions have carried through nothing short of a legal revolution. Contract lawyers only a few years ago were brought up to accept that all contractual terms were either conditions or warranties. Breach of a condition justified the other party in repudiating the contract; breach of warranty only sounded in damages. The distinction was, of course, enshrined in the Sale of Goods Act, but I think it is fair to say that most lawyers would have regarded the Act as merely stating the rules applicable in the general law of contract. It will be seen how this dichotomy reflected the desire to attribute the consequences of a breach of contract to the intention of the parties. It was the intention of the parties which determined whether a term was a condition or a warranty; and it was the characterisation of the term which determined the result of a breach. When a breach occurred one was thus compelled to go through the motions of looking at the contract as it was originally agreed, shutting out of one's mind the actual breach and its consequences.

In the law of sale of goods, as is well known, this dichotomy between conditions and warranties tended to produce the result that very trivial breaches often justified repudiation of the whole contract by the other party; this was because most terms in contracts of sale were treated as conditions—and indeed, all the implied terms in the Sale of Goods Act were originally conditions. For example, there were well known decisions like *Bowes* v. *Shand*[10]—predating the Sale of Goods Act—where it was held that a buyer could reject a cargo of rice on the ground that some of the cargo had been loaded a day or two early. In *Re Moore & Co. and Landauer & Co.,*[11] another extreme decision was arrived at by the Court of Appeal; it was here held that a buyer could reject a cargo of canned fruit on the ground that some of it was packed 24 cans to the case instead of 30 cans to the case, as required by the contract. This was the result of holding that there had been a breach of the implied condition that the goods should correspond with their description even though the correct total quantity of cans was delivered and it was found as a fact that there was no difference between the value of cans packed 24 or 30 to the case.

Then in *Hong Kong Fir Shipping Co. Ltd.* v. *Kawasaki Kisen Kaisha Ltd.,*[12] the first rumblings of a legal revolution were heard. In this case, which concerned a charterparty, the Court of Appeal declared that the traditional condition/warranty dichotomy was not exhaustive. There might, said the court, be innominate terms, the result of breach of which depended on the nature and gravity of the breach, and not on the nature of the term itself. Now it will be seen that this was a move away from the idea that it was for the parties to determine the consequences of a breach, and that the court played a purely passive role, interpreting and giving effect to the consent and intent of the parties. It now becomes possible to say that with these innominate terms it was for the court to make the active decision, as to whether the breach was sufficiently serious to justify repudiation. It seemed at first as though these new innominate terms might be rather rare beasts compared with the old familiars, conditions and warranties. But another twist was given to this tale in *Cehave N.V.* v. *Bremer Handelsgellschaft m.b.h.*[13] The Court of Appeal now declared that innominate terms were no rare creatures but that, on the contrary, the "vast majority" of contractual stipulations fell into this category. Even express contractual clauses in a contract of sale of goods were of this character. Only the implied terms under the Sale of Goods Act were strictly conditions in the traditional sense.

The next stage was the decision of the House of Lords in *Reardon Smith Lines Ltd.* v. *Hansen Tangen,*[14] where the *Cehave* decision was approved and the move away from the condition/warranty distinction was given further impetus. So far as contracts of sale of goods are concerned, the decision goes still further, for it lays down that not every departure from the contract description amounts to a breach of the implied condition that goods must correspond with their description. Thus matters which do not constitute a substantial ingredient of the identity of the goods are now excluded from the protective mantle of the statutory implied condition. Departure from the contract description on such matters becomes actionable in damages only. *Re Moore and Landauer* has been effectively overruled.

The result of all this is that what started by being the general rule—namely the division of contract terms into conditions and warranties—has been almost completely swept away. The general rule now seems to be that most terms are to be treated as innominate terms; only the implied terms under the Sale of Goods Act constitute an exception to this new approach, and even these terms cannot be treated as conditions with respect to all matters of description. I have used this series of cases to illustrate the way in which modern law is increasingly acknowledging that, even in the law of contract, the court does not merely play the passive role of giving effect to the intention of the parties. But it is worth adding that these cases also illustrate another major modern trend in the case law, namely an increasing move away from general principle towards rules that depend for their application on an examination of the particular circumstances of the case. The older rule may have promoted more certainty, but less justice; the newer rule may help courts to do justice, but at the expense of certainty. I developed this theme in my inaugural lecture at Oxford last year, under the title, "From Principles to Pragmatism," and I do not therefore propose to say anything more about it now.

I want now to say something about the protection of expectations. We have traditionally associated the law of contract with the protection of expectation rights; and it is also standard contract theory that expectation damages are the primary remedy for breach of contract. Moreover, in the case of wholly executory contracts, where no benefits have been rendered, and no reliance has taken place, there is no other basis on which damages can be awarded. Now in their celebrated article on "The Reliance Interest in Contract Damages" in the Yale Law Journal in 1936, Fuller and Perdue pointed out that there are in fact many situations in which the courts appear disinclined to award expectation damages, but are more willing to protect reliance and restitution interests. They observed that this was particularly the case with contracts which departed in some degree from the paradigm of the simple commercial contract. It may be too early to speak of a noticeable trend in this direction, but there are certainly some straws in the wind suggesting that there may be an increasing reluctance to award expectation damages where there has been no reliance or part performance, so that the plaintiff is simply suing on a wholly executory contract. One noteable recent decision which prompts reflections of this kind is *Lazenby Garages* v. *Wright*.[15] The defendant contracted to buy a secondhand car from the plaintiffs. He repudiated this contract before delivery, and the plaintiffs resold the car at a higher price. They nevertheless claimed for loss of profit, *i.e.*, they claimed expectation damages on the basis that the buyer who eventually bought the car at the second sale would probably have bought another car from them if that one had not been available. The Court of Appeal rejected this argument, holding that a secondhand car was unique; and that only one lot of profit could be made from its sale. I find the reasoning unconvincing. It is simply untrue to say that in a commercial sense a secondhand car is unique; secondhand car values are based on the assumption that such cars are virtually indistinguishable. It seems to me that decisions of this kind indicate some sympathy with a consumer who simply wants to change his mind and get out of a contract before there has been any performance or detrimental reliance.

But if the protection of pure expectations in contract is declining, it seems to me also apparent that there are other areas of the law in which expectations are actually being given enhanced protection. Some of these are statutory, *e.g.*, the law of unfair dismissal, but statute law is outside my brief so I say no more about them here. But even in the judicial sphere, we have an increasing tendency to protect certain expectations, for instance, in ordinary tort actions for personal injuries. For years it has been customary to award damages for losses of expected earnings, but recently it has become quite clear that you can recover not only for the earnings you were actually receiving before the injury but also for promotion prospects, and the like, though without allowance for inflation. Similarly, we now have explicit authority in the decision in *Moeliker* v. *A. Reyrolle & Co. Ltd.*,[16] that damages in a personal injury action can be awarded for a possible loss of earnings in the future even though the plaintiff is at present back in the old job, without loss of pay. So we seem to have moved quite smoothly into regular recognition that expectation losses of certain kinds are protected by tort law.

Moreover, there are other areas of the law, also, in which one finds employment expectations being given particularly high protection. A fascinating example is *Ebrahimi* v. *Westbourne Galleries*,[17] where the plaintiff had been in business with a partner for some years before they converted their business into a limited company, the two partners taking equal shares and being the sole directors. Shortly afterwards, they admitted a son of one of the partners as a co-director and shareholder. Disputes arose and the plaintiff was ejected from the Board by the other two; he petitioned for a winding up order on the ground that it was just and equitable that the company should be wound up. In effect the plaintiff's case was that his reasonable expectations about his participation in the business had been frustrated by the actions of the other two. They argued, on the other hand, that it was the terms of the articles of association which governed, and that the petitioner had been properly removed under the articles. The House of Lords upheld the petition thus in effect accepting the overriding importance of actual expectations as against the expectations which ought to have been entertained if the written word only were looked at.

My final illustration about the declining importance of the role of consent comes from the law of remedies. In recent years there have been a number of English cases which seem to me at least to suggest that there are some circumstances in which the courts are now willing to make a contract for the parties, contrary to the hallowed traditions of contract law. These three cases all concerned the enforcement of restrictive covenants, or rights of a similar character, namely, *Wrotham Park Estate Co. Ltd* v. *Parkside Homes Ltd.*,[18] *Bracewell* v. *Appleby*,[19] and *Shaw* v. *Applegate*.[20] In all of them, the courts declined to award specific relief and awarded damages in lieu. In theory there is nothing new about such a procedure. It has always been possible to leave a plaintiff to his legal remedy, and since 1858 Equity has had the power to award damages in lieu of specific relief. But what does seem to me to be new is that these three cases seem to show a new awareness of what may actually be involved in deciding whether to award an injunction or damages. For it is reasonably clear that in all three cases the real argument was likely to be about money; if specific relief had been given, the bargaining would then have proceeded, with one party in an immeasurably more powerful position. If specific relief is refused, the court fixes by way of damages the sum which it thinks is a fair price for the compulsory expropriation of rights which is involved. These cases, like many of those mentioned earlier, seem to me to reflect a changed set of values and ideologies. In the last century, a court would generally have taken the view that a person *prima facie* entitled to enforce a restrictive covenant was the only person who could decide at what price he would sell that entitlement. He could get his injunction and then bargain, if he wanted to, for whatever he thought his rights were worth. But the three decisions I have mentioned involved in effect compulsory expropriation, and then a judicial decision as to a fair compensation for that expropriation. Many American economists would, I suspect, welcome these decisions, because they all involved situations in which bargaining without the aid of the court is peculiarly difficult. They involved situations of bilateral monopoly, in which it is quite possible for the two parties to fail to come to an agreement, even though there is no doubt that an agreement which is beneficial to both parties is in principle possible. This is because, for various reasons, the bilateral monopoly is one of high transaction costs. There is, therefore, some ground for thinking that decisions of this character are desirable on economic grounds. All three decisions also suggest that where building operations in breach of a covenant or easement are in question, a plaintiff who fails to apply for interim relief may well be placing his right to specific relief in the end in great jeopardy. In all three cases, the fact that the defendants had continued with their operations at considerable expense, while the plaintiff knew what was happening, and failed to apply to the court, was held to be a major ground for denying specific relief. It will be noticed that this amounts to protection of the defendant against the consequences of detrimental reliance.

Reliance

Parallel with the declining importance of consent has been the increased protection accorded to reliance in recent years. And here we see perhaps the strongest examples of the tendency of modern law to depart from traditional categories. For reliance is protected today, sometimes in contractual actions, sometimes in tort actions, and sometimes by virtue of the doctrine of estoppel, or other similar doctrines such as acquiescence. The *Hedley Byrne*[21] decision which opened the door to many of these developments is, of course, conventionally classified as an action in tort. But it is just as possible to see it as a development of contract law. If we would be willing to expand our concept of what constitutes consideration, there would be no difficulty in seeing the plaintiff's actions in reliance on the negligent advice he received, as consideration. Two hundred and fifty years ago, this was more or less what Holt C.J. did in *Coggs* v. *Barnard,*[22] and that case does not differ so very much from the *Hedley Byrne* situation. At all events, what is quite clear today is that in cases of this general nature, the courts are increasingly disinclined to place any weight on the question whether the action lies in contract or in tort. Accountants, solicitors, investment advisers, architects and others have all in recent years been held liable for economic loss caused by negligent professional advice or information. And, indeed, in *Midland Bank Trust Co. Ltd.* v. *Hett, Stubbs and Kemp,*[23] the old rule in *Groom* v. *Crocker,*[24] that if you have a contract with a solicitor you must sue him in contract, has finally been overthrown. Whether these cases are looked at as contract or as tort actions, it is, I think, important to bear in mind how strongly reliance-based they are. The reason why these are such modern developments is not simply due to the greater adventurousness of modern judges, nor is it due to the greater freedom given by the use of tort doctrine as compared with contract doctrine. The reason, I venture to suggest, is closely bound up with differing values about what sort of reliance is reasonable and, still more, about when it is reasonable to throw the risk of reliance on other parties. A hundred years ago, decisions like *Hedley Byrne* would have been felt unreasonable because it would have been said, I think, that a man has no right to rely upon another in such a way as to throw upon him part of the risk of his business venture unless that other receives some benefit, some payment, for accepting that risk, and actually consents to do so.

I suspect that, in the last analysis, much the same sort of change in values underlies many of the modern estoppel, "standing by" cases, where a person's reliance has been "reasonable" in the ordinary popular sense, but where he has unfortunately failed to take the necessary legal precautions to protect his position. For instance, in *Crabb* v. *Arun District Council*,[25] the plaintiff was given a verbal assurance that he would have access to his land through a private road onto the main road, and, relying upon that assurance, he sold a part of his land so that the remainder became wholly dependent on this right of way. But, unfortunately, he never obtained a proper formal grant of the right of way, or even a contractual undertaking sufficient to satisfy the Statute of Frauds. But the Court of Appeal upheld his right, by using the doctrine of estoppel, where they felt unable to do so through the medium of contract—or perhaps I should say counsel felt unable to do so, because the case was simply not pleaded in contract. This decision, and it is representative of a great many others in recent years, seems to me to show the increased importance attached by courts to the fact of reasonable reliance, and a greater willingness to say that reliance is reasonable even where the plaintiff has failed to protect himself by using the formalities prescribed by law. If one looks at this case as a contracts lawyer might look at it, it does seem to me to represent a not uncommon situation where one has some sort of an agreement, which is very close to being a contract, but which would not be enforceable while it was still executory; on the other hand, once it has been acted on to the detriment of one of the parties, the agreement becomes enforceable.

When courts are willing to uphold rights based to some extent on the fact of reliance, or reasonable reliance, without stopping to ask if the reliance is justified by an actual promise, it is obviously not going to be long before they start imposing duties on contracting parties while they are actually in the negotiating stage. Of course, in classical contract law, this was confined within the narrowest possible limits. Apart from the law of fraud and misrepresentation, negotiating parties generally owed no duty to each other. Given that classical contract law so largely represented the law of the marketplace, this is hardly surprising. In the market, a man is not his brother's keeper. So classical contract law, for example, denied that a party owed duties of good faith to his co-contracting party while they negotiated, and duties of disclosures were extremely limited. Moreover, in classical contract law, these rules often came to be applied to situations where the morality of the marketplace was hardly appropriate. Isolated decisions of this kind are still to be found. For instance, in *Wales* v. *Wadham*,[26] it was held that a wife owed no duty to disclose to her husband, while they were negotiating a final settlement pending divorce, that she was intending to remarry a wealthy man when the divorce was finalised. I find this decision distasteful and contrary to the trend of much modern case law. Several recent cases have underlined that contracting parties do owe duties to each other even during the negotiating stage, well beyond traditional duties about fraud and misrepresentation. For instance, there is *Esso Petroleum* v. *Mardon,*[27] where the Court of Appeal held one contracting party liable *in negligence* for making inaccurate predictions concerning the sales potential of a filling station which was leased to the defendant. It is also relevant to note the kind of statement which was here held to constitute a misrepresentation, for this was basically a prediction, which must be a matter of opinion, rather than of fact. And traditional law has always said that statements of opinion cannot constitute a misrepresentation. But by switching into the tort arena, this argument seems to have been by-passed. The cause of action in tort is negligence, and negligent predictions may amount to the tort of negligence. Since then, several other decisions have suggested new avenues of approach as to the duties of negotiating parties. For instance, in *Daulia Ltd.* v. *Four Millbank Nominees Ltd.,*[28] the Court of Appeal provided authority for the proposition, hitherto resting solely on academic suggestions, that a person who makes a promise in return for an act may be held impliedly to promise in addition that he will not revoke the first promise once the promisee has commenced performance. I pause only to suggest that this liability is surely a reliance-based liability masquerading under the guise of an implied promise. Then we have had *English* v. *Dedham Vale Properties Ltd.,*[29] where the purchaser of some property sent off an application for planning permission a day or two before contracts were exchanged for the purchase. It was held that, in so acting, he must be taken to have acted as agent for the purchaser, so that when permission was granted and the land thus became more valuable than had been expected, the purchaser had to account to the vendor for the profit he had made. Two views could be held about the policy of the decision, but it seems one further move towards recognising duties of good faith between negotiating parties.

The most striking case of this nature is the case of *Midland Bank* v. *Box,*[30] decided earlier this year by Lloyd J. in the High Court. I only have information concerning it through the courtesy of one of the counsel. The defendant in this case sought a loan from the plaintiff bank for a business venture from which he expected to make a great deal of money. His bank manager advised him that the amount sought was outside his authority and would have to be submitted to the bank's head office; but the manager also led the defendant to believe that head office approval to the loan was something of a formality and could be confidently expected. He then allowed the defendant to anticipate head office approval by borrowing on overdraft a sum of about £40,000 though this was far below the total amount of the loan sought. Eventually the bank's head office declined to make the loan and the defendant lost the whole of his £40,000. When sued by the bank he counter-claimed for damages for negligence. He argued that the bank manager had negligently led him to believe that the loan would be forthcoming, and that, in the result, he had relied upon this advice or prediction by borrowing more on overdraft than he would otherwise have done. This argument was accepted by Lloyd J., who held that some £5,000 must be deducted from the bank's claim, this being the amount of the loss attributable to the negligence. When it was argued that a prediction could not be a misrepresentation, the judge pointed to the *Esso* v. *Mardon* case. The decision is altogether remarkable and is an excellent illustration of the way in which reliance *per se* is coming to be regarded as a ground of legal liability, if it can be said to be reasonable. Not long ago, the claim in this case would have been quite unarguable. It would have been said that the defendant has simply made an offer to borrow money which the bank had declined to accept; if the defendant had chosen to act in anticipation of the acceptance, it would have been said that he acted at his own risk. On the other hand, it is interesting to note how similar the overall pattern is to recent developments in America, as exemplified by the famous decision in *Hoffman* v. *Red Owl Stores.*[31]

Another decision, from a completely different social context, also illustrates the increasing tendency for reliance to be treated as a sufficient ground for imposing civil liability. In *Tanner* v. *Tanner,*[32] the plaintiff, a married man, formed an association with the defendant, a single woman, and she bore him twins. The defendant lived in a rent-controlled flat, but after the birth of the twins the plaintiff bought a house for her and the twins though he made it clear that he had no intention of marrying her. She did not herself contribute anything to the purchase price of the house though she spent some small sum on furnishings. She moved into the house with her children, but a year or two later the plaintiff married another woman, and he then sought to eject the defendant from the house; she was, he claimed, a mere licensee, and he terminated her license. It was held that by giving up her rent-controlled flat the defendant had furnished consideration, and that her license to occupy the house thus became irrevocable. But as the lower court had ordered the defendant to leave, and she had in fact left, the Court of Appeal awarded her damages in lieu. There was, said Lord Denning, no express contract that she should be allowed to live in the house for her life, or at least until her children grew up, but "the circumstances are such that the court should imply a contract by him [the plaintiff] or, if need be, impose the equivalent of a contract by him". As usual, Lord Denning has here blurted out the real truth. The court here imposed a contract on the parties, and the real ground for their decision seems to have been quite simply the belief that the plaintiff owed a moral duty to see that the defendant was housed, and, secondly, that she had acted to her detriment in reliance on him, by giving up her flat and moving into the house. Attempting to squeeze decisions of this kind into the traditional contract or tort categories seem to me to land one in fictions. To my mind, we are here in the process of drawing new lines for the imposition of civil liability, though one of the major grounds for imposing liability is the old factor of reliance.

Restitution

Turning to the other half of the doctrine of consideration, the benefit side, it seems to me that here too there are increasing signs that the notion of recompense for benefit, without any promise or even consent, is rapidly becoming established as one of the leading grounds for imposing civil liability on parties. One could begin by looking at a number of recent cases which in their social setting are not unlike *Tanner* v. *Tanner,* but in which both parties, whether married or not, have contributed to the purchase or improvement of a house. If they are married, and the question is one concerning the allocation of the property on divorce, the notion of imposing a constructive trust as a way of achieving a just division of the proceeds was approved by the House of Lords in *Gissing* v. *Gissing.* [33] It is true that a majority of the House here seems to have thought that there was nothing fictitious about such a constructive trust and that they were merely giving effect to real or inferred intentions, but it is impossible to share their belief in the reality of the intentions they were dealing with. And subsequent cases seem to bear this out. So far as married couples are concerned, the *Gissing* rule has now been largely superseded by statutory provisions, but it can still be invoked where the court is dealing with an unmarried couple. For instance in *Eves* v. *Eves,*[34] both parties had contributed, in money and work, to the purchase and improvement of their home, and when they split up the court divided the value of the property by imposing a constructive trust. Once again, there is some talk in the judgments of the existence of a bargain, but this was quite unreal and indeed contrary to the evidence, which was that the parties simply did not discuss what was to happen in the event of their separating. What married couple has any intention on that question when they are buying and improving their home?

A similar invocation of Equity in a slightly different context can be found in *Binions* v. *Evans,*[35] where the trustees of a charitable estate left the widow of an employee to live rent free in her cottage for her life; they sold the cottage, but subject to the widow's rights, and the buyer clearly paid a price commensurate with the belief that the widow was entitled to remain in the property. But no sooner had he bought the house than he gave her notice to quit, arguing that she had no legal right to stay. It was held that she was entitled to remain where she was; the fact that the buyer had paid a lower price in consequence of her supposed rights was surely the key to the decision.

Many other areas of law can be found in which the idea of restitution seems to be playing a much larger role than was formerly common. There are, of course, straightforward extensions of liability based plainly and simply on unjust enrichment ideas, as in *Greenwood* v. *Bennett,*[36] where it was held that a person who spent some £226 repairing a stolen car, which he had bought in good faith, was entitled to compensation for that expenditure when the car was handed back to the true owner. Then there is the lengthy and erudite judgment of Megarry V.-C. in *Tito* v. *Waddell (No. 2),*[37] during the course of which the learned judge enunciated and applied a completely new rule of contract law, to the effect that anyone who takes the benefit of a transaction must also accept the liabilities under it. Since this proposition was applied precisely because the judge was unable to find any assignments or novations to meet the problems that had arisen, it is plain that the liability he envisaged would be benefit-based, and not based on a promise, real or fictitious. More recently still, we have another Court of Appeal decision in *Swordheath Properties Ltd.* v. *Tabet,*[38] in which damages based on unjust enrichment principles were awarded in an action for trespass to land. In the old days it would have been said that the plaintiffs had waived the tort, and sued in quasi-contract. But to the Court of Appeal this seems to have been unnecessary; at any rate they said nothing whatever about waiving the tort. They seem to have taken the perfectly simple, and sensible, view that damage based on restitutionary, or unjust enrichment, principles could be awarded in tort where appropriate.

The Expansion of Liability for Omissions

There are two other major tort developments to which I wish to refer because these also strengthen my belief that we are witnessing a great redrawing of the lines in civil liability at the present day. I take first, the question of liability for omissions. Time was when liability for omissions was one of the distinguishing marks between contract and tort. In tort, of course, everyone has a duty to avoid harming his neighbour by positive, affirmative acts of negligence or other fault. But a person was not generally thought to be under a duty to act so as to render help to his neighbour unless he was paid for it. If you wanted a right to due care by affirmative conduct you generally had to pay for it in the last century. But this distinction has also been breaking down as the tort of negligence has been expanded in the present century. In *Home Office* v. *Dorset Yacht Co.,*[39] the plaintiffs' action, it will be remembered, was against the Home Office for negligently permitting the escape of the Borstal boys who damaged the plaintiffs' yacht. Now the Home Office did not itself cause any damage to the yacht; nor, of course, was it vicariously liable to the yacht owners for the wrongful acts of the Borstal boys. The plaintiffs' complaint was that by their negligent omissions the Home Office officials had permitted the Borstal boys to escape and do the damage. As Lord Diplock said in the House of Lords, the case raised the question how far a man is to be his brother's keeper. Liability was emphatically affirmed in this case, but it is, I think, unfortunate that the omission problem is so rarely recognized for what it is. Constant talk of foreseeability fails to provide any guidance whatever to decisions in this area, because the problem with omissions is not to decide whether certain precautions against harm should have been taken, but whose responsibility it is to take the necessary precautions. After all, to use the philosopher's old chestnut, if the flowers have died because they have not been watered, it does not help to fix responsibility on the gardener to say that he could have foreseen the result. The trouble is, that so could everybody else. Unfortunately, it still seems to be the case that omission cases are just not recognised as raising peculiar problems of legal difficulty. In another unreported decision in 1978, *Walton* v. *British Leyland*[40] the plaintiff sued in respect of injuries received when a wheel flew off a British Leyland car in which she was a passenger. The case seems to have been based, not on negligence in the initial design of the vehicle but on the failure of British Leyland to recall the cars after they had received information of over 100 similar cases. Liability was imposed but there is nothing in the brief newspaper report to indicate that the court was aware that any legal principle was involved. Yet we have no clear authority in our books to the effect that a person who creates a peril without negligence, comes under a duty to take reasonable steps to mitigate the peril if he thereafter comes to know of it. No doubt this is a reasonable enough proposition, but one would like to see some discussion of its limits.

The contemporaneous decision of the Supreme Court of Canada in *Arnold* v. *Teno*[41] shows a greater understanding of the issues involved, although this too was an omissions case of a kind. Here an ice cream vendor selling his wares from a mobile van was held liable for not warning a child about to run across the road after making her purchase, of the imminent danger from an approaching vehicle. Would the decision have been the same, one wonders, if the accident had happened while the child was crossing the road towards the ice cream vendor? Was this a duty arising out of contract or tort? The case was argued throughout as a tort case, and was not based on an implied term in the contract; yet a mere bystander who fails to warn another of danger is not normally liable in tort.

Liability for omissions has also shown signs in recent years of extending into the law of nuisance, where the basic issue remains, I think, much the same as it is in negligence. Is a landowner to be held liable for damage done by some hazard spreading from his land to that of the plaintiff without any active assistance of the landowner? In *Goldman* v. *Hargrave,*[42] it will be remembered, the Privy Council held that a landowner might be liable for allowing a fire to spread to his neighbour's land even though the fire was originally lit by lightning. More recently, in *Leakey* v. *National Trust for Places of Historic Interest or Natural Beauty,*[43] this decision was extended somewhat to a case where the defendants were held liable for damage done by earth falling from a large mound onto the plaintiff's house, onto which the mound abutted. The defendants had offered to allow the plaintiff to enter their land in order to remove the danger, so that it could not be argued that control in itself was a sufficient ground for imposing the liability. It seems that the underlying values here are simply that the ownership of land carried with it burdens and responsibilities. The defendant, as owner, took the benefit of the land, and must pay for damage done by it. I put it in this form, because the defendants themselves did absolutely nothing to create the danger which was entirely the result of natural causes.

Economic Loss

I turn finally to say something about the recent cases concerning the recovery of damages for purely economic loss. Here too there is a disintegration, or at least a blurring, of the dividing line between contract and tort. There has, after all, been nothing unusual about awarding damages for purely economic loss in contract. Indeed, this is the usual form of loss in contractual actions. But as is well known, in cases traditionally classified as tort, there has been felt to be more difficulty in obtaining damages for purely pecuniary losses, though the difficulty has never extended to cases in which the pecuniary losses depend upon and follow some physical damage or injury.

The *Hedley Byrne* case provided the first major breakthrough on this point, for the decision in that case necessarily meant that there are at least some cases in which damages for purely pecuniary losses can be recovered in tort. But the problem of setting limits to the kind of case in which this is permissible was not, I think, very clearly perceived in the *Hedley Byrne* case. And since that decision the courts, both in England and the Commonwealth, have been gradually groping their way towards some principles to govern this difficult question. It is now possible to begin to group the fact situations into various categories. First, we have cases which are so close to contract as to make it unreal to distinguish between contract and tort. I have already referred to *Esso Petroleum* v. *Mardon* and *Midland Bank* v. *Box*. Then there are cases in which a professional person gives professional advice in a relationship from which he expects to derive some indirect benefit, but for which he is not being directly paid by the advisee. Here, the element of benefit exists, notwithstanding that traditionally benefit of that kind may not satisfy the doctrine of consideration, and no court now seems to feel any qualms about imposing liability for negligent advice. Here we have decisions like those of the House of Lords in *Sutcliffe* v. *Thackrah,*[44] imposing liability on an architect who negligently certified building works to have been satisfactorily completed, and *Arenson* v. *Arenson,*[45] where the House of Lords held that an accountant who acted as a valuer in connection with a contract for the sale of shares was liable for negligence in the valuation. Still closer to contract is the decision in *Saif Ali* v. *Sidney Mitchell & Co.,*[46] in which the House of Lords finally set limits to the traditional immunity of the English barrister from actions for negligence, by restricting it to the actual conduct of litigation or the giving of advice which is intimately connected with the conduct of litigation.

The liability of accountants for negligence in tort is, in principle, indubitable after these cases, though the limits on that liability remain a matter of difficulty. In New Zealand, the Court of Appeal was divided in *Scott Group* v. *Macfarlane,*[47] as to the liability of auditors for negligently certifying the accounts of a company which was the subject of a take over bid by the plaintiffs. The majority denied liability, holding that the negligence was not sufficiently closely related to the take over bid. One of the majority judges also pointed out that the plaintiffs had made a profit from their take over, and that their only complaint was that they had not made as large a profit as they would have done if the accounts had been correct. To award damages for such a notional loss may well be thought to approach perilously close to awarding expectation damages, and although I have suggested that such damages are now sometimes awarded in tort cases, this is an area where there are surely good grounds for caution. Buying shares, whether in the form of a take over bid, or otherwise, is necessarily a somewhat speculative exercise. If the speculation succeeds beyond all measure, the successful speculator is unlikely to share his gains with those professional advisers on whom he has been relying. It does not necessarily seem just that he should be able to burden them with some of the loss where the speculation fails, or is only partially successful. In Canada, recent decisions of the Supreme Court *(Elderkin* v. *Merrill Lynch,*[48] and *Farish* v. *National Trust*[49]) have imposed liability in tort for negligent financial advice on stockbrokers and savings banks.

Liability of solicitors has recently raised—again in Canada—the question whether a disappointed legatee can sue where a will or a bequest fails because of negligence of the deceased's legal advisers. In *Whittingham* v. *Crease,*[50] liability in such a case was imposed by the British Columbia Court of Appeal. Here it must be noted that damages of this character are purely expectation damages; there is simply no question of any reliance loss, and no restitutionary interest to be protected. The liability protects the purest expectations; indeed, such a liability could well arise even if there have been no expectations, though in this particular case that was not the position.

Another class of cases in which liability for purely economic losses may be imposed concerns negligent certification cases. In New Zealand, for instance, liability has been imposed in recent years on a surveyor whose survey of a yacht was passed on to a prospective purchaser, even though the purchaser did not pay for it[51] and on the State for negligently issuing a certificate of roadworthiness of a heavy truck which was bought by the plaintiff in reliance on the certificate.[52] There is, without doubt, room for a massive growth in this area of liability for negligent misstatement, having regard to the extensive use of certificates of this general character, both private and public.

A third group of cases arises from negligent acts which cause physical damage to one person, and pecuniary loss to another. There is no doubt that these cases raise some of the most difficult problems facing the courts at the present day, and as yet, little in the way of principle seems to have emerged. In England, the *Spartan Steel* case,[53] is generally taken to deny liability for the pecuniary loss. In Australia, the High Court has held in *Caltex Oil (Aust.) Pty. Ltd.* v. *The Dredge Willemstad*,[54] that a ship which negligently severed a pipe line across a bay, was liable to an oil company for the economic costs imposed on it as a result, though the pipe line did not belong to it. On the other hand, in the comparable case of *Gypsum Carrier* v. *The Queen*,[55] the Canadian Federal Court dismissed an action by three railway companies who were put to great expense when a bridge which they normally used was negligently damaged by the actions of the defendant. In cases of this kind, the spectre of unlimited liability to an unlimited number of persons seems to loom very large; and for my part I cannot see any principle on which the *Caltex* case can be said to have been decided which would not equally entitle any road user to recover for his petrol when he is compelled to detour round a temporary obstruction caused by negligent driving. It is worth adding, perhaps, that the instinct which leads many of us to deny liability in such cases is not merely based on fear of being swamped by vast numbers of cases. It is based, surely, on recollection that one of the functions of tort law is to act as a loss distribution mechanism, and in cases of this kind, the loss is already well distributed. To invoke tort liability in such cases would concentrate and not distribute losses.

However, the infinity of circumstances raised by tort actions undoubtedly throws up cases from time to time in which recovery seems to be a reasonable solution, and no problem arises over the possibility of huge numbers of similar cases. One such case was *Yumerovski* v. *Dani*,[56] another Canadian decision, where the plaintiffs were travelling with their father in a car driven by their travel agent who was taking them to the airport to catch a charter flight for which the agent had booked them tickets. An accident occurred through the agent's negligence, the father was killed and the plaintiffs missed their flight. They forfeited their passage money and were held entitled to recover the cost in damages.

The most difficult questions of all in this field are perhaps those arising from the negligence of a manufacturer or builder, and here too, we are beginning to get a plentiful crop of litigation, though so far the problems are clearer than the solutions. As to buildings, we have the House of Lords decision in *Anns* v. *Merton London B.C.*,[57] imposing liability on a local authority for negligence in supervision of the building of a house. The plaintiff's claim was for damages for the actual defects in the house itself, a claim which the House of Lords was reluctant to classify as purely pecuniary. Because the house was in danger of collapse, and would thus endanger anyone continuing to live in it, it became possible to treat the loss as more in the nature of physical damage. This method of approach was extended somewhat in *Batty* v. *Metropolitan Property Realisations Ltd.*,[58] where the Court of Appeal held that the mere fact that the house was not in danger of imminent collapse did not deprive the plaintiff of his right to damages. I do not doubt that these decisions are wise, and represent a significant improvement in consumer rights particularly having regard to the difficulty of protecting oneself against such risks by insurance. But I have difficulty with the argument that the loss is really a physical one, and not a pecuniary one. Perhaps the case which goes furthest on these lines is the New Zealand decision in *Bowen* v. *Paramount Builders*,[59] where a builder was held liable to a subsequent purchaser of a building for the residual depreciation in value of the building, which remained uncurable after all repairs had been done. Here again, the decision seems to cut right across traditional lines between contract and tort. For, it is plain enough, the plaintiff surely would have had no cause for complaint if he had bought the building with full knowledge of the defects, and paid a price which fairly reflected the value of the building as it stood. Thus, the plaintiff's right to sue the builder seems to depend on the terms of his contract with the person from whom he purchased it. Moreover, as pointed out by Lord Wilberforce in the *Anns* case there is the awkward possibility of subsequent buyers also suing the builder for the same negligence if they too buy in ignorance of the defects, the first buyer having pocketed the damages and failed to perform the repairs.

With regard to chattels, we are still at the experimental stage. The leading decision here is, of course, *Rivtow Marine Ltd.* v. *Washington Iron Works*,[60] where the Supreme Court of Canada denied liability for the repair costs of a chattel negligently designed or manufactured. The court did, however, award damages for the additional pecuniary loss suffered by the plaintiffs because the defendants did not inform them as soon as they knew of the danger in the design, with the result that the plaintiffs suffered extra pecuniary loss, having to have the repairs done during their busy season, as the defendants could have foreseen. The denial of liability for the repair costs was followed in *Ital-Canadian Investments* v. *North Shore Plumbing & Heating*[61] and it has also been held in Canada that a plaintiff cannot recover extra repair costs which have been caused by his delaying the necessary repairs through his own impecuniosity: *Alberta Caterers* v. *R. Vollan (Alberta)*.[62]

As the decisions stand at the moment, therefore, we seem to be on the brink of establishing different rules for buildings and for chattels. But this is evidently only one of the many difficult issues in this area. Obviously I have no time for a full examination of the difficult questions arising from the continual incursions of tort law into the field of economic loss. But it is at least clear that the relationship between tort and contract will need to be defined anew in this field, as in so many of the others on which I have touched. Indeed, I am coming to hold the view that a total merger of contract, tort and restitution in a new law of obligations may not be far ahead. Certainly the case law of the last decade or so appears to be pointing in that direction.

NOTES

1. [1975] Q.B. 326.
2. [1974] 3 All E.R. 616.
3. [1937] 3 All E.R. 759.
4. [1978] 1 All E.R. 1158.
5. [1978] 3 All E.R. 758.
6. [1977] A.C. 239.
7. [1976] 1 W.L.R. 1187 (C.A.)
8. [1978] 3 All E.R. 37.
9. [1978] 3 All E.R. 1170.
10. (1877), 2 App. Cas. 455.
11. [1921] 2 K.B. 519.
12. [1962] 2 Q.B. 26.
13. [1976] Q.B. 44.
14. [1976] 1 W.L.R. 989.
15. [1975] 1 W.L.R. 459.
16. [1976] I.C.R. 253.
17. [1972] 2 All E.R. 492.
18. [1974] 1 W.L.R. 799.
19. [1975] Ch. 408.
20. [1978] 1 All E.R. 123.
21. [1964] A.C. 465.
22. (1703), 2 Ld. Raym. 909.
23. [1978] 3 W.L.R. 167.
24. [1939] 1 K.B. 194.
25. [1976] Ch. 179.
26. [1977] 1 W.L.R. 199.
27. [1976] Q.B. 801.
28. [1978] 2 W.L.R. 621.
29. [1978] 1 All E.R. 382.
30. Unreported.
31. (1965), 133 N.W. 2d 267.
32. [1975] 3 All E.R. 776.
33. [1971] A.C. 886.
34. [1975] 3 All E.R. 768.
35. [1972] Ch. 359.
36. [1973] Q.B. 195.
37. [1977] Ch. 106.

38. [1979] 1 All E.R. 240.
39. [1970] A.C. 1004.
40. *The Times*, July 13, 1978.
41. (1978), 83 D.L.R. (3d) 609.
42. [1967] 1 A.C. 645.
43. [1978] 2 W.L.R. 774.
44. [1974] A.C. 727.
45. [1977] A.C. 405.
46. [1978] 3 All E.R. 1033.
47. [1978] 1 N.Z.L.R. 553.
48. (1977), 80 D.L.R. (3d) 313.
49. (1975), 54 D.L.R. (3d) 426.
50. [1978] 5 W.W.R. 45.
51. *Gordon* v. *Moen*, [1971] N.Z.L.R. 526.
52. *Rutherford* v. *Attorney General*, [1976] 1 N.Z.L.R. 403.
53. [1973] Q.B. 27.
54. (1976), 11 A.L.R. 227.
55. (1977), 78 D.L.R. (3d) 175.
56. (1977), 83 D.L.R. (3d) 558.
57. [1978] A.C. 728.
58. [1978] Q.B. 554.
59. [1977] 1 N.Z.L.R. 594.
60. (1974), 40 D.L.R. (3d) 530.
61. [1978] 4 W.W.R. 289.
62. (1977), 81 D.L.R. (3d) 672.

3

The Rise of The 'Mareva' Injunction

G. H. Jones

"You cannot get an injunction to restrain a man who is alleged to be a debtor from parting with his property." These words of Cotton L.J. in *Lister & Co.* v. *Stubbs*[1] were, untill recently, thought to state for English lawyers a principle of general application. But this appears no longer to be so, at least if the debtor is resident out of the jurisdiction but has assets within the jurisdiction which the plaintiff fears he might quickly remove on notice of the plaintiff's claim. It is only in the last four or five years that the English courts have been prepared to enjoin the alleged debtor in these circumstances. On a number of occasions the Court of Appeal[2] has said that the court has power to grant these injunctions; and the Commercial Bar, which conceived them, is most anxious that they should continue. So, in the only case to reach the House of Lords,[3] counsel who sought to discharge the injunction did so on grounds which did not directly question its propriety. Initially the *Mareva* injunction (which takes its name from one of the formative cases)[4] gave rise to as many questions as it answered. What sort of *prima facie* case must a plaintiff show—a strong one or simply an arguable one? What evidence must he adduce to demonstrate that the defendant might remove the assets from the jurisdiction? What evidence must the defendant give in order to obtain the discharge of the injunction? And, fundamentally, why should the courts treat a plaintiff whose defendant is out of the jurisdiction more favourably than a plaintiff whose defendant is within the jurisdiction? The answers to some of these, and other questions, are still far from clear.

The Origin of the Mareva Injunction

Debtors are tiresome creatures, and debtors who reside out of the jurisdiction are particularly tiresome. If the common law courts and the Court of Chancery did not recognise this, some customary courts did. For example, there existed in the great mercantile cities, such as London, Bristol, Exeter and Lancaster, a custom which was known as Foreign Attachment. "The essence of its principle [was] to place an embargo on any property of the debtor, to ensure his appearance to answer the creditor's claim, and in default of such an appearance to take the property or part of it in satisfaction of the creditor's debt."[5] But by the late nineteenth century this custom had fallen into desuetude, although it continued to flourish in the United States, surviving attacks on its constitutionability.[6] The *Mareva* injunction is foreign attachment revived in all but name.

In two commercial cases, early in 1975,[7] the Court of Appeal granted an *ex parte* interlocutory injunction, pending the trial of the plaintiff's action, restraining a defendant resident out of the jurisdiction from disposing of assets within the jurisdiction. The background to these applications was the existence of one ship corporations registered abroad, charterers similarly incorporated, a depressed freight market, and the City of London where it was likely that the traceable assets of many such corporations could be found and where much international arbitration takes place. So, in *Nippon Yusen Kaisha* v. *Karageorgis*,[8] a ship owner sought an injunction against a charterer who, it was alleged, was in flagrant breach of the terms of the charter party. The ship owner deposed that, if the injunction were not granted, the charterer would remove money held to its account in an English bank. The court granted the injunction. Lord Denning M.R. said:[9]

> We are told that an injunction of this kind has never been done before. It has never been the practice of the English court to seize assets of a defendant in advance of judgement, or to restrain the disposal of them. . . . The time has come when we should revise our practice. There is no reason why the High Court or this court should not make an order such as is asked for here.

Browne and Geoffrey Lane L.JJ. simply agreed with Lord Denning M.R.

In the second case, *Mareva Compania Naviera S.A. of Panama* v. *International Bulk Carriers S.A.*,[10] Lord Denning M.R. did not hesitate to grant the injunction on somewhat similar facts. But Roskill L.J. had considerable doubts about the High Court's jurisdiction to do so; in his experience, such an injunction had always been refused and it was only the very special facts of *Mareva* which persuaded him to concur with the Master of the Roles.

In neither of these cases did the defendant appear or was he represented. Some months later, however, in *MPBXL Corpn.* v. *International Banking Corpn.*,[11] the grant of a *Mareva* injunction was successfully opposed. The Court of Appeal described the injunction as an "exceptional remedy," which should only be granted on clear evidence that the defendant had assets within the jurisdiction and where the plaintiff's claim was not disputed or seriously disputed.[12] The effect of that decision was to put something of a brake on applications for *Mareva* injunctions. It was not until 1977, in the *Pertamina*[13] case, that the High Court's jurisdiction to grant these injunctions was confirmed and indeed significantly enlarged. In *Pertamina* the Court of Appeal refused to exercise its discretion to grant an injunction for there was some doubt whether the assets which were to be the subject matter of the injunction belonged to the defendant. But it did not doubt that it would be "just and convenient" to do so in an appropriate case. For a foreign defendant was in a significantly different position from a defendant resident within jurisdiction. As Kerr J. said at first instance in *Pertamina*:[14]

> A plaintiff has what appears to be an indisputable claim against the defendant outside the jurisdiction, but with assets within the jurisdiction which he could easily remove, and which the court is satisfied are liable to be removed unless an injunction is granted. The plaintiff is then in the following difficulty. First, he needs leave to serve the defendant outside the jurisdiction, and the defendant is then given time to enter an appearance from the date when he is served, all of which takes several weeks or even months. Secondly, it is only then that the plaintiff can apply for summary judgement under R.S.C. Ord. XIV with a view to levying execution on the defendant's assets here. Thirdly, however, on being apprised of these proceedings, the defendant is liable to remove his assets, thereby precluding the plaintiff in advance from enjoying the fruits of a judgement which appears irresistible on the evidence before the court. The defendant can then largely ignore the plaintiff's claim in the courts of this country and snap his fingers at any judgement which may be given against him."

The principles established in *Pertamina* and refined in subsequent cases "gave a new dimension to the Mareva injunction".[15] Thereafter it was not an exceptional remedy; it became common place. "At present, applications are being made at the rate of twenty per month. Almost all are granted."[16]

The Principles Underlying the Grant of the Mareva Injunction

After *Pertamina* there have been three significant decisions. The first is that of the House of Lords in *The Siskina;*[17] and there are two of the Court of Appeal, *Cretanor Maritime Co. Ltd.* v. *Irish Marine Management Ltd.*[18] and *Third Chandris Shipping Corporation* v. *Unimarine S.A.*[19] From them the following propositions may be gleaned:

1. The jurisdiction of the High Court to grant an injunction rests on Section 45 of the Supreme Court of Judicature (Consolidation) Act 1925 which gives the High Court power to "grant a mandamus or injunction or appoint a receiver by an interlocutory order in all cases which it appears to the court to be just or convenient so to do".
2. The effectiveness of the application depends on it being made *ex parte;* otherwise the defendant would have the opportunity of removing the assets out of the jurisdiction.[20] But because the application is made *ex parte,* the defendant or his agent should be informed immediately that it has issued and he should be told that he is at liberty to have the in-

junction discharged at any time by notice.[21] Moreover the plaintiff should make "full and frank disclosure of all matters in his knowledge", and should give particulars of his claim against the defendant.[22] He must also give an undertaking to pay damages in the event that his substantive claim fails.

3. The plaintiff should give "some grounds for believing that the defendants have assets here".[23] At one time it was thought that the *Mareva* injunction could only restrain the defendant from removing assets described and identified by the plaintiff in his affidavit.[24] But in practice the form of the *Mareva* order was always wider, to restrain the defendant "from removing or taking any steps to remove *any assets* from within the jurisdiction of this court or otherwise disposing of same and, in particular," the assets specifically identified in the affidavit.[25] The Court of Appeal has now affirmed that it is enough that it is deposed that *prima facie* assets exist and where they may be found.[26] "In most cases the plaintiff will not know the extent of the assets. He will only have indications of them."[27] So, the injunction may relate wholly or in part to a body of unspecified but assertainable assets which might increase or decrease during the life of the injunction.[28]

   In most cases the plaintiff has sought to arrest money in a bank account. Indeed it appears to be enough that the defendant has a bank account within the jurisdiction even though the bank account may be overdrawn.[29] It lies against goods, although it has been said that the injunction should not readily be granted if the goods are part of the defendant's stock in trade and which could, if frozen by the injunction, bring the trade to a stand still. In *The Rena K,*[30] where the defendant sought unsuccessfully to resist the injunction on that ground, Brandon J. exercised the benefit of hindsight to conclude that, since the asset, a ship, had been released, the defendant ship owners had laid her up and had not attempted to use her as part of their trade.

4. It will be recalled that the *Mareva* injunction was originally only granted if the plaintiff's claim was not "seriously disputed".[31] In other words, one had to show a case so strong that, if the defendant was resident within jurisdiction, summary judgement would be given against him. In *Pertamina,* Lord Denning M.R. refused to limit the discretion of the court to cases "so plain that the plaintiff can get judgement under R.S.C. Ord. XIV".[32] Relying on the authority of the House of Lords in *American Cyanamid Co.* v. *Ethicon Ltd.*[33] he concluded that it would be enough that the plaintiff could show that he had "a good arguable case", that an award of damages would be an ineffective remedy, and the balance of justice and convenience demanded the grant of the injunction. In the court below Kerr J. had refused the injunction because the plaintiff's case was not strong

enough to have persuaded him to grant summary judgement if the defendant had been within jurisdiction; and the other member of the Court of Appeal, Orr L.J., also seemed to think that the court should take into account the apparent strength or weakness of the plaintiff's case.[34] However it would appear from *Third Chandris*[35] that Lord Denning's view presently prevails, even though this is the only occasion upon which the Master of the Rolls has enthusiastically followed the principles established by House of Lords in *American Cyanamid.*[36]

5. What evidence must the plaintiff adduce to demonstrate that it is likely that the defendant would remove assets from the jurisdiction before any judgement or award is satisfied? In *Third Chandris,*[37] Mustill J. answered the question in this way: "Prima facie by demonstrating that the asset is present, that it is moveable and that the defendant is abroad." He accepted that "some adverse inference" would have to be drawn from the mere fact that the defendant is abroad if the *Mareva* is to survive let alone flourish. The Court of Appeal refused to go this far. Lord Denning M.R., Lawton L.J. and Cumming-Bruce L.J. all agreed that "the mere fact that the defendant is abroad is not by itself sufficient".[38] Lord Denning and Cumming-Bruce L.J. gave very little guidance as to the quality of evidence which would satisfy the court; no "reputable foreign company" should "be plagued with a *Mareva* injunction simply because it has agreed to London arbitration".[39] Lawton L.J. was more specific. In his view, "an affidavit . . . should give enough particulars of the plaintiff's case to enable the court to assess its strength and should set out what enquiries have been made about the defendant's business and what information has been revealed, including that relating to its size, origins, business domicile, the location of its known assets and the circumstances in which the dispute has arisen".[40]
6. The converse to the previous question is this: what must the defendant do to secure the discharge of the injunction? In *Third Chandris* the defendant corporations failed, even though their affidavit stated that they were substantial corporations with about 100 ships on charter, that they had a good defence to the ship owners' claims, and that they could honour any judgement against them. However, they did not give any details of their financial position; there was no balance sheet or statement of account and no evidence was given by any director or officer of the company. A defendant must produce "solid evidence", and the defendant corporations had failed to do so.[41] Moreover the Court of Appeal was not deterred by the threat that, if the injunction were granted, the defendant corporation would move its business away from London.
7. In *The Siskina,*[42] the House of Lords refused to enjoin a defendant from dealing with the proceeds of an insurance claim which were

payable to him in London, in circumstances where the English courts had no jurisdiction whatsoever over the plaintiff's substantive claim. "In order to obtain a *Mareva* injunction there has to be in existence a substantive cause of action on which the plaintiff is suing or about to sue in the High Court in England or is enforcing or about to enforce by arbitration in England."[43] The dispute between the cargo owners and the ship owner was not justiciable in England for the bills of lading were governed by Italian law and the cargo was arrested *in rem* in Cyprus.

8. In *Cretanor Maritime Co. Ltd.* v. *Irish Marine Management Ltd.,*[44] the Court of Appeal allowed the debenture holder of the alleged debtor to apply for the discharge of a *Mareva* injunction which had been obtained by the plaintiff. The *Mareva* injunction was not an attachment in the sense that it enabled the plaintiff to seize the defendants' assets under some writ or like command. The *Mareva* injunction was, simply, "relief in personam".[45] "It does not affect the seizure of any asset. It merely restrains the owner from dealing with the asset in certain ways."[46] The court refused, therefore, to allow the plaintiff through a *Mareva* injunction to obtain indirectly the position of a secured creditor.

The Unresolved Questions

At first the *Mareva* injunction was regarded as a very special exception to the principle that you cannot restrain a person whom you allege to be your debtor from removing assets out of the jurisdiction. In *Pertamina,* Kerr J. attempted to justify its existence on the ground that his claim could otherwise be easily frustrated by the defendant quickly removing assets from the jurisdiction.[47] But a plaintiff may be equally vulnerable to the wiles of a resident defendant who is able to persuade the court to give him leave to defend. It was these considerations which led Lord Hailsham in *The Siskina*[48] to say that sooner or later the courts or the legislature would have to choose between two alternatives: either "the position of the plaintiff making the claim against an English based defendant would have to be altered or the principle of the *Mareva* cases will have to be modified".

Lord Denning M.R. would not hesitate to extend the *Mareva* injunction to restrain even a defendant resident within the jurisdiction from disposing of his assets so as to defeat a plaintiff's claim before judgement.[49] And in *Third Chandris*[50] he has said that the Court of Appeal has already done so, in the unreported case of *Chartered Bank* v. *Daklouche.*[51] If this is so, then the *Mareva* injunction will no longer be an exceptional remedy, and the principle of Cotton L.J. in *Lister & Co.* v. *Stubbs*[52] will be overthrown.

There is some force in the argument, particularly since England's entry into the E.E.C., that it is not tenable to apply different principles to govern the attachment of assets, depending upon whether the assets belong to a national who is normally resident within the jurisdiction or to a foreigner who is normally resident out of the jurisdiction.[53] But it is doubtful whether it would be wise to accept *Chartered Bank* v. *Daklouche*. The implications of any change would be profound, and would blur even further the boundaries between property and contract. A plaintiff has always been able to restrain a defendant whom he says is his trustee from disposing of assets which are alleged to belong to the trust. It is an entirely different question whether a defendant who is alleged to be a debtor should be similarly restrained from dealing freely with his own assets, particularly if the plaintiff has merely to show that he has an arguable case. There surely is something to be said for the reaffirmation of the principle that a plaintiff can obtain a *Mareva* injunction only if he demonstrates that he has so strong a case that he would obtain summary judgement if the defendant had been within the jurisdiction.

It is predictable that great commercial inconvenience may be caused by the grant of a *Mareva* injunction *ex parte*. In *Third Chandris*[54] Mustill J. accepted this but did not consider it to be conclusive. He said:

> The whole point of *Mareva* jurisdiction is that the plaintiff proceeds by stealth, so as to pre-empt any action by the defendant to remove his assets from the jurisdiction. This entails that the defendant finds that his bank account has been blocked before he has any idea of what is going to happen. This may have extremely serious consequences. Cheques or bills drawn on the account may be presented at a time when adequate funds are available to meet them, and may yet be dishonoured because the injunction inhibits the bank in making payment. Moreover the very secrecy of the procedure deprives the defendant of the opportunity to make a timely alternative arrangement for presentment or payment abroad. The dishonour of the defendant's paper may have disastrous consequences; and all this in a situation where the plaintiff has shown no more than an arguable case. An undertaking by the plaintiff for damages may not always be a sufficient indemnity for the loss the defendant may suffer. Again the blocking of an account may have very serious consequences for a defendant who is dependent on cash flow for his commercial survival. The case of a charterer provides an example. On a rising market the free use of his bank account is a crucial importance. The payment of hire may lead to the loss of a charter. It is of no consolation to say that he can apply to have the ex parte injunction discharged, if by the time his application is heard the damage may have been done.

Nonetheless, the judge found that "the considerations the other way," in particular the fact that the number of applications to discharge *Mareva* injunctions "is remarkably small," indicated that these potential hardships have not in fact materialised. But arguments based upon negative inferences are dangerous arguments. For example, as the judge admitted, the injunctions may have been voluntarily lifted because of the readiness of the defendant to provide financial guarantees rather than to have resource to the courts. In *Cretanor Maritime*,[55] the Court of Appeal rejected an attempt to manipulate the *Mareva* injunction so as to elevate the plaintiff into a position of a secured creditor. The court properly emphasised that the relief was relief *in personam*. "It does not affect a seizure of any asset. It merely restrains the owner from dealing with the asset in certain ways. . . . All that the injunction achieves is in truth to prohibit the owner from doing certain things in relation to the asset".[56] Yet if it is the case that an injunction may in practice be lifted only if the defendant provides security for the plaintiff's claim, that security may give the plaintiff a real preference if there is a foreign bankrupcy. In *Pertamina*,[57] Lord Denning viewed this with equanimity. But in *Cretanor Maritime*,[58] Buckley L.J. thought that it was a matter for debate whether "it is justifiable for the court to lend its authority in the exercise of a discretionary jurisdiction and one based fundamentally on equitable principles to bringing pressure to bear on a party in this way . . .". I share the Lord Justice's hesitations. The form of the injunction, referring to a body of unspecified assets which might increase during the term of the injunction and which might include money or goods of the defendant's stock in trade, in itself brings very considerable pressure to bear on any defendant.

Hitherto the *Mareva* injunction has been confined to commercial disputes. But there is no reason in principle to think that it should continue to be confined, in Lord Hailsham's felicitous phrase, to the "Arcadia of the commercial list".[59] For example, it could be a powerful weapon in disputes between estranged husbands and wives, particularly if the *Mareva* injunction is extended so as to reach defendants within the jurisdiction. There are indications that the courts are now realising some of the dangers of a promiscuous extension of *Mareva* injunctions. Lord Denning on more than one occasion has said "that we must be careful that it is not stretched too far, else we should be endangering it. It must be kept for proper circumstances and not extended so far as to endanger the proper conduct of business".[60]

The House of Lords has still to bless the jurisdiction to grant *Mareva* injunctions. Lord Denning has attempted to pre-empt that option by saying that "if the House had any doubts about our jurisdiction in the matter I should have expected them [in *The Siskina*] to give voice to them, rather than let the legal profession continue in error".[61] *Mareva* injunctions have now flourished for some years; and neither the legal profession nor the users of the commercial court will be anxious to kill the goose that laid the golden egg. They are now probably too firmly established to be overthrown. But the years that lie ahead may well see a restriction of the ambit and scope of the injunction rather than a further period of expansion. In my view, it should be sparingly exercised. In particular:

(a) the *Mareva* injunction should not be extended to attach the assets of defendants within the jurisdiction;

(b) the plaintiff should be required to show that his claim is so strong that it is not seriously disputed; and that the defendant is likely to remove assets from the jurisdiction;

(c) the *Mareva* injunction should not be used to circumvent indirectly statutory provisions.[62]

Addendum

This lecture was delivered in July, 1979. Since that time many of the "unresolved questions" have been resolved; for example, a *Mareva* injunction may now lie against a defendant resident within the jurisdiction[63] and the injunction is no longer confined to the "Arcadia of the commercial list".[64]

My forecast made 16 months ago, that the years ahead will see a restriction of the ambit of the *Mareva* jurisdiction has, therefore, proved quite wrong!

NOTES

1. (1890), 45 CL.D. 1, 14.

2. *Nippon Yusen Kaisha* v. *Karageorgis,* [1975] 1 W.L.R. 1093; *Mareva Compania Naviera S.A. of Panama* v. *International Bulk Carriers S.A.,* [1975] 2 Lloyds Rep. 509; *MBPXL Corp.* v. *International Banking Corpn,* unreported [1975] Court of Appeal Transcript 411; *Rasu Maritima S.A.* v. *Pertambangan Minyak Dan Gas Bumi Negera (Pertamina) and Government of Indonesia (as interveners),* [1978] Q.B. 644; *Cretanor Maritime Co. Ltd.* v. *Irish Marine Management Ltd.,* [1978] 1 W.L.R. 966; *The Assios,* [1979] 1 Lloyds Rep. 331; *Third Chandris Shipping Corpn.* v. *Unimarine S.A.,* [1979] 2 All E.R. 972.

3. *The Siskina,* [1977] 3 W.L.R. 818.

4. *Mareva Compania Naviera S.A.* v. *International Bulk Carriers, supra,* note 2.

5. Woodthorpe Brandon, *A Treatise upon the Customary Law of Foreign Attachment* (London, 1861), p. 7.

6. *Pennoyer* v. *Ness* (1877), 95 U.S. 714, 723-724, *per* Justice Field. In civil law jurisdiction the procedure is known as *saisie conservatoire.*

7. See text accompanying notes 8 and 9 *infra.*

8. *Supra,* note 2.

9. At pp. 1094-1095.

10. *Supra,* note 2.

11. *Supra,* note 2.

12. *Supra,* note 2, at 975, *per* Mustill J.

13. *Supra,* note 2.

14. *Supra,* note 2, at 660-661.

15. *Third Chandris Shipping Corpn.* v. *Unimarine S.A.,* [1979] 2 All E.R. 972, 976, *per* Mustill J.

16. *Ibid.*

17. [1977] 3 W.L.R. 818.

18. [1978] 1 W.L.R. 966.

19. [1979] 2 All E.R. 972.

20. *Supra.*

21. *The Assios*, [1979] 1 Lloyds Rep. 331.

22. *Third Chandris Shipping Corpn.* v. *Unimarine S.A. supra,* note 19, at 984, *per* Lord Denning M.R., citing *The Assios, ibid.*

23. *Ibid.*

24. *MPBXL Corpn.* v. *International Banking Corpn.*, [1975] Court of Appeal Transcript 411.

25. See *Cretanor Maritime Co. Ltd.* v. *Irish Marine Management Ltd., supra,* note 18, at 972.

26. *Supra*, note 22.

27. *Supra,* note 22.

28. *Cretanor Maritime Co. Ltd.* v. *Irish Marine Management Ltd., supra,* note 18.

29. *Third Chandris Shipping Corpn.* v. *Unimarine S.A.,* [1979] 2 All E.R. 972, 985, *per* Lord Denning M.R., 988, *per* Lawton and Cumming-Bruce L.JJ.

30. [1979] 1 All E.R. 397.

31. *Supra*, p. 31.

32. [1978] Q.B. 644, 661.

33. [1975] A.C. 396.

34. *Supra*, note 32, at 664. See also *Cretanor Maritime Co. Ltd.* v. *Irish Marine Management Ltd.,* [1978] 1 W.L.R. 966, 975, *per* Buckley L.J.

35. [1979] 2 All E.R. 972.

36. *Supra*, note 33.

37. *Supra*, note 35, at 977.

38. *Supra*, note 35, at 985, 987, 988.

39. *Supra*, note 35, at 985.

40. *Supra*, note 35, at 987.

41. *Supra*, note 35, at 985, 987-988.

42. [1977] 3 W.L.R. 818.

43. *Third Chandris Shipping Corpn.* v. *Unimarine S.A.*, [1979] 2 All E.R. 972, 983, *per* Lord Denning M.R.

44. [1978] 1 W.L.R. 966.

45. [1978] 1 W.L.R. 966, 974, *per* Buckley L.J.

46. *Ibid.;* as did the old procedure of foreign attachment.

47. *Supra*, p. 32.

48. *Supra*, note 42 at 830.

49. There are hints in *Pertamina*, [1978] Q.B. 644.

50. [1979] 2 All E.R. 972, 983-984.

51. March 16, 1979; unreported.

52. (1980), 45 Ch. D. 1, 14; *supra*, p. 1.

53. See Sir Michael Kerr's remarks in (1978), 41 M.L.R. 1, 14-15.

54. *Supra,* note 50, at 978.

55. [1978] 1 W.L.R. 966.

56. *Supra*, note 55, at 974, *per* Buckley L.J.

57. [1978] Q.B. 644, 662.

58. *Supra*, note 55, at 974-975.

59. [1978] 3 W.L.R. 818, 830.

60. *The Assios*, [1979] 1 Lloyds Rep. 331, 334. See also *Third Chandris Shipping Corpn.* v. *Unimarine S.A.*, [1979] 2 All E.R. 972.

61. *Supra*, note 60, at 983.

62. As was done in *Rena K.,* [1979] 1 All E.R. 397.

63. *Barclay-Johnson* v. *Yuill*, [1830] 3 All E.R. 190; *Abdul Rahman* v. *Abu-Taha*, [1980] 3 All E.R. 409.

64. *Allen* v. *Jambo Holdings*, [1980] 2 All E.R. 502. See also *Iraqi Ministry of Defence* v. *Arcepey Shipping Co.*, [1980] 2 W.L.R. 488; *A* v. *C,* [1980] 2 All E.R. 347.

4

London-Edinburgh and Ottawa-Québec: A Study in Parallels

The Honourable Jules Deschênes

Introduction

On March 1, 1979 the Welch electorate overwhelmingly turned down the devolution proposal that had been put forward by Westminster.

On the same day, the Scottish electorate gave the scheme a rather cool reception: there were more abstentions than either ayes or nays and the ayes even failed to reach the 40 percent level provided for in the Scotland Act.[1]

A month later, the Labour government was defeated in the House of Commons by a one-vote margin (311-310) and on May 3, the Conservatives were swept back into power.

Before the new Parliament, on May 15, 1979, Her Majesty read from the throne:

> My ministers will propose the repeal of the Scotland Act (1978), and all-party discussions will be held about the devolution of power from Westminster.[2]

On the other side of the Atlantic, Canada was living under a Liberal government committed to maintaining the unity of the Confederation when, on November 15, 1976, the *Parti Québécois* was elected to power in the Province of Québec. The very first article of the program of the *Parti Québécois* reads as follows:

> To realize the political sovereignty of Québec by democratic means and to propose to Canada a mutually advantageous economic association.
>
> [*Translation*]

There followed a period of fruitless continuous confrontation until the federal election of May 22, 1979 when the Conservative Party took 136 seats, *i.e.*, slightly less than a majority and were called upon to form the new government while the Liberals had captured 114 ridings, including all but eight of the 75 Québec seats.

Given those circumstances, both here and abroad, a superficial observer might be led to the conclusion that the pursuit of the topic of this lecture would amount to a mere exercise in futility. Yet on second thought one is brought to realize that the movement of history has not been stopped by those electoral events and that the nationalist forces which are at work in Scotland and in Québec will indeed continue to try and forge ahead.

Now it is of course well known that Scotland and Québec have not followed an identical path over the years in relation with the United Kingdom and Canada. Nevertheless a joint overview of their respective history opens up on striking similarities in many fields of human endeavour.

I therefore propose to examine with you two of those parallels in the fields of law and of politics after having briefly retraced, also in a parallel fashion, the course of the two countries.

Each of you will remain free to draw his own conclusions but our survey should form, I hope, a convenient backdrop for the discussions on devolution which are scheduled to follow.

Historical Parallel

The Indians were still roaming freely through the vast expanses of what would later become North America when King Robert Bruce I of Scotland defeated Edward II of England at Bannockburn in 1314. By the peace of Northampton in 1328 "the English for a time recognized a *fait accompli*"[3] and Scottish independence lasted nearly four centuries.

In the meantime the European perception of the world was quite materially evolving in the wake of the pioneering ships of the great adventurers of the 16th and 17th centuries. Colonial empires would rise and fall; men, countries and continents would be affected both at home and abroad. It does not fall within the purview of the present study to encompass all those events; a few relevant landmarks however deserve to be recalled.

In 1534, Jacques Cartier erected a cross with the coat of arms of the King of France on the peninsula of Gaspé, at the eastern tip of Québec.

Two years later, under Henry VIII, the Parliament of England enacted a statute providing for the incorporation of Wales into the realm of England,[4] thus confirming a situation which had in fact existed for some three centuries.

Towards the beginning of the next century, the effects of the marital *saga* of Henry VIII and the provisions of his will created an historical accident[5] as a result of which James VI, King of Scots succeeded Elizabeth in 1603 as James I[6] and united on his head the Crowns of England and Scotland. The gestation of Great Britain was beginning, though the independent Parliaments of Westminster and Edinburgh would continue to exist for another century.

Across the ocean, barely two years later, in 1608, Champlain founded Québec on the banks of the Saint-Lawrence River and in 1642 Monsieur de Maisonneuve established Montréal, under its original name of Ville Marie.

But while the French colony was slowly progressing, back in Great Britain the Scots were getting more and more restive under the rule of an absentee king and, at the beginning of the 18th century a war of nerves broke between the two Parliaments.

In 1703 the Scots moved to curtail in an unprecedented fashion the royal prerogative and to transfer to the Scottish Parliament the whole department of foreign affairs;[7] this was in truth a declaration of complete independence.[8]

The English Parliament retaliated in 1705 with an Act for the security of the Kingdom:[9] Westminster invited Edinburgh to a Conference on Union, but coupled its invitation with a threat that, failing union to materialize, the border would be closed to export of arms and to import of Scotch cattle, coal and linen.

Common sense prevailed and the two countries appointed Commissioners who finally agreed upon the terms of a complete union. The Scottish Parliament approved the plan on January 16, 1707 by a vote of 110 to 69.[10] The English Parliament in turn passed the Act of Union by a vote of 274 to 116 on February 28, 1707.[11] Royal assent was given on March 6 and the Union came into being on May 1, 1707 (art. 1).[12]

Henceforth Great Britain would have one flag, one King and one Parliament, common currency and standard of measures and freedom of trade and movement. The Acts of Union made however special provision for the independent continuance of the Church of Scotland and of the Scots legal and judicial system. We shall return later to this last condition of the Union.

From then on the colonial wars absorbed a growing part of the energies and resources of Great Britain, France, Spain, Portugal and the Netherlands and spread over their colonies. Around the middle of the 18th century, Great Britain scored victories in Europe, in America and in the Far East which culminated in the Treaty of Paris of 1763.[13] In article IV of the Treaty, France renounced Nova Scotia and ceded to Great Britain the whole of Canada.

Thus came to pass the most momentous event in the history of Canada when the colony changed allegiance from France to Great Britain: there was planted the seed of over two centuries of disagreements which, alas!, appear only to have grown with time.

The Conqueror had introduced his own laws into the former French colony.[14] This created insuperable difficulties which were remedied by the Québec Act of 1774.[15] The 1763 Proclamation was revoked (art. IV), property and civil rights would thereafter be determined according to the laws and customs of Canada, *i.e.*, the laws and customs in force before the conquest (art. VIII), wills could be drawn according either to the laws of Canada or the laws of England (art. X) and the criminal law of England would exclusively continue in force (art. XI).

But political trouble continued to brew and the clamor for representative government kept increasing; in 1791, the Colonial Office decided to break up the colony into Upper and Lower Canada[16] with the proviso that all laws would continue in force as before (art. XXXIII). This however did not solve the political problems of the colony.

On this side of the ocean, Great Britain was becoming the United Kingdom of Great Britain and Ireland in 1800[17] but, in Canada, pressure was mounting for a more responsible form of government until an armed rebellion erupted in 1837-38, which was quashed in bloodshed.

The Earl of Durham was then entrusted with the task of investigating the situation and reporting on the means for curing the same. He reported indeed:[18]

> I expected to find a contest between a government and a people: I found two nations warring in the bosom of a single state: I found a struggle, not of principles, but of races; and I perceived that it would be idle to attempt any amelioration of laws or institutions until we could first succeed in terminating the deadly animosity that now separates the inhabitants of Lower Canada into the hostile divisions of French and English. . . .
>
> The national feud forces itself on the very senses, irresistibly and palpably, as the origin or the essence of every dispute which divides the community; we discover that dissensions, which appear to have another origin, are but forms of this constant and all-pervading quarrel; and that every contest is one of French and English in the outset, or becomes so ere it has run its course.

The solution which Durham put forward was drastic:[19]

> A plan by which it is proposed to ensure the tranquil government of Lower Canada, must include in itself the means of putting an end to the agitation of national disputes in the legislature, by settling, at once and for ever, the national character of the Province. I entertain no doubts as to the national character which must be given to Lower Canada; it must be that of the British Empire; that of the majority of the population of British America; that of the great race which must, in the lapse of no long period of time, be predominant over the whole North American Continent. Without effecting the change so rapidly or so roughly as to shock the feelings and trample on the welfare of the existing generation, it must henceforth be the first and steady purpose of the British Government to establish an English population with English laws and language, in this Province, and to trust its government to none but a decidedly English Legislature.

Of course those recommendations were based on factual considerations of Durham's own observation, *e.g.*:

They (the English) have decided superiority of intelligence on their side;[20]

They (the French Canadians) can see no hope for their nationality.[21]

Be that as it may, the Imperial government promptly agreed with Lord Durham and in 1840 Parliament passed the Union Act[22] whereby the two provinces were reunited into the Province of Canada (s. 1), the laws and the courts were continued in force (ss. 3, 27, 46 and 47) but an equal number of members was provided in the Legislative Assembly for each of the former Upper and Lower Canadas (s. 12)—though the population of French Lower Canada was nearly half as considerable[23]—and, for the first time, English was imposed as the only language of the legislature (s. 41).

Of course the new regime stirred up the passions again, the United Kingdom Parliament was prevailed upon to abrogate in 1848 the "English-only" provision of the 1840 Union Act[24] and, on January 18, 1849 the Governor General Lord Elgin read the Speech from the Throne in both English and French.

Discussions on the future of the remaining North American colonies continued through the Conferences of Charlottetown and Québec in 1864 and London in 1866, finally to bring about the British North America Act of 1867[25] which still governs the Canadian federation today.

Canada has evolved from four provinces to ten provinces and two territories while the United Kingdom has taken its contemporary aspect following the secession of Ireland, less the six Ulster counties, in 1922.[26]

This bird's eye view shows marked differences in the political evolution of the two countries. Scotland has now been integrated for nearly three centuries in a unitary kingdom while Québec, after some tumultuous episodes, has enjoyed an autonomous government for over a century within the Canadian federation.

Yet both Scotland and Québec have evidenced—with various degrees of success, it must be admitted—a strong desire to protect and further the originality of their ancestral culture, their religion, their language, their system of education; enlightening parallels could be drawn in each of those fields. Let us pause and compare their legal situation.

Legal Parallel

As in the cases of Louisiana or South Africa, a study of the common origin and common perils of the laws of Scotland and Québec should help strengthen both systems against corruption due to outside influences.

But let it be made clear at the outset: this purpose does not proceed from, and should not be branded as a chauvinistic attitude. The comparative law method has long ago demonstrated its ability to bring different legal systems closer to one another and to enrich one by the novel solutions which another can offer and which are missing from the former's tradition.

The evil however that must be avoided at all costs consists in the blind importation into an autonomous legal system of solutions worked by a neighbouring legal system, without due regard to the inherent logic of each one and under the guise of a desirable so-called uniformity. Lord Cooper once made the point beyond reply:[27]

> In the last resort it does not greatly matter what solutions are found, but it does greatly matter that in any given country the law should develop systematically and logically so that its future trend and application shall be capable of reasoned forecast. Either oil or water is preferable to the unsatisfactory emulsion which results from attempts to mix the two.

Scotland and Québec share laws of romanistic origin; they also share the experience of common law infiltration, especially through the judicial process at the appellate level.

Prior to the 1707 Union, Scotland had perfected a legal system based essentially on Roman-inspired principles, learnt through the civilist tradition of France and the Netherlands. In the 14th century, the Scots students were numerous enough at Orléans to form a *nation* and, in the 17th and 18th centuries, no less than 1,600 Scottish law students received their training at Leyden.[28] No wonder that Scottish writers would quote freely from Pothier and Domat, from Grotius and the Voets.

By the same period, the Scottish courts were firmly established and no appeal lay from them to the Three Estates in Parliament, save exceptionally by means of the "protest for remeid of law" which, in any event, did not stay execution.[29] Indeed in 1674 the advocates who persisted to pursue direct appeals to Parliament were disbarred and banished from Edinburgh by the Lords of Session with the express support of Charles II.[30]

The 1707 Act of Union provided (art. 18) for the uniformity of commercial laws in England and Scotland and the continuance of the other Scottish laws, subject to alteration "by the Parliament of Great Britain; with this difference betwixt the Laws concerning Public Right, Policy and Civil Government, and those which concern Private Right, that the Laws which concern Public Right, Policy, and Civil Government, may be made the same throughout the whole United Kingdom; But that no alteration be made in Laws which concern private Right, except for evident utility of the Subjects within Scotland."

One might, in passing, compare this provision with the clauses of the B.N.A. Act, 160 years later, as to "peace, order and good government" in the federal powers and as to "property and civil rights" in the provincial powers.

The 1707 Act of Union also continued in existence the Scottish courts (art. 19) and provided "that no Causes in Scotland be Cognisable by the Courts of Chancery, Queen's Bench, Common Pleas, or any other Court in Westminster Hall; and that the said Courts, or any other of the like nature, after the Union, shall have no power to cognosce, review, or alter the Acts or Sentences of the Judicatures within Scotland or to stop the execution of the same''.

The Act was silent, however, concerning the possibility of appeals to the Judicial branch of Parliament. Immediately after the Union, the question arose and the House of Lords accepted to exercise an appellate jurisdiction over the Scottish Courts.[31]

Great difficulties would flow from this assumption of jurisdiction. For 160 years the law of Scotland would find its final exposition in a court where no jurist trained in Scottish law would ever sit, the law involved was openly taken as foreign and, too often, the point at issue was considered in the light of the inapplicable, but more readily-accessible English law.

Indeed some of the Law Lords would candidly admit their utter ignorance of the principles at stake; Lord Chancellor Erskine is reported to have once said in the House of Lords:[32]

> . . . that he knew something of the law; but of Scotch law he was as ignorant as a native of Mexico. And yet he was quite as learned in it as any one of their Lordships. . .

It was only in 1867—the year of Canadian Confederation—that the first Scottish Law Lord, Lord Colonsay, was appointed[33] and the year 1876 saw the passing of the Appellate Jurisdiction Act[34] which has been followed, as "a practical necessity",[35] by the presence of at least one Scottish peer (currently two) to hear appeals to the House of Lords from Scotland.

In Québec, where the civil laws were reinstated in 1774 after an 11-year unsuccessful experiment, the Judicial Committee of the Privy Council had served as the final court of appeal since the conquest by virtue of the Royal Proclamation of 1763.[36] Its jurisdiction was continued by s. 129 of the B.N.A. Act until its abolition in criminal matters in 1933[37] and in civil matters in 1949.[38]

In the interval, Canada had established the Supreme Court of Canada in 1875.[39] Until recently, it usually sat as a Bench of five and not until 1949 did the Québec judges ever form a majority in hearing civil law cases.[40]

Similar difficulties were therefore likely to arise in the treatment of Québec civil law as in that of Scottish law and similar protests would be heard from time to time on either side of the Atlantic. Listen to Lord Justice-Clerk Home in 1852:[41]

> The more I am able to collect of English law, I am only the more confident that we do not understand nine out of ten of the (English) cases which are quoted to us, and that in attempts to apply that law, we run the greatest risk of spoiling our own by mistaking theirs.

Listen now to Mr. Justice Mignault in 1918:[42]

> May I say, with all possible deference, that I would deprecate, on a question under the Quebec law, relying upon a decision, even of the Privy Council, rendered according to the rules of the English law. It would first be necessary

to shew that there is no difference between the two systems of law by referring to authorities binding under the French law, and this has not been done. Very earnestly, I am of the opinion that each system of law should be administered according to its own rules and by reference to authorities or judgments which are binding on it alone.

And again Mr. Justice Mignault:[43]

Il me semble respectueusement qu'il est temps de réagir contre l'habitude de recourir, dans les causes de la province de Québec, aux précédents du droit commun anglais, pour le motif que le code civil contiendrait une règle qui serait d'accord avec un principe du droit anglais. Sur bien des points, et surtout en matière de mandat, le code civil et le *common law* contiennent des règles semblables. Cependant le droit civil constitue un système complet par lui-même et doit s'interpréter d'après ses propres règles. Si pour cause d'identité de principes juridiques on peut recourir au droit anglais pour interpréter le droit civil français, on pourrait avec autant de raison citer les monuments de la jurisprudence française pour mettre en lumière les règles du droit anglais. Chaque système, je le répète, est complet par lui-même, et sauf le cas où un système prend dans l'autre un principe qui lui était auparavant étranger, on n'a pas besoin d'en sortir pour chercher la règle qu'il convient d'appliquer aux espèces bien diverses qui se présentent dans la pratique journalière.

Due to historical circumstances beyond their control, both Scotland and Québec were thus exposed to an outside influence which would naturally tend to assimilate different original systems into the one with which the court of last resort—be it the House of Lords or the Privy Council—was most familiar.

The approach usually followed the same line of reasoning based on a pseudo-comparative method that reduces all other systems to common law as though, to quote Professor T. B. Smith,[44] "the ultimate revelation of legal wisdom had been given to one chosen people at one particular period in time".

Thus in a Scottish appeal where, strangely enough, he chose to consider first the English authorities, Lord Chancellor Cranworth then said:[45]

I consider, therefore, that in England the doctrine must be regarded as well settled; but if such be the law of England, on what ground can it be argued not to be the law of Scotland? The law, as established in England, is founded on principles of universal application, not on any peculiarities of English jurisprudence; and unless, therefore, there has been a settled course of decision in Scotland to the contrary, I think it would be most inexpedient to sanction a different rule to the north of the Tweed from that which prevails to the south.

One could hear the same doctrine in Canada towards the turn of the last century. In 1894 the Chief Justice of Canada (Strong C.J.), examining a question which fell to be decided by the civil law of Québec, commented as follows after having quoted from various English precedents:[46]

> The two systems of law are, as I have said, identical as to the liability here invoked being one arising from the breach of an incidental duty towards inferior proprietors appertaining to the ownership of property and not dependent upon any delict or quasi-delict in the nature of personal negligence. I see therefore no reason why the courts of the province of Quebec in administering their own law should not be content to adopt the principle of these English authorities founded upon reasons which must certainly commend them to every judicial mind.

More recently the Supreme Court of Canada came to the defence of the morality of Québec, as embodied in art. 1056 of the Civil Code, on the occasion of a suit in damages by a mother following the death of her natural son;[47] and here again, after referring to English law which held that the word "child" refers only to a legitimate child, the Chief Justice of Canada (Anglin C.J.) added:[48]

> We can conceive of no reason why a different intention should be imputed to the legislature of Quebec. It would be a libel on that province to suggest that (except, perhaps, in the particular covered by art. 237, discussed below,) illegitimacy is there less disfavoured by law than it is in England, or in any province of Canada whose legal system is based on the English common law.

This attitude, which I would dare call imperialistic, forced upon the legal systems of Scotland and Québec institutions and constructions which were foreign to their spirit and detrimental to their integrity. A simple mention of a few instances in both countries will suffice.

In the matter of *Gordon of Park*[49] which, admittedly, goes back a long way, Lord Chancellor Hardwicke, speaking on behalf of the House of Lords and reversing the Court of Session, gave to the word "heir" a meaning foreign to the law of Scotland. He then wrote to one of his friends that he feared his decision "would be of difficult digestion with the professors of the law of Scotland".[50]

A full century later the House of Lords, again reversing the Court of Session, imposed on Scotland the law of common employment.[51] It would take 90 years of complaint and a special statute[52] to restore the *status quo*.

In this century—this last example will sound quite familiar to the ears of Québec civilian lawyers—the English categories of invitees, licensees and trespassers were judicially imposed in 1929[53] on the Scottish system of *culpa*, or fault which is also embodied in art. 1053 of the Québec Civil Code. Again it took special legislation to remedy the situation.[54]

But Scotland is not alone to suffer from those inadmissible incursions of common law over its civil law heritage.

Early this century the Privy Council was pondering a question of burden of proof[55] where the Supreme Court of Canada had considered and relied upon ten judgments of the French Courts, seven of which were in the *Cour de Cassation*.[56]

Now unbelievable as it may appear, counsel were commended for their failure to discuss those authorities before the Judicial Committee. Lord Macnaghten said:[57]

> As recent French decisions, though entitled to the highest respect and valuable as illustrations, are not of binding authority in Québec, the learned counsel at the bar very properly abstained from examining in detail the cases referred to by Girouard J.

Later in the celebrated case of *Québec Railway Light, Heat and Power* v. *Vandry*[58] the Privy Council had to examine the meaning and effect of art. 1054 of the Québec Civil Code concerning the responsibility of a person for a thing under that person's care. Lord Sumner said:[59]

> Natural as this may be, the statutory character of the Civil Code of Lower Canada must always be borne in mind.
>
> . . .
>
> . . . (it) is and always must be remembered to be the language of a Legislature established within the British Empire.

Now it has repeatedly been pointed out since then that such is a wrong approach: the Civil Code is not a statute, it calls for a liberal construction and to apply to it the rules of statutory interpretation is to betray its very nature and function.

Again this approach led the Privy Council into refusing to consult what, in civilian tradition, is a most important source for the true construction of the Code: the Reports of the Codifiers. Lord Moulton took occasion of another celebrated case involving, this time, the provisions of the Civil Code concerning marriage[60] to state categorically:[61]

> If it were permissible to regard the intentions of the codifiers as expressed by their reports, their intention to leave the law unchanged would be equally evident, but this is a dangerous and doubtful proceeding and their Lordships decline to adopt it.

Mr. Justice Mignault, one of the most respected exponents of the Civil Law tradition in Québec, severely criticized this refusal:[62]

> J'ai indiqué plus haut quelques règles d'interprétation. Je veux insister encore sur l'autorité qu'on doit reconnaître dans ce cas aux rapports des codificateurs. On en a toujours fait usage dans la Province de Québec ainsi qu'à la Cour suprême pour découvrir l'intention du législateur. Nos juges disent souvent que ces rapports fournissent le meilleur commentaire du texte. Il n'y a pas d'analogie entre ces rapports et les débats au Parlement dont on ne peut faire état devant les tribunaux. J'ai déjà dit que les rapports des codificateurs ont un caractère officiel. Il n'y a pas lieu de croire qu'on cesse jamais de s'en servir chez nous. Certainement le fait de s'y référer ne constitue pas, dans notre système juridique, une erreur de droit.

Then after referring to the Privy Council's attitude, Mr. Justice Mignault added:[63]

> Le but de cette étude est d'exprimer avec toute déférence possible mon opinion personnelle. Je me permettrai donc d'insister sur ce que je viens de dire. L'usage des rapports des codificateurs pour découvrir la volonté du législateur existe chez nous depuis la confection du Code. Je soumets qu'il est conforme non seulement à une pratique judiciaire constante, mais encore aux méthodes qu'emploie le droit civil partout où il forme le droit commun. La pratique du droit anglais est différente, je le reconnais, mais dans une matière comme celle-ci, notre droit a des méthodes qui lui sont propres.

Fortunately this "historical association with an English court . . . is now passé,"[64] our legal literature is flourishing and our court of last resort for the last 30 years, the Supreme Court of Canada, has resolutely turned to a truly civilian approach of the Civil law appeals which come from Québec.

Yet it is a mutually stimulative exercise to compare the very similar difficulties under which Scotland and Québec have had to labour in order to preserve and even enhance the specific character of their traditional legal systems. This originality stands as one of the basic ingredients of our respective societies; and our common will at preserving our legal tradition, together with our other traditional institutions, goes a long way to explain the political parallel to which we will now direct our attention.

Political Parallel

In his recent book on Scotland,[65] John Mercer wrote:

> The natural allies of the Scots nationalists are the Quebec separatists and the European minorities;

Elsewhere in his book, Mercer analyzed the social background of the S.N.P. (Scottish National Party) candidates in the 1974 British general elections and noted:[66]

> This is remarkably similar to the composition of the candidates put up by Canada's separatist Parti Québécois, recently successful in the Québec province election.

Even though the two movements are rooted in a much different soil, one should not be surprised at their common complexion, at least in many particulars. They are both driven by closely-related forces; they are both trying to find solutions to the acute problems which Vernon Bogdanor has so sharply outlined in his provocative book, earlier this year, on *Devolution*:[67]

> How is national unity best secured—through centralized government, or through the dispersal of power? Is the recognition of a sense of nationality in one of the component parts of a state compatible with the continued unity of that state? These are the kinds of issue that lie behind the contemporary debate. . . .

So let us now try together to grasp the situation, to understand the much talked about "devolution" and to shoot tracers into the darkness of the future.

In the middle of 1977,[68] there were 55,852,000 people in the United Kingdom, of whom 5,196,000, *i.e.*, 9.3 percent lived in Scotland.

The Scots are rightfully proud of their national achievements.

Since the Act of Union, they have preserved the freedom of the Presbyterian Church of Scotland, the establishment of which constituted a fundamental condition of the Union.

They have also preserved, in spite of the difficulties which we have reviewed earlier, their original legal and judicial system and have launched a considerable effort in order to revitalize the teaching and the development of law.

They can boast of a rich cultural heritage: Adam Smith, David Hume, Robert Burns, Sir Walter Scott, among others. In our times, Edinburgh is a leader with its International Festival and Québecers will learn with amazement and a hint of jealousy that the Scottish opera benefits from an annual grant of about £1,000,000 plus £175,000 for playing in England.

They also have a claim to an ancestral language: the Scottish form of Gaelic which, a hundred years ago, was spoken by about 6 percent of the population of Scotland. It however appears that this figure has now dropped to 1½ percent.[69] Of course Gaelic has no claim to international usage outside of Ireland and, to some extent, French Britanny but its continued presence nevertheless gives rise occasionally to various incidents; witness a protest to the B.B.C. that one of its programmes "separated Christ from his Disciples by English and Scots speech".[70]

The situation of French Canadians bears much resemblance to that of the Scots, except that we represent a substantially larger proportion of the total population of our country.

In October 1978, Canada had 23,548,000 inhabitants, of whom 6,285,400 *i.e.*, 26.7 percent lived in Québec.[71] But one has to superimpose here the figures relating to languages, mainly English and French. According to the 1976 Census, 61.4 percent of the Canadian population reported English as their mother tongue and 25.6 percent French. Of these, 4,989,245 were living in Québec where they formed exactly 80 percent of the population.[72]

Those 5,000,000 French Canadians—or, as they are more often referred to today, Québecers—together with their compatriots spread across Canada (897,960 in 1976) and the hundreds of thousands who emigrated to the New England states towards the end of last century, are the descendants of the 60,000 colonists who were left by France on the shores of the St. Lawrence River in 1763.

As the Scots, we have kept our church, though it must be admitted that it has lost many followers during the last 25 years or so.

As the Scots also, we have kept our legal system. Thanks to the large number of scholars who have matured during the last generation, civil law in Québec is most vigourous and the Civil Code Revision Office has produced in 1978 a monumental draft of a new code adapted to our new society.

As the Scots, we cherish our cultural heritage. Numerous are our authors, composers and performers who have now won international recognition and the French TV network of Radio-Canada, which services about ¼ of the country's population, has produced last year 12 percent more original programmes than the total of which its English counterpart can boast.[73]

Finally, as the Scots, we love our maternal tongue, but I owe it to the truth to say that we have done better than the Scots in that particular respect since French is the actual daily language of my 5,000,000 compatriots in Québec and we can, through it, communicate freely with a large audience the world over and share in one of the richest cultures that the Western civilization has known.

Yet, strangely enough, both Scotland and Québec have collided with England.

Scots and Québecers can demonstrate without fear of contradiction that the 1707 Union and the 1867 Confederation were consummated without popular consultation and in spite of serious objections which were forcefully voiced at the time.

Here, many Scots complain that the Union has consistently played in favour of England; in Canada, many Québecers complain that Confederation has consistently played in favour of industrialized Ontario and the Western prairies.

In Scotland and Québec, the weight of a stronger partner is always felt, economically and culturally.

In Scotland and Québec, the wish and the will steadily grow to become masters in one's own house and to entertain free international contacts.

But in Scotland and in Québec, many people fear the unknown morrows of radical political changes.

Both Scotland and Québec accounts, based as they are on figures which are often incomplete and calculations which are often arbitrary, have led only to useless verbal fights and inconclusive debates.

Yet there is felt a deep unrest in both countries and, in each of them, a nationalist party is aiming broadly at the same results.

Due however to the very different constitutional and political situation which obtains here and abroad, each party had to follow a different strategy.

In Scotland, the movement began towards the middle of the last century[74] when the Reverend James Begg, of the Free Church in Edinburgh, called for the preservation of Scotland's status "not as a conquered province of England, but a distinct independent kingdom, which was united with England on equal terms, and under a clear and solemn treaty''.[75]

During the next hundred years, the movement knew various ups and downs. One curious incident occurred in 1912. Winston Churchill had suggested during the previous year, while he was Home Secretary, a policy of devolution—here is the ''sacred'' word. In September of 1912, he was soberly discussing the proposal in his riding of Dundee when he was interrupted by suffragette demonstrators.[76] The question of the women's vote carried the day over that of devolution.

In due course the S.N.P. came out of the merger of the Scottish Party and the National Party in 1934. In 1946, under the inspiration of Doctor Robert McIntyre it published an extensive programme providing, *inter alia,* for the setting up of a Scottish Parliament under the Crown as soon as a majority of S.N.P. members would be elected to Westminster; the programme also foresaw ''a particularly intimate relationship with the other countries of the British Isles'': across the Atlantic, others would later label such a programme ''Sovereignty-Association''. The S.N.P. programme also looked to direct relations with the Dominions and membership in the United Nations Organization.[77]

The S.N.P. entered the electoral field in 1945 but failed to make any significant impact during the next 20 years. Nevertheless its ideas were slowly gaining ground and, in April 1969, the government created a huge 16-member Royal Commission of Enquiry on the constitution under the chairmanship of Lord Crowther and, after the latter's death, of Lord Kilbrandon.

In 1970, the S.N.P. took 11.4 percent of the vote in Scotland, won one seat and ran second in nine constituencies.

On October 10, 1973 the Kilbrandon Commission filed its report[78] where it recommended, among other matters, that several powers be devolved to a Scottish elected assembly (#173) and that Executive authority be exercised by Ministers appointed by the Crown and drawn from members of the Assembly (#177).

In the General elections which followed in February 1974, the S.N.P. increased its proportion of the vote to 22 percent, elected seven members and ran second in 17 ridings.

Then came the elections of October 1974. The S.N.P. announced in its manifesto that it ''would support the establishment of a Scottish Assembly only as a step on the road to full self-Government''.[79] The S.N.P. was contesting all the 71 Scottish seats. It increased its share of the vote to 30 percent, elected 11 members and ran second in no less than 42 ridings. The S.N.P. was now obviously a force to be reckoned with.

In Québec, nationalist effervescence can be traced as far back as the conquest. It had its first violent eruption in the 1830's. It then listened to its tenors: Henri Bourassa at the turn of the century, Canon Lionel Groulx for the first half of the 1900's. It gained ground during the economic recessions and during the military crises of the last two wars. It even made a brief incursion into the political arena with André Laurendeau and the Bloc Populaire during the last war. Only however during the recent years, as in Scotland, did it display real political force.

One must however take into account that Canada is not a unitary State, but a Federation comprising a central and ten provincial governments. Since 1867, Canadians have voted for two levels of government. Now the powers are shared between them in agreement with the division provided for in the B.N.A. Act and the Privy Council has stated clearly that the B.N.A. Act has conferred upon the provincial legislatures "powers not in any sense to be exercised by delegation from or as agents of the Imperial Parliament, but authority as plenary and as ample within the limits prescribed by sect. 92 as the Imperial Parliament in the plenitude of its power possessed and could bestow. Within these limits of subjects and area the local legislature is supreme, . . .".[80]

Far therefore from trying to gain access to the Federal Parliament, the natural strategy for the nationalist movement led it to concentrate its efforts on the Government of Québec which could later on be used as a most powerful lever to achieve its aims.

The now uncontested leader of the movement, René Lévesque, had been a Minister for some five years in the Liberal government of Jean Lesage when he broke away, in October 1967, on the matter of Québec sovereignty. The following month he founded the "Mouvement souveraineté-association" and still 11 months later the "Parti Québécois". Within two weeks, a merger followed with the other force of importance, the R.I.N. (Rassemblement pour l'indépendance nationale) and the scene was set for the political battle.

In 1970, the P.Q. (Parti Québécois) won seven ridings on 23 percent of the votes. In 1973 it took 30 percent of the votes, but only six seats as against 102 by the Liberals. Came then November 15, 1976 when, after a campaign based at least as much on good government as on a platform of independence, a dramatic reversal gave 40 percent of the popular vote to the P.Q. Premier Bourassa was defeated in his own riding, the Liberals lost 76 seats and the P.Q., with 71 members elected out of 110, emerged as the new Government of Québec. For the first time in history, the party in power and the government did not include a single anglophone and were committed to a drastic re-appraisal of the political arrangements in Canada.

But events were also moving fast in the United Kingdom. The government had to face up to the challenge of the rising influence of the S.N.P.; its answer was the magic word: devolution.

The Kilbrandon Commission had examined the various alternatives to the *status quo* with which, obviously, a large number of Scots were dissatisfied.

It first discarded separatism, whereby Westminster would "transfer" to Scotland "complete sovereignty in all matters, in effect creating a separate independent state".[81]

It went on also to set aside federalism, whereby Westminster would "transfer" to Scotland "sovereignty in certain matters only, retaining sovereignty in other matters, such as defense and foreign affairs".[82] Such a division of powers and its related taxation scheme are of course familiar to Canadians.

But the Kilbrandon Commission considered favourably devolution whereby, "while retaining sovereignty in all matters", Westminster "could delegate to Scotland the exercise of selected powers".[83] In such a system, the central Parliament would retain its supremacy, but it would transfer some of its functions to a subordinate elected body.

Devolution in turn may be broadly legislative or, more restrictively, executive. The Kilbrandon Commission recommended legislative devolution including a number of fields more properly regional, to be dealt with by an elective Scottish Assembly. The Assembly would however have no taxing power and the system would be financed by means of a block grant by Westminster.[84] Thus would be created the strange situation of an elected Assembly armed with the power to spend, but denied the power to tax.

In a White Paper of November 1975,[85] the government foresaw the system as follows:

> 99. The Government accordingly intend that Scottish public expenditure should be settled as part of the annual public expenditure review for the United Kingdom as a whole. The amount will be a matter for political judgment, on the basis of an assessment of relative needs made jointly with the Scottish administration through close and continuous collaboration. Once the relative amounts of public expenditure are established, Parliament will be asked to vote the appropriate element for the devolved services in the form of a block grant. In 1974-75 public expenditure on the services proposed for devolution was about £2,000 million, with a further sum of more than £100 million met by local authorities as loan charges. Had the proposed financial arrangements been in operation this would have involved a block grant of more than £1,300 million, local authority taxation of £300 million and borrowing of about £500 million. Expenditure on the devolved services would have come to nearly three-fifths of total identifiable public expenditure in Scotland.

A first Scotland and Wales Bill to implement the scheme was published on November 29, 1976. It was however halted at Committee stage on February 22, 1977.

Separate Bills were later introduced and the Scotland Act (1978) was finally assented to on July 31, 1978.[86]

For Canadians, who know by experience the infinite possibilities of litigation and the hundreds of cases that have arisen under the relatively short provisions bearing on the division of powers between federal and provincial authorities in the B.N.A. Act, the Scotland Act will remain as a source of perpetual amazement.

To deal with the issue of devolution, Parliament needed no less than 87 sections supplemented by 17 schedules.

Devolution must be restrictively interpreted; in any event, no power is devolved to the Scottish Assembly that would bear on extraterritorial matters or on the powers to borrow or to tax. The prerogative of mercy and the field of international affairs are also excluded.

Then the nice schedule #10 lists, in its Part I, 25 groups of devolved matters; in its part II, 25 groups of exclusions and, in its part III, 18 pages of specific *in*clusions or *ex*clusions.

It comes as no surprise that the Act sets out a detailed procedure to litigate devolution issues up to the Privy Council.[87]

The Act also provided for a referendum where at least 40 percent of the eligible voters should approve of the measure. We now know that this level of consensus was not reached. Further events are part of the country's recent history, but it should be noticed that in the 1979 general elections the S.N.P. lost half of its electoral support and kept only two of its previous 11 seats at Westminster.

Conclusion

The question may now be asked: Where do these parallels between Scotland and Québec lead us?

History shows that nationalist feelings will not be abated by electoral drawbacks.

Furthermore as to Scotland, the oil and gas discoveries in the North Sea provide a powerful incentive for the search of more regional freedom with a view to larger financial rewards: witness Shetland. However Glasgow Professor John P. Grant has shown that, upon turning independent, Scotland might well not be able to establish title, under international law, to the larger part of the oil fields off its coasts.[88] But the question remains debatable.

Be that as it may, the political programmes of the S.N.P. and the P.Q. show striking points of contact.

They both claim access to international personality and, even in the event of a restricted devolution, the S.N.P. would press Scotland into supporting Québec's theory that the treaty-making executive power corresponds to the legislative competence. It is interesting to remember that the Constitution of West Germany has negatived this theory and subordinates the external activities of the Länder to a veto power of the federation.[89]

The S.N.P. programme also qualifies for the designation of the aim of the P.Q. programme: Sovereignty-Association. Both pursue:

(a) full independence from their present ties, with exclusive power of legislation and taxation;

(b) a renegotiation of their relations with the rest of the United Kingdom or the rest of Canada, on the basis of equal partnership;
(c) a customs union;
(d) free movement of labour, goods and capital.[90]

At its convention of June 2, 1979 the P.Q. also called for a monetary union between Canada and Québec. The S.N.P. programme appears to be silent on the subject.

In these various connections, it should be noted that the customs union, the free movement of labour, goods and capital and the monetary union already exist in fact in the United Kingdom and in Canada.

As to the prospective association between the new states and their former co-constituents, realistic criticisms have been levelled on both sides of the Atlantic.

The Kilbrandon report says, in part:[91]

> If Scotland and Wales were to become independent in the full sense, so that Great Britain consisted of three completely sovereign states, it would then be open to the three states to make agreements and to co-operate in the way which many Scottish and Welsh nationalists would like to see. But it cannot be taken for granted in advance that they would do so. And even if they co-operated initially they might later change their minds.
>
> . . .
>
> Political and economic relationships with England could be changed also. Nationalists usually assume that as independent states Scotland and Wales would join with England to form a British common market, within which there would be no military frontiers or passports and no barriers to the free movement of people, goods or money.
>
> . . .
>
> But both Scottish and Welsh nationalists claim the ultimate right, in all matters, not to co-operate with England. Nor can it be taken for granted that a separated England would always feel able to co-operate with Scotland and Wales. Even if an ideal partnership existed at the outset, circumstances could change, leading to disagreements;

In Québec, the leader of the Liberal opposition party, Claude Ryan, echoed those words on October 11, 1978[92] in a statement which he made in answer to a declaration of policy by Premier Lévesque:

> In a system of straight economic association, the rules of the game would no doubt be common, but the relations would be strictly determined on the basis of the relative strength of the parties. In this form of partnership, Québec would concretely figure in the proportion of 1 to 3.
>
> . . .
>
> Once sovereignty has been chosen, no guaranty for the time being can be offered whether the other partners would eventually accept an association and under what conditions.
>
> [*Translation*]

The point was succinctly made by Mr. David Steel M.P.:[93]

> They (the separatists) believe that Scotland should establish a customs and tariffs union with England. Since England is overwhelmingly the more powerful economic unit, this would mean in effect accepting such an arrangement dictated on English terms. There would be no reason for England to be altruistic and damage her own interests to benefit an independent Scotland.

Yet it must be conceded, as a counter-argument, that countries the world over are continuously engaged in political or economic discussions, quite irrespective of their various sizes and nobody ever questions their independent status and their right to be considered, legally, as equals.

Mr. Ryan was equating the relationship Québec-Canada with the terms of 1 to 3. But the relationship of Canada to the U.S.A. stands on the basis of 1 to 11; nevertheless nobody will deny Canada's sovereignty and there could be given numerous examples of treaties or agreements of all kinds freely entered into by the two countries on an equal to equal basis. Of course economic forces do play their part, but they could not be more dangerous for Québec facing Canada than they are for Canada facing the United States.

Those economic forces point however to another factor common to Scotland and Québec, which may also play a substantial part in their future development: it is the importance of American investments in both countries.

Canada, including Québec, ranks as the first country in the world with regard to the importance of American investments. What is less known is that it is not English companies, but American interests that have the largest stake in Scotland.[94]

One can surmise that the U.S.A. would not remain indifferent to break-away movements in either country and this concern should explain the considerable efforts which the Québec Government has displayed over the past two years to reassure American public opinion of the peacefulness and security of its intentions.

At this time, no more can be said concerning the Scottish problem. The initiative now rests with the Conservative Government which, after all, has increased by 6.7 percent its electoral support in Scotland last May.

But one must not lose sight of the fact that, even under the most advanced devolution programme, Scotland would still not reach to the degree of self-government which Québec has enjoyed and consistently enlarged over the past hundred years; so the game, on this side of the Atlantic, is far from over.

At least, an answer ought to be given to the latest Scottish grievance that "golf clubs have carried purchase tax—but not so cricket bats!"[95]

In Québec, there persists the lingering memory of 100 years of litigation concerning language and religion in New Brunswick, Manitoba,

Saskatchewan, Ontario and Québec;[96] the most recent examples are the matters of *Blaikie* in Québec and *Forest* in Manitoba,[97] both of which are currently pending before the Supreme Court of Canada. English is now largely considered in Québec as the language of conquest and exploitation and redress is sought through the Charter of the French Language[98] enacted on August 26, 1977.

Québec is also suffering from economic difficulties: high rates of unemployment and inflation, high level of public spending in the past few years, higher rates of taxation on higher income than in other provinces of Canada, persistence of estate duties which have been abolished in sister provinces, alleged flight of commercial head offices; all those diverse factors combine to create a climate conducive to extreme reactions.

Yet in the Canadian elections of May 22 last, when the rest of Canada by and large let down the Liberal Party which had been at the helm for 16 years, the same Québec that had elected the P.Q. in 1976 remained faithful to the Liberals and their leader Pierre Elliot Trudeau at the federal level, gave them 62 percent of its votes and returned 67 Liberal members to the House of Commons out of 75 Québec seats. That was the party which had made Canadian unity its main electoral platform!

Now the Québec Government is planning a referendum on the constitutional issue. Three weeks ago (June 21, 1979),[99] Premier Lévesque officially announced that it would be held in the spring of 1980. The question however is not yet known, still less the probable result.

So the parallel between Scotland and Québec persists: As Galbraith has said, we are living in "the age of uncertainty".[100]

NOTES

1. Scotland Act 1978: An Act to provide for changes in the government of Scotland and in the procedure of Parliament and in the constitution and functions of certain public bodies, 1978 Eliz. II, c. 51 (31st July 1978).

2. At the time of writing, the House of Commons had passed the repealing Act on June 20, 1979 by a vote of 301 to 206, but the Bill had not yet been considered by the House of Lords.

3. John Bowle, *The English Experience* (New York, 1971), p. 174.

4. 27 Henry VIII, c. 26.

5. Taswell-Langmead—Plucknett, *English Constitutional History,* 10th Edition (London, 1946), p. 563.

6. 1 Jac. I, c. 1.

7. Scots Act Anent Peace and War, 1703, c 5.

8. D. Oswald Dykes, *Source Book of Constitutional History from 1660* (New York, 1930), p. 11.

9. English Act for the Security of the Kingdom, 1705, 3 & 4 Anne, c. 7.

10. A.P.S. XI, 406, c. 7: see text also in T. B. Smith, *Scotland—The Development of its Laws and Constitutions* (London, 1962), p. 869.

11. An Act for the Union of the Two Kingdoms of England and Scotland, 1707, 6 Anne, c. 11.

12. Some of those documents bear the date of 1706, others that of 1707. This is due to the overlapping effect of two historical events which occurred in the period of 1750-1752: (a) the change in Great Britain from the Julian Calendar to the Gregorian Calendar (24 Geo. II, c. 23 and 25 Geo. II, c. 30); (b) the change of the beginning of the year in England from 25th March to 1st January, whilst 1st January had been adopted in Scotland as from 1600 (see *Encyclopedia of the Laws of Scotland* (Edinburgh, 1933), Vol. XIV, p. 441). The author has decided, for purposes of clarity, to retain the year 1707 throughout.

13. *Documents, relating to the Constitutional History of Canada, 1759-1791*, Canadian Archives, 2nd ed., part 1, 1918, p. 97 (French text) and p. 113 (English translation).

14. Royal Proclamation, George III, October 7, 1763, *ibid.*, p. 163, at p. 165; Ordinance Establishing Civil Courts, Québec, September 17, 1764, by Governor James Murray, *ibid.*, p. 205.

15. An Act for making more effectual Provision for the Government of the Province of Québec in North America, 14 Geo. III, c. 83 (U.K.).

16. An Act to repeal certain Parts of an Act, passed in the fourteenth Year of his Majesty's Reign, intituled An Act for making more effectual Provision for the Government of the Province of Québec, in North America; and to make further Provision for the Government of the said Province, 31 Geo. III, c. 31 (U.K.) (The Constitutional Act, 1791).

17. An Act for the Union of Great Britain and Ireland, 39 & 40 Geo. III, c. 67 (U.K.), 2nd July 1800.

18. *Report on the Affairs of British North America,* The Earl of Durham, 1839, (Ed. Lucas), pp. 16 and 17.

19. *Ibid.,* p. 288.

20. *Ibid.,* p. 291.

21. *Ibid.*

22. An Act to re-unite the Provinces of Upper and Lower Canada, and for the Government of Canada, 3 & 4 Vict., c. 35 (U.K.)—(The Union Act, 1840).

23. At the time of Union, Lower Canada had a population of 650,000, *i.e.,* 200,000 more than Upper Canada: Thomas Chapais, *Cours d'histoire du Canada,* Vol. IV, p. 297.

24. 11 & 12 Vict., c. 56 (U.K.).

25. An Act for the Union of Canada, Nova Scotia, and New Brunswick, and the Government thereof; and for Purposes connected therewith, 30 & 31 Vict., c. 3 (U.K.)—(The British North America Act, 1867).

26. An Act to give the force of Law to certain Articles of Agreement for a Treaty between Great Britain and Ireland, and to enable effect to be given thereto, and for other purposes incidental thereto and consequential thereon, 12 & 13 Geo. V, c. 4 (Irish Free State Agreement Act, 1922). Irish Free State Constitution Act, 1922, 13 Geo. V, session 2, c. 1.

27. Cooper, *The Scottish Legal Tradition,* 1949, p. 23.

28. T. B. Smith, *British Justice: The Scottish Contribution,* the Hamlyn Lectures, London, 1961, p. 12.

29. See Robertson's preface to 1707 Scotch Appeal Cases, p. xii, ss.

30. See the narration of the event by Robertson, *ibid.,* pp. ix to xi.

31. *Roseberrie* v. *Inglis* quoted by A. D. Gibb in *Law From Over the Border* (Edinburgh, 1950), pp. 4 and 5.

32. Hansard, *The Parliamentary Debates,* Vol. IX, 1823, House of Lords, p. 1322.

33. See Gibb, *ibid.,* p. 82.

34. 39 & 40 Vict., c. 59 (U.K.).

35. Quoted by Gibb, *op. cit. supra,* note 31, p. 84.

36. See also An Act for the better Administration of Justice in His Majesty's Privy Council, 3 & 4 Will. 4, c. 41 (1833) and The Judicial Committee Act, 7 & 8 Vict., c. 69 (1844); according to the Public Record Office, the first appeal from Québec to the Privy Council was taken on May 29, 1765 in a case involving—appropriately enough for a former French colony—the importation of sundry wines as contraband goods (after a letter to the author from C. J. Kitching, Search Department, Public Record Office, London, June 29, 1979).

37. An Act to amend the Criminal Code, 23 & 24 Geo. V, c. 53, s. 17 (Canada). See also *British Coal Corporation* v. *The King,* [1935] A.C. 500.

38. An Act to amend the Supreme Court Act, 1949, 2nd session, c. 37, s. 3 (Canada). See also *Attorney-General for Ontario* v. *Attorney-General for Canada and Attorney-General for Québec,* [1947] A.C. 127.

39. 38 Vict., c. 11.

40. Jean-Louis Badouin, *"L'interprétation du Code civil québécois par la Cour suprême du Canada."* (1975), 53 Can. Bar Rev. 715, at p. 716, note 4.

41. *McCowan* v. *Wright* (1852), 15 D. 229, at p. 232 as reproduced in *The Scots Revised Reports,* Court of Session, 2nd Series, Vol. VIII, p. 109.

42. *The Colonial Real Estate Company* v. *La Communauté des Soeurs de la Charité de l'Hôpital Général de Montréal* (1918), 57 S.C.R. 585, at p. 603.

43. *Hospice Desrosiers* v. *His Majesty the King* (1919), 60 S.C.R. 105, at p. 126.

44. *Supra,* note 28, p. 43.

45. *Bartonshill Coal Company* v. *Elizabeth Reid* (1858), 3 Macq. 266, at p. 285.

46. *The City of Québec* v. *Her Majesty the Queen* (1894), 24 S.C.R. 420, at p. 445.

47. *The Town of Montreal West* v. *Dame Sarah Hough,* [1931] S.C.R. 113.

48. *Ibid.,* at p. 120.

49. *L.A.* v. *Gordon* (1754), 1 Paton 558.

50. Quoted by Gibb, *op. cit. supra,* note 30, p. 22.

51. *Supra,* note 45.

52. Law Reform (Personal Injuries) Act, 1948, 11 & 12 Geo. VI, c. 41.

53. *Dumbreck* v. *Addie & Sons (Collieries) Limited,* [1929] S.C. (H.L.) 51.

54. The Occupier's Liability (Scotland) Act, 1960.

55. *McArthur* v. *Dominion Cartridge Company,* [1905] A.C. 72.

56. (1901), 31 S.C.R. 392.

57. *Supra,* note 55, at p. 77.

58. [1920] A.C. 662.

59. *Ibid.,* at p. 671.

60. *Despatie* v. *Tremblay,* [1921] A.C. 702.

61. *Ibid.,* at p. 711.

62. P. B. Mignault, "Le Code Civil de la Province de Québec et son Interprétation", (1935-36), 1 U. of T. L. J., p. 104.

63. *Ibid.,* p. 126.

64. Edward McWhinney, "Comparative Law and Jurisprudence at the University of Toronto" (1956-57), 9 Journal of Legal Education 99, at p. 101.

65. John Mercer, *Scotland: The Devolution of Power* (London, 1978), p. 149.

66. *Ibid.,* p. 141.

67. Vernon Bogdanor, *Devolution,* (Oxford University Press, 1979), p. 1.

68. The Government Statistical Office, London, England: *Monthly Digest of Statistics,* #397 (January, 1979), p. 15.

69. Quoted by Mercer, *op. cit. supra,* note 58, p. 57; see also *Britain: Official Handbook,* 1979, pp. 11 and 12.

70. *Ibid.,* at p. 81.

71. Statistics Canada, *Canadian Statistical Review* (Ottawa, February 1979), p. 14.

72. Ministry of Industry, Trade and Commerce, *Canada Year Book 1978-1979,* Ottawa, p. 160.

73. 2746 hours by the French TV network as against 2458 hours by the English TV network: C.B.C. 1977–78 Annual Report, pp. 19-20.

74. H. J. Hanham, *Scottish Nationalism* (London, 1969), p. 74.

75. James Begg, "A violation of the Treaty of Union the Main Origin of our Ecclesiastical Divisions and Other Evils", 1871, as quoted by Hanham (*supra,* note 74), p. 75.

76. See Hanham, *op. cit. supra,* note 74, at p. 97 for a recital of the incident.

77. Quoted *in extenso* in Hanham, *op. cit. supra,* note 74, at pp. 213 to 230.

78. Report, *Royal Commission on the Constitution* (London, October 1973), Cmnd. 5460.

79. 1974 Keesing's Contemporary Archives, *Weekly Diary of World Events,* 1974, p. 26746.

80. *Hodge* v. *The Queen* (1883), 9 App. Cas. 117, at p. 132.

81. Report (*supra,* note 78) p. 133, no. 423.

82. *Ibid.*

83. *Ibid.*

84. *Ibid.,* p. 337 ss.

85. *Our changing Democracy: Devolution to Scotland and Wales,* (London) Cmnd. 6348, p. 20, no. 99.

86. See *supra* note 1.

87. Section 65 and Schedule 12.

88. John P. Grant, "Oil and Gas," in *Independence and Devolution* (Edinburgh, 1966), pp. 86-99.

89. Tony Carty, "A Place for Scotland in International Law?", *ibid.,* pp. 100-123.

90. See the statement of Premier René Lévesque in the Québec National Assembly on October 10, 1978: Québec, *Journal des débats,* Vol. 20, no. 60, p. 2889 ss.

91. Report, *supra* note 78, p. 134.

92. *Le Devoir,* Montréal, October 12, 1978, p. 8.

93. David Steel, "Federalism", in *The Scottish Debate,* Ed. Neil MacCormick (London, 1970), p. 80, at p. 83.

94. See Mercer, *op. cit. supra,* note 65, p. 117.

95. *Ibid.,* p. 2.

96. On recent Québec Jurisprudence concerning the language of education, see the comments of Professor Edward McWhinney, *Quebec and the Constitution 1960-1978* (Toronto, 1979), pp. 65-77.

97. *Blaikie* v. *Le Procureur général de la Province de Québec et al.,* [1978] C.S. 37, 85 D.L.R. (3d) 252; confirmed by a unanimous seven-member bench of the Court of Appeal, [1978] C.A. 351; affd. by [1979] 2 S.C.R. 1016; *Forest* v. *The Attorney General of Manitoba et al.*, unanimous decision of the Court of Appeal of Manitoba, April 25th 1979, [1979] 4 W.W.R. 229; affd. [1979] 2 S.C.R. 1032.

98. 1977 L.Q., c. 5.

99. Québec, *Journal des débats,* 1979, Vol. 21, no. 48, p. 2632.

100. Boston, *Houghton Miffin,* 1977, based on a 1977 B.B.C. Television series.

Additional Bibliography

Duncan H. MacNeill, *The Historical Scottish Constitution (Edinburgh).*

Andrew Dewar Gibb, *A Preface to Scots Law,* 4th ed. (Edinburgh, 1964).

David M. Walker, *The Scottish Legal System,* 4th ed., revised (Edinburgh, 1976).

Norman F. Cantor, *The English: A History of Politics and Society to 1760* (Simon and Schuster).

Wade & Phillips, *Constitutional Law,* 3rd ed. (London).

André Maurois, *Histoire d'Angleterre,* (Paris).

Jacques Patey, *La Commission Judiciaire du Conseil Privé du Roi d'Angleterre* (Paris, 1938).

R. MacGregor Dawson, *The Government of Canada,* 5th ed. (Norman Ward, Toronto).

W. P. M. Kennedy, *Statutes, Treaties and Documents of the Canadian Constitution, 1713-1929,* 2nd ed., revised (Toronto, 1930).

Edward McWhinney, *Canadian Jurisprudence* (Toronto, 1958).

Peter W. Hogg, *Constitutional Law of Canada* (Toronto, 1977).

Louis Baudouin, *Le droit civil de la province de Québec, Modèle vivant de Droit comparé* (Montréal).

Albert Mayrand, "A quand le trépas du 'trespasser'?" (1961) Revue du Barreau, p. 1.

J.-G. Castel, "Le Juge Mignault défenseur de l'intégrité du droit civil québécois" (1975), 53 Can. Bar Rev. 544.

Jean-Louis Baudouin, "L'interprétation du Code civil québécois par la Cour suprême du Canada" (1975), 53 Can. Bar Rev. 715.

Reynald Boult, "Aspects des rapports entre le droit civil et la 'common law' dans la jurisprudence de la Cour Suprême du Canada," (1975), 53 Can. Bar Rev. 738.

Fernand Ouellet, "Les Fondements historiques de l'option séparatiste dans le Québec," in *Liberté,* IV, 21 March 1962, p. 90.

Vêra Murray, *Le Parti Québécois: de la fondation à la prise du pouvoir* (Montréal, 1976).

Thomas McCord, *Preface to the Civil Code of Lower Canada* (Montreal, 1867), at p. ix: "The conversion into English of those titles, especially, which are derived from the old French law was not unattended with difficulties, and to overcome these the terms of the Scotch law were in many instances made use of."

5

Devolution in Britain—A Scottish Perspective

The Right Honourable Lord Murray

The United Kingdom is generally said to be a unitary state. Certainly it has a powerful centralism embodied in the sovereignty of Parliament. But closer scrutiny of the origins and functions of Westminster parliamentary government somewhat modifies this picture.

The sovereignty of Parliament as a constitutional principle is rather more than just the naked annexation of power by the Commons from the King. Of course, that is virtually what Parliament, under Cromwell, did in the Civil War, when Charles I was vanquished and executed and the British nations were united by force of arms. But afterwards there was a revulsion against the Commonwealth which Cromwell had imposed and the Stuarts were restored in 1660. It is a measure of the depth of this revulsion that all the legislation of the period was then expunged from the statute book. It has disappeared without trace, as if it had never been. Juridically, then, the unity of the present kingdom owes nothing to Cromwell's constitutional settlement.

The juridical—as distinct from political—origins of Parliamentary sovereignty lie, I think, in the revolution settlement of 1688/89. To set this in perspective we have to look back beyond Cromwell to 1603, when James VI of Scotland became James I of England. This union of the crowns, it should be noted, was strictly a personal union. James succeeded to the Scottish Crown by the Scottish law of royal succession. He succeeded to the English Crown by the English law of royal succession. But the succession law of neither country was altered and no legal provision was made for a single succession in future. As there were some differences in the respective succession laws, there was nothing to stop the Crowns diverging again, as indeed happened to the Crowns of the United Kingdom and Hanover on the accession of Queen Victoria in 1837, for females were excluded in the

Hanoverian succession. The risk of the Crowns of England and Scotland diverging was one of the factors which led to the Treaty of Union, 1707.

The revolution of 1689, the "Glorious Revolution", was, in contrast with Cromwell's conquest, an exercise of Scottish as well as English political power. There were in fact two separate revolutions, an English one and a Scottish one, for there were still two separate kingdoms. Both wanted to be rid of James Stuart, but there was no *a priori* reason why the respective Parliaments should have chosen the same successor.

In fact they did. The English revolution was embodied in the Bill of Rights whereby the Parliament of England declared that James had abdicated the throne of England by his flight and then invited William and Mary of Orange to accept the vacant throne, praying them to observe certain stated rights and liberties. The Bill of Rights is part of the current statute law of England. However it remains a Bill. It could not logically be an Act of Parliament, for no royal assent could be given until it had already taken legal effect. (It was retrospectively validated by the Crown and Parliament Recognition Act, 1689.)

A parallel, but rather more forthright, constitutional revolution took place in Scotland. The Scottish Claim of Right is still part of the statute law of Scotland, though like the Bill of Rights, its juridical effect does not depend on the royal assent of a normal Act of Parliament. The Claim of Right roundly condemned the misdeeds of James VII as unlawful and unconstitutional; and bluntly proclaimed that, by acting contrary to law, James had forfeited all right to the Crown, leaving the throne of Scotland vacant. The Parliament of Scotland then, in effect, offered the throne of Scotland to William and Mary on condition that they would rule lawfully and comply with the declaration of rights and liberties set out in the Claim. (The Claim was retrospectively validated by an Act of the Scottish Parliament in 1703.)

By these enactments the legislature, not feudal succession, became the juridical basis of the monarchy in each country. Though Ann of Denmark was the designated successor to the throne of each country, their succession laws remained distinct. In addition, as the monarch was now the juridical creature of the parliaments of separate and sovereign states, the Crowns were no longer a guarantor of unity between Scotland and England as they had been, subject only to the differing succession laws. Any basis for a unitary Crown would henceforth have to be explicitly agreed and enacted by the respective parliaments of the two countries.

This is precisely what happened in 1706 when commissioners for each country were appointed to negotiate a basis for legal and constitutional union. It is well known that the English wanted an incorporating union, the Scots a federal union. English constitutional lawyers generally assume that the English got their way. Scottish constitutional lawyers—and some Irish ones, too, I am happy to say—see the matter rather differently.

Terms of union, subject to minor alterations, were agreed by the English and Scottish Parliaments. The initial Articles of Union were signed by the commissioners of the two kingdoms on 22 July 1706. Each Parliament ratified the agreement by its own Act of Parliament. Strictly speaking, the so-called "Act of Union, 1706" does not exist. The Scottish Parliament passed a Union with England Act, 1707, on 16 January that year. This brought the Union into juridical effect within the realm of Scotland. Then on 6 March of the same year the English Parliament passed the Union with Scotland Act, 1706, which gave the Union juridical effect in England. Both Acts remain on the current statute book and each has been separately revised in minor detail by separate procedure. It takes two consents to make a marriage and to keep it in being. You may wonder why the English Act, which came later, has the year 1706 appended, while the earlier Scottish Act is dated 1707. The answer is simple. Scotland, and almost all christendom except England, had adopted the Gregorian in place of the older Julian calendar. So New Year's day in England was on March 25 and this anomaly remained until 1752 when England, too, went Gregorian and adopted January 1.

The Articles of Union contain some provisions which are stated to be "for ever". In modern terminology we would call them entrenched provisions. These provisions are clearly significant in determining the character of the Union, for they were plainly thought, at the time, to be of special and lasting importance.

Article I contains the first entrenched provision. I quote from the Scottish text which states "The two kingdoms of Scotland and England shall, upon the first day of May next ensuing hereof, and *forever after,* be united into one Kingdom by the name of GREAT BRITAIN. . . ." [Emphasis added.]

Article II, which has to be read along with Art. I, also contains words of entrenchment. It provides for a single lawful succession to the merged and united Crown and makes certain exclusions from the succession *for ever.*

Article III, which provides for a united Parliament, has, in contrast, no words of entrenchment. It merely provides that the United Kingdom of Great Britain shall be represented by one and the same Parliament "to be styled the Parliament of Great Britain". The provision for the united Crown is entrenched, but not the provision for the united Parliament. With deference to the history books, 1707 would appear to be more a union of the Crowns than a union of the parliaments. (Incidentally there would appear to be no repugnancy to Art. III in having a Scottish or a Welsh legislature provided that it was devolved from Parliament and that the whole kingdom continued to be represented by one and the same Parliament.)

I should refer to two further provisions of the Articles of Union. Article XIX reserves the existence and jurisdiction of the Court of Session as the supreme court of Scotland *in all time coming* and excludes the jurisdiction of the English courts. The reason why appeals could be taken to the House of Lords after the Union was because in Scotland, prior to the Union, there was an ultimate appeal to the Scottish Parliament "for remeid of law" in civil actions. Appeal to the House of Lords was taken to be the post-Union equivalent. As criminal causes could not be appealed "for remeid of law" there was not, and still is not, any appeal to the House of Lords from a Scottish criminal court. This entrenchment of the Scottish courts ensured continuation of the common law of Scotland as well as its courts. Article XVIII emphasises this point. After providing that the laws concerning the regulation of trade are to be the same after the Union, the Article continues: ". . . all other laws in use within the Kingdom of Scotland do, after the Union and notwithstanding thereof, remain in the same force as before (except such as are contrary to or inconsistent with this Treaty) but alterable by the Parliament of Great Britain; with this difference betwixt the laws concerning public right, policy and civil government and those which concern private right, that the laws which concern public right, policy and civil government may be made the same throughout the whole United Kingdom, but that no alteration be made in laws which concern private right, except for the evident utility of the subjects within Scotland".

Apart from the juridical basis of the Union itself, the public law of Scotland, and the institutions which derive authority from it, remain unaltered by the Union though liable to change by United Kingdom legislation. The Union, then, did not incorporate the public institutions of Scotland into those of England—it merely provided a basis upon which they could be made the same. No systematic incorporation has ever been carried out; so that to this day the countries of England and Scotland remain legally, and to a considerable extent institutionally, separate. It is hard to avoid the conclusion that some semblance of Scottish—and English—statehood continues to subsist and that this subsistence was foreseen. Indeed the Treaty's final entrenched provision, at the end of Art. XXIV, lays down that "the crown, sceptre and sword of state of Scotland, and all state records, shall continue to be kept in Scotland in all time coming". Is this to be attributed to mere sentiment, devoid of constitutional significance?

Because the Union was not federal, Scotland's legislature was removed 400 miles away to Westminster. This created a constitutional vacuum. For Scotland retained within her boundaries two of the dimensions of statehood, namely, an executive administration and a complete legal system, but lacked the third, a domestic legislature. From then on Scotland had in effect to work with an absentee legislature. This constitutional imbalance, though somewhat reduced by improved communications, has been increased by the growth of central government during the past century. The requirements of effective administration in Scotland have given rise to new organs of central government located in Scotland. The Scottish Office, based in Scotland, is now an establishment of 10,000 or more civil servants carrying out departmental functions in the fields of home affairs, health, education, local government, agriculture, fisheries, crime, police, legal administration, planning, land, land use, roads, and regional development. Critics have pointed out that, although these departments are under the control of Crown ministers who are Scottish Members of Parliament at Westminster, democratic accountability and scrutiny cannot be effectively operated from 400 miles away in Westminster. Furthermore the increasing volume of United Kingdom legislation reduces the already limited time available for Scotland-only legislation and debate.

As the United Kingdom comprises three quite separate legal jurisdictions, or law districts, for England, Scotland and Northern Ireland respectively, there has to be separate legislation for each, from time to time, as well as United Kingdom legislation for the whole. In particular Parliament enacts a material number of statutes each year applying exclusively, or largely, to Scotland. There is a special procedure for Scottish legislation at Westminster whereby much of the process is carried out by Scottish ministers and Scottish Members of Parliament. There is a special team of Scottish Parliamentary draftsmen at Westminster. Scottish government departments are directly responsible for Westminster legislation in their own fields. Even a United Kingdom Act, applying to the whole country, has to be tailored so that it slots separately into the legal systems of each of the three national jurisdictions. So too the House of Lords on appeal does not apply a superior British law—it applies English law in an English appeal, Scots law in a Scottish appeal, and so forth. There is, of course, a considerable measure of identity, but that does not affect the point.

In this constitutional perspective it is possible to view the currents of public opinion which made devolution for Scotland and Wales a live political issue, at least for the life of one Parliament. Home rule for Scotland had been an abiding, though secondary, political aspiration for a minority of Scots since Victorian times. Certain recent developments gave it added momentum. Increasing centralisation has led generally to demands for more democratic control and accountability of central government to those who are affected by it. The discovery of North Sea oil, largely in waters off the Scottish coasts, has made it possible to conceive of an independent Scotland as a wealthy, or at least solvent, state. Accession to the European Community has highlighted the institutional benefits which could accrue to Scotland within the Common Market if she were independent. Within the United Kingdom, Scotland is not directly represented in any Community organ and has eight of the 81 British members of the directly-elected European Assembly. In contrast the Republic of Ireland, with a population less than 60 percent of Scotland's, is directly represented in the

Council of Ministers, the Commission, and the Luxembourg Court of Justice, and has 15, compared with Scotland's eight, members of the European Assembly.

In that general context it is not altogether surprising that the Scottish National Party (S.N.P.), who seek independence, made a spectacular electoral advance between June 1970, when they had one Member of Parliament, and October 1974, when they obtained 11 out of the 71 Scottish seats. Although their numbers have been reduced to two in the recent general election they still command the votes of roughly one-fifth of the Scottish electorate.

Both the major British political parties had taken early steps to counter the anticipated threat of the S.N.P. In 1968 the Conservative Party established a constitutional committee under Sir Alec Douglas-Home, now Lord Home, to consider the problems which had given rise to a demand for devolution in Scotland. It reported in favour of a directly-elected assembly with powers of interrogation and scrutiny, and with limited powers to carry out some stages of Westminster's Scottish legislation in Scotland. In 1969 the Labour government set up a Royal Commission on the constitution which came to be known as the Kilbrandon Commission. At the end of 1973 it produced a comprehensive report dealing with devolution proposals in regard to the whole of the United Kingdom, though its Northern Ireland remit had been curtailed. The Commission made a majority recommendation for a full-blooded legislative devolution for Scotland roughly comparable with Northern Ireland's Stormont constitution; and a minority report which recommended a much more restricted scheme with no delegation of legislative functions.

The public got little time to digest the far-reaching Kilbrandon proposals, for only a few months after the report was published there was a general election, in February 1974, which returned a minority Labour government in a House of Commons where S.N.P. representation had risen from one to seven. The new government immediately embarked on plans to legislate on the basis of the majority Kilbrandon proposals. A series of white papers were issued setting out the alternatives and later the government's proposals. At the ensuing general election in October 1974 Labour was returned with a very small majority and S.N.P. representation rose from seven to 11. There followed the long campaign of political attrition which led to the enactment of the Scotland Act and the Wales Act in 1978 and to their repeal in 1979.

In reaching their majority view the Kilbrandon Commission considered and rejected two alternatives for dealing with the problem of Scottish government, separatism and federalism. They did not consider a third alternative for which nobody was asking, that is, the total re-fashioning of the constitution to transform the country into a completely integrated British state. That alternative probably looked quite unreal then. It may look a little less unreal now, with Northern Ireland under direct Westminster rule and with full representation in the House of Commons to come.

Kilbrandon gave separatism short shrift, relying on both economic and political considerations.

On the economic aspect, the difficulties which faced the Republic of Ireland were cited. In view of the recent success of the Republic's economy, as the fastest-growing one in Western Europe, this argument does not look as persuasive now as it did then; particularly when one bears in mind that Scotland's economy is more broadly-based than that of the Republic of Ireland.

Two main political points weighed heavily with the Commission. Firstly, they found that only a small minority of the Scottish people supported independence as an option. Secondly, they felt that, on independence, there was no way in which it could be guaranteed that both England and Scotland would be willing to take the steps necessary to ensure common economic arrangements and common social standards so as to prevent divergence which, they judged, could in the long term only harm Scotland.

The first point would appear to carry less force than formerly. While only a minority (no longer small) of the electorate remain S.N.P. supporters, that minority remains large enough to constitute a standing threat to the political security of the major parties. As regards the second point, with the experience of the Scotland Act behind us, I think that we can say that devolution on the Kilbrandon model would have thrown up continuing problems of divergence which need have been no easier to solve than home rule for Scotland coupled with reciprocal bilateral agreements on common economic arrangements and common social standards. The Commission laid great stress on the apparent contradiction between complete home rule and the organic unity of the British economy. Yet the Isle of Man, whose Parliament celebrated its millennium in 1979, and the Channel Island states enjoy complete home rule, with control of their own budgets and tax laws, which make them tax havens, without any apparent disruption of the British economy, of which they form part though constitutionally and politically outside the United Kingdom.

The option of federalism did not fare much better at the hands of the Kilbrandon Commission. In contrast with devolution, which may be defined as the delegation of central government powers without relinquishing sovereignty, federalism implies the division of sovereignty between two or more levels of government according to a formula which is fixed or at any rate especially difficult to alter. The Commission judged federal constitutions to be increasingly unworkable today because of new functions which central government had acquired in all modern states, and because of increasing demands for equality of social standards and economic treatment in every provincial unit—which in practice have to be provided and funded by central government. In this process provincial sovereignty is progressively eroded so that even in a federation such as the United States, founded on the sovereignty of the federating units, it can be said that states' rights have become something of a legal fiction in face of Washington's increasing power.

The Commission relegated the federal concept to the constitutional level appropriate for an early stage in the transition from an association of sovereign states towards a larger unity; and they therefore ruled it out for decentralisation in an over-centralised (and supposedly unitary) state like the United Kingdom.

They also found substance in two other objections. Firstly it was said that disputes between the constituent parts of a federation tended to take the form of litigation about constitutional rights. Important policy decisions were thus in effect decided by unelected judges who were set in authority over elected bodies who ought to be deciding controversial policy matters. This was at once undemocratic and tended to bring the judiciary into politics. The second objection was more fundamental. No federal constitution, it was said, could be devised or would work in which one of the provinces contained 85 percent of the population and more than 85 percent of the present economic power; and where the other partners, with supposedly equal status, were small and economically weaker countries like Scotland, Wales or Northern Ireland.

Though the force of the first objection can be blunted by observing that some federations are more flexible than others and give limited scope for judicial intervention, the second objection is difficult to meet without proposing that England itself should be carved up into a number of provinces—for which there is no present political demand in England at all—or that a new type of federal structure needs to be devised to meet the problems set by such great disproportion. It is perhaps unfortunate that the Kilbrandon Commission did not pursue the last point a little more fully. For, after all, it is precisely the economic and political imbalance in favour of urban southeastern England which has contributed to the demand for institutional change to counter it. Such institutional mechanisms are built in to federations, but they are conspicuous by their absence in centralist constitutions. To adapt federal forms would seem to be a more promising line of advance than to invent entirely novel institutions. We should be seeking constitutional devices, it may be said, where they are most likely to be found. The Parliamentary debates on the Scotland Bill time and again threw up illustrations of the parallels between specific problems of devolution and federation. In the end the Scotland Act had a noticeably more federal flavour than the original Bill.

With that preamble, consideration may now be given to some of the main features of constitutional interest in the Scotland Act, 1978. It bears at least superficial comparison with the Government of Ireland Act, 1914, which like the Scotland Act was enacted and took its place on the statute book only to be repealed before it could come into effect. But unlike the Scotland Act, the Irish Act of 1914 conferred on the Irish legislature power to make laws for the peace, order and good government of Ireland in terms familiar in other Commonwealth constitutions which have been enacted by Westminster.

The pattern for the Scotland Bill was deliberately different. Indeed the first clause contained a key-note declaration in these terms: "The following provisions of this Act make changes in the government of Scotland as part of the United Kingdom. They do not affect the unity of the United Kingdom or the supreme authority of Parliament to make laws for the United Kingdom or any part of it." This clause was defeated in the House of Commons on the basis that it was misleading and hypocritical in political terms and that it was superfluous in law. The latter point at least had force.

The principle of devolution adopted was that the delegated powers were to be exhaustively enumerated. Whatever was not enumerated remained with Westminster. To avoid any taint of federalism the government set its mind against any enumeration of reserved matters.

Some of the less transparent features of the Act can be attributed directly to this deliberate decision. Thus s. 18 provides for the legislative competence of the Assembly and the key passage is as follows: "Any question whether a provision is within the legislative competence of the Assembly shall be determined in accordance with Schedule 2 to this Act." Turning to Schedule 2, we discover that a matter is within the legislative competence of the Assembly if it is a devolved matter. To trace devolved matters, one has to follow the interpretation provisions to s. 63 which enacts: "In relation to the legislative competence of the Assembly, a devolved matter is one which is included in the Groups in Part I of Sched. 10 to this Act." In Schedule 10 are to be found three pages where 25 groups are specified in some detail. But the three pages of Part I are further qualified by 3½ pages of Part II and 17½ pages of Part III. In other words, some 24 pages of closely printed text have to be read to determine if a matter is devolved to the Assembly and, if so, subject to what restrictions. In contrast, s. 2 of the Irish Act of 1914 qualified the general power to legislate for the peace, order and good government of Ireland by 1½ pages of major reservations and a small number of minor ones specified elsewhere in the appropriate sections of the Act. On the other hand this way of drafting the Scotland Act does correctly reflect the fact that express delegation, that is, express enumeration of devolved matters, is easy in principle but difficult in demarcation.

The difficulties generated by ruthless maintenance of the principle of express delegation could be seen in the so-called "over-ride" power in cl. 45 of the original Scotland and Wales Bill. This sought to give Westminister a quick way of vetoing Scottish Assembly legislation even though it might fall within the delegated powers. The veto, which was subject to affirmative Parliamentary resolution, was to be available against a provision which "would or might affect, directly or indirectly, a matter with respect to which only Parliament has power to legislate" and which Westminster deemed not to be in the public interest. Because of the principle of express delegation, what only Parliament could legislate upon had to be determined by subtracting what was expressly delegated. When that difficult task had been completed one was not necessarily much the wiser. For the demarcation was often too crude to cope with overlaps and borderline cases in just the areas where clash of policies between the two legislatures could be envisaged.

Take trade, for instance. Only Parliament, one would assume, was to have power to legislate for that. But the Scottish Assembly was given extensive powers over the private law of Scotland, including contract and other obligations. Legislation to reform Scots law in this area, even on a matter which was already different from English law, could affect trade: through contracts of sale, for instance. Unfortunately the same thing could be seen as an enumerated devolved matter and, in a different perspective, as a matter on which only Parliament could legislate. In effect, then, the veto could be used to strike at anything which Westminster disliked, even if it fell foursquare within the Assembly's legislative powers. To take an extreme example: a purely internal Scottish educational measure could be vetoed because it conflicted with purely English educational policy, the latter undoubtedly being a matter for which only Parliament could legislate.

Intense criticism of this "Governor-General's" veto produced an amendment which apparently breached the principle of express delegation. By s. 38 of the Act the veto was limited to cases where the provision would or might affect a *reserved* matter. The breach was more apparent than real, however, for "reserved matter" was defined later in the section as a matter which concerns Scotland but with respect to which the Scottish Assembly has no power to legislate. This definition is almost circular, but not quite—it would exclude abuse of the veto of the kind given in the last example.

The problem of *vires* emerged as an important issue. One option for the original Scotland and Wales Bill had proposed that the validity of Scottish Assembly enactments could not be challenged in a court of law. This proposal, which looked very like the conferment of a sovereign legislature's privilege, had been attacked from all sides even before the Bill was published. Responding to this criticism, the Bill and the subsequent Scotland Bill provided for scrutiny of the *vires* of Assembly measures before royal assent, and for reference of doubtful cases to the judicial committee of the Privy Council for determination. The offending exclusion of the courts was rejected.

This was still not enough for those who maintained, I think rightly, that the citizen should have the clear right to challenge in the ordinary courts abuse of power by the Assembly affecting him. A government amendment to provide specific machinery for such judicial review was passed by an overwhelming majority in the House of Commons—the Bill's most favourable vote in that House.

Another interesting problem arose from an innocent-looking provision in cl. 62 that the prerogative of mercy was not devolved—an apparently unnecessary adumbration of the principle of express delegation. This raised queries about an earlier provision in the Bill relating to the powers of the Assembly's executive. The government were determined to withhold from the executive members the status of ministers of the Crown which might encroach on Westminster's sovereignty. How then were executive members to operate the present prerogative powers of ministers in the devolved areas? The solution appeared to be to transfer these prerogative powers. The provision in cl. 21(3) of the original Scotland Bill was as follows: "Such of Her Majesty's prerogative and other executive powers as would otherwise be exercisable on behalf of Her Majesty by a Minister of the Crown shall, if they relate to devolved matters and are exercisable in or as regards Scotland, be exercisable on behalf of Her Majesty by a Scottish Secretary." On the face of it, this provision could be said either to raise Scottish secretaries to the status of ministers of the Crown or to excise the delegated powers from the undifferentiated residue of powers which constitutes the royal prerogative and convert them into specific statutory powers. Either alternative was equally unacceptable. The answer finally adopted was to delete the reference to prerogative powers, so that Scottish secretaries could exercise in the devolved areas the executive powers which a minister of the Crown could have exercised, leaving the royal prerogative at least formally intact and undefiled.

Two other distinctive features of the Act arose as the result of determined anti-devolution opposition.

The first was an attempt to answer the so-called "West Lothian question" which was pressed with remorseless persistence and untiring repetition by Tam Dalyell M.P. for West Lothian. It posed a paradox of devolution, first stated by Enoch Powell M.P., which seemed insoluble. If devolution debarred English M.P.'s in Westminster from voting on Scottish housing, health or other devolved matter, how could English M.P.'s, in the long run, tolerate Scottish M.P.'s voting on English housing, health and so forth, and by their votes overruling the wishes of the majority of English M.P.'s? The question was neither academic nor idle for Labour would not have had a majority in the Commons for any of its legislation in that Parliament without the support of Scottish Labour M.P.'s. Section 66, an amendment carried against the wishes of the government, sought to limit this evil by providing that, if a domestic English Bill passed the Commons merely because of the votes of Scottish members tipping the balance against the wishes of English members, it would be deemed not to have had a second reading unless it was confirmed by the House after an interval of at least 14 days. This change was hardly more than cosmetic.

The other major change forced against the government was the provision that there should be a referendum of the Scottish electorate before the Act came into force. There was a parallel provision for the Wales Act. This in the end destroyed the government's legislation. For once the government, yielding to pressure, had tabled the referendum clause there was grafted on to it, by opponents of devolution, a passage in the following terms: "If it appears to the Secretary of State that less than 40 % of the persons entitled to vote in the referendum have voted 'yes' . . . . or that a majority of the answers have been 'no' he shall lay before Parliament the draft of an Order in Council for the repeal of this Act". The government's whole legislative exercise hinged upon the assumption that an overwhelming majority of the Scottish electorate wanted devolution of roughly the kind contained in the Bill. Opinion polls seemed to bear this out. The 40 percent hurdle, designed to call this bluff, could be presented as a perfectly reasonable test of opinion before launching out upon a constitutional venture whose long-term consequences for the United Kingdom could not be foreseen. In the event 33 percent of the Scottish electorate voted "yes", 31 percent voted "no", and 36 percent did not vote or were not entitled to vote. The referendum was won, but the Act was lost—damned by faint praise. In Wales there was a massive "no" majority.

Any attempt to explain the referendum result is bound to be speculative. But it cannot be denied that some electors who wanted devolution voted against the Act because they thought that the particular package was a bad one (Lord Home, the former Prime Minister, is an outstanding instance). It would be interesting to know how many electors voted "no" for that reason. For the Scotland Act's allocation of functions between Westminster and Edinburgh reflected existing departmental divisions. Many of the more obscure checks and balances in the Act could be viewed as designed to protect existing departmental interests. To what extent did the unsatisfactory nature of these existing departmental responsibilities affecting Scotland mirror itself in an unattractive devolution package? We shall never know the answer to this question, nor shall we know how many electors voted as they did, on one side or the other, for purely tactical party political reasons. That, of course, is the trouble with referendums.

Is there a moral to be drawn from the life and death of the Scotland Act? There are perhaps two constitutional lessons: firstly, that it is unwise to attempt major constitutional reform without broad cross-party support in the legislature and in the country; and secondly, that the orthodox doctrine of the sovereignty of Parliament may have outlived its usefulness in the United Kingdom and may now be an obstacle to progressive institutional reform. The Scottish referendum may itself have damaged the integrity, if not the sovereignty, of Parliament. For it can hardly enhance Parliament's power or reputation that it remitted to the Scottish people an important constitutional measure dominating two parliamentary sessions while committing itself to a formula which, in the event, required it to disregard the will of the majority in Scotland.

The problems of identity and difference which the Union of 1707 created for Scotland will have to wait a little longer for their resolution.

6

Devolution, Delegation, Centralization and Decentralization of Powers as Seen by the Pepin-Robarts Commission

Gérald A. Beaudoin

When a secessionist government is elected in a province like Quebec which constitutes 28% of the whole Canadian population, the least that we can say is that there is a problem in Canada.

Introduction

As we intend to say a few words on the centralization and decentralization of powers in Canada, as seen by the Pepin-Robarts reports, in the framework of a seminar on devolution and delegation, we shall make at the outset the following basic distinctions:

(1) The United Kingdom has a unitary form of government, where the Parliament at Westminster is supreme in principle and may by a statute delegate legislative powers to a legislative assembly, be it in Scotland, Wales or Northern Ireland. The United Kingdom is in no way a federal state and the devolution of legislative powers contemplated in that country does not change that basic character.

(2) Since 1867, Canada is a federal country where the constitution is the supreme law of the land and where the Parliament and the provincial legislatures are supreme only in the spheres allocated to them by the Con-

stitution and where delegation of legislative powers cannot take place between Parliament and legislatures horizontally[1], but between Parliament or legislatures *and* a subordinate body, in a vertical[2] or oblique[3] manner. The legislative powers attributed to each order of government are mutually exclusive. A delegation may take place *vis à vis* a subordinate body, be it provincial or federal.

(3) When the Parliament of the United Kingdom, by a statute, attributes powers to a legislative body, it is a legislative delegation; it is of the same nature as a legislative delegation in Canada by either the Parliament or a provincial legislature to a subordinate body. The delegator may take powers back at any time[4].

In Canada, the courts have stated that since parliament and provincial legislatures have a "plenary" power within their constitutional sphere, they may delegate a power to a subordinate body like for example a municipality. Parliament and legislatures each within their allocated sphere are sovereign and equal in principle[5].

Sir Barnes Peacock, in the *Hodge* case remarked:[6]

> They (provincial legislatures) are in no sense delegates of or acting under any mandate from the Imperial Parliament. When the British North America Act enacted that there should be a legislature for Ontario, and that its legislative assembly should have exclusive authority to make laws for the Province and for provincial purposes in relation to the matters enumerated in sect. 92, it conferred powers not in any sense to be exercised by delegation from or as agents of the Imperial Parliament, but authority as plenary and as ample within the limits prescribed by sect. 92 as the Imperial Parliament in the plenitude of its power possessed and could bestow. Within these limits of subjects and area the local legislature is supreme, and has the same authority as the Imperial Parliament, or the Parliament of the Dominion, would have had under like. . . .

Lord Watson in the *Maritime Bank* case remarked:

> The object of the Act was neither to weld the provinces into one, nor to subordinate provincial governments to a central authority, but to create a federal government in which they should all be represented, entrusted with the exclusive administration of affairs in which they had a common interest, each province retaining its independence and autonomy.[7]

and:

> But, in so far as regards those matters which, by sect. 92 are specifically reserved for provincial legislation, the legislation of each province continues to be free from the control of the Dominion, and as supreme as it was before the passing of the Act. . . .
>
> It (provincial legislature) derives no authority from the Government of Canada, and its status is in no way analogous to that of a municipal institution, which is an authority constituted for purposes of local administration.[8]

In the *Mellenger* case, Lord Denning wrote:

> The British North America Act 1867 gave Canada a federal constitution. . . . Each provincial government, within its own sphere, retained its independence and autonomy, directly under the Crown. The Crown is sovereign in New Brunswick for provincial powers, just as it is sovereign in Canada for dominion powers. . . . It follows that the Province of New Brunswick is a sovereign state in its own right, and entitled, if it so wishes, to claim sovereign immunity.[9]

(4) The word "devolution" is not generally used by the courts in Canada. Mr. Justice Rinfret, (as he then was) however refers to it in the *Chemicals Reference*[10] in speaking of the War Measures Act:

> The Act constitutes a devolution of the legislative power of Parliament. . . .

But as stated by Chief Justice Duff:

> Under the *War Measures Act* the final responsibility for the Acts of the Executive rests upon Parliament. Parliament abandons none of its powers, none of its control over the Executive, legal or constitutional.[11]

The court came to the conclusion that the authority vested in the Governor General in Council by the War Measures Act is legislative in its character. An order in council passed in conformity with the conditions prescribed by that Act has the effect of an Act of Parliament.

(5) In Canada, part of the present political and constitutional debate centers on the distribution of legislative powers. The said distribution made mostly by ss. 91 to 95 of the B.N.A. Act 1867, as amended, can be modified only by a formal constitutional amendment. The power to amend those sections of the B.N.A. Act is still vested in the U.K. Parliament. Only that Parliament at the request of Canada, following a Joint Address of both federal houses may validly amend ss. 91 to 95 of the B.N.A. Act. Formal centralization or decentralization of legislative powers can only take place by constitutional amendments. Of course, the Courts in construing ss. 91 to 95 may centralize or decentralize the powers in delimiting, circumscribing or in enlarging the ambit of the words used in the said sections. As we all know, the U.S. Supreme Court centralized the American Constitution in interpreting the famous "commerce clause". But to change the wording of ss. 91 to 95 of the B.N.A. Act we need a formal amendment.

(6) The amendments to the distribution of legislative powers in Canada are the object of negotiations between the Prime Minister and the ten Premiers. The constitutional revision is conducted by the executive branch of the State. This is what many political scientists and jurists call "executive federalism". In the United Kingdom the devolution is the affair of Parliament and of legislators mostly; the executive and the legislative branches are both called upon to act.

(7) The procedure of referendum, although used widely in Australia, is not used often in the United Kingdom and in Canada. Referendum is not part of the Canadian constitutional process, although nothing preludes the holding of a consultative referendum by the federal and provincial governments acting within their sphere of legislative jurisdiction.[12].

With this in the background we may now consider briefly how the Task Force on Canadian Unity sees the Canadian constitutional crisis and the remedies that it advocates.

The Main Constitutional Propositions of the Task Force on Canadian Unity[13]

The Task Force on Canadian Unity (of which the author was one of the eight members) was established on July 5, 1977 to listen to the Canadian public and to offer advice to the Government of Canada on questions of Canadian unity. After having visited 15 cities in all parts of Canada, received 849 briefs and more than 3,000 letters, this Task Force which legally speaking was a Royal Commission made three reports which were unanimous.

The first report "A Future Together" was published on January 25, 1979. It includes our observations and 75 specific recommendations. The second report published on February 4, 1979 is entitled "Coming to Terms". It is a glossary, a dictionary of political and constitutional terms. So far, it is probably unique in Canada. It is a scientific effort to define the major terms of the debate on the future of our country—What is a federation? What is a Confederation? What is the distribution of powers in Canada? What is a "nation", a "state", a "referendum"? How do we define "self-determination", "sovereignty", "common market", etc. There is so much confusion in Canada about all those terms that it was thought necessary to publish a lexicon. And finally, the third report published on March 21, "A Time To Speak" is a resumé of what the Canadians in this country said to us.

"A Time to Speak" was supposed to be the first report; the second, "Coming to Terms" and the third, "A Future Together". We reversed the order of publication; the last report was ready before the first one, and, in December 1978, we decided to publish our final report two months ahead in order to be pertinent to the constitutional debate, that is before the Constitutional Conference of February 5, 1979. It became obvious that governmental authorities in Ottawa and in the provincial capitals, that the media and, the public, were desirous to have some imput from the Commission. Furthermore as the federal general elections were coming, it was thought advisable not to publish during an electoral campaign.

Our diagnosis was that the Canadian political crisis is deep—it concerns our *vouloir-vivre* together. The biggest threat to the survival of

Canada, as a political entity, comes from those who want to change nothing and from those who want to change everything. The first and most important thing is: are the diverse elements of our country desirous to stay together? This is why we have intituled our first report: "A Future Together".

Fifteen years ago Monsieur André Laurendeau, in his beautiful blue pages of the B & B preliminary report affirmed that Canada was in the midst of a political crisis. The crisis became acute in November 15, 1976. That event was the *causa causans* of the establishment of our Commission. It is very urgent to do something to resolve our constitutional problem and for the Pepin-Robarts Commission to do something is to draft a new Constitution for Canadians.

Three basic criteria should govern the drafting of any new Constitution for Canada: dualism, regionalism and power sharing and benefit.

The principle of dualism (or duality) is solidly imbedded in the Canadian history. It is older than the Confederation of 1867. It could be traced to the Quebec Act of 1774, two years before the American Revolution when the United Kingdom recognized in a constitutive and organic statute, that there are two basic systems of law in Canada, the civil law and the common law. The two main communities in Canada have also different languages. The principle of duality or dualism is profoundly inscribed in the history of Canada. In our lexicon we have defined the term "dualism".[14]

The second principle is "regionalism". Canada is not a homogeneous country: regionalism is strong in this country. This principle of regionalism which is at the same time a "fact" and a "value" should be the second pillar of the constitutional structure of tomorrow.[15]

It is only in Quebec that the federal system itself is questioned. In the other provinces it is the working of federalism that is questioned. This being said, regionalism in Canada should not be overlooked.

The third principle is "power sharing". To keep Quebec in the Canadian federation a power sharing shall be devised.

The new Canadian Constitution if it is going to endure should reflect those three basic principles.

The Distribution of Legislative Powers

Quebec has since three decades ago considered that topic as the most important aspect of any constitutional revision. It is a *constante* in its revendications. The threat to Canadian unity comes firstly although not uniquely from Quebec. So, it is that topic that should retain our attention first.

In that field the Task Force on Canadian Unity has devised a philosophy. We did not have the specific mandate nor all the expertise and the time to draft new ss. 91 and 92, nor to make complete blue prints for a new constitution. We started with three basic criteria: the principal roles and responsibilities of the central government, the needs and responsibilities of the provinces, and, the particular case of Quebec. On that basis, we outlined a philosophy for a new distribution of legislative powers.

In our opinion, the central government should have all the essential powers to keep this country together and to assure the well being of its citizens, like national defense, the preservation and enhancement of the integrity of the country, the strengthening of Canadian identity, the overriding responsibility for the conduct of external affairs, the redistribution of income, and the direction of the Canadian economy. The essential powers of the provinces are property and civil rights, the management of territory, the regional economic development, the social and cultural well-being of their communities.

Quebec, because of its specificity should also have all the essential powers that it needs in the Canadian federation for its well-being like culture, language and generally the preservation of its french *patrimoine*.

We have too many "grey areas" in our Constitution, too many "silences" too many "obsolete provisions". So, we should at the beginning clarify the distribution of legislative powers and when it is not possible to attribute a power to the provincial legislatures or to the central Parliament exclusively, then, and only then, the legislative power should be concurrent.

We have now in the Constitution of Canada in s. 94 and s. 95 some concurrent powers like immigration, agriculture, old age pensions: sometimes the preponderance or paramountcy is federal; sometimes, it is provincial. It should be that way also in the future for the concurrent powers.

We have provided that we shall have in Canada a clause of delegation of legislative power enabling a province to delegate to Ottawa and vice versa some powers that it does not intend to use;[16] we constitutionalized the "opting out" formula, invented in the early 1960s, but with fiscal compensation.

It is then possible for each province in using the delegation clause, the opting out formula and the paramountcy to acquire a distinctive status, according to its needs.

So, in the field of legislative powers it is not what we call a "particular status" *de jure*. It may be in practice a distinctive status *de facto* and this, for any province, depending whether a province wishes to take advantage of the clause of delegation of powers, or of the stipulated paramountcy, or, of the "opting out" formula. It is asymetric federalism *de facto* and not *de jure*.[17] It is only if all provinces reject such a scheme, that, in our opinion, Quebec, because of its specificity should really have a particular status *de jure*. This is quite different. It should not be presumed at the outset that the other provinces would reject such a scheme for them; it should not be presumed also that some will not want distinctive status to a certain degree.

The residual power would become provincial as is already the case in nearly all other federations. The federal declaratory power would be used only with the consent of the province concerned. An emergency power in peace time and an emergency power in wartime would be inscribed expressly in the Constitution and their exercise would be described. The two emergencies would differ in nature and in their ambit. The federal spending power in fields of interest to the provinces would be exercised only with the consent of a majority of two thirds of the new second House.

The economic union would remain strong. It is not true that our proposals may balkanize the country. On the contrary we suggested a strong central economic power. The direction of economy remains in the hands of central government. Furthermore the equalization payment formula would be entrenched in the constitution, as well as the principle of federal jurisdiction in the field of regional disparities. The movement of persons and capital from one province to another would be strengthened. Section 121 of the B.N.A. Act would be clarified.

Finally in addition to all those objectives the distribution of powers should take account of the following criteria as stated in Recommendation 36:

general and particular concern;
effectiveness, efficiency and responsiveness
common agreement
continuity
overall balance.

The Second House

We have stated that Canada is not an homogenous country and that our regions are strong. For the second House we have suggested a *Council of the Federation.* That proposal is not very far away from propositions made by British Columbia or the Advisory Committee of Ontario. This Council is destined to favour the harmony of federal-provincial relations. It would not be primarily or entirely a legislative chamber, but a second House composed of delegates appointed by the provinces. Sometimes the members of that chamber will have a veto power that may be suspensive for areas concerned with provincial competence; sometimes, they may have an absolute veto, for example for the ratification of appointment of the Supreme Court judges.

The purpose of our new "second House" is to represent adequately the value and the fact of regionalism in Canada. People in some parts of Canada contended that they were not present enough in the centre of the decisions of this country. So, we suggested a new Council of the Federation with provincial appointees and delegates. Such a solution is aimed at the sensibilization of the centre to the regional needs and at the sensibilization of the regions to the needs of the whole country.

The Tribunal of Last Resort

Closely related to the distribution of legislative power is the court of last resort. It is a distinctive character of all federations that an organism should rule on the interpretation of the division of legislative powers. In Canada the Supreme Court is the final arbitrator in the distribution of legislative powers. A decision of the Supreme Court is like a *de facto* amendment to the Constitution, because the court is enabled to say what is the meaning of the terms and words used in a Constitution. For example, the central Parliament has the power to legislate on "criminal law" and the provincial legislatures on "property and civil rights". But what authority is going to say what "criminal law" includes and what "property and civil rights" means: in the final analysis, it is the Supreme Court of Canada. So, that institution is vitally important for the Canadian federalism of tomorrow. The Canadian "dualism" should be strongly represented in the Supreme Court. We have already seen that we have two systems of law in Canada. This dualistic character should be reflected more adequately in our constitution.

The existence of the Supreme Court should be provided for in the Constitution. It shall continue to be a general Court of Appeal for both civil law and common law. Secondly, the central government alone shall not appoint the judges. We suggest another procedure of appointment. The judges would be appointed by the central government after consultation with the Attorney General of the province concerned and the selection of judges would be ratified by the new second House composed of provincial appointees or delegates. So, in that sense, the provinces would clearly participate in the process of appointment of Supreme Court judges. Both federal and provincial authorities should have full confidence in the final arbitrator of the Constitution. So it is necessary to modify its structures.[18]

The structures of the court should be such that the people in Quebec will feel quite secure about this vital institution which tomorrow will orientate the federalism. Duality should be strongly represented in the Supreme Court of Canada, perhaps more than in any other institution. The credibility of the court should be complete.

We have suggested also that this court be composed of 11 judges, six from common law and five from civil law background. A civil law Chief Justice would succeed to a Common Law Chief Justice, by rotation.

The existence and independence of the judiciary should be consecrated in the Constitution.

Superior Court judges and Appeal Court judges would be appointed by the provincial government after consultation with the federal government.

A Better Balancing of Powers

In the future Constitution we should say clearly that the two orders of government are equal, each in its own legislative sphere allocated by the

Constitution. In a federal system the Constitution is supreme and each order of government is supreme in its domain. There is no superior nor inferior government. We should speak of "order" and not of "levels" of governments. All governments in a true federation are sovereign in their own sphere. The *Hodge* case and the *Maritime Bank* case and more recently the *Mellenger* case, already referred to, illustrate that basic principle of balanced federalism. This should be clearly stated in the next Constitution. As a consequence, the federal powers of reserve and dissallowance which participates in the nature of a unitary state should be abolished. If "some" hybridity is required it should be borrowed from confederate instead of unitary models. The recommendations related to the second House and the court of last resort constitute perhaps good examples.

The overriding federal powers like the emergency power, the declaratory power, should be described with more precision. Parameters should be set for their exercise in order to maintain the equilibrium of the Constitution.

The House of Commons

History shows that in the federations which collapsed the federal parties often ceased first to be "national". In order to correct that situation, we suggest the status quo for the election of our 282 members but we recommend that 60 additional members of Parliament be elected under the principle of proportional representation. What it would mean is this. In the provinces where a party has received a fair percentage of the vote and just one or two members of Parliament, additional members would be elected, according to lists drafted before the elections. It would mean for example, that in Quebec where the Conservative party has only a few members with perhaps 14 percent of the vote, that party would have additional conservative members; in a province like Alberta where the Liberals have no member with perhaps ten, 15 or 20 percent of the vote they will have additional members of parliament. With that scheme our political parties will remain more national.

The General Formula of Constitutional Amendment

Closely related to the distribution of legislative powers and their interpretation by the tribunal of last instance, is the general formula of amendment. It concerns the formal amendment of *inter alia* the competences which constitute the core of federalism.

Canada has been in search of a formula of constitutional amendment since 1927. In 1931, at the time that Canada became an independent country, we should have entrenched in our Constitution the general formula of amendment. In spite of repeated efforts, like the Fulton Favreau formula, the Trudeau formula, the Victoria formula, we have not yet succeeded.

The Task Force on Canada Unity has suggested a new formula of amendment. It would be possible to amend the Constitution by a constitutional amendment bill adopted by the House of Commons and the second House and ratified by a national referendum. Both Ottawa in the House of Commons and the provinces in the second House (Council of Federation) would then have a right of initiative.

The constitutional amending process would start with a bill, either in the first House which represents the federal authority or in the second House which represents the provinces. When it is adopted in those two houses by an ordinary majority, like any other ordinary statute, it would go before the Canadian people which by a national referendum will say "yes" or "no". In order to protect the regions of Canada we have provided that this Bill shall obtain a majority of votes in each of the four Canadian regions, that is, in Quebec, Ontario, the Maritimes and the West. We think that this new device is better than the unwritten formula that we now have, where a single government may *de facto* block the whole system and where the right of initiative belongs to the central authority only. In our proposal the last word would rest with the Canadian people. The formula seems more democratic and no government may make a deadlock.

An Entrenched Bill of Rights

Civil liberties are protected in Canada by federal and provincial statutes, by the unwritten part of our Constitution and to a certain extent by the decisions of the courts.

We have suggested that a Bill of Rights be entrenched in the Canadian Constitution. It is obvious for us that democratic values, the principles of the equality before the law, the rule of law, the freedom of speech, and other well-known "classic rights," are so vital in our parliamentary democracy that they should be enshrined in the Constitution and beyond the reach of governments and parliaments except through a formal constitutional amendment.

This is quite possible in our system of parliamentary democracy. In our opinion it would be an improvement.

Linguistic Rights

In that explosive field, we have recommended at the federal level the entrenchment of the two official languages, that is, French and English in the laws of Canada, in the federal courts, the right to have T.V. programs in French or in English wherever possible and we have protected the language of service and the language of work as far as possible. It cannot be otherwise if Canada is going to remain one country. At the provincial level we suggested something different. In more than one federation the linguistic rights differ in the federal and in the regional orders of government. Quebec now is bound by s. 133 of the B.N.A. Act and Manitoba by a provision similar in principle to s. 133, but, as we know, the latter provision (s. 23 of the Manitoba Act) has not given what was expected from 1890 to 1979. New Brunswick adopted in 1969 an Official Languages Act. Ontario is unilingual but now some trials may take place in French, for example, in Sudbury, Ottawa and some other cities and I think that the government is considering giving more services in French in certain areas.

The situation differs from one province to another, and has greatly changed since 1867. The Pepin-Robarts Commission came to the conclusion that the proper solution for the time being is to recommend that each province guarantees linguistic rights by statute, in having regard to its own context, and, once the provinces agree, those linguistic rights should be entrenched in the Constitution. Our philosophy in that field is a question of strategy first, because we come to the conclusion that if the provinces do not protect linguistic rights by their own statutes they will not agree to entrench them in the Constitution. We hope of course that the provinces will guarantee linguistic rights in their own legislation. We suggest entrenchment in a different way; that is entrenchment by consensus; gradual entrenchment.

The Preamble of the New Constitution

In the future Constitution a preamble much more inspired than the one we now have should refer to the two main linguistic communities, to the specific character of Quebec, to the distinctive character of the Indians and Eskimos, to the democratic values under which this country has been erected and finally, to the fundamental rights, and the rule of law. We shall not minimize the educational value of a well drafted preamble and we shall remember that in a few cases the judges and courts have referred to the preamble of our Constitution.

The Question of Self-Determination

We have treated in our first report the right of self-determination and a word of explanation is here necessary. We came to the conclusion that, in law, a formal constitutional amendment is necessary to allow a province to secede. Such an amendment may be adopted by the Parliament of Westminster. In the field of public international law we said that the question of self-determination for Quebec is a controverted question. Some say that Quebec has the right to do it while others contend that Quebec has no such right. However, we expressed the view that the problem is more political than legal, in practice, and that if by an appropriate referendum Quebec chooses independence, then, for democratic reasons that choice should be respected. We shall not use force to keep Quebec in Confederation. Our position has not perhaps been well understood by the public. We made a clear distinction between the legal situation and the political situation. We recommended a new constitution for Canada in order to keep Quebec *de plein gré.*

A Constituent Assembly?

The Pepin-Robarts Commission came to the conclusion that for the moment, the federal provincial conferences shall continue to take place in the field of the constitutional revision. The new Constitution of Canada should be devised and drafted by the elected representatives, that is the Prime Minister of Canada, the ten Premiers, and ratified thereafter by the Canadian people. If we fail to have a new constitution in that way, then we will have to consider other processes—a ''constitutional commission'' charged with the specific mandate of writing a new constitution, or, a ''constituent assembly'', that is, an assembly made of delegates with a special mandate to draft a new constitution for Canada. This has been done in some countries, for example in the United States in 1787. A constituent assembly of the 13 states was established and it has enacted a new Constitution after four months of debates. Each of the 13 states was called upon to ratify the new Constitution.

The Task Force on Canadian Unity concluded that we were not at this stage yet. The political leaders of this country should once again try to make a new Constitution and it is only if they fail that we shall consider the establishment of a constitutional commission or a constituent assembly. But the difficulty with a constituent assembly is its composition. Who is going to be a ''delegate''? Are the provinces going to have the same number of delegates irrespective of their population? Is Quebec going to be one out of ten or 11, or, one out of four, or even one of two as the sovereignists suggest? It is perhaps as difficult to devise the constitution of the constituent assembly as to make the constitution itself.

Conclusion

A federal Canada is possible and quite desirable for the Pepin-Robarts Commission, but with a different division of powers and with reformed central institutions. I hope that a federal provincial conference will be convoked before the referendum of 1980 in order than Quebec knows what the other parts of Canada are ready to do. Quebecers shall not have the choice between the constitutional *status quo* and the ''sovereignty'' of Quebec but between a new restructured Canadian federalism and the sovereignty of Quebec. This is what our Commission has tried to do: to offer an alternative, to offer a solution between the *status quo* and the ''sovereignty of Quebec''. We were not a constituent assembly, we had no mandate to draft a new Constitution. We offered guidelines, we devised a philosphy.

People are more sensibilized than in 1968 when Prime Minister L. B. Pearson started the constitutional revision. We must now act fast. We are perhaps one constitutional crisis behind. We shall without delay adapt our federal constitution to the needs of today. We cannot provide for everything in the Constitution, true. But a federal constitution shall not include too many silences. There must be a *modus vivendi* between those who suffer from legal claustrophobia (those who fear to be imprisonned by legal enactments) and those who want to foresee everything.

The Pepin-Robarts Commission has taught that there is a path between those who want to change nothing and those who want to change everything.

NOTES

1. *A.G. (Nova Scotia)* v. *A.G. (Canada),* [1951] S.C.R. 31.

2. *Hodge* v. *The Queen* (1883), 9 App. Cas. 117.

3. *P.E.I. Potato Marketing Bd.* v. *Willis,* [1952] 2 S.C.R. 392.

4. "Decentralization" "Devolution" and "Deconcentration" are defined at p. 27 of the second report of the Pepin-Robarts Commission intituled "Coming to Terms". "Delegation" is defined at p. 63.

5. *Hodge* v. *The Queen, supra* note 2; *The Liquidators of the Maritime Bank* v. *The Receiver General of New Brunswick,* [1892] A.C. 437; *Edwards* v. *A.G. (Canada),* [1930] A.C. 124; *In Re The Initiative and Referendum Act,* [1919] A.C. 935, at p. 942; *British Coal Corp.,* [1935] A.C. 500; *Mellenger et al.* v. *New Brunswick Development Corp.,* [1971] 2 All E.R. 593. "Within its appointed field, the Provincial Legislature is as supreme as any other Parliament", said Lord Atkin in *Shannon* v. *Lower Mainland Dairy Products Bd.,* [1938] A.C. 708, at p. 722. See an article of Louis-Philippe Pigeon (now a Supreme Court judge) "Are The Provincial Legislatures Parliaments?" (1943), 21 Can. Bar Rev. 826.

6. *Supra,* note 2, at p. 132.

7. *Supra,* note 5, at p. 441.

8. *Supra,* note 5, at p. 442.

9. *Supra,* note 5, at pp. 595-6.

10. [1943] S.C.R. 1, at p. 19.

11. *Ibid.*, at p. 12.

12. See an article of Gérald A. Beaudoin: "Les aspects constitutionnels du référendum". Etudes internationales, Université Laval Volume III, no. 3. Juin 1977, pp. 197-207.

13. For a more lengthy and complete outline of the subject, read an article of Gérald A. Beaudoin: "La philosophie 'constitutionnelle' du Rapport Pepin-Robarts" (1979), 57 Can. Bar Rev. 428.

14. Pages 9 and 10.

15. "Regionalism" is defined in "Coming to Terms" at pp. 10 and 11.

16. The Committee on the Constitution of the Canadian Bar Association in its report of August 1978 recommended against the insertion in the Constitution of a clause of legislative delegation of powers. One of the reasons invoked is that it may lead to a particular status for a province.

17. The term "asymetric federalism" is defined in "Coming to Terms" at pp. 83 and 84.

18. We may perhaps apply here for constitutional law the principle enunciated in the famous case *R.* v. *Sussex Justices,* [1924] 1 K.B. 256. At p. 259, Lord Hewart C.J. notes: ". . . a long line of cases shows that it is not merely of some importance but is of fundamental importance that justice should not only be done but should manifestly and undoubtedly be seen to be done."

7

Devolution

Douglas McK. Brown

When we speak about devolution, we are talking about the stuff of which history is made. Power is acquired by devolution and equally it is destroyed in the same way.

The instruments of devolution are revolution, conquest, transfer and death. It is, however, the underlying causes that attract the playwright and the historian. Devolution is attractive because it signals the great movements and upheavals of history, the downfall of monarchs and regimes. It involves the whole range of human motivations, to which you can attach your own adjectives.

With Brutus and his friends—Fear and ambition
With Coriolanus—Pride
With Quebec and Wales—Language and culture
With Scotland—Culture and legal institutions

Devolution is a process, it is evolutionary. It requires a predecessor and a successor. In private affairs, it has to do with property. In public affairs, it has to do with sovereignty. The latter is our present concern. It would appear that the instrument in this country is transfer; an agreed transfer from the central government.

This is described in the White Paper as:

> The creation of elected as well as administrative institutions destinctive to Scotland and Wales. This is what devolution means.

It seems to me that there must be an element of permanence in devolution. In its purest form, as it occurs upon intestate succession, the predecessor is gone and the successors acquire everything. This is also the result where conquest has occurred.

Something more is involved than the delegation of authority which occurs at the municipal level.

The legal precedent is not the Book of Job.

> The Lord gave and the Lord has taken away. Blessed be the name of the Lord.

The extent of reserved power is an important element but here the intention may be more important than the words used.

The B.N.A. Act

In this respect the transfer of sovereignty under the British North America Act may be usefully referred to. It is a model of orderly transfer of authority. The reservations are primarily to be found in:

Section 9

> The Executive Government and Authority of and over Canada is hereby declared to continue and be vested in the Queen.

Section 55

> Where a Bill passed by the Houses of Parliament is presented to the Governor General for the Queen's Assent, he shall declare, according to his Discretion, but subject to the Provisions of this Act and to Her Majesty's Instructions, either that he assents thereto in the Queen's Name, or that he withholds the Queen's Assent, or that he reserves the Bill for the Signification of the Queen's Pleasure.

The Act then divides and bestows the whole of sovereignty with limited exceptions upon the provinces and the Dominion. They are, to use K. C. Wheare's definition of federalism, "Within a sphere, co-ordinate and independent."

The comprehensiveness of this constitutional document connotes permanence. Where the whole of the sovereignty has once been bestowed, it is doubtful if it can be recaptured without great political turmoil. While reservations may be noted in the document, the Legislative Powers of the Dominion and the provinces *vis-à-vis* each other are each sovereign in its field.

The fleeting character of the reservation was underlined in 1929 when the Conference on Operation of Dominion Legislation applying the principles laid down in the Imperial Conference Report of 1926 recommended:

> That his Majesty's Government in the United Kingdom do not advise His Majesty to give the Governor-General any Instructions for reserve bills presented to him for assent and that it would not be in accord with constitutional practice for advice to be tendered to his majesty against the views of the Government of the Dominion.

The Statute of Westminster and abolition of appeals to the Privy Council completed the process to the extent that the Committee on the Constitution opined that the creation of a new constitution by action taken wholly in Canada would be an important unifying symbol.

No question of international law was raised by the devolution of Canada and its provinces.

Quebec

The present crisis over Quebec separation raises questions of international law as well as constitutional law.

It is the avowed intention of the present party in power in Quebec to separate completely from Canada. There is to be a unilateral declaration of independence.

It must be important to the governing party to be perceived as acting legally. If they can be so perceived by the international community, then they will have met an important test.

The "right" to self-determination is referred to in the charter and resolutions of the United Nations. It has been deferred to and implemented in the practice of states who made up the body of international law, and it has been recognized in the International Court of Justice (Southwest Africa and Western Sahara, Namibia).

Self-determination in this century has been seen for the most part in a colonial context. The concept has been used to break up the colonial empires. However, the language of the charter refers to peoples without distinction and the right of "self-determination" may be appealed to by groups seeking political recognition, even if not in a colonial context.

Professors Claydon and Whyte of Queen's University have pointed out that self-determination is important.

> Because the judgments about whether it applies to the Quebec case may influence both support for and opposition to independence itself.

People, and particularly the law-abiding citizens of Quebec, would feel disinclined to opt for separation, if they felt they were acting contrary to recognized bodies of law.

The Question Is—Has Such a Case Been Made Out?

It is at this point that constitutional law and international law become interdependent. Will the international community be prepared to accord the benefits of recognition to Quebec, if that province by a unilateral declaration is acting outside a constitutional framework.

A claim that a province can constitutionally declare independence must be rejected. Such a declaration, if carried into effect, would contravene important rights of citizenship possessed by all citizens of the country, not the least of which are the free passage of goods and services and the right to reside and dispose of one's labour in any part of the country. In the *Winner* case, the right to use the highways was protected. Without elaborating, I believe it can be said that constitutional authorities would reject the idea. The international community would wish to have very valid reasons for concurring in a secession. The fact that a declaration took place over the protests of the federal government would be important.

The questions have been posed this way. Is the "self" in self-determination Quebec or Canada as a whole? Are other aspects of international law involved, such as human rights? Which result would be most likely to discourage international violence and enhance human rights? Would the claimant be economically and politically viable in the world community? Are there separate ethnic identities that are politically salient? Has there been significant integration in economic, political and other spheres over a long time? If secession were to be honoured, what would the consequences be for the rest of Canada? What are the benefits to the world community?

It must be conceded that the government of the law-abiding people of Quebec would not in all likelihood endanger human rights. No doubt they are a viable economic and political unit as ordinarily understood. They have a separate ethnic identity and have significant integration in political and economic spheres.

These facts in themselves, while important, do not guarantee approval by the world community. On the other hand, Canada is a valued member of the world community and an important factor in its stability. What would the effect be on Canada?

This can only be described as tragic. The fragmentation so caused would put the very existence of Canada as a nation in doubt. The land mass would be divided and an East Pakistan-West Pakistan type of geography created. It is doubtful if this situation would contribute to world community interests.

I have barely touched upon this subject but perhaps enough to express the view that in the short term and perhaps the medium term the benefits of recognition would probably be denied.

Scotland and Wales

In practical terms the impact that is likely to be felt as a result of the devolution proposals depends largely on the range of subjects that are devolved in the Assemblies. In this respect, the scheme of devolution resembles the distribution of powers that takes place between the different levels of government in a federal system, and some interesting comparisons can be made between, on the one hand, the subjects which were to have been devolved to the Assemblies, and on the other hand, the matters over which the provinces have jurisdiction under the Constitution of Canada.

A complete list of the devolved subjects is contained in Schedule 10, Part 1, of the Scotland Act, Schedule 2 of the Wales Act. Reference will only be made, however, to the more significant areas.

Law and the Legal System

In this area, the separate character of Scots law facilitated the.delegation of extensive authority to the proposed Scottish Assembly. Under the proposals, the Assembly would have legislative power over almost the whole range of civil and criminal law. There would be some exceptions to this general power, but these would be of a fairly limited nature. For example, the Assembly would not have jurisdiction over labour relations, nor would it have any authority in relation to offences against the state. Despite these limitations, the Assembly would nevertheless enjoy considerably greater power than that currently enjoyed by the Canadian provinces, which are excluded altogether from the field of criminal law.

As regards the court system, it was decided, after some debate, that the administration of the courts should be fully devolved. However, the Westminster parliament would retain exclusive authority over such important subjects as the appointment and conditions of tenure of judges and sheriffs, the basic structure of the court system and all aspects relating to the jurisdiction of the courts.

Financial Arrangements

Under the proposals, the Westminster parliament would retain close control over the financial resources available to the Assemblies. The devolved services would be financed by a block fund voted by parliament, after consultation with the Scottish and Welsh administrations. This fund would be drawn from the national pool of taxes. The Assemblies would therefore have no independent revenue raising powers but would be totally reliant upon the funds allocated to them by Westminster. In the White Paper of 1975, it was proposed that the Assemblies should be able to supplement the block fund by levying additional taxes on local rates. However, these proposals were abandoned when the legislation was drawn up.

This financial dependence on Westminster represents a significant limitation on the powers of the Assemblies. The importance of some measure of financial independence is clearly recognized within most federal systems. For example, in Canada the provinces enjoy some measure of independence in raising their own revenues, particularly in the area of direct taxation.

Natural Resources

This topic is closely associated with the previous one and is relevant to both the U.K. and Canadian situations. Much of the impetus for greater self-determination in Scotland stemmed from the hope that North Sea oil would guarantee for that country a prosperous economic future independently of the rest of the United Kingdom. In this expectation the proponents of devolution were sadly disappointed as the proposals allowed the Assembly scarcely any measure of control over the country's resources, either on shore or off shore. By contrast, the Canadian provinces own their on-shore resources and are able to exercise considerable control over them.

Other Matters

Other devolved matters include responsibility for health, housing, local government, social welfare and pollution. The Assemblies would also have considerable control over education, although after much debate it was decided that this control should not extend to the university system or any other method of post-secondary education.

Reserve Powers

A considerable amount of discussion was generated by this topic. We have already seen that the powers of the Assemblies would, in practice, be much restricted on account of the retention of sovereignty by the Westminster parliament and by the armlock that Westminster would have over the purse strings of the newly-created bodies. In addition, however, it was proposed that there should be further means of control written into the legislation itself relating directly to the matters that have been devolved. As originally proposed, these powers would have been very sweeping. The Secretary of State for Scotland, a member of the U.K. Executive, would have been able to reject any Assembly Bill which he judged, on the advice of the law officers, to be *ultra vires*. This decision would not have been subject to any form of judicial review. Moreover, the U.K. government would have had an unqualified general reserve power to reject any Assembly Bill on grounds of policy. Finally, in relation to executive functions exercisable by the devolved administrations, it was envisaged that the U.K. government would be able to simply take back devolved functions. The U.K. government would also have been able to alter or annul subordinate legislation passed by the local executives.

These proposals were sharply criticized by the proponents of devolution, who argued that they represented a gross insult to the stature of the proposed Assemblies. On account of this criticism, the government decided to make significant changes to their original proposals. Firstly, as regards the legality of Assembly legislation, it was decided that this question would no longer be left to the subjective determination of the Attorney-General. Instead, if there was any dispute as to the constitutionality of Assembly legislation, this would have to be resolved by reference to the courts. Schedule 12 of the Scotland Act sets out a procedure whereby the Attorney-General would be able to institute proceedings for the determination of a devolution issue. This schedule provides that the Privy Council will be the court of final review.

As regards any policy objections to Assembly legislation, s. 38 of the Scotland Act prescribes a procedure for preventing the passage of certain Assembly Bills. If the Secretary of State is satisfied that a Bill might directly or indirectly have repercussions for a reserved matter, and that this would not be in the public interest, he can suggest to parliament that the Bill should not be given Royal assent. East House of Parliament is then given 28 days within which to pass a resolution that the Bill should not be given Royal assent. This procedure is much narrower than that previously proposed, although the vagueness of such determinations as whether a provision would indirectly have repercussions for a reserved matter, or whether a particular provision would or would not be in the public interest, necessarily means that the Westminster parliament retains considerable discretion in deciding whether Assembly legislation should be allowed to proceed.

Thirdly, in relation to the executive functions of the devolved administration, s. 39 of the Scotland Act gives the Secretary of State certain overriding powers. These powers are very similar in nature to the powers exercisable in relation to Assembly legislation in s. 38 of the Act. In other words, the Secretary of State is able to prevent action being taken by the devolved administration where, in his opinion, this action would directly or indirectly affect a reserved matter and would not be in the public interest. Again, this exercise of power must within 28 days be approved by both Houses of Parliament. A similar procedure is described in s. 40 where the U.K. government wishes to revoke a statutory instrument made by the devolved administration.

The existence of these reserve powers could perhaps be compared with the power of the federal parliament of Canada to pass laws for the "Peace, Order, and good Government of Canada", contained in s. 91 of the B.N.A. Act. It seems quite clear, however, that the U.K. reserve power offers considerably more opportunity for intervention on the part of the U.K. government than that which is available to the federal government by virtue of s. 91.

Judicial Review

After much discussion, it was finally decided that the constitutionality of Assembly legislation should be open to review by the courts at the instance of any litigant. Therefore, not only the Attorney-General, but also any interested party can raise the validity of Assembly Legislation in the courts. In this respect, the situation resembles that in Canada where the constitutionality of federal and provincial legislation is subject to review by the courts. In both situations it will be necessary for an individual litigant to establish that he possesses sufficient standing to challenge the legislation in question, and again in this area there is also much similarity between the laws of England and Canada.

Wales

The proposals for Scotland and Wales are, in many respects, very similar. There are, however, one or two significant differences, most important of which would be that the proposed Welsh Assembly would not be able to exercise any legislative powers. It would be able to make statutory instruments in any of the devolved areas, but, unlike the Scottish Assembly, it would have no power to pass primary legislation in any field. The range of devolved matters also differs from that established under the Scottish scheme, noticeably in the area of law and the legal system. The Welsh Assembly would not be able to exercise any powers in these areas.

Conclusions and Observations—The U.K. and Canadian Situations Compared

We have seen that the devolution proposals for Scotland and Wales fall far short of creating a federal scheme on the Canadian model. There are areas of similarity but on the whole a comparison of the two situations is apt to be misleading. In one sense, on a general level, it might be said that both situations deal with basically the same issue, namely, to what extent is recognition to be given to the interests and aspirations of identifiable regions or communities within a country? The great historical and constitutional differences between the two countries dictate that the approach which is taken will vary greatly in each case.

It would be pointless to recite the constitutional differences which exist between Canada and the United Kingdom—most of them are obvious. However, mention should be made of one factor that has become very relevant to the U.K. situation, namely, that country's membership in the E.E.C. There were repeated references during the course of the devolution debate for the need to ensure that in any devolution scheme the U.K. parliament would retain sufficient power to enable it to ensure that its obligations under the Treaty of Rome were capable of being met. Moreover, there was also a feeling that membership of the E.E.C. had significantly eroded the traditional sovereignty of parliament and many people were unwilling to see this process carried any further through to extensive devolution of power to regional Assemblies.

It is presumed in the case of Scotland and Wales that the powers reserved and the matters devolved, all of which are within a constitutional framework, do not attract the attention of the international community, provided the United Kingdom membership in the E.E.C. is not interfered with. From a Canadian standpoint the devolution as proposed even for Scotland appears to be a relatively mild affair. Presumably the voters thought differently in their rejection of the proposals.

8

*The Pearson Report: A Personal Comment**

J. A. Jolowicz

The Report of the Royal Commission on Civil Liability and Compensation for Personal Injury, generally known as the "Pearson Report," was published in March 1978, five years after its members were appointed. During the intervening period the Commission received a vast amount of evidence, its members visited a large number of foreign countries, and they held a total of 225 meetings, some of the full Commission, some of committees, and varying in length from quite short sessions to working week-ends. The result of these labours is the publication of three substantial volumes: the main Report and Recommendations in Volume I, statistics and costings in Volume II, and, in Volume III, brief descriptions of a number of overseas systems.

The industry of the Commission is beyond criticism and the collection of information contained in the Report is of great value, but the sad fact is that the Report itself satisfies scarcely anyone. To some extent disappointment with the Report of any Royal Commission is inevitable because of the compromises it is bound to contain. Blame must also attach in the present instance to the Commission's terms of reference which were in some respects surprisingly restricted: the Commission was to consider to what extent, in what circumstances, and by what means compensation should be payable in respect of death or personal injury suffered (a) in the course of employment; (b) through the use of a motor vehicle or other transport; (c) through the manufacture, supply or use of goods or services; (d) on premises occupied by another; (e) otherwise through the act or omission of another where compensation under the present law is recoverable only on proof of fault or under the rules of strict liability. These terms of reference

* For a fuller statement of the author's position, see Allen, Bourn and Holyoak, (ed.) *Accident Compensation After Pearson* (1979, London, Sweet & Maxwell), pp. 31-82.

contain a number of significant omissions. In the first place they exclude all damage to property, and so draw a distinction between personal injury and property damage which is not drawn by the present law of civil liability for tort or breach of contract. Secondly, they draw a distinction between personal injury and illness which, though familiar to most existing systems of social security or national insurance, is not self-evidently justifiable when the source of compensation is found in public money administered by the state: practical considerations may demand that the distinction be maintained, but if so that should emerge as a conclusion at the end of an enquiry on the scale of that entrusted to the Pearson Commission rather than taken as given at the beginning. Thirdly, they exclude a major category of accidents, namely, accidents suffered in the home which, according to the Commission's own figures, account for 29 percent of all deaths following injury and 27 percent of all injuries sufficiently serious to prevent the victim from working for four days or more.

The Commission itself considered that its terms of reference precluded the possibility of a recommendation even that all injury, let alone all injury and disease, should be covered exclusively by a global social security scheme, but whether or not the Commission's opinion on this was right, a major failing of the Report, and one of the reasons for my own disappointment with it, is the absence from its pages of any discussion in depth of the theory or philosophy of compensation or of the ways in which it may be made available. Even if it is accepted as axiomatic that a civilised society will not always leave losses to lie where they fall, and even if it is accepted, in accordance with the Commission's terms of reference, that losses due to personal injury or the death of another fall into a special category of their own, it might still have been hoped and expected that the Commission would at least go behind the appearances of what we have in our present law and attempt to throw some light on what, in the late 20th century, we ought to be trying, as a society, to do. Unfortunately, however, and notwithstanding its great attention to detail on particular matters such as the assessment of damages, the Report accepts and even exaggerates some of the more glaring misdescriptions which are built into our existing legal terminology, and largely overlooks the way in which the existing law actually operates in the conditions of today. The Report and its recommendations rest far too much on inarticulated assumptions, on unquestioned but out-dated notions of the rationale of civil liability, and on inadequate analysis of the way in which the law of civil liability for unintended damage actually functions in the modern world.

One of the most striking and one of the most unfortunate consequences of these failures lies in the Commission's own choice of terminology to describe the two principal sources of compensation available other than those which depend on the foresight of the victim himself (self-insurance) or on the voluntary action of others (simple charity, occupational insurance schemes and so on.). These sources are, of course, on the one hand, the system of civil liability for damages and, on the other, state operated compensation schemes funded by compulsory contributions—national insurance or social security. For myself, the phrases "civil liability" and "social security" seem perfectly satisfactory and I shall use them in the course of this lecture, but for some reason the Commission preferred the word "tort" to "civil liability" and it preferred the phrase "no fault" to "social security".

Under the Commission's recommendations both sources are to continue to exist, though the balance between them is to be altered, and one of the aims of the Commission is to achieve greater co-ordination between them. This is a proper objective, but the Commission's choice of terminology makes it even more difficult of achievement than it need have been, for "no-fault" does not mean to the Commission what it means to North American writers such as Professors Keeton and O'Connell: "no-fault" is a system of obtaining compensation directly from a pre-existing fund instead of by legal proceedings brought against a person legally responsible for the injury; "tort" is the system of obtaining compensation through the legal process, and, though it includes such matters as liability for breach of a strict contractual or statutory duty, though there are proposals for the introduction of new rules of strict liability in tort, the contrast between "no-fault" and "tort" implies both that the normal and proper criterion for civil liability should continue to be fault and that the accident victim should have, in addition or as an alternative, a right to claim on a fund which arises independently of fault on the part of anyone. The dichotomy thus presupposed is, I believe, at best misleading and at worst fundamentally false. I shall return to this criticism in due course.

In general terms the system of compensation now prevailing in England consists of the body of law governing civil liability for damages for personal injury—tort (including breach of statutory duty) and breach of contract—on the one hand, and social security on the other. Workmen's compensation was abolished with the introduction of the first of the post-War National Insurance Acts with the result that civil actions for damages brought by injured workmen against their employers are common, and in appropriate circumstances an accident victim may recover both damages and the compensation allocated to him by national insurance or, as it is now called, social security. The only provision concerning overlap between the two is the rule contained in the Law Reform (Personal Injuries) Act 1948 which provides that there shall be deducted from any damages recoverable for loss of earnings an amount equal to one half of the value of the plaintiff's rights to social security benefits. The explanation of this is that it is a rough compromise which, though applicable in all classes of case, is particularly apt in actions in respect of industrial injuries where the employer is defendant since in those cases each party has contributed to the fund from which the benefits are paid. Reference may conveniently be made at once, therefore, to an important recommendation of the Commission, namely, that in future, and with certain qualifications, the whole of any social security benefit to which a plaintiff may be entitled should be deducted from his damages. In principle a better solution would have been to deduct any damages recoverable from the social security benefits, but that would be difficult to implement in practice, and the Commission's recommendation on this point should not give rise to serious controversy.

So far as the benefits actually available under the social security system are concerned, it is unnecessary for present purposes to enter into detail on such matters as "special hardship allowance," "mobility allowance" and so on; what matters is the general basis of entitlement, and for this two broad categories of benefit must be taken into account. First there is "sickness benefit" to which any "insured" person, that is, broadly, any person in employment, is automatically entitled if he is prevented from working by injury or illness and, secondly, there is "industrial injury benefit" which is available to a person whose injury arises "out of and in the course of" his employment. The distinction was intended, for a variety of reasons, to create the so-called "industrial preference" and, although the difference between the values of the two classes of benefit has been reduced since they were originally introduced, "industrial preference" remains a feature of social security at the present time.

The Report contains numerous proposals for change in the benefits which should be available through social security, but it is necessary to mention here only the salient features of the Commission's proposals, namely, first, that "industrial preference" should remain but should be extended to "commuting" accidents and, secondly, that an entirely new scheme of social security benefits should be introduced to cover other accidents on the highway. With one dissentient the Commission recommends that this scheme should be financed by a special levy on petrol, and it is calculated that at January 1977 prices a levy of one penny per gallon would suffice.

On the civil liability side of things, a surprisingly large part of the Report is given over to the assessment of damages—a total of five chapters out of 33, and 71 out of 188 listed recommendations. Here too, however, time prevents detailed analysis: it is the Commission's consideration of the principles of liability to which I wish to devote the time at my disposal.

As the Commission's choice of terminology indicates, fault, that is, ordinarily, "negligence," is considered by the Commission still to be both the natural and the residual basis of liability in damages, and there is, in particular, no proposal for any major change in the law as it relates either to road traffic accidents or to accidents at work: both, as has been mentioned, will have preferential social security schemes if the Commission's proposals are accepted, and both will continue to have their civil actions for tort, subject, under the proposals, to deduction in full of the social security benefits available. For road traffic accidents this means that liability will continue to depend on proof of negligence, but as regards accidents at work there is already in existence a heterogeneous collection of strict statutory duties contained in the Factories Act and similar legislation. The introduction of new rules of strict liability in tort is, however, recommended for a number of particular cases.

The recommendations for strict liability fall into two categories. In the first place strict liability is recommended for certain rather specialised types of case such as accidents caused by movement of railway rolling stock, injuries caused to volunteers for medical research or clinical trials and the victims of vaccine damage where vaccination has been recommended by central or local government. Secondly a rule of strict liability is recommended for two large classes of case, "product liability" and what the Report calls "exceptional risks". For product liability the Commission's recommendations are broadly in line with those contained in the Council of Europe's Convention, the proposed Directive of the E.E.C. and the Report of the Law Commissions for England and Scotland, namely that the producer of a product which is shown to be "defective" and to have caused injury should be strictly liable. A product is "defective" if it "does not provide the safety which a person is entitled to expect, having regard to all the circumstances including the presentation of the product." "Producer" includes component manufacturers as well as final producers and it also includes importers and persons who market products as "own brand". As to "exceptional risks," the Commission's idea is that strict liability should be imposed "on the controller of things or operations in each of two categories—first those which by their unusually hazardous nature require close, careful and skilled supervision, the failure of which may cause death or personal injury; and secondly, those which, though normally by their nature perfectly safe, are likely, if they do go wrong, to cause serious and extensive casualties". Because of the difficulty of defining more closely the things and operations included within these categories, however, the Commission proposes that this kind of strict liability should be introduced by way of a "parent" statute enabling particular things and operations to be subjected to strict liability by statutory instrument.

Looking broadly at the overall scheme envisaged by the Commission, its most striking feature is, of course, that it contemplates the continuation of the duality of sources of compensation—social security and civil liability, or "no-fault" and "tort". This was not in fact to the liking of all the members of the Commission, but although the Commission as a whole considered that its terms of reference precluded a recommendation for the removal of civil liability from the field of personal injury compensation, most members felt that in any case a system of civil liability retained real value in cases of serious injury, both as a supplement to what should be available through social security and because the civil liability process enables the individual case to be more accurately dealt with than is possible under social security alone. From the point of view of an author of a text book on the law of tort, implementation of the Commission's proposals will not reduce the size of his book and may even increase it; from the point of view of practice, on the other hand, it is the expectation that the various increases in the social security benefits which are proposed, the offset against damages of all social security benefits and the introduction of a new and somewhat controversial rule that no damages for non-pecuniary loss should be awarded in respect of the first three months following an injury, will substantially reduce the number of claims for damages. The Commission itself calculates that implementation of the proposals would reduce total expenditure on damages by 20 percent and that it would cut out all claims other than those in respect of death or serious and lasting injury. Social security, in the Commission's view, should become the principal source of compensation with civil liability having a generally subsidiary and supplementary role.

To the victim of personal injury the source of his compensation is a matter of comparative indifference: the two things that matter to him are the amount of his compensation and the ease with which he gets it. If, then, social security is seen as a system whereby a person claims against a fund and is required only to show that he qualifies for payment while civil liability is seen as a system whereby a plaintiff has to establish the legal liability of another, usually by proving negligence, then it seems evident that social security will serve the accident victim better, exceptional cases only apart.

The Commission's general assumption is that, with limited exceptions, civil liability depends on proof of fault and should continue to do so. What is more, given the clear notion that civil liability should supplement social security and that it can deal more accurately with serious cases, it is difficult to avoid the conclusion that the Commission believes that the victim of fault has a better title to individualised and supplementary compensation than has the victim of a faultless accident. This, no doubt, is a still prevalent idea and it is closely related to that which holds that a wrongdoer should pay for the damage which his wrongdoing has caused. And that, in turn, has the apparently logical corollary that before a person is required to put his hand in his pocket to compensate another he should normally be shown to have behaved in a manner which the society in which he lives is prepared to condemn as morally culpable. So, in a modern, caring, society, the victims of faultless accidents must have another source of compensation and, given the expense and inefficiency of litigation about fault, that other source might as well be used generally, leaving civil liability with, at best, a subsidiary role.

The trouble with this is that it rests upon a false premise: the cases in which a judgment in damages results in an individual human being having to pay from his own pocket more than an insignificant amount such as the loss of a no-claims bonus under an insurance policy are extremely rare. In any case, the combined effect of the corporate ownership of virtually the whole of our transport and industrial undertakings and the principle of vicarious liability means that the only substantial class of case in which the person whose negligence is alleged to have caused damage is even the nominal defendant in an action is that of accidents involving private motorists. And in that class of case the real defendant is invariably an insurer.

This basic fact destroys the moral foundation of civil liability founded on fault, and most of the case against liability without fault, but it does more than that: it undermines if it does not altogether destroy the distinction seen as fundamental by the Commission between civil liability and social security, namely that under the latter the victim claims against a pre-existing fund while under the former he claims against an individual whose legal liability he must first establish. The truth is that in both cases he claims against a fund, and the real distinctions lie only in the mechanisms of the claim and the way in which the fund is financed.

It is, of course, true that the form of civil litigation calls for a defendant as well as a plaintiff, but the impact of insurance today is such that virtually all nominal defendants in actions for damages for personal injury, by the payment of insurance premiums, have contributed, in advance of the particular injury in respect of which they are sued, to the fund from which the damages awarded, if any, will actually be paid. The defendants do not pay the damages; they pay contributions in advance, just as do those persons who are called upon to pay contributions to the social security fund which does not, of course, get its money out of the air. What is more, such is the impact of insurance that we should no longer envisage the rules of civil liability for personal injury—whatever those rules may happen to be—as rules for deciding whether or not a particular identified individual should be called upon after the event to pay damages in respect of a particular injury: we should see them as rules which allocate the cost of bearing risks—the inevitable risks that accidents will happen and that people will get hurt.

This point is seen, and well taken, in some parts of the Commission's Report. In the Chapter on Product Liability, for example, there is clear recognition of the fact that producers insure their potential liabilities and can be expected to pass on the cost of insurance to their customers. And, the Commission concludes, "We think it justifiable and sensible that consumers as a whole should pay for the cost of insuring against injuries caused by a product from which they benefit, just as they pay for its other costs." Again, in relation to "exceptional risks," the Commission says, "Most personal injury accidents relate to risks which are capable of being covered by insurance: and it is generally more practicable and less expensive for the controller of a specific thing or activity to insure against its miscarriage (whether or not by reason of his negligence) than for every potential victim to take out first party insurance against that risk. We think that the case for strict liability is stronger where a person is in control of a thing or operation in the course of a business. . . . The incidental cost of personal injuries can then normally be charged to the cost of the business and so ultimately spread over all the consumers of the goods or services in question." The Commission does not, however, explain why this sort of reasoning is applicable only to "exceptional risks".

If what I have been saying thus far, and what I have just quoted from the Report, is even approximately correct, then not only is the contrast between social security and civil liability less stark than seems to be supposed by the Commission, but the choice between them—or the allocation of roles between them—turns out to be little more than a choice between methods of securing that compensation funds are available. Either we do it by one or more kinds of taxation to feed a centrally administered fund on a national basis or we reformulate the rules of civil liability—removing almost entirely those rules which make liability dependent on proof of fault—in such a way as to place the risk of having to pay compensation where we think it should lie in the first instance, leaving it to the chosen risk bearer, through insurance and pricing, to protect himself and thereby, in appropriate cases, to distribute the cost of compensation over his customers in proportion to the use they make of the goods or services he supplies.

It is at this point that political preferences cannot fail to influence one's approach, and I should not disguise my own preference for restricting the intervention of the State to circumstances in which nothing else will serve. This means that I should prefer to see the role of civil liability expanded, rather than that of social security, but, even trying to discount my own preferences, it seems clear that civil liability, properly applied, must lead to a more accurate distribution of the cost of risk-bearing over those who benefit from the risk created than can any method of raising funds for a system of social security. No doubt the cost of social security contributions, like the cost of insurance premiums, is reflected in the prices charged by the manufacturing and service industries, and a social security system, if it were to differentiate between high- and low-risk industries in fixing contribution rates, could go some way towards the desirable end of linking prices with the risk involved in providing the goods or services in question. The insurance industry, however, can go much further in this direction, for it knows how to adjust premiums by reference to a wide variety of factors, factors which are particular to the individual assured as well as those of general application, and it has the enormous advantage of fixing premiums from time to time by contract with the assured, not by cumbersome legislative techniques.

When all is said and done, however, the case for the retention of the system of civil liability for accidental injury, suitably amended to meet modern conditions, still rests upon a moral foundation, though not the moral foundation that was formerly thought to justify the imposition of liability for fault. The principle to be invoked is that we must accept responsibility for the consequences of our actions and of our decisions.

The imposition of civil liability for unintended damage does not, in today's world, often involve condemnation of the actual defendant's behaviour, and should not be thought of as doing so; still less should it be seen as the application of some kind of punishment for misconduct. In the individual case, even under the present law, an order that the defendant pay damages to the plaintiff is normally no more than the outcome of the law's judgment concerning the amount and the source of the plaintiff's compensation and as such is morally neutral. But the law itself should not be morally neutral about the creation of risks. On the contrary, it should insist that a person who creates a risk—however blameless or even meritorious he may be in doing so—must be aware of the risk that he creates and of his responsibility to those who may suffer injury in consequence of what he does. This extends from elementary individual acts such as the acquisition of a motor car for use on the highway through ordinary commercial or industrial undertakings to government or government-inspired activities, in respect of which the common law urgently needs to develop an equivalent to the French administrative law concept of *égalité devant les charges publiques*. In a complex mechanised society accidents resulting in personal injury or death will continue to happen however careful we all may be, and it is essential to the health of society that individuals, including individuals in charge of corporations, learn to recognise their responsibility for the consequences of all that they do, not only for the consequences of their "faults".

The sense of individual responsibility has been gravely weakened by the development of collectivist ideas and, while collective responsibility in the shape of social security for the victims of accidental injury, amongst others, is in itself an admirable thing, if it is so expanded as to relieve individuals of their own responsibilities for the consequences of their actions where it is unnecessary to do so, that is, where the victim can be adequately compensated without it, then it cannot but be harmful: that the private motorist would not notice the penny per gallon of petrol necessary to finance the Commisson's proposed "no-fault" scheme for accidents on the highway, for example, is not an advantage but a disadvantage of the scheme. Properly reconstructed—with the outmoded insistence on fault eliminated to the maximum possible extent—a system of civil liability can do as well for most accident victims as can social security, and at the same time it can encourage the sense of individual responsibility; society cannot afford to let it disappear. The one major class of case for which social security seems the only solution, if the victim is not to rely wholly on his own resources, is that of accidents in the home, and accidents in the home were, for some inexplicable reason, excluded from the Commission's terms of reference.

The implementation of some of the Commission's recommendations will, no doubt, bring improvement to the present unsatisfactory situation, and the retention of civil liability alongside social security does at least leave open the possibility that the principles of liability will one day receive the careful and complete revision that they deserve. But the Report itself does not provide the kind of study in depth of the problem for which we might have hoped after so long a period of preparation, and it does not get us much further in finding a solution to the question how a modern state—a state with a mixed economy, a belief in individual freedom and thus, by necessary implication, in individual responsibility—should deal with accident compensation as a whole. It is an overstatement, but it is not entirely untrue to say that the Report's proposals amount to little more than tinkering in accordance with no discernible principle with the illogical and inadequate system we now have.

9

The Law Commission

The Honourable Mr. Justice Kerr

Over the last 15 years or so, we in the Commonwealth have become used to the concept and institution of Law Commissions, bodies set up by statute to keep the law under review and to make recommendations for reform. I believe that the first such body was in fact in Canada, but the main international model was no doubt the establishment of the Law Commission of England and Wales and the Scottish Law Commission by the Law Commissions Act 1965. To-day I will be speaking about the English Commission, of which I have the honour to be the present Chairman, though of course we are in close touch with our Scottish colleagues in relation to all matters affecting the United Kingdom as a whole. The reason for a separate Law Commission in Scotland, as you will know, is that Scottish law differs in many respects from English law, and is generally regarded by our fellow lawyers north of the Border as being superior to ours. (I hasten to add that I am fortunately unable to express any view on this question, even if I were prepared to do so.) However, before dealing with the English Law Commission in some detail, it is necessary to set its creation, and its achievements and failures, into the perspective of history—or rather into the perspective of our nonhistory so far as systematic law reform is concerned.

One of the greatest paradoxes of the English legal system is that while our courts and administration of justice have enjoyed world-wide respect and influence over many centuries, there has always been great clamour, with every justification, for some systematic means of reforming the law in order to make it simpler and more intelligible and accessible to the public. However, these calls for reform were left virtually unheeded by countless governments and parliaments until they finally bore fruit, to a limited extent, in 1965.

As long ago as the beginning of the sixteenth century Francis Bacon—both before and when he was Lord Chancellor—tried hard to produce some order. He wished, already then, to reduce the volume of statutes, which were "so many in number that neither the common people can practise [sic] them nor the lawyers sufficiently understand them'', and about a decade later, still in his time, Parliament was invited by James I to consider the reform of the laws "so that they might be cleared and made known to the subjects''. Indeed, Bacon called for "Law Commissioners'' to revise the laws and keep them up to date, but nothing came of any of these initiatives.

A further attempt was made under Cromwell in 1652 when Parliament set up a Law Commission under the chairmanship of Sir Matthew Hale "to take into consideration what inconveniences are in the law''; this sat for five years and prepared draft statutes on many topics, but none of them saw the light of day. During Henry Brougham's great speech on law reform to the House of Commons in 1828, over 170 years later, he read out their long forgotten titles. He called for reform of the common law in a speech which lasted over six hours and which is perhaps the greatest landmark in this field. However, he was also unsuccessful, and equally so when he became Lord Chancellor shortly thereafter. Although a "Royal Commission on the Consolidation of Statute Laws'' was set up in 1833 and reported in 1835, nothing was done to implement its recommendations. Another 20 years later Lord Cranworth tried again; he asked the Chancellor of the Exchequer for a paltry annual sum and a small office for a "Board for Consolidating and Digesting the Statute Law'', but this again produced no result. When Lord Gardiner introduced the Law Commission's Bill as Lord Chancellor in the House of Lords in 1965, he had a copy of Lord Cranworth's letter with him for the occasion!

Then what are the reasons for these centuries of extraordinary failure? There is no single or simple answer, but a combination of reasons which between them produced this result with virtual inevitability. First, we have nothing analogous to a Ministry of Justice. Many of its functions, but by no means all, are collected in the office of the Lord Chancellor and of his department, but virtually all other government departments also have responsibilities involving aspects of law reform on matters with which they are concerned. There is no focal point, let alone any single agency. Next, Parliament itself must bear a great deal of the responsibility. It has ultimate sole control over the form and content of statutes, and of course, over its procedures. Neither of these are in the least bit suitable for any systematic approach to law reform. The traditional form of Acts of Parliament, particularly under the influence of our parliamentary draftsman—who are few in number, high in intellect, wield great power, and are largely conservative in their techniques—is to try to cover every possible eventuality by some legislative provision. Our system is totally opposed to the continental approach of codes which lay down principles in general terms and then leave it to the courts to work them out and apply them in individual cases. Thus, alone in the company of Eire, I believe, the United Kingdom still has no Criminal or Penal Code such as your Code of 1970, nor any visible prospect of getting one in the foreseeable future. To virtually every other country in the world it must seem extraordinary that under our system people can still be convicted of offences solely on the basis of the views of judges as to whether some particular conduct was or was not criminal at common law.

Another and quite different reason is our hallowed common law system, and for the moment I include in it the principles of equity. For centuries the development of the law was in effect left to the judges, with only sporadic interventions by Parliament to pull together a few topics here and there and restate them in statutory form when they had become too complex, unsatisfactory or out of date. Chief Justice Coke regarded the common law as "the perfection of reason". He was, of course, not referring to the law in his time or at any one point of time, but to the jurisprudential concept of developing the law on a case-by-case basis, with the judges threading their way on lines of principle through distinguishable precedents in order to do justice in individual cases. However, from the point of view of making the law simple, intelligible and accessible, this is a very imperfect system, because it leads inevitably to a vast accumulation of case law, with never a pause for any form of consolidation in the widest sense of the word. Even the invention of equity was no more than a typical pragmatic compromise, though without it we could never have got along at all. When the common law had become too rigid and formalistic to be adaptable for situations in which it provided no fair answer, successive great Lord Chancellors, such as Bacon, Nottingham, Hardwicke and Eldon, were forced to inject into it the expediency of equitable solutions. But for this device Parliament would have had to intervene radically centuries ago. But equity in its turn developed like the common law; it grew slowly on the same piecemeal basis of a mixture of innovation and binding precedents until, in its turn, it became too rigid and unwieldy to provide any systematic solution. All that could then be done was finally to fuse the two systems in 1873, but even this process took nearly 300 years.

Under the guidance of many great and distinguished judicial minds the combination of common law and equity has produced a vast and complex fabric of law, admirable in much of its detail, but far too complex to be encompassed by the public which it is designed to serve. It is one of our great cultural heritages and has produced judicial giants such as Coke, Mansfield, Blackstone and, among others in our time, Lord Denning. In the early days of the Law Commission he made no secret of the fact that he saw it as an unwieldy instrument of law reform in comparison with the powers of a strong Court of Appeal. When I once said in a speech at some public function that real law reform could now only come through Acts of Parliament, he said: "But then I am out of a job!" I admire him as one of the great men of our time. He has made an enormous and perhaps unique contribution to the development of our law in this century. However, from the point of view of systematic reform, no judges or courts can do anything like enough, even with occasional collective reforms and restatements by Parliament.

The result of this shapeless process was that by 1965 we had over 350,000 reported cases, more than 4,000 statutes which were in force, and about 100 volumes of delegated legislation. These figures were mentioned by Lord Gardiner during the passing of the Law Commissions Act. This had been preceded by yet another compromise; the recognition that something had to be done, but—typically under our system—no more than a half-way house towards real change. During the period immediately before and after World War II, successive Lord Chancellors had come to accept that in order to move the law forward in some systematic way, something new had to be introduced to add to the lawmaking powers of the judges and of piecemeal initiatives by government departments. Two standing committees were set up, the Law Reform Committee and the Criminal Law Revision Committee. It was their function, under references from the Lord Chancellor and the Home Secretary, to examine specific topics of the law which were badly in need of reform and to recommend changes. But the members—distinguished judges, barristers, solicitors and academics—were acting merely on a voluntary and part-time basis, holding such meetings as could be fitted in with their ordinary commitments. Both committees did—and still do—invaluable work, and many important reforms are due to their efforts. But once again it was only a partial and inevitably imperfect solution.

The great new departure came with the concept of the Law Commissions Act 1965, the creation and long-cherished ideal of Lord Gardiner, L.C. After more than 350 years, and countless governments and Lord Chancellors, a radically different line was finally taken. To-day, only 14 years later, we perhaps already take it for granted; but the radical nature of the new concept can be seen from the definition of the Law Commissions' functions under s. 3 of the Act. This is:

> to take and keep under review all the law . . . with a view to its systematic development and reform, including in particular the codification of such law, the elimination of anomalies, the repeal of obsolete and unnecessary enactments, the reduction of the number of separate enactments and generally the simplification and modernisation of the law.

What this amounts to in effect is something quite new and revolutionary in our legal history. In relation to the whole of our law, Parliament was thereby entrusting to an independent body the task of recommending to Parliament legislation to be enacted by Parliament. However, perhaps not surprisingly, the idea was received with a good deal of scepticism from many quarters. Lord Reid thought that it was a pity that such very wide language had been used, which "raised many false hopes unlikely to be fulfilled". While no one in either House ultimately opposed the Bill, and many were enthusiastically in its favour, the general tone was nevertheless perhaps best reflected in the speech of Sir John Hobson, a former Attorney

General, who said: "Certainly the Bill will do no harm, although I doubt very much whether it can do much good."

What was doubted, rightly as things turned out, was the ability of a small body of lawyers, even working on a full-time basis, of making any real impact on the vast fabric of our law and, above all, the logistic difficulties of getting its recommendations backed by government and put through Parliament. I will have to say something about both these aspects hereafter, but first I must briefly explain the structure and methods of work of the Law Commission, which have now been adopted in principle in many parts of the Commonwealth, including in particular Canada and Australia.

The Act provides for a Commission consisting of a Chairman and four other Commissioners to be appointed by the Lord Chancellor. They must be suitably qualified by holding judicial office or by experience as a barrister or solicitor or as a teacher of law in a university. (The latter words are noteworthy as the first and only statutory recognition of the qualification of academic lawyers to play an official part in the life of the law.) All Commissioners are appointed for a fixed term not exceeding five years, and any judge who may be appointed cannot be required to sit in court during his term of office unless his appointment otherwise provides, which has so far never happened.

The pattern of appointments over the last 14 years has been broadly the same throughout. Three High Court judges, of whom I am the third, have been the Chairmen; there has always been a Queen's Counsel with experience of criminal and general common law work, a practising solicitor with experience of conveyancing, land law and equity, and usually two academics in specialised fields, at present Private International Law in the one case and Family Law in the other. All work on a full-time basis. In addition there is a staff of some 20 civil service lawyers and five parliamentary draftsmen who come to us on secondment from Whitehall for a period of about two years at a time. The fact that we have their highly specialised services, which are in enormous demand and short supply, is perhaps the greatest recognition of the stature which this new body was intended to have. We also have a secretary with the rank of Under Secretary in the Civil Service, a librarian with an excellent library, and a full supporting staff in good premises just behind Gray's Inn; the total number in the building is about 45.

The work which we do falls into three main parts. First, a number of general programmes for law reform were evolved in the early days, including the reform of Family Law and the Codification of the Criminal Law and of the law of Landlord and Tenant. These programmes were laid before Parliament pursuant to the Act, and within them we are in theory free to recommend whatever legislation we see fit. In practice, however, our projects are evolved in consultation with the Lord Chancellor, and in relation to the Criminal Law with the Home Secretary, and their departments.

Secondly, we are required "to provide advice and information to Government Departments and other authorities or bodies concerned at the instance of the Government with proposals for the reform or amendment of any branch of the law". In this connection we do two main things. We receive and deal with references on specific topics of law reform from the Lord Chancellor, and we provide *ad hoc* advice and comments to government departments whenever we feel able to do so. The latter aspect of our work has increased enormously as the result of our entry into the Common Market; this was a dimension which had not been foreseen when the Law Commission was set up, but unfortunately it provides a steady flow of requests for comments which interrupt our regular work and with which we often cannot comply. Thirdly, we are required to receive and consider any proposals for law reform which may be made to us from any source. However, we are in no way bound to act upon them, and in many cases we can do no more than to refer them to the appropriate department for consideration.

Within this broad framework, and despite the all-embracing definition of our functions as expressed in the Act, there are many topics with which we do not deal at all and which we could not effectively tackle at present. Thus, we do not at present deal with Labour Law, Tax, Civil or Criminal Procedure or Company Law, which remain the responsibilities of the various departments concerned. Some years ago the Law Commission sought to propose wide-ranging reforms for our Administrative Law (such as it is), but this proposal was in effect blocked by the government of the day, the only occasion on which there was some real divergence of views and the exercise of something like a veto. In theory the Commission might have persisted in a full-scale exercise, including draft legislation. But it has no direct access to Parliament, and in practice it is dependent on the cooperation and support of ministers and government departments, except occasionally when a Private Member's Bill may take up our recommendations. Even then, however, this would have no prospect of making any progress without government support.

Internally we work in "teams" specialising in particular topics, with at least one Commissioner on each team. The basic task of the team, apart from its day-to-day contacts with government departments, professional organisations and the general public, is to work up topics for consideration by the five Commissioners collectively. In effect nothing is published otherwise than under the auspices of all the Commissioners.

Our method of work on law reform projects falls into two stages and has set a pattern which is now widely adopted throughout the public sector. The first stage is consultative. We produce Working Papers for consultation. These contain a fully researched review of the present law on the topic in question, followed by an analysis of its defects and of the criticisms which have been made of it. We then explain the "field of choice" for reform and usually express provisional views on preferred solutions. These Working Papers are then published, and hundreds of copies are sent out for comment to professional and other organisations, government departments, the judiciary, the professions, the universities, etc., as well as being on sale by HMSO. We then allow a consultation period of three to six months for comments to come in. These are then analysed by the team, and on the basis of the comments received the team produces its policy solution on the reform in question, which may often differ from the provisional views expressed in the Working Paper, for the consideration of the Commissioners. The team drafts a Report with recommendations and (usually) a draft Bill which are often further revised by the Commissioners. The final product is then a definitive Report with recommendations by the Commissioners and a draft Bill. This goes to the Lord Chancellor and is published as a Command Paper which is laid before Parliament. At this point the Commission is formally *functus officio* in relation to the topic in question; the problem is then what happens—or does not happen—thereafter.

In the 14 years of its existence the Commission has undoubtedly done a great deal of work and achieved a substantial measure of reform, most of which would not have seen the light of day if the Commission had not been set up. Our modern divorce law owes its existence largely to the efforts of the Commission in its early years, and there have been substantial reforms and restatements in the fields of contract, tort and crime. Some 70 Working Papers and 90 Reports have been produced. The latter include Reports concerning statutes (which I must mention in a moment) as well as our 13 Annual Reports; but of the Reports containing proposals for law reform about 70 percent have already been enacted in whole or in part, and many of the remainder are still under active consideration. In this respect we have been more fortunate, I think, than our sister organisations in the Commonwealth.

Apart from the reform of the general law, the Commission performs another crucially important function in the purely technical process of modernising what we euphemistically refer to as our "statute book", which in fact consists of countless volumes of legislation. We have two means of making some impact on this shapeless mass of statutes, many of them centuries old. Neither involves changing the existing law, and this is why Parliament has been content to allow its traditional controls and procedures to be by-passed in a more manageable way. The first is by means of "Statute Law Reform" which consists of the repeal of archaic, obsolete, spent and unnecessary enactments. By this means over 2,000 legislative provisions, including more than 900 whole Acts of Parliament, have been repealed in successive Statute Repeals Acts, which do no more than cutting out the dead wood and slightly slimming the volumes of statutes. The second is by Consolidation Acts, which gather together in one Act the provisions on any particular topic which are spread over a number of statutes and which can be conveniently collected together and brought up to date. However, no change of any kind in the substance of the law is permitted in such cases except to rectify obvious errors, omissions or other anomalies. The process is extremely useful, but inevitably limited in its function.

This dual process of modernising our statutes to some extent is only successful because it is not subject to the ordinary procedures of Parliament. All Statute Law Repeal Bills and Consolidation Bills are automatically referred by Parliament to a Joint Standing Committee of both Houses. This considers the Bills in great detail, with the assistance of the draftsman concerned, and then sends them back to both Houses with a report on their acceptability on the ground that they contain no changes in the substance of the existing law. Unfortunately, however, there is nothing analogous for law reform proposals. These have to compete for a place in the legislative programme with all other measures which are introduced or supported by the government, and they then have to weather the full parliamentary process whereby, in particular, any amendment can be put down and debated provided that it is within the ambit of the "long title" of the Bill in question.

Looking at the picture as a whole after 14 years of the Law Commission's existence. I think that it can fairly be summarised as follows. There has been a substantial achievement of reform, simplification and modernisation, for which the Commission has received considerable public praise; indeed it has rightly been described on several occasions as by far the most important and useful piece of law reform in this century, and probably in the whole of our history. On the other hand, if these achievements are set against the background of s. 3 of the Act, which defines the right objective but in terms which are purely utopian, then the achievements pale almost into insignificance in comparison with what is really needed.

There are three main problem areas, and no real solution is at present in sight for any of them.

First, when the resources of the Law Commission are set against the spectrum of what needs to be done, and what the Act rightly requires to be done at least in theory, what has been done and what can be done is extremely limited, and little more than a drop in the ocean. We cannot begin to fulfil the task "to take and keep under review all the law".

Secondly, there has so far been a total failure of "codification", one of the main objectives laid down in the Act. This term can mean different things, but what it was no doubt intended to mean was the production of comprehensive codes of principles and rules on different topics, which would take the place of the vast mass of law distilled in our text-books from thousands upon thousands of decided cases. However, such attempts as have been made to produce any such codes have so far been wholly unsuccessful. One of the highest original priorities of the Commission was to produce a Contract Code on the lines, for instance, of the Indian Contracts Act

1872. But after about five years or so the work had to be suspended indefinitely, for two reasons. First, it proved impossible to agree, in many respects, on what should be the content of such a code; the objectives of definition, restatement and reform, all at the same time, proved to be impossible to achieve. Secondly, even if such a code had materialised, it was hard to imagine its passage through Parliament because—as already mentioned—Parliament traditionally does not legislate in the form of general principles and rules but in enormous and complex detail. The same fate befell an attempt to codify the whole of the law of Landlord and Tenant (apart from the political legislation for the protection of tenants, in particular the Rent Acts). An experienced barrister in this field was instructed, with the assistance of others, to produce a code. He drafted some 660 propositions of a code which was intended to contain about 880, but when he then died the project was effectively abandoned, at any rate for the foreseeable future.

What has been achieved, and is now sought to be done, under the name of codification is something quite different. It is to embody in statutes, partly by way of restatement and partly by way of reform, aspects of our law under various topics which are particularly unsatisfactory. Thus, parts of the law of Landlord and Tenant have been the subject of Law Commission Reports. The same has happened and is happening in the field of contract, and in the field of criminal law we are beginning to approach the stage when all offences will at least have a statutory foundation. However, instead of producing anything in the nature of a real code, this process is like producing or piecing together individual bits of string which, between them, are intended to cover those parts which are at present judged to be most in need of reform. Moreover, what has to be borne in mind throughout is that the resulting statutes take the traditional form of immense detail and complexity, with no real coherence of principle or terminology between them. These in their turn give rise to all the traditional problems of interpretation, modernisation, consolidation, etc. In effect, it is a never-ending and basically unsatisfactory process.

The third and perhaps the most important problem area relates to the implementation of Law Commission recommendations. Up to now, and in particular in the early years, the record of implementation has been quite impressive. However, as time goes on it is clear that an increasing backlog is going to arise. We have been fortunate, from the point of view of law reform, in having had a more or less "hung" Parliament for some years, during which governments found it difficult to enact much politically controversial legislation and therefore found relatively more parliamentary time for law reform measures. But this is clearly not an acceptable long-term solution; something new is needed. One possibility which is frequently mentioned is something in the nature of an annual Law Reform (Miscellaneous Provisions) Bill. But this could do little in practice except to tinker with small points here and there. What is needed is some special parliamentary procedure for law reform Bills. Admittedly, no law reform is wholly uncontroversial; virtually nothing is pure "lawyers' law". Admittedly, also, the last word must rest with Parliament. But something should be done to secure access to Parliament in a more direct form, and some simpler procedure for law reform Bills should be devised. The need for this was clearly foreseen during the passage of the Law Commission's Act in 1965, and the government gave assurances in both Houses that some special procedure would be considered. What had evidently been evisaged was that a Joint or Select Standing Committed would consider law reform Bills put forward by the Law Commission and report to Parliament with a view to their enactment with the minimum of time and debate thereafter. However, this has not happened.

Without some change on these lines the general picture is unsatisfactory. While the Law Commission's Reports and Bills are invariably laid before Parliament, there is no obligation on anyone to do anything about them. Although Private Members can take them up, if successful in the ballot for Private Members' Bills, they are usually more interested in measures which have a greater political and social impact than the reform of the law. Moreover, the fact that draft Bills produced by the Law Commission, pursuant to their statutory duty, are no one's responsibility creates something of a vicious circle. It means that Ministers and their departments may pay little or no regard to them, since they anticipate the difficulties of parliamentary time from the outset. This in turn means that they may take little interest in Law Commission proposals during their formative stages. We do not get any sufficient reaction to our Working Papers, and in many cases we only discover departmental and ministerial policy attitudes to our proposals after months of work in preparing Final Reports with draft Bills.

What is needed is the sanction of some new simple and speedy parliamentary procedure for law reform Bills whereby the departments concerned, and the government of the day, would in effect be held responsible to Parliament for ensuring that the recommendations are fully considered at every stage and introduced into Parliament unless there are real policy objections to the proposals. Having established the new concept of an independent agency for the reform of the law, both the executive and the legislature should accept some constitutional commitment to the implementation of Law Commission recommendations. This is what is still lacking; here, in Canada and Australia, and no doubt in other countries as well. After centuries of inaction we have at last taken a positive step forward; but only in principle, not yet in reality. The reality can only be transformed if we find and adopt logistic solutions which give real effect to the concept which has at last emerged. These solutions have not yet been found, but, unless they are, the Law Commissions will be able to produce relatively little towards the overall reform which is greatly needed.

10

The European Economic Community—Some Salient Features

Kurt Lipstein

For a Canadian lawyer, accustomed to a constitutional instrument which relies on the separation of powers in government, whether federal or provincial, and between the powers vested in the federation and the member provinces, the first question must be how the E.E.C. fits into such a constitutional structure. The answer is, at first glance, that it is based on a treaty between sovereign states, at least in the contemplation of its founders. There is no separation of powers between the organs of the community in the traditional sense. Instead of the usual horizontal division of legislative, executive and judicial functions there is a vertical one consisting of the functional integration of certain areas of human activity through the co-operation of the political and the administrative or executive organs, the Council and the Commission respectively, advised by an assembly of representatives of state Parliaments and controlled by a court whose function is primarily that of an administrative tribunal controlling executive legality.

In substance the treaty deals, directly, with the free circulation of goods, capital, workers, services and the establishment of business or professional people, indirectly with the abolition of discrimination in the public and private sector of the economy, of customs duties and quantitative restrictions, with the control of cartels and monopolies, of subsidies and dumping practices, with the elimination of discriminatory tax legislation and, generally, with the adaptation, co-ordination and harmonization of all laws which have a direct bearing upon the operation of a common market and, still more indirectly, through the co-ordination of economic policies and activities of the member states, such as rates of exchange, the movement of capital, rectification of any imbalance of exchange, uniform policy in foreign trade and the development of common policies in agriculture, transport and social services.

The Council has the function of co-ordinating the general economic policies of the member states and of taking decisions (Art. 148). In addition it carries out the individual functions mainly in the field of decision-making allocated to it in the various articles. It consists of representatives of the member states, being either ministers or their deputies or, originally in the case of Germany, Permanent Under-Secretaries of State (who are civil servants). In all matters, including budget, the foreign ministers will participate, but one half of the meetings will also concern the ministers dealing with the economy and two-fifths require the presence of the ministers of agriculture. Each specialized section of the Council represents the Council as a whole. While the ministers are of course instructed by their governments, the latter are themselves bound by the treaty (Art. 5) to observe the latter's policies. A first step had already been taken to make the treaty the master of its founders. The Council is presided over by one of the ministers who is elected for six months, or his deputy. His function is januslike: he must serve the organization as well as his own people. In order to coordinate the Council's functions a committee of permanent representatives (COREPER) operates under the chairmanship of a national of the state whose representative occupies the presidency of the Council. It does not enjoy delegated powers (such powers can only be delegated to another member of the Council) but deals with routine business, which it channels for the use of the Council according to a scheme which divides uncontroversial from controversial business. Special and *ad hoc* committees of the Council, but no subcommittees, exist and a secretariat assists the Council. The latter's functions in dealing with the budget and in preparing the Council's business overlap with those of the Commission. The Council's powers are partly executive (co-ordination of economic policies) and partly legislative, but it is also the final authority for the Community's external relations and the budget. Its meetings are periodic, covering on the average 40 days per annum, each of two-four days. The agenda is prepared by the President and the sessions are attended by the Commission. The Council has the right to be heard by the assembly which, in turn, has no right to put questions, although it has this right as regards the Commission.

Although the treaty provides for decisions by a simple or qualified majority, it has become a convention (arising out of the Luxembourg Agreement of 28-29 June 1966) that where important state interests are involved, an agreement acceptable to all must be sought within a reasonable time. The question remains as to what happens if a reasonable time has elapsed and no agreement has been reached. The French answer is: wait, until agreement is reached.

It is obvious that as the political organ, principally entrusted with decision-making, the Council occupies a dominant position. This has been further increased in importance by the emergence of what is now known as the *European Council.* It developed outside the provisions of the treaty, out of decisions of the representatives of the governments assembled on the occasion of a Council meeting, but dealing with matters which are reserved by the treaty for the governments acting outside the Council or which were not foreseen by the treaty (such as appointment of members of the Commission, judges, execution of treaties, amendments of the treaty itself, acceleration of its operation, etc.). Stimulated by France, it grew into a meeting of heads of governments three times a year to deal with political co-operation and economic integration. Its functions are not defined: are they decision-making, appellate or merely stimulating? Its decisions are mainly of the character known as "framework" and their binding force is in doubt. They have covered such diverse items as New Zealand butter, direct elections for the Assembly, passports, budget and finance, the presidency of the Commission, economic and monetary action, energy policy, terrorism, Portugal, fishing limits of member states and European Union—all topics outside the immediate range of the Treaty. In particular by its wide power of initiative this new "Super Council" can by-pass the Commission which is the normal initiating agency (Art. 55). Moreover, since it operates on the highest political level, compromises and package deals tend to supersede the singleminded Commission proposals, and the nature of such wrapped-up decisions renders it more difficult for national parliaments to ask their ministerial representatives to account for their actions.

Parallel to the Council operates the *Commission*, which consists of 14 members, not more than two from each country, appointed for four years, but re-eligible. They are completely independent, must not follow any other occupation and enjoy extensive immunities. Unlike the Council, the members of which are exclusively responsible to the national parliaments, the Commission is subject to a limited, but drastic control by the Assembly. Upon a notion of censure of the latter, the Commission must resign *en bloc.*

Its functions are primarily executive, but also legislative in so far as either the treaty or the measures taken thereunder by the council confer such a power, and it exercises judicial functions in supervising restrictive practices and monopolies. Its main function, however, is to ensure that the treaty and the measures taken by the institutions are applied. Its wide range in substance is reflected in topics which are treated in various departments (called Directorates General) on economy, finance, industrial and scientific technology, competition, social affairs, agriculture, transport, development and co-operation, internal market, financial institutions and taxation, regional policy, energy, credit and investment, budget and finance.

The Commission is therefore unlike any previously existing institution; it is not an executive arm of the Council in the nature of a secretariat, government or ministry. It remains what it was intended to be: the guardian of the treaty and of the subordinate legislation of the community, the proposer of recommendations and opinions, enjoying a monopoly of initiative in the community, acting normally in close collaboration with the member states. In 1965, a clash between an independent Commission initiative on financing the agricultural programme and France led to the so-called Luxembourg Agreement which confirms that in making important proposals the Commission should act in contact with member states. It enjoys also an autonomous decision-making power, enabling it to take protective measures in the sphere of the economy and to control competition. Indirectly it is also the protector of the smaller member states, since its monopoly of initiative uninfluenced by national policies can only be overridden by a unanimous vote of the Council. Externally it represents the Community by negotiating agreements with other states, subject to authorization by the Council, and serves as a link between the Community and various international organizations. Finally, it represents the Community as a legal entity in the member states.

Neither should the *Assembly* be regarded as a legislature. True, its members are now chosen by direct elections and vote on party lines, but its function is advisory and consultative. It can censure the Commission and dismiss it *en bloc*, but it has no control over the Council. It exercises a limited control over the budget, in so far as it concerns expenditure, but not supply. Even this control extends only to the so-called "free items", *i.e.*, the expenditure other than that fixed by precise financial commitments, mainly for agricultural support (which covers up to at least 90 per cent of the total). Supply is excluded altogether, since it consists of the customs revenues, external levies and a proportion of the indirect value added tax raised in each member state.

The *court* has a variety of functions, most of which are judicial. It ensures that "in the interpretation and application" the law is observed (Art. 164). At first glance this appears to require the court to control the legality of the acts and measures of the community organs and of the member states in executing their duties or obligations. This conclusion is confirmed by further provisions which confer jurisdiction on the court to determine whether a member state has *failed* to carry out its obligations under the treaty and by other provisions which enable individuals under limited circumstances to challenge the validity of community organs by a procedure much influenced by continental administrative law; in addition there is some advisory and appellate jurisdiction. If these were the original functions of the court, the latter has enlarged them considerably by ensuring not only (as the treaty intended) that the treaty, when applied, is applied correctly and that when wrongly not applied, a failure to observe it is declared. Instead, the court has taken it upon itself, in the case of a failure of a member state to apply the treaty or measures taken thereunder, to hold that the treaty or the measure has become part of the law of the member states and that in certain circumstances its provisions and not only the legislative measures taken thereunder (called regulations Art. 189) are directly applicable as part of domestic law, without the need for domestic implementation, and may be directly effective in conferring rights upon individuals to be enforced in national courts. Moreover, once a topic has been claimed by community law, the latter has pre-empted the subject matter.

This practice, introduced by judicial interpretation early in the 1960s, completely altered the nature of the treaty, the measures taken thereunder, the function of the court and the place of domestic law. For by incorporating community law as a whole into domestic law and not only treating regulations as binding upon member states without implementing legislation, the court had bridged the gap between the community and the member states, between the treaty and national law, between duties of the states under a treaty and rights of individuals thereunder. A dual system had become a unitary one, not unlike that of a federal system. Not only the control of the application of the treaty and the power to declare the failure of a member state are exercised by the Community Court. It has also taken upon itself to enforce directly those provisions of community law which the member states have failed to implement. From being the guardian of the legality of its application, the court had erected itself as the instrument of stimulating its implementation, by enforcing those rules which member states had either neglected to embody in their own law or had actively contravened in their own legislation. The treaty itself allowed in such cases no more than an action for declaration of failure to conform, coupled with the requirement of remedial action by the member state concerned. The court, impatient with this somewhat ineffective remedy, anticipated the absence of governmental action by treating as done what ought to have been done and by making individuals the instrument of enforcement which was lacking in the treaty. The lesson for members of a federal state is clear. The repercussions in the laws of the member states, particularly when conflicting domestic legislation or, to make matters worse, a conflicting provision of the Constitution bound the local court, are easily envisaged. But the Community Court has persisted in its practice, and on joining the community, the United Kingdom accepted this judicial extension of community law. Community law and the laws of the member states are no longer co-existent, the one binding on, the other binding in, member states, sovereign each in its own sphere, but community law has arrogated for itself a substantive place in domestic law. The technique by which this was achieved will be described later on.

The Community is a functional organization, restricted to ensuring the free circulation of goods, capital, workers services and the unimpeded establishment of business and professional people. Its powers must be exercised within this framework as part of the treaty, reminding a Canadian lawyer of articles 91ff. of the British North America Act 1867. However, a very broadly formulated article offers residual powers to take "action . . . necessary to attain in the course of the operation of the Common Market one of the objectives of the Community and [if] this Treaty has not provided the necessary powers." (Art. 235) Thus the purpose of the treaty justifies every means for achieving it. However, there is one safeguard: the Council must act unanimously and, thus, no one member state can be coerced. In addition, provision is made in the treaty for the conclusion of conventions on double taxation, the mutual recognition of companies, and the retention of their legal personality in the event of a transfer of their seat and, for the mutual recognition and enforcement of judgments. The latter convention is already in operation.

The treaty provides expressly (Art. 222) that the rules governing the system of property ownership in the respective member states are not to be affected. However, by drawing a distinction between the categories of property rights—which were not to be affected—and the exercise of property rights—which were not exempt from the operation of the treaty—the Community Court imposed its control over patent copyright and trade mark licensing agreements which either constituted restrictive practices or more frequently contravened the rule against the imposition of quantitative restrictions by carving up the markets.

Where the treaty considers the conclusion of agreements between the community and other states or an international organization (Art. 228), the United Nations, its specialized agencies or GATT (Art. 229) or any cooperation with the Council of Europe (Art. 230) or the Organization for European Economic Development (Art. 231) the commission is entrusted with powers of negotiation or liaison. However, once again the Community Court has, by its interpretation, enlarged these powers so as to extend to all negotiations for international agreements, and not only those in which the treaty itself refers to agreements on specific topics, once the subject matter to be dealt with by an international agreement has become the object of a uniform regulation in the community as a result of the activities of the community organs.

The efficacy and supremacy of community law is assured by a number of measures available to the community—rules of general application which are operative without local implementing legislation *(regulations),* orders addressed to one or more member states which are binding as to the result but leave the member states free to choose the means of achieving the result *(directives),* orders binding in their entirety upon the addressee *(decisions)* and recommendations and opinions which are without binding force (Art. 189).

The remedies differ according as member states or community organs have failed to observe the rules of the community.

As regards member states, the Community Court can issue declaratory judgments establishing the failure to carry out the state's obligations (Arts. 169, 170), but the treaty is *lex imperfecta* (Art. 171) for it is not enforceable.

As regards the community itself, member states, other community organs and, in somewhat limited circumstances, individuals and corporations can challenge binding community measures on grounds identical with those of French administrative law (Art. 173) or for failing to act when so required by community law (Art. 176).

In exercising a concurrent jurisdiction on the merits with the courts of the member states over individuals in matters of restrictive practices and monopolies (Art. 172) where community organs may impose penalties for the violation of a community measure, the judgments of the Community Court are enforceable in the member states in accordance with the local rules of procedure (Arts. 187, 192).

However, the greatest influence not only in controlling the application and interpretation of the treaty and the measures taken thereunder, but also in introducing the treaty and these measures where local law and local courts had failed to implement them (a development described above) was exercised by the Community Court in deciding what are called Preliminary Rulings (Art. 177). These concern the interpretation of the treaty and the validity and interpretation of community measures. Such preliminary ruling *may* be requested by municipal courts or tribunals if a question of this type is raised and *must* be asked for if the court involved is one of last resort. The question to be put to the Community Court must be formulated in abstract terms, must refrain from introducing a question of fact, must not ask for an interpretation of domestic law or whether domestic law is compatible with community law and cannot seek to obtain an answer on the merits. On the other hand, it is irrelevant whether in the view of the Community Court the question is relevant and the court can consider the facts as presented by the national court in order to elucidate the purport of the abstract question presented to it and in order to extract those aspects of community law which require consideration. The notion of a court or tribunal is wide, but it is not clear whether it includes arbitral tribunals. If it does, it will be easy to evade the operation of Art. 177 by establishing it in a country outside the community.

The formulation of the question to be submitted to the Community Court is therefore not always easy and requires skilful insight into the possible implications of Community Law, and the quality of the form in which problems have been put varies considerably. The limited practice of English courts is a useful guide.

By this device the Community Court has instructed the courts of member states with what community law claims to be binding effect that community law is part of the law of the member states, must prevail in a conflict with national law, be it even the Constitution, if directly applicable and, if directly effective, and allows individuals to seek its enforcement in national courts. Thus the failure of a member state to abolish certain duties by maintaining the previous regime of national law was met by the advice that any community measure which is complete and legally perfect, unconditional and not open to any discretionary treatment, takes its place in domestic law and supersedes any conflicting national law. Individuals have been able to assert the right, denied to them by local law, to be admitted to a profession without possessing local nationality; women have been accorded equal treatment in employment contrary to local law and nationals of member states have been freed from restrictive conditions of residence.

It is another matter whether the national courts in receipt of this interpretative instruction will give precedence to community law. A reference for a preliminary ruling by the Community court by a lower national court may be balanced by an appeal to a higher national court in reliance on national law or even the Constitution to the contrary effect. The practice of the highest national courts of the member states has vacillated; while some accepted the supremacy of community law either because so required by national law or for jurisprudential considerations developed by the courts themselves, others have hesitated to commit themselves wholeheartedly, while accepting the Preliminary Ruling in the particular circumstances.

Another, indirect means of introducing community law into the law of the member states is provided by the process of harmonization, coordination and approximation of the domestic law of the member states which directly affect the establishment or functioning of the Common Market. By these means such diverse topics as company law, indirect taxation, transport, human and animal processed food, motorcar construction and measuring instruments, have been rendered uniform, to mention only a few.

In giving a Preliminary Ruling the Community Court will also apply public international law as part of community law if it is embodied in a treaty which is directly applicable in national law; possibly it must also be directly effective by conferring rights upon individuals. But the Community Court has gone further and, contrary to its basic tenet that it does not interpret or apply the domestic law of the member states, has stated, if perhaps only *obiter,* that it takes into consideration the basic constitutional guaranties of the member states. This would constitute another step forward in the integration of community law and the law of the member states to an extent which might be regarded as a fusion.

Enough has been said about this process to raise the interest of those outside the E.E.C. with experience in the development of law in a federation and to invite speculation as to the ultimate structure of the community which is constantly evolving and whose legal structure owes so much to a small body of constitutional and administrative lawyers.

11

Industrial Tribunals

The Honourable Sir John Donaldson

In 1973 I was invited to give a talk in Toronto at Osgoode Hall. At that time I was President of the now defunct National Industrial Relations Court. My hosts chose the title for my talk—"How to live with the Confederation of British Industry, the Trade Union Congress and Her Majesty's Government without actually getting lynched". It was a topical question then and I think that it still is. "Industrial Tribunals" are a factor in answering the question. But they are only one factor and I should like today to consider the problem on a rather wider basis.

I sometimes think that many of our problems stem from the 1870's. This was the time when workmen began to combine as a means of redressing very real grievances at the way they were treated. But such industrial action necessarily involved the torts of conspiracy and inducing breaches of contract. The courts, if asked to intervene, were bound to find against the workforce. Parliament had a choice. It could do nothing, but this would have produced unacceptable conflict. It could legislate giving the workforce basic rights enforceable in the courts whilst prohibiting self help by unlawful means. Or it could give workers a limited immunity from civil action.

It chose to confer immunity from civil action. This was a cardinal error from the point of view of the rule of law. The emerging trade unions acquired no rights justiciable in a court of law. They did not need the courts. They did not want the courts. Their only connection with the courts was as defendants—never as plaintiffs. It was quite different for the employers. They could appeal to the courts whenever the unions and the workers overstepped the limits of the immunity. Small wonder that the judges were regarded as being anti-trade union.

In fairness it should be added that there was then and still is today, a basic philosophical difference in approach between the judges and the trade unions. The judges are individualists, brought up by professional training, rather than social origin, to believe in the supreme sanctity of the rights of the individual. The trade unions and their more active and vocal leaders are essentially collectivists, believing in the supreme sanctity of the majority decision, even if it is a majority of three to two, 95 not voting. Curiously the trade unions do not take this to its logical conclusion, namely that group decisions in the form of a general election or a parliamentary statute are necessarily equally binding. The trade union rule books which are evolved by a series of majority conference decisions are considered sacred, but my cry that the law is the nation's rule book has sometimes fallen on deaf ears.

It is, of course, a recipe for disaster to refight the battles of bygone wars. We cannot echo the Irishman who when asked the way to Dublin said: "Well, I wouldn't start from here." We have to start in 1979, but I would hope that during the 1980's parliament will try to cast the courts more in the role of a friend of labour. I hope that it will remember that in almost all other fields in which the courts are required to discourage self help—for example, the motorist who wishes to recover compensation after a crash or the citizen who thinks that his neighbour is committing a nuisance—the courts are allowed and indeed required to provide the aggrieved citizen with an alternative and better remedy. This approach is crucial to the maintenance of the rule of law.

From the 1870's until 1971, labour law, as such, scarcely existed. An employee could resort to the County Court or the High Court to complain that he had been wrongly dismissed as a matter of contract. If the contract specified one month's notice, the issue was whether he had received that notice or money in lieu or whether his conduct was such as to justify dismissal without notice. The courts also dealt with personal injury and workman's compensation scheme claims, but that was all.

Apart from this there were only two statutes which gave him any special rights. The first was the Contracts of Employment Act, 1963. This specified a minimum period of notice of between one and four weeks for employees who had been in the same employment for two or more years. It also required employers to give their employees a document setting out the principal terms of their employment. The second was the Redundancy Payments Act of 1965 which gave an employee the right to a fixed sum if his employment ended as a result of redundancy. The sums were not large, varying between one and one half a week's wages and one half a week's wages for every year of continuous employment. They were simply intended to compensate the employee for the disruption involved in seeking other employment. Claims by workers under either of these statutes were made to industrial tribunals. Such tribunals had three members—a lawyer, as chairman, and two lay members, one drawn from each side of industry.

But the courts main involvement was in policing the statutory immunity in respect of action in contemplation of furtherance of an industrial dispute. This consisted of an immunity from action for the tort of conspiracy if the act would not have been actionable if done by an individual alone and for any other tort in so far as the cause of action was based only on the fact that the conduct complained of induced some other person to break a contract of employment or was an interference with trade. This immunity was and still is known to trade unionists as "the golden formula"

By the late 1960's it was apparent to everyone that this system really did not work. The country was faced with widespread strikes and other industrial action, some official and some unofficial. A Royal Commission under Lord Donovan was set up and duly reported in 1968. The Labour government under Sir Harold Wilson produced a White Paper "In Place of Strife" which proposed a comprehensive industrial relations law. The details do not matter, but the proposal was to tackle a wide range of industrial relations problems, such as recognition disputes, the right to belong to trade unions, the need for cooling off periods before strike action was taken, taking ballots before calling of strike, making collective agreements legally enforceable in certain circumstances and providing the employee with a legal right not to be unfairly dismissed even if his dismissal was not in breach of contract. The principal instrument was to be a Commission on Industrial Relations, but to some extent these reforms were to be backed by legal sanctions. As a *quid pro quo,* it was proposed that the golden formula be widened to protect not only action to induce breach of a contract of employment, but also breach of a commercial contract. This was important because the trade unions had found that if there was a dispute with, for example, a motor manufacturer, one of the best methods of bringing pressure to bear was to induce the employees of a components manufacturer to cut off supplies of components.

The trade unions took the view that the package was an unacceptable restriction upon their *de facto* freedom to take industrial action and they lobbied for the withdrawal of the proposal. What happened then has not yet been officially revealed. But according to the newspapers, there was a split in the Cabinet and it is a fact that the proposals were withdrawn with the explanation that the T.U.C. would take the necessary steps to achieve many of the desired objectives.

The following year—1970—there was a general election and the Conservatives under Mr. Heath were returned to power. They set about introducing a comprehensive system of labour law. It is impossible to summarize the Act and I can only point to its more outstanding features. It established three new institutions—the National Industrial Relations Court, The Commission on Industrial Relations and the Registrar of Trade Unions.

The court was of equivalent status to the High Court and sat in divisions consisting of a High Court judge and two experienced industrial members. These members should have come from both sides of industry. Unfortunately, the trade unions refused to allow their members to accept appointment. The court was the Appeal Court for the industrial tribunals and also had an original jurisdiction.

The Commission on Industrial Relations was an investigatory and advisory body but was concerned, in the main, with collective bargaining rights.

The Registrar of Trade Unions had the duty of approving applications by trade unions to be registered, the test being independence and rules which gave the members the bare minimum of rights. For example, the right not to be disciplined by procedures which contravened the rules of natural justice. Registration was voluntary but conferred substantial privileges.

Individual workers obtained entirely new rights against both employers and trade unions to which they belonged. They became entitled to compensation for being unfairly dismissed or being unfairly treated by their unions. They also became entitled to join or to refuse to join a union as they wished.

Registered trade unions also obtained new rights. Whilst pre-entry closed shops were abolished, they were able to obtain approval for a post-entry closed shop agreement from the Industrial Court. Again on application to the Industrial Court and after an investigation by the Commission on Industrial Relations and a ballot of the workers, registered unions could establish an agency shop despite opposition by the employer. By a similar process registered unions could obtain collective bargaining rights.

And the public too obtained rights. When industrial action threatened vital national interests, the Secretary of State could apply to the Industrial Court for an order requiring a cooling off period and/or a ballot of all the workers involved.

But perhaps the most far reaching reform was in relation to the golden formula—the trade union's right to take industrial action without fear that they would be sued in tort. In general *registered* trade unions retained freedom of action wherever, as in the case of a claim for increased wages, the legislation did not provide an alternative and better remedy. Unregistered unions were not, however, allowed to take industrial action short of a strike and strike action had to be preceded by notice of the same length as was necessary to terminate the contract of employment. In addition there were restrictions on secondary industrial action—action against suppliers to and customers of the employer who was at the centre of the dispute.

The trade unions rightly recognized that this Act offered them enormous advantages, but that it was as much a threat to their unbridled independence of the law as was "In Place of Strife". Their problem was that they had great difficulty in finding a rallying point. Some unions wanted to use one part of the Act and others another. Eventually they all agreed upon a campaign against the Act based upon a concerted refusal to register under the Act. The Act itself was reasonably well balanced on the assumption that trade unions registered. By refusing to register the unions made it wholly unbalanced and thus apparently very pro-employer.

The Act lasted from 1 December 1971 until 31 July 1974. It was a vastly interesting, busy and sometimes turbulent period in the history of the law in the field of industrial relations. I should hate not to have been involved, but it was not an easy position. I regarded it as an essential part of my job to explain what the court was doing and why it was doing it. To explain that parliament rather than the courts made the law and that the courts and not parliament administered that law. In the midst of the political argument, I hoped that my contribution would seem to be independent, non-political and even sensible. So it might have been but for an imbalance in the political argument. Those who opposed the Act, used the court, and me as its President, as a useful symbol and target for abuse. That it is contrary to natural justice to shoot the pianist because you do not like the music that he is required to play is beside the point. But it had the unfortunate result that anything said by me by way of explanation or defence of the court was readily misinterpreted as a political utterance. I make no complaint. This is an occupational hazard. I mention it merely because it has to be taken into account if hereafter the judges are to be involved in politically sensitive areas.

Three quarters of the court's work consisted of hearing appeals from the industrial tribunals in cases concerned with the new law of unfair dismissals and redundancy. As each appeal came up, we did not confine ourselves to deciding that case. We used it as a vehicle for laying down broad principles of general application and teaching the basic rules of good industrial relations. It is a fact that many of these decisions have stood the test of time and are still the leading authorities in the field. We also produced a procedure for speedy "do it yourself" litigation which has remained unchanged to this day and is now used both by the County Court and by the new Employment Appeal Tribunal. In a word, we were pioneers and in many respects successful pioneers.

But the courts' popular reputation differs from its record to an extent which is scarcely credible. By repute the opposition of the trade unions was so intense that it was never used. In fact it disposed of 1,096 cases in under three years. By repute the unions did not recognise the court. Non-recognition was supposed to take the form of attending only in defence of their vital interests. It did not work out quite like that. On three occasions T.U.C. unions actually appeared as applicants. On 176 occasions they appeared "in defence of their vital interests". But in many of these cases they had arranged for a member to take proceedings against the employer with the sole object of being brought in as respondent and, having got before the court, seeking the remedies for which they could not apply directly as applicants. As a court we pretended to be wholly ignorant of this manoeuvre.

By repute it was a court of confrontation. Any Englishman can tell you about the vast fines imposed upon the unions and the imprisonment of the five dockers. In fact, only two unions were fined.

At a very early stage the T.G. & W.U. stopped all unlawful opposition and subsequently appeared in and settled a large number of cases before the court. The A.E.U.W. alone continued to defy the court to the end. Of the 141 complaints to the court under its original jurisdiction 101 were settled amicably, 27 were dismissed and only 13 were decided against the unions. Of these only four gave rise to "confrontation" in any shape or form.

February 1974 saw the election of a new government pledged to repeal the Act and abolish the court. Running a court under sentence of death is a ticklish operation. The rule of law required it to enforce the law until that law was changed. But the public and the unions regarded the law as having already been changed. The only solution seemed to be to keep our heads down, to try to avoid making orders which would be defied and finally to kick for touch by adjourning cases until a date by which we were confident that we should have ceased to exist.

The new government was publicly pledged to sweep away the whole edifice of industrial law created by the Conservatives and to restore the pre-1971 position. And to this day most people think that it did just that. The reality is somewhat different. The new legislation retained and expanded the law in so far as it favoured individuals or trade unions against employers. But it did far more than go back to 1971 in giving the trade unions freedom of action unfettered by the law.

The individual worker retained his protection from being unfairly dismissed. Indeed, this protection was increased by lowering the qualifying period of employment. He—or rather she—obtained new rights to maternity leave and the right if she wished to return to her job after the confinement. But the worker lost all rights against his union, other than such as could be spelt out of the union's rules. The closed shop was legalised and encouraged and there was no protection for the man who refused to join a union unless it was on the ground of religious belief.

The trade unions obtained new rights to advance information on redundancies. Their shop stewards obtained extensive rights to time off for union activities. It is within my own knowledge that one health service shop steward devoted the whole of his employers' time to these activities and then applied for overtime payments in respect of additional union work. He did not actually succeed, but he was very aggrieved.

The Commission on Industrial Relations was abolished. Instead a new body was set up charged with the duty of encouraging collective bargaining—the Arbitration, Conciliation and Advisory Service (A.C.A.S.). A trade union could apply to the service for recognition rights. The employer who resisted recognising one or perhaps two or more competing unions had no right to such assistance. The service could recommend recognition and if the employer did not agree could refer the matter to a Central Arbitration Committee. That Committee could then impose on the employer the terms and conditions of employment sought by the union.

But the biggest change was in "the golden formula". It was not a case of "back to 1971". Trade union immunity from suit was extended to inducing breaches of commercial contracts in contemplation or furtherance of a trade dispute. And "trade dispute" was redefined so that it did not have to be a dispute between worker and worker or worker and employer. You could have a contented work force which was paid twice the union rate and wanted to have nothing to do with the union. But if the union objected, there was a trade dispute. There was even a trade dispute if the employer lay flat on his back and said "I surrender". And the dispute did not have to be in the United Kingdom. A trade dispute in Canada would justify industrial action in this country in support of it—for example, a refusal to handle Canadian wheat.

One change that was more apparent than real related to collective agreements. Under the 1971 Act they were legally binding unless the parties otherwise agreed. In practice, all unions had rubber stamps stating that the document was not legally binding. I am told that these were applied to every piece of paper in sight—even to those which came in rolls. Under the new legislation the position was reversed and it required express provision before any collective agreement was binding. Such a provision is, I think, unknown.

The new government retained the industrial tribunals. Indeed, over the last five years their jurisdiction has been significantly widened and their work load has increased by 100 percent. They now deal with unfair dismissals (which account for about 80 percent of their work load) redundancy payments, equal pay, sex discrimination and race relations. They received 40,000 applications a year and 70 tribunals are sitting at any one time in different parts of the country.

But what about the National Industrial Relations Court? It was duly swept away. But this created a problem. Someone had to hear appeals from industrial tribunals. The High Court was the obvious candidate, but it showed itself to be supremely unfitted for the task. Delays grew rapidly. And, dare I say it, some of my brother judges were unfamiliar with the work. So what was to be done? The solution was breathtakingly simple. Take the relevant sections and schedule to the Industrial Relations Act of 1971 which created the Industrial Court and re-enact them striking out the words National Industrial Relations Court and substituting Employment Appeal Tribunal wherever they occurred. This was something totally new and different. It was not a court, it was a tribunal. True the small print said that it was a superior Court of Record with status equal to that of the High Court, but who reads the small print? It was not concerned with National Industrial Relations, but with Employment Appeals. No one listened when, *sotto voce,* I remarked that if imitation was the sincerest form of flattery, what could one say about reincarnation?

Well, the experiment has lasted for just over five years. Industrial action became more ambitious. The control exercised by trade unions over their shop stewards and members became more tenuous. There were some well publicized instances of victimization of trade union members who refused to follow the collectivist line. But curiously enough it was picketing which perhaps created the greatest public disquiet.

I say "curiously enough" because there has been no material change in the definition of "peaceful picketing" for years. There is and remains a right to attend anywhere other than where the picketee lives for the purpose only of peacefully obtaining or communicating information or peacefully persuading him to work or to abstain from working. But picketing became widespread and violent. Indeed, last winter we had a situation in which goods could only be moved from place to place if the lorry driver had a permit from local union committees. There were four reasons for this phenomenon.

The first is that peaceful picketing is only permissible in contemplation of furtherance of a trade dispute. Widen the concept of trade dispute and you widen the area for people to peacefully picket. The second is that trade unions did not understand the law. They thought that picketing involved a legal right to require people to stop and be persuaded. Third, in the same period the "demo" or demonstration had come to be an accepted method of political expression. If a picket became so numerous and threatening as to be neither a picket nor peaceful, it became a "demo". Fourth, and most fundamental, if the public is told day in and day out that the law has no place in industrial relations, it is an inevitable consequence that the authority of what little law remains is wholly undermined.

By their vote in the May general election, the public showed that it had had enough. This week the Thatcher government has taken the first, perhaps faltering, steps towards the re-introduction of the law into the No Go areas of industrial relations. You may not think that they are very ambitious and you might be right. But the fact is that in the last analysis the rule of law has one sanction and one sanction only—the power of public opinion. The 1971 legislation went too far and too fast. It outstripped the essential support from public opinion. So it is probably right to hasten slowly at this stage.

The discussion papers published by the government this week cover three topics—the closed shop, the use of public money to meet the expense of trade union ballots and picketing.

The closed shop is a fact of life. It is supported by both sides of industry. It could not be abolished, although it could be driven underground. The government therefore proposes to confine itself to tackling the hardships caused to individual workers by the closed shop. It suggests that this is best done by widening the liability of an employer to compensate an employee who is dismissed as a result of a union membership or closed shop agreement.

At present the employer is only liable if the worker refuses to join the union because of his religious beliefs. It proposes to widen this category to include workers who have deeply held personal convictions that they should not join any trade union or possibly a particular union. It also proposes to include employees who are not members of a union when a closed shop comes into force.

So far as new closed shop agreements are concerned, it proposes to ensure that they conform to the best practice and are only introduced if supported by the overwhelming majority of the workforce expressed in a secret ballot. The sanction will be that no other closed shop agreement will provide the employer with a defence if he dismisses an employee for refusing to join the union.

But the government also recognizes that employers will often yield to union pressure and will dismiss workers in the category which is entitled to refuse to join a union. They propose, therefore, to give the employer a right to join the union as an additional defendant to the workers' claim for unfair dismissal. This in theory enables the union to be ordered to pay all or part of the compensation awarded. I say "in theory" because the 1971 Act contained a similar power which was never used. The unions persuaded the employer that to use it would be an unfriendly act which would produce dire and expensive consequences. I have no reason to believe that the situation has changed.

The government also wants to encourage secret ballots in the case of the election of full time union officials, changes in the union rules and calling or ending strikes. Taking decisions by open votes at branches or mass meetings has two results. It opens the way to undue pressure on the union members. It also tends to result in very important decisions being taken by a tiny minority of the membership.

The proposal is to remove the cost objection to secret ballots, which is considerable, by making public money available. But there would be some control of eligible ballots by a public official, the Certification Officer, and this may render the proposal unacceptable to the unions.

But the most controversial proposal concerns picketing. The government takes the view that there is no need to change the criminal law. Violence, threatening behaviour, obstruction and breach of the peace are already offences. They may be right, but in practical terms the law has proved difficult to enforce.

The government's proposals are therefore confined to civil liability. The idea is to limit the right of peaceful picketing to workers who are a party to the dispute which occasions the picketing and to carrying out picketing at their own place of work. This limitation, if observed, would have enormous consequences. In recent years we have been afflicted by motorised pickets which move from factory to factory by the coach load and concentrate on suppliers to and customers of the employer at the heart of the dispute—secondary picketing as it is called.

An alternative proposal which, if it were adopted and the law were observed, would have an even more far reaching effect is to restrict the "golden formula" in a similar way. Almost all industrial action would then become unlawful unless it was by the workers involved in the dispute and took place at their place of work.

There are proposals for a code of practice to give moral and detailed support to the change in the law, but the crunch point is, as always, how you enforce it. The government proposes to leave this to employers, who it believes would seek injunctive relief from the High Court. I fear that the answer is that employers would be unlikely to do any such thing. I say this because there is a matrimonial relationship between the two sides of industry. They will fight to the death, but will unite to repel any interference by a third party. If employers do resort to the High Court, other problems will arise. The court's orders will sometimes be defied, but there is no certainty or even likelihood that the employer will take the necessary steps to enforce the orders. The result will be that the public will read in the newspapers that the court's orders are useless bits of paper and the rule of law will be undermined. For this reason the National Industrial Relations Court resorted to a system for policing and enforcing its own orders, but I cannot see the High Court doing so. For my part, I should have preferred to see this jurisdiction transferred to the Employment Appeal Tribunal, but there may well be political objections to that course.

As Canadians, you have your own industrial relations problems. Some may appear similar to ours. Others are obviously different. But even though the problem appears the same, the solution will be different in our two countries. Industrial relations are only human relations in the workplace. And human relations are the product of social and historical factors which differ widely between countries. So any simple transplant of industrial relations laws or practices between Canada and the United Kingdom will fail and the rejection symptoms will be violent. But this is not to say that we should not study each other's problems and solutions. Comparative studies stimulate ideas which can be developed and adapted to the home environment and may then well work.

12

The Ombudsman

Sir Alan Marre

I take it as a compliment to have been invited to give this lecture, on the Ombudsman, to so distinguished an audience. It is the more flattering because I do know how active you have been in Canada in developing the Ombudsman concept. British Columbia has now joined eight other provinces—that is, all except Prince Edward Island—in setting up its own Ombudsman office and, unless your change of government alters the picture, there is, I believe, a distinct prospect that an Ombudsman also will be appointed at the federal level where hitherto complaints-handling offices have served only specialised purposes.

The Canadian interest in general, and that of the legal profession in particular, has also been underlined by the establishment of an International Ombudsman Institute by the University of Alberta, with the aid of a grant from the Alberta Bar Association. I am sure that that Institute will help to promote a wider knowledge and understanding of the scope and potential of this type of office, and enable different countries to profit from the experience of others.

I cannot myself claim to have knowledge in depth of the international scene. I take my remit to be to talk to you about the British scene, though I do propose in passing to comment on some of the features that distinguish our system from many or all of the systems which function elsewhere.

Let me start by defining my terms. The word "Ombudsman"is, as most of you know, Swedish in origin. It can, I understand, be used there to signify a spokesman or representative for any kind of group or organisation. As applied to their parliamentary Ombudsmen, of whom they have four, it signifies someone specially appointed to represent the general public in their difficulties with officialdom. And in that sense it came to be adopted in the many countries which have, in their own ways, followed Sweden's example. Different writers have developed slightly different definitions of the essential features of this kind of office. My definition is that it is an office created with an independent status, by statute or some other public instrument, charged with responsibility for investigating complaints made by aggrieved persons against public authorities, and endowed with sufficient powers to discharge that responsibility effectively.

In this country—Great Britain—we have three types of office which satisfy that definition: the Parliamentary Commissioner for Administration (the first such office to be created here, in 1967), who investigates complaints against government departments; the Health Service Commissioner (created in 1973), who investigates complaints against the special health service authorities which run our National Health Service; and the Commissioner for Local Administration (created in 1974), who investigates complaints against municipal authorities.

When I say we have the three types of office, I do not mean to imply that there is one holder of each. In fact, although there is only one office of Parliamentary Commissioner for Administration, there are three Health Service Commissioner offices—one each for England, Scotland and Wales; but all these four offices are currently held by the same man. I myself held them all—the Parliamentary Commissioner office from 1971 to 1976 and the Health Service Commissioner offices from the time of their creation in 1973 to 1976 also. By contrast there are five Commissioners for Local Administration, three of whom function in England, one in Scotland and one in Wales.

All the British Ombudsmen offices have a great deal in common. The legislation creating the later offices was closely modelled, though with some significant changes, on the Parliamentary Commissioner Act of 1967. I propose to concentrate on what seem to me to be the main points that might interest you in relation to the office of the Parliamentary Commissioner for Administration, who in the eyes of most people *is* our national Ombudsman, and afterwards refer, more briefly, to the other offices.

Perhaps, since I am addressing an audience of lawyers, I ought to start by saying that, as I see it, the office of Parliamentary Commissioner for Administration, like the other British Ombudsman offices, is totally separate and distinct from our legal system. It functions mainly (though not exclusively) in matters for which the law itself provides no easy remedy. There is no charge for its services, and its procedures are not those of a court of law. For example, the 1967 Act specifically requires that its investigations must be carried out in private. And, although obviously the Commissioner does his best to make sure that everyone concerned has the fullest opportunity to present his case, this is normally done by arranging for them to be seen—or getting their written comments—individually; an adversarial procedure as practised by the courts—though there is nothing in the statute to bar it—has not been felt appropriate.

Some of your other speakers may be commenting upon proposals that have from time to time been put forward for the creation in this country of a system of administrative courts, or an Administrative Division of the

High Court, which would be integrated into our legal system. But the Ombudsman would, I think, continue to remain outside that system even if it were introduced. Certainly other countries that have administrative court systems—among others, Sweden and France,—still have their Ombudsmen.

The central provision of the 1967 Act that prescribes the basic function of the Parliamentary Commissioner for Administration is s. 5(1). That it lays down:

(a) first, that the only investigations it is open to the Commissioner to undertake are into allegations of injustice caused by a department's maladministration;
(b) secondly, that the alleged maladministration must have been in connection with action taken in the exercise of the department's administrative functions; and even so, under a separate provision in the Act, there are certain types of administrative action specifically excluded from the Commissioner's purview by the Act;
(c) thirdly, that he can only act if the complaint is referred to him by a member of the House of Commons.

I think it is worth spending a little time examining these and other requirements and limitations and commenting on the controversy to which they have given rise in some quarters.

Is the scope of the office too narrowly conceived, and should it sensibly be widened?

For my part, although I think there are some needless restrictions, the underlying approach—that the office concerns itself with complaints of injustice caused by maladministration—is sound and suitable in the circumstances of this country. It is sometimes argued that this remit is too narrow when judged against the remit of, for example, the New Zealand Ombudsmen. Their legislation authorises them, to question any decision, recommendation, act or omission which, in their opinion, was "unreasonable, unjust, oppressive or improperly discriminatory;" and the legislation which governs the creation of the various Canadian Ombudsmen offices for the most part follows that wording very closely. But in my view, on a reasonable construction, the wording of the British provision, though more general, enables the Parliamentary Commissioner to challenge decisions and acts or omissions characterised by the defects spelt out in the New Zealand and Canadian legislation. There is, in our 1967 Act, no definition included of what is meant by either injustice or maladministration. The late Mr. Richard Crossman, who, as Lord President of the Council, had the job of piloting the Bill through the House of Commons in 1966 and the early part of 1967, had his own shot at describing to Parliament what *he* thought might be included in maladministration: he suggested that among its features were "bias, neglect, inattention, delay, incompetence, ineptitude, perversity, turpitude, arbitrariness" and, for good measure, he added "and so on". The Parliamentary Commissioner is, in no sense, bound by Richard

Crossman's definition, but, as experience shows, he certainly in practice interprets his remit no less widely. As to injustice, that is taken to include any kind of detriment which the act complained of may have caused; and that means not simply financial loss but any other kind of deprivation and even frustration that the complainant may have suffered.

One provision of our Act that has caused some raising of eyebrows is the specific declaration that the Parliamentary Commissioner may not question the merits of a decision taken by a government department in the exercise of a discretion they have, if it was taken without maladministration. To me that provision serves no more as a reminder of what the basic remit of the Commissioner in fact is. It does not, of course, inhibit the Commissioner from investigating a claim that a discretionary decision *was* taken with maladministration. As a broad working rule, I followed the line that a decision was taken without maladministration if it was taken properly, with full knowledge of the facts and after due consideration of the arguments. This still leaves plenty of room for a flexible approach. What is *due* consideration? I had no hesitation in looking at this in a broad way. I can illustrate this by telling you about a planning case I had to deal with where it was difficult to point to any specific maladministration, but yet a decision I had to criticise had been taken.

It was a case in which the complainant had applied to develop a property in a rural area. An appeal against rejection of the application by the local planning authority had been made to the responsible government minister and remitted for decision to a planning inspector of the department. He had decided to reject the appeal, on one ground only—that the access proposed as part of the development was unsatisfactory because it caused traffic problems; he specifically said that in his view the development would not impair the local amenities. So the complainant went away and revised his plan so as to improve the access arrangements, put it forward again, was again turned down by the local planning authority and again appealed. This time the appeal was remitted for decision to a different planning inspector. He conceded that the access difficulties had been removed but nevertheless also rejected the appeal on the ground that, in *his* view, the local amenities *would* be impaired, the very opposite of the view taken by the other inspector. Both inspectors had clearly looked fully and carefully at the plan, but they had arrived at incompatible decisions, and even if I could not point to a specific act of maladministration, I had to criticise the result.

In the outcome arrangements were made for the case to come forward again and it was eventually decided by the Minister, personally this time, in the complainant's favour.

Another limitation that has been criticised in the Parliamentary Commissioner's scope is the absence of any power to initiate investigations; he has first to wait for a complaint to be duly submitted. If it is a weakness for an Ombudsman to lack this power, it is not confined to this country. Although quite a number of Ombudsmen in other countries have this power, many do not. In Canada I think some of your Ombudsmen have it, but most do not. And when you consider the circumstances of this country, with (with France) far and away the largest population of any country with an Ombudsman, I think a general power to initiate investigations without a formal complaint (on the basis, for example, of a newspaper report or some publicly voiced criticism) could divert his energies over a wide field, which would often be unrewarding. Better to encourage those who genuinely feel aggrieved to put their complaints forward; there is no doubt that, despite the considerable efforts to publicise the work of the office, the Commissioner's services are not used nearly as much as they could be.

Before I go on to mention some extensions that I *would* favour, there are two other statutory provisions that I would like to draw attention to. The first is the provision that debars the Commissioner from investigating a complaint made more than a year after the complainant became aware of his grievance, unless he considers there are special circumstances which make it proper for him to carry out an investigation. The reasons for having some time limit are obvious and, in principle, sound. But the question arises whether the discretion to waive the time limit is too highly qualified. The legal advice I was given was that I ought to proceed on the basis that the discretion should be only rarely exercised: that Parliament's intention was clearly that the time limit was to be the general rule and that the circumstances in which it could rightly be waived had really to be special. And it was rare for me to use that discretion. But I was interested to read that, in the course of a judgement given by the Court of Appeal on 31 July 1978 in a case involving one of our Commissioners for Local Administration—I shall be saying more about them later, and the only point I need make here is that a similar time limit applies to them also—Lord Denning said: "time limits are not to be enforced rigidly against a complainant where justice requires that the time be extended and his complaint heard". That view no doubt reflects current trends in legal thought, and it might, had it been stated in my time, have influenced me to accept a few more out-of-time complaints than I did.

The other statutory provision I want to draw attention to is also one which specifies a limitation on the Parliamentary Commissioner's scope, but gives him a qualified discretion to waive it. One of the underlying concepts about his office is that it is not intended to supplant other existing remedies, but to offer an additional, new, means of redressing a grievance which otherwise would remain unremedied. Consistently with that concept the 1967 Act lays down that the Parliamentary Commissioner shall not investigate a complaint about any action in respect of which the aggrieved person has or had a right of appeal to a statutory tribunal or a remedy by way of proceedings in a court of law; once more he is given a power to waive the limitation, if he is satisfied that, in the particular circumstances, it is not reasonable to expect use to be made or to have been made of that right or remedy. Here again my legal advice was that the Commissioner ought to proceed on the basis that the discretion was one that should rarely be exercised. On Lord Denning's approach, he might now feel disposed to be a little less inhibited in using the discretion.

I come now to changes that I *would* like to see made. I mentioned earlier that there are certain types of administrative action specifically excluded from the Commissioner's purview by the 1967 Act. With some of these exclusions it is difficult to quarrel; for example, the exclusion of actions relating to the security of the state or connected with international relations. But other exclusions are more debatable. Two which have attracted most attention are, first, personnel matters—that is, action taken by the government, as employer, in relation to its employees (present, past and future)—and, second, action taken in connection with commercial and contractual transactions. The government's justification for these exclusions is, basically, that our Ombudsman system is intended to operate between the executive and those whom it governs, and not between the government and its suppliers or between the government and those whom it employs. They argue also that it would not be in the general interest that the government's commercial activities should be open to Ombudsman investigation when other parties are free from it, and that means of redress exist already, for dissatisfied Civil Servants, and also for intending or past employees. I find the arguments unconvincing and to some extent specious, and I should like to see the Commissioner's scope widened by the removal of these exclusions. Whether our new government will adopt a more sympathetic approach to this than their predecessors remains to be seen.

There is one other, more fundamental, change that I would like to see made, and that is the method of access to the Parliamentary Commissioner. This, under the 1967 Act, has to be through a Member of the House of Commons. The reason for this requirement was twofold: first, when the office was set up, it was seen as an additional weapon in the armoury of our Members of Parliament, who have themselves a traditional and well-established role of acting as local trouble-shooters on behalf of their constituents; and, second, there was a fear that the new office might get overwhelmed with complaints without some such protective screen as Members of Parliament would provide.

There is no doubt that our Parliamentary Commissioner office is closely integrated—as the name implies—into our parliamentary system. He is required to submit to parliament annual reports and free to submit also other reports, which he does quite regularly; and these reports are considered by a specially appointed all-Party Committee of the House of Commons—the Select Committee on the Parliamentary Commissioner for Administration. He himself is examined on these reports by the Committee, who also call in for examination a selection of the Permanent Secretaries of Government Departments whose actions have come under scrutiny and criticism from the Commissioner. They can also thus lend their own support to recommendations by the Commissioner which departments may have shown some reluctance to take up and may even press upon the government proposals for changes in practices or even policies which—whether or not maladministration has been established—have been shown to give rise to injustice or hardship. The Select Committee is a powerful follow-up and supporting feature of our system which I think is not paralleled in many other countries.

But, important as the parliamentary connection is, it does not follow that access to the Commissioner must continue to be only through a Member of the House. Many people do not understand this requirement and often approach the Commissioner direct. They used to be referred back to Members in these cases. There is now a procedure under which they are, where appropriate, asked if they would like the Commissioner to send on their complaints to a Member, with whose agreement the Commissioner would carry out an investigation. This is an advance, but only a small one. It affects only people who start by following the wrong procedure. And that is hardly sufficient. I would like to go the whole way now and allow direct access generally. My experience, and the experience of other of our Parliamentary Commissioners, has been that different Members had different views about the circumstances in which the Parliamentary Commissioner could be of help to them and so made very different use of his services. In the last annual report I presented to parliament for the year 1975, I reported that about 250, or something like 40 percent of the sitting Members had referred not a single complaint to me during the year. In my preceding annual report for 1974 I reported that, in the whole of the lifetime of the previous Parliament, which lasted nearly four years, about 125, or about 20 percent of the Members, had submitted no complaints to me. And in any year the number of references submitted by individual Members varied from nothing to a dozen or more. There must be many explanations for the differences, but it seems to me that these figures show that, under the present system, in different areas, people do not find the Commissioner equally accessible. As to the argument that the Commissioner might be overwhelmed if we changed over to direct access, it must be true that the numbers that reached him would increase. But I am not convinced that they would reach overwhelming proportions. Certainly the experience of the Health Service Commissioner office—which I shall soon be coming to—has not so far been that direct access leads to an impossibly heavy workload. If there really was considered to be a serious risk, various checks could be devised. But my guess would be that, even if direct access was introduced, we should still find that MP's would often continue to act on behalf of their constituents; the difference would be that they would not be the exclusive channel of access.

I think most outside observers have now come to the view that it would be better if we moved over to a system of direct access. But I have to say also that, in a recent report, the Select Committee themselves rejected this view, standing by the original reasons which led to the introduction of the present system. And the former government supported the Select Committee's stand. So I am not optimistic that we shall see any early change.

There are one or two other aspects of the Parliamentary Commissioner's work that I want to comment on, before I go on to the other British Ombudsmen office.

First, he is armed with effective powers to enable him to carry out his investigations as thoroughly as he sees fit—powers no less wide than those possessed by our judges. He can require the production of any documents, and the attendance of any witness, if this will help him in his task; the only exception is that he cannot call for documents relating to Cabinet or Cabinet Committee proceedings.

There was only one case that I can recall in my time in which the exception caused certain documents to be withheld from my scrutiny; but even in that case I was furnished by the Secretary to the Cabinet with a note of the outcome of the Cabinet discussion, and I had no hesitation in expressing the view that it would have made no difference to my findings even if I had seen the Cabinet papers.

One power the Commissioner does not possess is the power to enforce his findings. There are a few Ombudsmen in other countries who do have an enforcement power of some kind, but not the great majority. In our own country the absence of this power did produce a fair amount of criticism, particularly in the early days; the Parliamentary Commissioner was described as a toothless tiger, and one newspaper carried the headline "Ombudsman or Ombudsmouse". The criticisms have, over the years, tended to diminish, as it became clear that a castigation by the Parliamentary Commissioner made a very strong impact and that under pressure if necessary from the Member of Parliament or the Select Committee and under fire from the press or other media, a government department would hesitate long and hard before rejecting a remedy proposed by the Commissioner. There have been a few cases in which they have done so, but in the vast majority they have accepted his view. And it is a tenable view that, given the other sorts of sanction, the absence of a power of enforcement is a strength rather than a weakness.

What sort of a background does our Parliamentary Commissioner need for carrying out these duties? In most other countries the choice seems to fall usually on someone with a legal background of some kind. In Canada your Ombudsmen have had a variety of earlier occupations. According to an analysis in a book published last year there were eight of your former or serving Ombudsmen who had had a legal background, as judges, university teachers of law, practising lawyers or, in one case, as a lawyer in provincial government service; one had been a businessman and parliamentarian; two had been clergymen; two had been senior police officers; and one had been the head of a University and a professor of French. In this country, for our first three Parliamentary Commissioners, including myself, the choice fell on former senior civil servants; one had had, in addition, experience as our Comptroller and Auditor General, also an officer attached to parliament with the function of rooting out financial weaknesses or failures. There seems to be an obvious advantage in appointing a former Civil Servant; he knows the ropes and he knows personally many of the senior people in departments whose actions he will be investigating and often how best to handle them. But there was the obvious criticism that, coming from the same stable, he might not be altogether unbiased in considering his former colleagues' action. And there have been odd occasions when actions in which he might have been remotely involved in his Civil Service capacity, years previously, have figured as part of a set of actions in which complaints have later come to be made to him. For our fourth Parliamentary Commissioner, the current one who took up office in January last, the choice fell on a practising lawyer, a Queen's Counsel. I have had more than one informal chat with him, and I have gathered his approach is not likely to prove fundamentally different from that of his predecessors. What I am quite sure is that it makes sense not to look upon the office as the preserve of any particular type of person. Previous experience is relevant, but in the end you are looking for a man, or, of course, a woman, not a type.

It may serve to give you a clearer picture of the scope of the Parliamentary Commissioner if I quote some actual examples of the kinds of maladministration that he is asked to investigate. It is not easy to put these into meaningful categories—they are so wide and varied. But delay by a government department in providing information or giving advice or a decision—or the provision of inaccurate information or advice—or following imperfect procedures in the course of taking decisions, or basing decisions on incomplete information are among the commonest types of allegation. And though such allegations are made on occasion against most government departments, the three that have always figured most prominently in the Parliamentary Commissioner's postbag are the Board of Inland Revenue (our direct taxation Department), the social security side of the Department of Health and Social Security, and the Department of Environment (the department concerned with planning appeals). It need be no surprise that these departments come at the head of the list, since they are those who are, far and away, most commonly in contact with the general public. Often nothing more than an apology may be the result of an investigation.

But in a fair proportion of cases more than that—often a financial remedy—may be called for. Let me mention one or two of these, since they usually attract most interest. On the taxation side, a fairly common complaint—surprising at first sight—was the belated discovery by the tax inspector that he had undercharged you, through a mistake on his part, for several years. The reason for the complaints was, of course, that he now proposed to recover the arrears, as the law allows, for up to six years. As a result of a series of investigations by the Commissioner which showed the hardship that this could cause and the support of the Select Committee, the government agreed to waive their legal entitlement and forgo the arrears in whole or in part for people whose income was modest. This, which is a continuing concession year by year, has benefited many thousands of people already. On the social security side, dozens of war pensioners have had their awards backdated, after the department had originally refused to do this, because the Commissioner has established that they should have been awarded earlier but for a departmental mistake. One hundred thousand people who had been misled by a badly worded form issued by the Department of Transport and had delayed applying for renewal of their vehicle licence until a higher duty came into operation were each refunded £10. At the other extreme a single trader misled by wrong information from our Board of Customs and Excise to invest abortively in manufacturing a new product was given £6000 compensation. In many cases procedures for handling correspondence or forms sent in by the public have been changed at the Commissioner's suggestion. And the arrangements for allowing prisoners access to legal advice when they claim to have been injured by a prison officer have been liberalised. This is not meant to be a representative selection of cases, but I hope it brings out not only the varied nature of the work but its impact, going often far beyond an individual complaint. It is perhaps in this wider impact, and the general "tonic" effect that the office can be presumed to have on the approach by government officials to their work, that the greatest value of the office lies.

I have not left myself much time to deal with the other Ombudsman offices we have in this country. I have already explained that their operations, their scope (including the exclusions) and their powers, as laid down in the legislation which governs them, are based on those of the Parliamentary Commissioner. Let me, therefore, pick on what I see as the main differences.

For the Health Service Commissioner—and when I talk of the Health Service Commissioner, I include all three of those offices—much the most significant difference is that complainants are not required to approach him through their Members of Parliament. They can go to him direct. The only stipulation is that (except in one special type of case) they must first have given the relevant health service authority a reasonable opportunity to investigate and reply to the complaint.

Why the difference? Why did parliament allow direct access to the one Commissioner when it was denied to the other? The underlying logic seems to have been that, whereas Members of Parliament have a close relationship and continuous correspondence on behalf of their constituents with government departments and they ought therefore to be associated with the operations of the Parliamentary Commissioner system, their connection with the health service authorities was more distant and did not require them to be involved with the Health Service Commissioner. There may be some validity in this distinction, but not in my view a great deal. It is true that ministers are at the end of the day answerable to parliament, and health service authorities are not. But the health service authorities are constitutionally carrying out their responsibilities on behalf of ministers, who are equally answerable to parliament for the way they do so. And many Members of Parliament have no hesitation in dealing direct with the authorities. It is also the fact that the Health Service Commissioner has in other ways much the same relation to parliament as does the Parliamentary Commissioner. He makes annual and other reports which have to be laid before parliament and are considered by the same Parliamentary Select Committee.

Another difference in the legislation governing the Health Service Commissioner's office gives him an apparently wider remit than the Parliamentary Commissioner's remit to investigate complaints of injustice sustained through maladministration in connection with the exercise of administrative functions. The Health Service Commissioner's remit is expressed as to investigate complaints of injustice or hardship sustained in consequence of an alleged failure in a service provided by an authority; of an authority's failure to provide a service that it was its function to provide; or of maladministration connected with any other action taken by an authority. In practice, however, on a reasonably broad interpretation, I did not myself attribute any major difference of meaning to the differences of wording.

But there is one specific exclusion from the Health Service Commissioner's remit which does have great significance. He is debarred from investigating action taken in connection with diagnosis or care or treatment in the exercise of clinical judgment. This exclusion, made in deference to the views of the medical profession, is in one sense logical enough. What a doctor does in the exercise of clinical judgment would not normally be thought to be an act of the same nature as an administrative act of the kinds listed in the Health Service Commissioner's remit. Nevertheless its exclusion gives rise to problems. Complaints to the Health Service Commissioner frequently include criticisms of clinical judgment as well as criticisms of administrative action, and it is often not easy to confine a coherent investigation to the latter alone, though the attempt has to be made. And there may be uncertainty about the dividing line. If an operation is delayed, for example, it may be because the doctor thought delay clinically necessary, or because an administrative mistake of one kind or another was made, or a mixture of both. There is no doubt in my mind that a more satisfactory investigation could in many cases be carried out if this particular exclusion was ended. This has been recommended by the Select Committee. They made it clear that what they had in mind was that the Commissioner should be empowered only to call in question actions or judgments which were unreasonable in all the circumstances, not those which, even if they turned out to be mistaken, were perfectly reasonable at the time they were taken. Certainly the Commissioner would need to have adequate help from qualified people, if he were to take this on. But it is strongly opposed by the medical profession, who point out doctors are already exposed to the risk of being sued for negligence for damage caused by clinical error and have expressed the fear that any new additional form of investigation may only encourage what they call "defensive" medicine.

However that particular, important, issue is sorted out the Health Service Commissioner has a varied sphere of operation in matters clearly within his remit: including, to quote again but a few examples, complaints of faulty admission procedure; needless delays in fixing appointments or in causing people to wait to be seen in clinics or in providing treatment; failures in the meals service; loss of patients' property; failure to organise aftercare; and above all perhaps a variety of communication failures. Patients have not been told what is wrong with them, why they are or are not being admitted, or what to expect from a particular form of treatment. Relatives have not been told how ill a patient was or have not been summoned when his condition deteriorated and he was dying. Adequate information has not been exchanged between members of the staff or to others who will take over responsibility for care when a patient leaves hospital. A depressing list—but the Commissioner sees the unhappy side of things. And that, of course, goes also for the Parliamentary Commissioner, and equally for our local commissioners, whom I now come to.

The appointment of local commissioners—Commissioners for Local Administration to give them their full title—completed the organisation of a system of Ombudsmen for complaints against what might be called collectively the public services in this country: first central government, then the National Health Service, and finally local government. The five local commissioners chosen included four with some background of experience in local government, either as member or officer, two of whom were also legally qualified and three of whom (in addition to the fifth commissioner) had also had experience of service outside local government. The Ombudsman system has not been applied to the wider public sector, public corporations or nationalised industries, for example, which do come under the Ombudsmen's scrutiny in many other countries; and I would like to see them brought within the system in this country too. Nevertheless the inclusion of local government filled a large gap.

Once again the legislation which created local commissioners followed closely in most respects the provisions of the Parliamentary Commissioner Act of 1967. But there are again some significant differences. Access to the local commissioner is not through a Member of Parliament. Nor for that matter is it, normally, direct. The complainant is required to ask a local councillor to put his complaint to the local commissioner. The basis for this requirement is that, in this country, the local councillor is expected to exercise much the same role in seeking redress for members of his local electorate who are aggrieved as the Member of Parliament does for his constituents. But there is, at least in theory, a constitutional awkwardness here. The local councillor is not simply an elected representative; he is also a member of an executive authority and shares collective responsibility for actions or decisions taken by them or on their behalf. Is it right to make him the channel of complaint when he shares some responsibility for the action complained of, even if (as is usual) he was not personally involved. The problem, for what it is worth, is met by a provision that the local commissioner can at his discretion investigate a complaint if a councillor has refused to forward it. So to that extent, and it is in practice a very limited extent, direct access is allowed.

Perhaps the other most significant difference is the absence of any direct parliamentary link. The local commissioners' annual reports, for example, do not have to be laid before parliament, and do not therefore come up for consideration by the Parliamentary Select Committee. They are made instead, in the different parts of Great Britain, to bodies representative of the local authorities whose actions are subject to their scrutiny. It follows that they do not have the powerful backing which that Select Committee can provide for the recommendations of both the Parliamentary Commissioner and the Health Service Commissioner. On the other hand their individual reports do receive considerable local publicity; and, if a local authority does not act upon them, they are required to make a further report which is liable to attract greater attention still from the press. Although some local authorities resent criticism, it is fair to say that the great majority do act upon the local commissioners' reports.

Naturally enough complaints which the local commissioners investigate reflect predominantly dissatisfaction in those matters falling within the Commissioner's scope on which the public have the most regular contact with local authorities. Far and away the most common are complaints of delays and failures relating to local planning applications. You may be kept waiting months or years for a decision on an application to develop some property; or you may think somebody else has been given a development permission unreasonably to your detriment. Next come decisions in the field of housing—why have you been kept waiting so long to be allocated a house, or why has someone been given one ahead of you! Complaints connected with the allocation of children to schools also come quite high up on the list. And, as with the other commissioners, where fault is found, the action recommended can vary from a call for an apology to financial compensation.

There are many features of our Ombudsmen offices I do not have time to go into. I want to conclude by drawing some of the threads together and looking ahead.

There is a not uncommon misconception in this country about the nature of the Ombudsman system. It does not exist to put right all grievances whatever their origin or cause. Before he was brought into being, a complex variety of methods for seeking redress of grievances already existed—action through a court of law, whether under the common law or under statute, rights of appeal to independent tribunals of various kinds, making use of the help of advisory bodies, some statutory (for example in connection with national industries), some voluntary (for example Citizens' Advice Bureaux) and, very important, the services of our Members of Parliament or local councillors. Ombudsmen have been added not to take their place but to fill gaps that even that armoury of support left. And their scope has been defined by statute to fit in to that role. I have mentioned some areas where I think the legislation is too restrictive. But the basic concept seems to me generally sound, and I think it is more widely understood now. Certainly their reports are quite widely publicised and often applauded.

But, notwithstanding the Select Committee's view, I remain unhappy about the arrangements for access to our Ombudsmen other than the Health Service Commissioner. It is only in this country and in France that direct access is not the rule. It is true that, in terms of population, our two countries are by far the largest to have Ombudsmen. It is no doubt true that the restrictions on access do limit the number of cases they have to handle. I do not propose to inflict statistics on you, but if I did they would show that, proportionally to population, our Ombudsmen handle many fewer cases than most of those in other countries. But the access arrangements are only part of the reason for that. And even if we did need more to handle an increased flow, I think we ought to face that. Indeed, even as matters stand, I believe the time may not be too long delayed before a separate Health Service Commissioner appointment is needed.

What I think is particularly objectionable is the fact that we have a variety of different methods of access: through the Member of Parliament to the Parliamentary Commissioner, direct to the Health Service Commissioner and through a local councillor normally to the local commissioners. Members of the public could be forgiven for finding the total picture pretty confusing. Moreover, the arrangements can put them to considerable inconvenience if, as can and sometimes does happen, they want to ask for the investigation of complaints ranging over two or more of the services which come within the purview of different commissioners. Though I think it was sensible and natural for our system to grow up by stages as it has done, there is so much that is common to the spheres of all the commissioners that I would like to see us move in the not too distant future to a more co-ordinated total system, in which each individual commissioner would remain independent in carrying out his investigations, but all would be brought together into a single institute or college which would provide administrative co-ordination and unified procedures. Already systems of this kind exist in Sweden and New Zealand. The three local commissioners for England are similarly organised into a single commission, with the Parliamentary Commissioner also present *ex officio*, but the commission has no function outside the area of English local government. If we had a fully co-ordinated system of the kind I would like to see, direct access would be an integral part of it. This view of mine may not find general acceptance yet—there are a number of interests that would prefer to leave matters as they are—but I think it would certainly underpin and strengthen an office which has proved its value.

13

The Role of the Court Within the European Communities

J. P. Warner

In this paper the court within the European Communities is discussed with emphasis on its institutional role.

Perhaps the first thing to mention, very briefly, is the fact that the formal name of the court is "the Court of Justice of the European Communities", in the plural.

That reflects the legal situation.

There are, in law, three communities, to each of which each of our member states belongs. At present, as you know, there are nine member states. Soon, with the accession of Greece, there will be ten. Then, probably, with the accessions of Portugal and of Spain, there will be 12.

Of the three communities the first in date of creation was the European Coal and Steel Community (the "ECSC"). That was created by the Treaty of Paris of 1951, which entered into force in 1952. It was that Treaty that gave birth to the court. So, in its early years, the court was simply the Court of Justice of the ECSC.

Then, in 1957, came the two Treaties of Rome, one creating the European Atomic Energy Community (Euratom) and the other the European Economic Community (E.E.C.). Those treaties entered into force in 1958. As a result of them the court became the court of the three communities.

In practice the E.E.C. is the most important of the three communities. Indeed it is often popularly thought to embrace the other two. Journalists, for instance, often refer to the E.E.C. even when they are writing about coal or steel or nuclear energy.

For that reason I propose to refer in the main to the E.E.C. Treaty. In general the provisions about the court are the same or similar in the three treaties.

Article 164 of the E.E.C. Treaty states the function of the court in these terms:

> The Court of Justice shall ensure that in the interpretation and application of this Treaty the law is observed.

From the reference there to "the law", one can infer that the authors of the treaty had in mind an existing (albeit developing) body of legal principles against the background of which and with due regard to which the treaty should be interpreted and applied. In other words the treaty is not to be approached as if in a legal vacuum.

That is important because it has enabled the court to treat as fundamental in community law a number of general principles which are nowhere expressly stated in the treaty, but which, under different labels, and with slight differences, are recognized in the legal systems of all or most of the member states. Among those principles are those that common lawyers generally call the principles of natural justice. It has also enabled the court to hold, in no uncertain terms, that the safeguard of human rights is inherent in community law, so that any act of a community institution that infringes any of those rights is void. In identifying them the court draws inspiration from the constitutions and constitutional traditions of the member states, and from international agreements for the protection of human rights to which those states are parties, especially of course the European Convention on Human Rights.

The jurisdiction of the court is, on paper, very diverse, as any of you who have read the treaties and some subsequent conventions will know.

I should mention first, I think, its advisory jurisdiction under Art. 228 of the E.E.C. Treaty. That Article is about the negotiation and conclusion of agreements between the community and non-member states or international organizations. It provides that, where such an agreement is envisaged, the council, the commission or any member state may seek, before it is entered into, the opinion of the court as to whether it is compatible with the provisions of the treaty.

We have not had many cases under Art. 228, but those we have had have been of far-reaching importance. That is because, essentially, what the court has been asked to do in those cases is to define the limits of the community's competence in the international sphere—to say, in other words, in what fields the community is competent, to the exclusion of the member states, to negotiate and conclude agreements with non-member states; in what fields the competence of the community and of the member states is concurrent; and in what fields the community has no competence so that the member states remain independent. For example, the court has before it at the moment the question whether the proposed international rubber agreement should be entered into by the community to the exclusion of the member states or by the community and the member states jointly.

The exercise by the court of that jurisdiction has sometimes caused violent indignation among the defenders of state rights in the member states. In particular a recent ruling of the court under Art. 103 of the Euratom Treaty (which roughly corresponds to Art. 228) has provoked an astonishingly virulent reaction among some French politicians.

So far as contentious business is concerned, the greatest single source of work for the court is Art. 177 of the E.E.C. Treaty.

That Article empowers any court or tribunal of a member state—and, in the case of a court or tribunal whose decision will be final, obliges it—to refer to the European court for what is called a "preliminary ruling"—it would be better called an "interlocutory ruling"—any question of community law that arises in a case before it. It may be a question of interpretation of the treaty or of an act of a community institution (such as a regulation, or a directive, of the council or of the commission) or it may be a question as to the validity of such an act.

In practice we get references from a wide variety of courts and tribunals in all the member states, and on a wide variety of topics, such as the regulations giving effect to the common agricultural policy; the social security regulations; the transport regulations; the Common Customs Tariff; the rules about freedom of movement of goods between member states, including cases about the exercise of industrial and commercial property rights, about state commercial monopolies and about indirect taxation; the rules about freedom of movement of persons and services within the community; community competition law; and so forth.

The importance of preliminary rulings is twofold.

First they go a long way towards ensuring that community law is interpreted and applied uniformly throughout the community. The importance of that hardly needs emphasis. Take for example the freedom to provide services. It would be intolerable if the rules about it were interpreted more restrictively by the courts of one member state than by the courts of another, so that (say) it was open to a Belgian theatrical agent (I am thinking of a particular case) to offer his services in France, but not to a French theatrical agent to offer his in Belgium.

Secondly the preliminary ruling procedure does a great deal to ensure detailed compliance by the member states with the rules of community law. Of course there are provisions of the treaty (and I shall come to them) that enable the commission to bring an action before the Court for a declaration that a member state has failed to comply with the treaty in this or that respect, and there are provisions enabling another member state to do same. But a private person who is (say) assessed to a particular tax by the authorities of a member state and is advised that that tax is incompatible with community law, or one who is denied, by the authorities of a member state, a right to which he considers himself entitled by virtue of community law, such as a right to an agricultural subsidy or to a social security benefit, or the right to work in that state, can obtain a ruling of the European court on his case much more swiftly and effectively if he can appeal to the appropriate court or tribunal of that state and persuade it to order a reference under Art. 177.

Article 177 has in fact proved to be a major instrument for securing the correct application of community law in the member states. It requires close co-operation between the European court and the courts and tribunals of member states. That that co-operation has been forthcoming is one of the most remarkable and agreeable features of the community judicial scene, even though it is unfortunately true to say that there are still here and there, in some of the member states, courts that have not yet got used to it.

While on the subject of references for preliminary rulings, I should perhaps mention that there is provision for such references to be made also by courts and tribunals in the member states that find themselves called upon to interpret the Community Convention on Jurisdiction and the Enforcement of Judgments in Civil and Commercial Matters, commonly called "the Judgments Convention". We have had quite a few cases under that convention.

I turn from references for preliminary rulings to what we call direct actions.

I mentioned earlier that there were provisions enabling the commission to bring an action before the court for a declaration that a member state had failed to comply with the treaty in a particular respect. Those provisions are in Art. 169 of the E.E.C. Treaty.

Article 169 has always supplied a small but important part of the court's business, and there are signs that the commission is making increasing use of it. Actions under Art. 169 vary in atmosphere. Most of them are cases in which there is genuine disagreement between the commission and a member state as to the interpretation of this or that provision of community law. In one case at least, we gathered that both the commission and the defendant state, which was the Netherlands, were uncertain what the provision in question meant, so they agreed to have a friendly action to have it decided by the court. In quite a number of cases where the defendant has been Italy, there has been a plea of guilty, together with an explanation that the failure to comply was not deliberate but due to the slowness of legislative processes in Rome. But there have been cases where a member state has deliberately flouted the treaty and waited to see how long it could get away with it.

One thing that can be said, however, is that no member state has ever, once the court has declared it to be in breach of the treaty, failed to take steps to put its house in order—though it has in some cases taken a bit of time. The United Kingdom is going through that process, at present, over tachographs.

Article 170 of the treaty is the one that enables a member state to bring an action against another for a declaration that it is in breach of the treaty. Before such an action can be brought, the matter must first be submitted to the commission for its opinion.

Article 170 has been very little used. In fact it was never used at all until 1977, when Ireland brought an action against France about French restrictions on imports of mutton and lamb. That action was settled. There is at the moment before the court an action brought by France against the United Kingdom about British restrictions on fishing.

The majority of direct actions are brought under Art. 173 of the treaty, which confers on the court jurisdiction to review the legality of acts of the council or of the commission.

Actions under Art. 173 are generally of two kinds: on the one hand those brought by a member state against the council or the commission, or by one of those institutions against the other, and, on the other hand, actions brought by a private person, usually a trading company, against one or other institution, usually the commission.

Actions under Art. 173 brought by member states have been few and far between; and far fewer have been those that have succeeded. Perhaps the most important ones recently have been a group of actions in which three member states (France, Germany and the Netherlands) challenged aspects of the commission's accounting in connexion with the European Agricultural Guidance and Guarantee Fund (more generally known as "the Farm Fund"). They all failed.

There have to date been, I think, only three actions between the community institutions themselves. Each of them has been brought by the commission against the council. The first of them was the famous European Road Transport Agreement case (*ERTA*). It was the first case in which the court had to consider the limits of the competence of the community and of the member states respectively to negotiate agreements with non-member states. The other two were about council legislation concerning the remuneration of members of the staffs of the community institutions. The commission won one and lost the other.

Actions by private persons under Art. 173, on the other hand, constitute an important part of the court's business. They are actions in which a person challenges a decision that is of direct and individual concern to him.

The most frequent type is an action by way of appeal against a decision of the commission that a named undertaking or group of undertakings has infringed community competition law. Since such a decision often also imposes a fine, the appeal is generally both against the finding of infringement and, in the alternative, against the amount of the fine, which the court has a complete discretion to cancel, reduce, increase or leave alone. One feature of these competition cases is that the appellants often include concerns established outside the community, because community competition law applies to them if what they do has effects in the community. American and

Swiss companies particularly have often been appellants before the court, and in one case the appellant was a world wide association of manufacturers of a particular product: marine paint.

Recently we had a group of appeals brought under Art. 173 by Japanese manufacturers of ball and roller bearings against whom the council and the commission had taken anti-dumping measures. This drew from me the longest Opinion I have ever written as an Advocate General, let alone at the Bar. It ran, if I remember rightly, to over 120 pages. The appeals succeeded.

That covers what I think are the main heads of the court's jurisdiction. There are others that I can deal with more briefly.

Article 175 gives the court jurisdiction to declare that a failure by the council or the commission to take action in a particular respect is a breach of the treaty. So far as I know, the court has never made such a declaration—perhaps surprisingly.

Article 178 gives the court jurisdiction to award damages where a community institution incurs liability otherwise than for breach of contract. There have been many claims under that Article, but none has so far ever succeeded.

Then there is Art. 179 which confers jurisdiction on the court in what we call "staff cases," that is in disputes between officials of the community institutions and their employing institutions. We are there acting as a kind of industrial tribunal. I cannot imagine that a discussion of the staff cases could be of much interest to you, but it is fair to say that it is in those cases that the court has largely developed the principles according to which it will review administrative decisions; and those principles apply also to, for instance, decisions of the commission in competition cases. The court is soon to be relieved of much of the burden of the staff cases by the creation of a tribunal to hear them, at first instance.

Lastly, Arts. 180 to 182 confer jurisdiction on the court in disputes involving the European Investment Bank and in disputes between member states submitted to it by special agreement. But those Articles have never given rise to any actual cases.

That, I think, covers the essentials, and I do not think that there is any useful way in which it can be summed up.

14

Major Trends in the Case Law of the Court of the European Communities

(Free Movement of Goods)

The Honourable Lord Mackenzie Stuart

Introduction

When I undertook the subject of the major trends in the case law of the Court of the European Communities, I failed to realise the magnitude of my task.

In the calendar years 1977 and 1978 the European Court of Justice delivered 101 and 98 judgements respectively. In subject matter they ranged from the common customs tariff applicable to orange skin and pith[1] to the ruling given at the request of the Belgian government on the compatibility with the Euratom Treaty of Belgium's unilateral adherence to the Vienna Convention on the Physical Protection of Nuclear Materials.[2]

Accordingly I would propose to restrict myself to the topic of free movement of goods within the European Community. By free movement of goods I mean the removal of all artificial barriers to trade between member states. This, itself, I am sure you will agree, is a broad enough topic indeed and which I can only treat in outline although for those of you who are interested I have available, by way of an appendix, a series of more detailed references.

Why this particular topic? Because the free movement of goods, in the widest sense of that term, is one of the fundamental objects of the Treaty of Rome and, moreover, it seems to me that community developments in this field may have particular interest for you as Canadian lawyers with your substantial case-law concerning inter-provincial transactions and, for those of you who are comparative lawyers, similar problems are to be found in the case-law of both the United States of America and the Commonwealth of Australia.

Indeed as long ago as 1964, when the work of the European court was only a fraction of what it is today, Professor Sutherland of Harvard, in his foreword to Professor Mackinnon's excellent book on *Comparative Federalism* had this to say,

> In a world of increasing economic complexity and inter-relation, some form of organisation resembling the federal structure of Australia, of Canada, or of the United States, is quite likely to grow up among large groups of nations now discrete. The Common Market in Europe follows the pattern of growth of federal union on the North Atlantic seaboard between 1755 and 1789, not because of imitation, but out of the sheer necessity of societal growth.

Whether Professor Sutherland would express himself in exactly the same way today is perhaps another question but his percipience in observing the common ground is unquestionable.

Free Movement of Goods and the Treaty of Rome

As you know, by Art. 2,

> The Community shall have as its task, by establishing a common market and progressively approximating the economic policies of Member States, to promote throughout the Community a harmonious development of economic activities, a continuous and balanced expansion, an increase in stability, an accelerated raising of the standard of living and closer relations between the States belonging to it.

In Art. 3 we find the means by which these aims are to be achieved. Of these, the first two are concerned with the free movement of goods, namely "(a) the elimination, as between Member States, of customs duties and of quantitative restrictions on the import and export of goods, and of all other measures having equivalent effect;" and "(b) the establishment of a common customs tariff and of a common commercial policy towards third countries." It is only at a later stage that the treaty makes provision for such matters as the abolition of obstacles to the freedom of movement of persons, service and capital or the adoption of a common policy in the field of agriculture.

From these quotations it is apparent that the foundation of the European Economic Community rests upon a customs union. As has often been said by the court, the abolition between member states of customs duties and charges having equivalent effect constitutes a fundamental principle of the common market with the result that any possible exception, which in any event must be strictly construed, must be clearly laid down.[3] A customs union is, of course, something more than a mere free trade area. In a free trade area, the member states provide merely for the removal of all customs duties and quotas on goods moving between one member state and another.

This leaves each member state free to import goods from third countries, according to the terms prescribed by its own external customs tariff. It is obvious that without further agreement, distortions of trade can thereby occur.

The European Economic Community, however, is far more than just a customs union. It is a common market, that is to say, it involves a series of other freedoms than just the freedom from imposition of internal customs duties or their equivalents combined with a common external tariff. The Treaty deals with the freedom of movement of persons, services and capital; there are provisions relating to a common policy in agriculture and transport; there are provisions relating to taxation; there are the provisions which ensure that competition in the common market is not distorted.

As regards the specific topic of the free movement of goods, not only does the treaty require the abolition of customs duties and measures having equivalent effect to customs duties as between member states, by the chapter beginning at Art. 30 it prohibits quantitative restrictions on imports and all measures having equivalent effect. This must be read along with Art. 95 which contains the important provision that no member state shall impose, directly or indirectly, on the products of other member states internal taxation of any kind in excess of that imposed, directly or indirectly, on similar domestic products. Moreover the same chapter provides that where products are exported to the territory of any other member state the repayment of internal taxation is not to exceed the internal taxation imposed on them. That is to say member states may not subsidise their exports under the guise of a tax refund. Finally, in this context, Arts. 97 and 98 contain provisions designed to ensure that internal taxation should in the long run be harmonized.

The treaty, moreover, by Art. 37 deals with the problem of state monopolies which as you may well imagine are, or were, in a position to distort the normal flow of commerce and which for certain products in certain countries are of great commercial importance. Indeed the power of the individual state to affect commerce whether internally or externally is fully recognized by the treaty. Article 90 deals with the problems which may arise from the case of public undertakings and undertakings to which member states grant special or exclusive rights and Arts. 92 onwards deal with the question of state aids.

The list of factors affecting the free movement of goods does not end there. For example, to take state purchasing policy: Is a policy of "buy British" or "buy French" or "buy German", as the case may be, truly compatible with the proper functioning of a common market? If you look at the 1977 General Report of the Commission you will see that they have currently under scrutiny cases of "administrative circulars and statements by public authorities in several Member States to encourage the purchase of home-produced goods'' (p. 78). Lastly, and I only mention it to show that it cannot be neglected in this context, we have a chapter of the treaty which deals with cartels and other measures which private undertakings may adopt in order to reduce the force of competition within the market. Thus Art. 85 prohibits agreements which may affect trade between member states and Art. 86 prohibits the abuse by any undertaking possessing a dominant position in any substantial part of the market.

May I then, within the limits of the time available to me, say something about each of these topics in turn.

Customs Duties on Exports and Imports

The effect of Arts. 12 to 16 of the treaty is that since 1961 all customs duties and ''charges having equivalent effect'' have been abolished between Member States.

''Charges having equivalent effect'' has been defined by the court as one which is imposed on goods ''by reason of the fact that they cross a frontier,''[4] and by altering the price of an article exported or imported ''has the same restrictive effect on the free circulation of that article as a customs duty''.[5]

On the other hand in the very recent case of *Pigs and Bacon Commission* v. *McCarren and Company Ltd.*[6] what was in issue was a levy imposed by the Irish government on all bacon produced in Ireland. If, however, bacon of specified quality known as ''specials'' was exported through the agency of the Pigs and Bacon Commission the producer received a bonus. It was argued that the combined effect of the levy and the possible bonus was a charge on exports—but as the Advocate-General, Mr. Warner, said, since the greater part of the levy was a burden on home sales ''it would be an abuse of language to describe the levy/bonus system as a charge on exports''.

In the field of charges having equivalent effect to a customs duty one of the more important cases has been that *Les Commissionnaires Réunis*[7]. By its judgement, and here I quote the 1978 General Report of the Commission, ''the Court rejected definitively the widely held view that the Community institutions are empowered, even after the end of the transitional period, to set up or to retain, at least temporarily, obstacles to trade within the Community, where such measures are considered necessary to achieve the objectives assigned to the Common agricultural policy under the Treaty''.

This case arose out of the dispute between Italy and France about excessive—in the French view at least—imports of Italian wine into France. France imposed a charge on such imports invoking powers conferred by a safeguard clause forming part of a Council Regulation. For such a safeguard clause to be valid, said the court, express warrant in the treaty would have to be found in the provisions relating to the agricultural sector. None were to be found. Thus the Regulation in question

> in so far as it authorizes producer Member States to prescribe and levy, in intra-Community trade . . . charges have an effect equivalent to customs duties, is incompatible with . . . the Treaty and is consequently invalid.

Article 95

It is probably convenient at this stage to mention Art. 95 which, as I have already indicated, provides that

> No Member State shall impose, directly or indirectly, on the products of other Member States any internal taxation of any kind in excess of that imposed directly or indirectly on similar domestic products.

It is sometimes difficult to know whether a fiscal imposition is to be regarded as a customs duty or a charge having equivalent effect or whether it fell, as a matter of internal taxation, to be judged according to the provisions of Art. 95.

This problem had to be considered in two cases.[8] The cases concerned certain charges known as the *sovraprezzo* and the *sovraprezzo extraordinario* imposed by the Italian government on holdings of sugar at a given date, the proceeds of which were intended to finance aids to the Italian sugar beet producers and the sugar producing industry generally. For the first time the court made it clear, that one and the same scheme of taxation could not belong simultaneously to both the categories mentioned, having regard, as it said, "to the fact that the charges referred to in Articles 9 and 13 must simply be abolished, whilst for the purpose of applying internal taxation, Article 95 provides solely for the elimination of any form of discrimination, direct or indirect, in the treatment of the domestic products of a Member State and of products originating in other Member States". A financial charge within a general system of internal taxation which applies systematically both to domestic and to imported products according to the same criteria are not normally to be considered as having charges having equivalent effect to a customs duty. Apart from anything else the charge in such a case does arise by reason of the passage of a frontier.

The situation may be different, however, if such a duty, limited to particular products, has the sole purpose of financing activities for the specific advantage of the taxed domestic product, so as to make good, wholly or in part, the fiscal charge imposed upon them. In such a case, said the court, such a device would only have the appearance of a system of internal taxation and accordingly by reason of its protective character be deemed to be a charge having effect equivalent to customs duties, so as to fall under the prohibition of Arts. 9 and 13. For this to arise, however, there would have to be a clearly established connection between, on the one hand, the collection of a fiscal duty, levied without distinction on the products in question, whether domestic or imported, and, on the other hand, the advantage which ensures only for the benefit of domestic products by reason of that one and the same duty. The exceptional nature of the charge in question, however, was underlined. It is only where there is an obvious and direct link between the charge and the domestic market that there is brought into play the prohibition against charges having equivalent effect to a customs. In all other cases, a charge which bears equally upon imported domestic products is to be considered in the light of Art. 95.

Quantitative Restrictions on Imports and Exports and All Measures Having Equivalent Effect

The treaty prohibits, as between member states, quantitative restrictions on imports (Art. 30) and exports (Art. 34) and "all measures having equivalent effect".

The expression "measures having equivalent effect to a quantitative restriction" is not to be found in any of the other community treaties and nowhere is it defined. An equivalent expression, equally undefined, is to be found in Art. 10(11a) of the convention establishing EFTA.[9] The concept itself has been defined by the commission as "all laws, administrative provisions and administrative practices which hinder imports or exports which would otherwise take place including those provisions and practices which make importation or exportation more difficult or costly than the disposal of domestic production".

The court, itself, in Case 8/74[10] defined measures equivalent to quantitative restrictions as being

> All trading rules enacted by Member States which are capable of hindering, directly or indirectly, actually or potentially, intra-Community trade . . . .

Obviously, as with all broad formulations, specific cases are bound to present problems. Other considerations, too, such as the need adequately to protect designations of origin have to be kept in mind. In the case of *Dassonville* the question at issue was the right in Belgium to sell what in fact was genuine Scotch whiskey, but which had been imported via France and was not accompanied, as Belgian law requires, with a certificate of origin from the British Excise authorities.

In the result the court had this to say:[11]

> In the absence of a Community system guaranteeing for consumers the authenticity of a product's designation of origin, if a Member State takes measures to prevent unfair practices in this connexion, it is however subject to the condition that these measures should be reasonable and that the means of proof required should not act as a hindrance to trade between Member States and should in consequence, be accessible to all Community nationals.

The commission was not satisfied, however, that the system of certificates demanded by the Belgian government measured up to this test and they initiated proceedings under Art. 169 against Belgium for failure to comply with the treaty obligations. The gravamen of the commission's complaint was that if Belgium were prepared to accept bottles with appropriate labelling and fitted with the type of capsule which had to be destroyed in opening the bottle all administrative difficulties for the importer would be eliminated and the authenticity of the product assured. This the Belgian government would not accept. It would be only too easy, they said, to falsify labels and capsules. In the end the court held that Belgium was not in breach of Art. 30. There had been certain changes in the certificate procedure (which everyone agreed was an effective way to assure the authenticity of the product) making parallel imports posssible and in these circumstances the court was not prepared to hold that the Belgian system was unreasonable.

Article 36

As you know this provides that the prohibition on quantitative restrictions and measures having equivalent effect

> shall not preclude prohibitions of restrictions on imports, exports or goods in transit justified on grounds of public morality, public policy or public security;

Moreover such restrictions may be justified on grounds such as

> the protection of health and life of humans, animals or plants; the protection of national treasures possessing artistic, historic or archeological value; or the protection of industrial or commercial property.

However, Art. 36 concludes with the important qualification that:

> such prohibitions or restrictions shall not, however, constitute a means of arbitrary discrimination or a disguised restrictions on trade between Member States.

Article 36 has been the subject of many recent decisions by the court and will no doubt continue to be regularly invoked. The reason for this is not far to seek. Article 36 may provide a member state with *prima facie* justification for a barrier to trade introduced in fact for purely protectionist reasons. As one experienced administrator has explained:

> Trade barriers such as bans on imports, quotas, customs duties and monopolies now belong to outdated autarkic eras which are inconceivable at the stage of economic integration reached after twenty years of the Community's existence.
>
> They are instruments of protection which are too obvious and blatant still to be used by States which intend, for instance, to discourage imports or encourage a national sector of production.
>
> The devices used come from an arsenal of measures spread among a wide

variety of different rules. To the uninitiated observer, they are usually cloaked by a demure veil of legality; they apply, in almost all cases, to national as well as imported products and appear not to contain any discriminatory or protective element. Moreover, the objective which they are designed to attain is always very praiseworthy: the protection of human life and health, the campaign against pollution, consumer protection, the protection and improvement of the environment, the fight against inflation, standardization, the raising of the quality of products, etc.[12]

On the other hand there are many situations in which the Article may be legitimately invoked. For example, in matters of sanitary control where a community scheme is not in being a member state may impose its own conditions where necessary to achieve the objects referred to in the article.[13]

On the other hand where a community scheme is in being national measures are no longer "necessary" and thus a member state's right to base itself on Art. 36 is excluded.[14]

Article 36 is an exception to the fundamental principle of the free movement of goods and must, therefore, be interpreted in such a way that its scope is not extended any further than is necessary for the protection of those interests which it is intended to secure.[15]

Moreover such measures must always be in proportion to the end to be achieved. That is to say, they must not be excessively rigid when other means would suffice.[16]

Price Control

The prohibition of measures equivalent to quantitative restrictions has also been recently considered in the context of national measures prescribing maximum or minimum selling prices for certain products. There may often be good social reasons for the one or another. Minimum prices may be made compulsory in order to prevent undercutting by large business to the detriment of the small shopkeeper; maximum prices may be imposed in an attempt to hold down the cost of living.

At the same time, however, a minimum price fixed at a specific amount, although applicable without distinction to domestic and imported products, may be capable of having an adverse effect on the marketing of the latter, if it be cheaper to produce since it prevents the lower cost price from being reflected in the retail selling price. The imposition of maximum prices, however, may have the result that a foreign product, costing more to produce, is totally excluded from the market.

The court had recently to consider national measures imposing minimum prices in the case of *Openbaar Ministerie of the Netherlands* v. *Van Tiggele.*[17] Dutch legislation had provided for a minimum retail selling price for certain types of gin. As the Advocate General explained:

It is both well known and accepted that widely-consumed products sold in a large self-service store are generally offered at lower prices than in businesses

> where customers are served individually by a shop assistant. Such lower prices are the results of economies in staffing costs brought about by the self-service system of marketing and generally through the discounts which large stores can obtain when purchasing goods since their orders are in bulk and usually greater than of small-scale traders. Furthermore the greater volume of sales permits large stores to restrict their profit margin per unit as compared with that required by small businesses. Thus since the imposed price in question prevents unrestricted competition from lowering the price of alcoholic beverages to such a level that it would no longer be profitable for small-scale retailers it constitutes a measure of support for the latter.

The court drew a distinction, however, between the fixing of a minimum profit margin at a specific amount and the fixing of a specific minimum price. The former case it said, if applicable without distinction to domestic products and imported products, is incapable of producing an adverse effect on imported products which may be cheaper. "On the other hand", said the court, "this is not so in the case of a minimum price fixed at a specific amount which, although applicable without distinction to domestic products and imported products, is capable of having an adverse effect on the marketing of the latter in so far as it prevents their lower cost price from being reflected in the retail selling price."

State Aids and State Monopolies

A number of important cases have arisen recently involving Art. 92 to 94 which, with certain limited exceptions, prohibit the granting of state aids without the prior approval of the commission. These cases have been frequently complicated by the existence of state monopolies. In the case of state monopolies of a commercial character member states are required to ensure that they are so adjusted that no discrimination exists between nationals of member states as regards the conditions under which goods are procured and marketed.

For example in *Pigs Marketing Board (Northern Ireland)* v. *Redmond*[18] and in *Pigs and Bacon Commission* v. *McCarron,*[19] which I have already mentioned, the court had to consider the compatibility with a number of treaty provisions, including those relating to state aids, of the state pig marketing systems of Northern Ireland and the Irish Republic respectively. In these cases, however, since there is a common community scheme for pork and bacon the court preferred to approach the problem by first considering the nature of that scheme and whether the national marketing systems were compatible with the community scheme since

> the provisions of the Treaty relating to the common agricultural policy have precedence, in the case of any discrepancy, over the other rules relating to the establishment of the common market.[20]

Again an analogous approach was adopted by the court in *Hansen* v. *Hauptzollamt Flenburg.*[21] There is, as you know, a state alcohol monopoly in Germany. Certain categories of producer—largely the small-scale producers of fruit based liqueurs—make and sell their products without being required to pass them through the monopoly and pay a slightly lower tax than that generally levied on spirits sold by the monopoly and by importers of foreign produced alcohol. In an earlier case the Advocate-General said that "Article 37 is the sole criterion for judging monopoly charges and monopoly equalization since Article 37 is the *lex specialis* in relation to Article 95."[22] In *Hansen* the Advocate-General did not agree. "In my view", he said, "it is preferable to take account also of Article 95, the general provision concerning tax discrimination" and the court followed this approach.

"It appears preferable", the decision ran, "to examine the problem raised by the national court primarily from the point of view of the rule on taxation laid down in Article 95, because it is of a general nature, and not from the point of view of Article 37, which is specific to arrangements for State monopolies."

Viewed from the point of view of Art. 95 the court concluded that any preferential aspect of the German tax system must be extended without discrimination to spirits coming from other member states.

Conclusion

I began by underlining the importance for the working of the European Economic Community of the free movement of goods. I have indicated a number of recent cases where the court has sought to amplify the meaning of the relevant community rules. No doubt it will be called upon to do so many times more.

Nonetheless in this field above all it is for the community administrator and legislator and not the community judge to take the leading role. Much has certainly been accomplished but one has only to read the commission's publications—and I particularly commend the report on the 1977 conference on the Customs Union from which I have quoted—to realize how much hard administrative work remains to be done even after 20 years of operating the treaty.

Even more telling is the 1978 Annual General Report of the Commission at paragraph 100:

> On 18 October the Commission, conscious of the imperative need to sound the alarm in face of the repeated attacks by the Member States on the free movement of goods within the Community, approved a letter on protection of free trade within the Community and sent it to each of the Member States, the President of the Council and the President of Parliament.
>
> In its letter the Commission drew attention to the fact that the free movement of goods has been and continues to be impeded by more and more restrictive measures applied by public authorities to curb imports. At the end of 1978 the Commission was investigating our four hundred cases of barriers to the free movement of goods, mostly under Articles 30 to 36 of the EEC

Treaty. And even this figure, which is more than four times as many as four years ago, represents only the tip of the iceberg. Aware of the need to safeguard free trade—a vital factor for the operation and development of the internal market—the Commission has decided to act firmly and promptly and has set this as one of its priority tasks.

In this important field the judicial function is important but secondary. The court's task of interpreting Community law can only be properly performed if it is given adequate material to interpret. Indeed if there is available sufficient and well-prepared community legislation judicial interpretation might not even be required. So, let me end by emphasizing this, as in many other fields, nothing can replace a wise exercise of his powers by the community legislator and administrator and genuine co-operation by member states.

Free Movement of Goods

Check-list of the more recent Report Cases— 1975, 1976, 1977 European Court Reports. 1978 so far as published to June 1979.

	NATURE OF THE MEASURES INVOLVED	PROVISIONS AT ISSUE
Case 31/74, *Mr. Filippo Galli,* [1975] E.C.R. 47	Italian price-control measures affecting *inter alia* agricultural products covered by common organisations of the market	EEC Treaty, Arts. 2, 3, 5, 30, 39(1) & 40(3) Regulation 120/67/EEC of the Council Regulation 136/66/EEC of the Council
Case 51/74, *P. J. Van der Hulst's Zonen* v. *Produktschap voor Siergewassen,* [1975] E.C.R. 79	Dutch internal levies on sale of flower bulbs and their effect on export sales as compared with sales inside the Netherlands	EEC Treaty, Arts. 16, 40(3) & 95 Regulation no. 234/68 of the Council
Case 63/74, W. Cadsky SpA, [1975] E.C.R. 281	Imposition of pecuniary charge on exports of fruit and vegetable products where revenue is used to cover expenses relating to quality control at frontier	EEC Treaty, Arts. 9, 12, 13 & 16 Regulation no. 159/66 of the Council, Art. 13
Case 94/74, *IGAV* v. *ENCC,* [1975] E.C.R. 699	Duties claimed under Italian legislation by Italian public body at the marketing stage of paper products coming from other member states	EEC Treaty, Arts. 13(2) & 95

	NATURE OF THE MEASURES INVOLVED	PROVISIONS AT ISSUE
Case 4/75, *Rewe-Zentralfinanz eGmbH* v. *Landwirtschaftskammer,* [1975] E.C.R. 843	Phytosanitary inspections carried out at the frontier of the Federal Republic of Germany on imports of apples from other member states	EEC Treaty, Arts. 30 & 36 Commission Directive no. 70/50/EEC, Art 2(2) Council Directive no. 69/466/EEC, Art. 11
Case 21/75, *Schroeder* v. *Oberstadtdirektor der Stadt Köln,* [1975] E.C.R. 905	Pecuniary charges levied for public health and veterinary health inspections of productions imported from third countries	EEC Treaty, Art. 13(2) Regulation no. 121/67/EEC of the Council, Art. 17(2) Regulation no. 805/68 of the Council, Art. 20(2)
Joined cases 89/74, 18 & 19/75, *Procureur Général, Bordeaux* v. *Arnaud and Others,* [1975] E.C.R. 1023	Application by France, by way of a national measure of control, of a presumption in law of over-alcoholization of wine based on the proportion of alcohol to dry extract	EEC Treaty, Art. 30, Regulations 816/70 and 817/70 of the Council Regulation no. 1539/71 of the Commission
Case 59/75, *Pubblico Ministero* v. *Flavia Manghera and Others,* [1976] E.C.R. 91	Italian state monopoly for "the manufacture, preparation, import and sale of tobacco". Monopoly's exclusive right to import from other member states	EEC Treaty, Art. 37(1)
Case 87/75, *Conceria Daniele Bresciani* v. *Amministrazione Italiana delle Finanze,* [1976] E.C.R. 129	Pecuniary charge levied in Italy for the purpose of a compulsory public health inspection of raw cowhides upon importation	EEC Treaty, Arts. 9, 12 & 13(2)
Case 45/75, *Rewe-Zentrale des Lebensmittel Grosshandels GmbH* v. *Hauptzollamt Landau/Pfalz,* [1976] E.C.R. 181	German spirits monopoly. Surcharge on imported spirits designed to contribute to monopoly costs	EEC Treaty, Arts. 95 & 37
Case 91/75, *Hauptzollamt Göttingen und Bundesfinanzmünster* v. *Wolfgang Miritz GmbH & Co.,* [1976] E.C.R. 217	Special equalization charge on imports into the Federal Republic of Germany of alcoholic products. Charge forming part of the adjustment of the state monopoly in alcohol undertaken by the Federal Republic	EEC Treaty, Art. 37
Case 65/75, *Riccardo Tasca,* [1976] E.C.R. 291 Joined Cases 88 to 90/75, *Società SADAM and Others* v. *Comitato Interministeriale dei Prezzi and Others,* [1976] E.C.R. 323	Unilateral fixing by the Italian state of maximum prices for the sale of sugar	EEC Treaty, Art. 30 Regulation no. 1009/67 of the Council, Art. 35
Case 104/75, *Adriaan de Peijper,* [1976] E.C.R. 613	Dutch rules and practices governing the importation of pharmaceutical products into the Netherlands	EEC Treaty, Arts. 30 & 36

	NATURE OF THE MEASURES INVOLVED	PROVISIONS AT ISSUE
Case 51/75, *EMI Records Ltd.* v. *CBS United Kingdom Ltd.,* [1976] E.C.R. 811; Case 86/75, *EMI Records Ltd.* v. *CBS Grammophon A/G,* [1976] E.C.R. 871; Case 96/75, *EMI Records Ltd.* v. *CBS Schallplatten GmbH,* [1976] E.C.R. 913	Exercise by proprietor of a trade-mark in all the member states of the community of his right to the mark in order to prevent the importation of similar products bearing the same mark coming from a non-member country	EEC Treaty, Arts. 9(2), 10(1), 36, 110, 85(1), & 86
Case 119/75, *Terrapin (Overseas) Ltd.* v. *Terranova Industrie C.A. Tapferer & Co.,* [1976] E.C.R. 1039	Exercise by proprietor of trade-mark and commercial name registered in the Federal Republic of Germany of right to prevent importation of products of firm established in England bearing a name giving rise to confusion with the German mark and name	EEC Treaty, Art. 36
Case 127/7', *Bobie Getränkevertrieb GmbH* v. *Hauptzollamt Aachen-Nord,* [1976] E.C.R. 1079	German beer tax applied at graduated rate to home-produced beer and at a flat rate to imported beer	EEC Treaty, Art. 95
Case 41/76, *Criel, née Donckerwolcke and Henri Schou* v. *Procureur de la République and Director General of Customs,* [1976] E.C.R. 1921	French rules providing for measures of customs monitoring comprising, for products in free circulation by virtue of the provisions of the treaty, an indication of the country of origin	EEC Treaty, Arts. 9, 30, 31, 32 & 115
Case 46/76, *Bauhuis* v. *Netherlands,* [1977] E.C.R. 5	Fees charged by the Dutch authorities for veterinary and public health inspections on livestock destined for exportation	EEC Treaty, Arts. 12, 13, 16, 30 *et seq.* & 95 Council Directive No. 64/432/EEC
Case 53/76, *Procureur de la République* v. *Bouhelier,* [1977] E.C.R. 197	Requirement imposed upon French exporters of watches and watch movements to obtain a licence or a standards certificate	EEC Treaty, Art. 34
Case 20/76 *Schöttle* v. *Finanzamt Freudenstadt,* [1977] E.C.R. 247	German tax on the carriage of goods by road according to the distance covered on the German territory and the weight of the goods transported	EEC Treaty, Art. 95
Case 68/76, *Commission* v. *France,* [1977] E.C.R. 515	Introduction by the French government of a measure rendering exports of potatoes conditional upon submission of an export declaration previously endorsed by a branch of the administration	EEC Treaty, Art. 30 *et seq.*

	NATURE OF THE MEASURES INVOLVED	PROVISIONS AT ISSUE
Case 74/76, *Iannelli* v. *Meroni,* [1977] E.C.R. 557	Levy charged *inter alia* on domestic and imported wallpaper by a body governed by Italian public law, the proceeds of which are used to finance a system of state aids to newspaper publishers	EEC Treaty, Art. 30 *et seq.* EEC Treaty, Art. 95
Case 78/76, *Steinike und Weinlig* v. *Germany,* [1977] E.C.R. 595	German tax levied *inter alia* on domestic and imported fruit juices on their being processed into more elaborate products	EEC Treaty, Art. 95
Case 77/76, *Cucci* v. *Avez,* [1977] E.C.R. 987 Case 105/76, *Interzuccheri* v. *Rezzano e Cavessa,* [1977] E.C.R. 1029	Italian taxes levied on white sugar, whether home-produced or imported, the proceeds of which are used to finance a subsidy to Italian sugar industry	EEC Treaty, Arts. 13(2) & 95 Regulation no. 3330/74 of the Council
Case 89/76, *Commission* v. *Netherlands,* [1977] E.C.R. 1355	Fees for phytosanitary inspections charged by Dutch authorities on the export to other member states and third countries of plants and certain products of plant origin	EEC Treaty, Arts. 12, 16 & 30 *et seq.*
Case 5/77, *Tedeschi* v. *Denkavit,* [1977] E.C.R. 1555	Control over undesirable substances and products contained in feeding-stuffs	EEC Treaty, Art. 36 Council Directives nos. 70/524/EEC and 74/63/EEC
Case 52/77, *Cayrol* v. *Rivoira,* [1977] E.C.R. 2261	Restrictions on the importation into France of table grapes of Spanish origin put into free circulation in another member state	EEC Treaty, Arts. 30 & 115 Agreement between the EEC and Spain Regulation no. 2513/69 of the Council
Case 82/77, *Openbaar Ministerie of the Netherlands* v. *van Tiggele,* [1978] E.C.R. 25	Dutch regulation fixing minimum prices for the marketing of spirits	EEC Treaty, Art. 30 *et. seq.*
Joined Cases 80 and 81/77, *Commissionnaires Réunis* v. *Receveur des Douanes,* [1978] E.C.R. 927	Imposition by the French government on the basis of Art. 31(2) of Regulation no. 816/70/EEC of a tax on imported Italian wines	EEC Treaty, Art. 12 *et seq.* Regulation no. 816/70 of the Council, Art. 31(2)
Case 102/77, *Hoffmann La Roche* v. *Centrafarm,* [1978] E.C.R. 1139	Exercise by a manufacturer of pharmaceutical products of trademark rights in order to prevent the importation of products marketed in another member state and repacked for sale in the member state of importation by a third party.	EEC Treaty, Art. 30 *et seq.*

	NATURE OF THE MEASURES INVOLVED	PROVISIONS AT ISSUE
Case 142/77, *Statens Kontrol med Aedle Metaller* v. *Larsen,* [1978] E.C.R. 1543	Levy calculated on the basis of consumption of precious metal (imported or domestically produced) imposed by Danish law on undertakings, manufacturing, importing or dealing in articles of precious metal	EEC Treaty, Arts. 16 & 95
Case 154/77, *Procureur du Roi* v. *Dechmann,* [1978] E.C.R. 1573	Belgian regulation on fixing maximum prices for retail sales of beef, veal and pigmeat	Regulation no. 121/67 of the Council
Case 148/77, *Hansen* v. *Hauptzollamt Flensburg,* [1978] E.C.R. 1787	German tax legislation providing for exemptions and reduced rates of taxation in favour of certain domestic producers of spirits	EEC Treaty, Art. 95
Case 3/78, *Centrafarm* v. *American Home Products Corporation,* [1978] E.C.R. 1823	Exercise by the owner of a trademark registered in one member state of trademark rights in order to prevent attempts by a third party to import under the said trademark products marketed by the owner of the mark in another member state under a different trademark	EEC Treaty, Art. 30 *et seq.*
Case 13/78, *Eggers* v. *Freie Hansestadt Bremen,* [1978] E.C.R. 1935	Requirement imposed by a German legislative provision that an official designation of quality for spirits, which is indicative neither of origin nor of source, may be awarded only if one or more stages of the production process have been carried out on the German territory	EEC Treaty, Art. 30 *et seq.* Commission Directive no. 70/50
Case 7/78, *Regina* v. *Thompson,* [1978] E.C.R. 2247	Ban on the export from the UK of silver alloy coins, which have been legal tender in the UK, and the melting down or destruction thereof; ban on the importation of gold coins into the UK	EEC Treaty, Art. 30 *et seq.*
Case 83/78, *Pigs Marketing Board* v. *Redmond,* [1978] E.C.R. 2347	Northern Ireland regulation on the marketing of pigs prohibiting *inter alia* the sale of pigs otherwise than to the Pigs Marketing Board, an official body, and the transport of pigs otherwise than subject to the authorization of said Board	EEC Treaty, Art. 30 *et seq.*, 40 Regulation no. 2759/75 of the Council

NOTES

1. Cases 69 and 70/76, *Dittmeyer,* [1977] E.C.R. 321.

2. Ruling 1/78, [1978] E.C.R. 2151.

3. See, in first instance, Joined Cases 90 and 91/63 *Commission* v. *Grand Duchy of Luxembourg & Kingdom of Belgium,* [1964] E.C.R. 625, at p. 633 and more recently, Joined Cases 80 and 81, *Commissionaires Réunis* v. *Receveur des Douanes,* [1978] E.C.R. 927, at p. 945.

4. Case 63/74, *Cadsky,* [1975] E.C.R. 281; Case 87/75, *Bresciani,* [1976] E.C.R. 129; and Case 78/76 *Steinike & Weintig,* [1977] E.C.R. 595.

5. Case 7/68, *Commission* v. *Italy,* [1968] E.C.R. 423 and 429.

6. Case 177/78, Judgement 26th June 1979, unreported.

7. *Supra,* note 3.

8. Cases 77/76 and 105/76, *Cucchi* v. *Avez* and *Interzuccheri* v. *Rezzano,* [1977] E.C.R. 987.

9. For a useful discussion, see "The concept of measures having an effect equivalent to quantitative restrictions" 1977, European L. Rev., p. 105, by A.C. Page.

10. *Procureur du Roi* v. *B. & G. Dassonville,* [1974] E.C.R. 837.

11. *Ibid.,* at p. 852.

12. "The Customs Union: Today and tomorrow." Conference held in Brussels, 6, 7 and 8 December 1977. Paper by Dr. Pierre Schloesser, Deputy Director-General, Directorate General for Internal Market and Industrial Affairs.

13. Case 5/77, *Tedeschi* v. *Denkavit Commerciale,* [1977] E.C.R. 1555:

> 33 National measures regulating the composition of feeding-stuffs may in certain cases constitute measures having an effect equivalent to quantitative restrictions which are however capable, where they are justified by the protection of animal or human health, of coming within the application of Article 36 of the Treaty.
>
> 34 Article 36 is not designed to reserve certain matters to the exclusive jurisdiction of Member States but permits national laws to derogate from the principle of the free movement of goods to the extent to which such derogations is and continues to be justified for the attainment of the objectives referred to in that Article. (p. 1576)

14. Case 35/76, *Simmenthal Spa* v. *Italian Minister for Finance,* [1976] E.C.R. 1871.

15. Case 13/78, *Eggers* v. *Freie Hansestadt Bremen,* [1978] E.C.R. 1935, at p. 1956.

16. See *Simmenthal, supra;* also Case 104/75 *Adriaan De Peijper,* [1976] E.C.R. 613, at pp. 635 and 636.

17. Case 82/77, [1978] E.C.R. 25.

18. Case 83/78, [1978] E.C.R. 2347.

19. *Supra,* note 6.

20. *Supra,* note 18, at p. 2368.

21. Case 148/77, [1978] E.C.R. 1787.

22. Case 45/75, REWE, [1976] E.C.R. 202.

15

*The Trend to Subjectivism in English Criminal Law**

J. C. Smith

In this paper I propose to review recent developments in English law concerning one of the fundamental questions as to the nature of the fault required to give rise to liability for serious crime. Should we apply an objective or a subjective test? Should the defendant be treated as if he had foreseen all the consequences of his conduct which a reasonable man in his situation would have foreseen and as if he knew of all the circumstances which a reasonable man would have known? Or should the court or jury be required to attempt to ascertain what he in fact foresaw or what he in fact knew? Should the standards by which the defendant's state of mind is to be classed as criminal or lawful be the objective standards laid down by the law or the jury; or should the outcome depend on the defendant's own standards in the matter?

Because of the way in which the law has developed it is convenient to consider first the question of the defendant's foresight of consequences and then that of his knowledge of circumstances, before dealing finally with the matter of standards.

Foresight of Consequences

My starting point is the decision in *D.P.P.* v. *Smith*[1] in 1961. Some judges have professed to find difficulty in ascertaining the true meaning of this case[2] but to my mind it laid down a strictly objective test of foresight of consequences in the clearest possible terms. A police constable noticed some property in the back of a car which was stopped at traffic lights. Rightly suspecting the property to be stolen, the constable told the driver, the defen-

* This is an expanded and updated version of a paper delivered at the Conference in Cambridge of the Canadian Institute of Advanced Legal Studies on Tuesday, 17 July, 1979.

dant, to pull in to the nearside. When the lights changed, the defendant drove off. The constable jumped on to the car which pursued an erratic course until he was thrown off in the path of an oncoming vehicle and killed. The defendant was charged with murder. His defence was accident. Donovan J. directed the jury that if the defendant must as a reasonable man have contemplated that grievous bodily harm was likely to result from what he did and that death in fact resulted, the defendant was guilty of murder. He referred to the presumption that a man intends the natural consequences of his acts and did not tell the jury that the presumption was rebuttable. The defendant was convicted but the Court of Appeal quashed his conviction.[3] The question for the jury in their opinion was whether the defendant really did, during the relevant ten seconds, realise what was the degree of likelihood of serious injury, not whether a reasonable man would have done so; and, once the language of presumption was used, it was essential to explain that the presumption was rebuttable. The House of Lords restored the conviction for murder. Viscount Kilmuir with whom all their Lordships agreed said[4]:

> The jury must, of course, in such a case as the present make up their minds on the evidence whether the accused was unlawfully and voluntarily doing something to someone. The unlawful and voluntary act must clearly be aimed at someone in order to eliminate cases of negligence or of careless or dangerous driving. Once, however, the jury are satisfied as to that, it matters not what the accused in fact contemplated as the probable result or whether he ever contemplated at all, provided he was in law responsible and accountable for his actions, that is, was a man capable of forming an intent, not insane within the M'Naghten Rules and not suffering from diminished responsibility. On the assumption that he is so accountable for his actions, the sole question is whether the unlawful and voluntary act was of such a kind that grievous bodily harm was the natural and probable result. The only test available for this is what the ordinary responsible man would, in all the circumstances of the case, have contemplated as the natural and probable result. That, indeed, has always been the law. . . .

It would be difficult to find a clearer formulation of an objective test of foresight than that: " . . . it matters not what the accused in fact contemplated or whether he ever contemplated at all. . . ." But, to make the point, if possible, even clearer, the Lord Chancellor went on[5] to affirm that the presumption that a man intends the natural consequences of his acts is, in the case of a mentally normal person, irrebuttable.

> Whether the presumption is one of law or of fact or, as has been said, of common sense, matters not for this purpose. The real question is whether the jury should have been told that it was rebuttable. In truth, however, as I see it, this is merely another way of applying the test of the reasonable man. Provided that the presumption is applied, once the accused's knowledge of the circumstances and the nature of his acts has been ascertained, the only thing that could rebut the presumption would be proof of incapacity to form an intent,

insanity or diminished responsibility. In the present case, therefore, there was no need to explain to the jury that the presumption was rebuttable.

The decision provoked a storm of criticism.[6] The High Court of Australia was so outraged by it that they declared that they could not in future regard themselves as bound by decisions of the House[7]. To what extent the decision represented general judicial opinion in England it is difficult to say. A strong Court of Appeal (Byrne, Sachs and Winn JJ.) had firmly laid down a subjective test and Mr. Buxton's researches[8] suggest that trial judges took little notice of the decision and continued to direct juries in subjective terms—a course they could then take with impunity because we had not yet invented the machinery of the Attorney General's reference[9] which enables a too-favourable direction resulting in an acquittal by a jury to be challenged in the Court of Appeal, though the acquittal itself is still, of course, final.

What was not clear about the decision in *Smith* was whether it laid down a rule of the law of evidence, that is a rule about the proof of foresight generally, or a rule only as to the law of murder.[10] The language used was certainly capable of application throughout the criminal law with the effect that proof of actual foresight of consequences on the part of the defendant would never be required—everyone who was not mentally abnormal would be conclusively presumed to intend the natural consequences of his acts. The retreat from this position of extreme objectivity began almost immediately. The decision was held to have no application on charges of attempted murder,[11] causing grievous bodily harm with intent to do so or unlawful wounding.[12] It was not applied in any reported case other than a murder trial. The effect was that the decision acquired the appearance of a rule of the substantive law of murder, and this view was supported by the fact that *Smith* did require a subjective element of intention in one respect—"The unlawful and voluntary act must clearly be aimed at someone in order to eliminate cases of negligence or of careless or dangerous driving."[13] This suggested that once it was proved that the defendant in fact "aimed at someone" (as the jury presumably found that Smith did by attempting to shake off the constable) the only remaining test was as to the nature of the act.

The Criminal Justice Act 1967, Section 8

The decision was referred to the Law Commission who produced two recommendations[14]—first, that the *mens rea* of murder should be re-defined by statute and, second, that it should be made clear that there is no irrebuttable presumption that a man intends or foresees the natural consequences of his acts. Only the second proposal was accepted. It was enacted by s. 8 of the Criminal Justice Act 1967 which provides:

> A court or jury in determining whether a person has committed an offence,

a) shall not be bound in law to infer that he intended or foresaw a result of his actions by reason only of its being a natural and probable consequence of those actions; but
b) shall decide whether he did intend or foresee that result by reference to all the evidence drawing such inferences from the evidence as appear proper in the circumstances.

If, then *Smith* laid down a rule of the substantive law of murder, this section had no effect whatever on the decision. Section 8, as the courts have subsequently affirmed,[15] relates to *how* intention and foresight must be proved, not *when* they must be proved. In order to ascertain when intention and foresight must be proved we must refer to the definition of the particular offence; and, when we turned to murder, the leading authority was *Smith* which said that there must be an unlawful and voluntary act aimed at another person, but no foresight whatever beyond that. Surprisingly, this point did not seem to be appreciated by Parliament when it enacted s. 8, although distinguished members of the judiciary participated in the debate in the House of Lords[16].

It was assumed that the effect of the Bill was that *Smith* was being in some way reversed. The courts soon made the same assumption. Within a month of the section coming into force the Court of Appeal applied it in *R.* v. *Wallett.*[17] Since the section was not in force when the killing occurred the court must have considered that it made a change in the law of evidence, not in the substantive law. The judge had directed the jury that the defendant was guilty if he did the act, "knowing quite well at the time that he was doing something [which] any ordinary person like himself would know was doing her really serious bodily harm". The Court of Appeal held that this was a misdirection. The reference to "any ordinary person" was an error. The question, since s. 8 came into force, was no longer what any ordinary person would foresee was likely to be the result of an action but what the defendant actually foresaw. The problem of the construction of s. 8 was apparently not brought to the court's attention in that case but, when the law of murder was next considered by the House of Lords, the point was argued. In *Hyam* v. *D.P.P.*[18] the defendant, Mrs. Hyam, in order to frighten away a certain Mrs. Booth who was her rival for the affections of a man, put blazing newspaper through Mrs. Booth's letterbox and caused the death of two of Mrs. Booth's children. Ackner J. directed the jury as follows[19]:

The prosecution must prove, beyond all reasonable doubt, that the accused intended to (kill or) do serious bodily harm to Mrs. Booth, the mother of the deceased girls. If you are satisfied that when the accused set fire to the house she knew that it was highly probable that this would cause (death or) serious bodily harm, then the prosecution will have established the necessary intent. It matters not if her motive was, as she says, to frighten Mrs. Booth.

The question in the House of Lords was whether an intention to do an act knowing that it was highly probable that it would cause serious bodily harm was a sufficient *mens rea* for murder. By a majority of three to two the House held that it was and the conviction was upheld. The minority thought the direction wrong because the law of murder required foresight of danger to life, not merely serious bodily harm. Ackner J. had directed the jury to apply a subjective test so that this issue did not arise in the House of Lords. It seems clear, however, that the majority of their Lordships accepted that s. 8 required them to apply a subjective test and, though Lord Hailsham referred to the difficulties discussed above[20], none of their Lordships offered any explanation as to how this change in the law had been achieved. Viscount Dilhorne who, as Sir Reginald Manningham-Buller, the Attorney General, had argued successfully for the restoration of Smith's conviction in the House of Lords, seems to have considered that *Smith* may still represent the law.[21] On a true construction of the section, it is submitted that, if so, he was right; but, as a practical matter, we are now most unlikely to go back to it. *Hyam* lays down a strict law of murder but is at least subjective. However illogically, s. 8 is taken to have changed the law of murder. It has not changed the law of any other crime.

The Criminal Damage Act 1971

After the Criminal Justice Act 1967, the next significant step was the Criminal Damage Act 1971, replacing the Malicious Damage Act 1861. The 1971 Act was a product of the Law Commission, the body charged with the duty of reforming and codifying English law, and so it is likely to be the pattern for future legislation in criminal law. It is clearly stated in the Act that the mental element is intention or recklessness but these terms are not defined. There was some risk that "reckless" might be interpreted in an objective sense to mean gross negligence but in 1976 in *R.* v. *Briggs*[22] the Court of Appeal held that a man was reckless only if he did a deliberate act *knowing* that there was some risk to property. There is, however, a judicial reluctance to allow a man to escape liability for the natural and probable consequences of his acts and this emerged the following year in *R.* v. *Parker*[23]. The defendant attempted to make a telephone call from a public call box. He became irritated at his inability to get through. Twice he slammed down the receiver and on the second occasion he smashed the telephone. He was observed by a policeman. He said that he did not intend to damage the telephone and it did not occur to him that he might do so. The judge directed the jury that "a reckless act is one done without thought for the consequence of it". Parker's appeal, relying on *Briggs* and arguing that the judge had applied an objective test, was dismissed. The Court of Appeal pointed out that Parker was aware of all the circumstances; he knew that he was handling a bakelite receiver, that the cradle was of similar material and of the degree of force that he was using. The court asserted that, if he did not know there was some risk of damage, he was closing his mind to the obvious and that was the equivalent of knowledge. He could not escape liability for the consequences of his action by saying "I never directed my mind to the obvious consequences because I was in a self-induced state of temper." Accordingly the court added to the definition in *Briggs* so that it read:

> A man is reckless in the sense required when he carries out a deliberate act knowing *or closing his mind to the obvious fact that* there is some risk of damage resulting from that act but nevertheless continues in the performance of that act.

Now the concept of "wilful blindness" is well established in the criminal law and is indeed generally recognised to be the equivalent of knowledge.[24] It connotes that the defendant deliberately avoids finding out some fact, the existence of which he would prefer not to know. There are many ways of formulating the principle but one of the words, "wilfully", "purposely" or "deliberately" is almost invariably used. A man cannot deliberately refrain from ascertaining the existence of a fact without adverting to, at least, the possibility of its existence. It is not enough to attract the operation of the doctrine that the defendant ought to have known of the fact. If the possibility of its existence never crossed his mind he cannot be said to have been wilfully or deliberately blind or to have purposely abstained from ascertaining the existence of the fact. The man who is wilfully blind knows that there is at least the possibility that the fact may exist and he deliberately takes the risk.

The concept is perfectly satisfactory when applied to knowledge of facts; but the knowledge required by the test laid down in *Briggs* was not knowledge of a fact, it was knowledge of the existence of a risk. It is submitted that the doctrine of wilful blindness cannot properly be grafted on to that. A person cannot deliberately close his mind to the existence of a risk—as the court requires—without first knowing that there is a risk. The court disclaimed any intention to apply an objective test; yet the effect of their decision is that a man who knows that he is putting down a bakelite telephone receiver on a bakelite cradle with such force as, whether at that moment he realises it or not, is sufficient to break it *must* be taken to have deliberately closed his mind to the existence of the risk. This looks like the application of a subjective test as to the existence of circumstances and an objective test as to the knowledge of circumstances which is precisely the same as the doctrine of *D.P.P.* v. *Smith*, by now discredited.

Parker was heavily criticised and caused difficulties in the application of the law because of the difficulty—the writer would say impossibility—of reconciling it with *Briggs*. Naturally, it was not long before the issue came before a court again. In *Stephenson*[25] the defendant was convicted of arson, contrary to subss. 1(1) and (3) of the Criminal Damage Act 1971. The same test of intention or recklessness applies on a charge of arson as on any other charge of criminal damage. The defendant went to sleep in a straw stack. He felt cold and lit a fire within a hollow in the stack. Not surprisingly, the stack went up in flames and some £3,500 worth of damage was caused. The jury were directed as to the meaning of recklessness in the words used by the Court of Appeal in *Parker*.

There was evidence that the defendant had a long history of schizophrenia and may not have had the same ability to foresee or appreciate risk as a mentally normal person. The Court of Appeal quashed his conviction, saying that a man is reckless when he carries out a deliberate act, appreciating that there is a risk which it is unreasonable for him to take that damage to property may result from his act. The appellant, because of his mental condition, may not have appreciated the risk which would have been apparent to any normal person. The question was not clearly left to the jury to decide. If the defendant had been a mentally normal person it is possible that the conviction would have been upheld by the application of the proviso to s. 2 of the Criminal Appeal Act 1968;[26] but the direction would still have been wrong. The decision makes it clear that the defendant must know that there is a risk. The alternative to "knowing" stated in *Parker*, "or closing his mind to the obvious fact that . . .", could only mean that the defendant need not actually know that there was a risk of damage to property. It now appears clear that there is no alternative to knowledge of the risk. After the judicial hesitation in *Parker*, it seems clear that we have now returned to a purely subjective test of recklessness in the law of criminal damage.

The Principle Extended

Of course the possibility of further lapses such as that in *Parker* cannot be ruled out but it seems likely that *Stephenson* has now established the principle to be applied in all modern statutes using the word "recklessly" in relation to some forbidden result; but that is not the limit of its application. The same principle has now been held to apply to an offence under the Offences against the Person Act 1861 where the word which describes the *mens rea* is "maliciously". It has, of course, long been recognised that this word bears a technical meaning, far removed from its ordinary, popular meaning. In *Flack* v. *Hunt*[27] it was held that the principle of *Stephenson* is equally applicable to a charge of malicious wounding, contrary to s. 20 of the 1861 Act. The defendant, a gamekeeper, fired a shot into a bush with the intention of forcing a suspected poacher to come out of hiding. The man, who was concealed in a bush, was wounded. It was found as a fact that the defendant believed that there was no one in the line of fire or within range of the gun and he did not think there was any risk of causing direct physical injury to anyone. No doubt he intended to frighten. On these facts he was not reckless. *Stephenson* and *Flack* v. *Hunt* mark important steps towards a rational and consistent theory of *mens rea* in English criminal law.

The Exception for Intoxication

One exception to the subjective principle has become firmly established in our law through the decision of the House of Lords in *D.P.P.* v. *Majewski*:[28] where the defendant relies on evidence that he was intoxicated by drink or drugs voluntarily taken to show that he lacked the *mens rea* of the offence charged, that *mens rea* need not be proved, unless the crime is one requiring "specific intent" which is distinguished from "basic intent". This, the House decided, is a rule of substantive law and so not affected by s. 8 of the Criminal Justice Act 1967 which is concerned only with how intention or foresight must be proved, not when. Criminal damage, contrary to subs. 1(1) of the 1971 Act is not a crime of specific intent so that a voluntarily intoxicated defendant may be convicted of the offence although he neither intends nor foresees any damage whatever.[29] On the other hand, the aggravated offence under subs. 1(2) of the same Act, intentionally or recklessly damaging property, intending thereby to endanger life or being reckless whether life would be endangered, is a crime of "specific intent" and the intoxicated defendant who did not foresee danger to life may not be convicted of this offence.[30] If this is right it will be observed that a crime may be one of "specific intent" although the definition of the offence requires no element of intention; a sober defendant may be convicted under subs. 1(2) although he is only reckless whether he causes damage and only reckless whether he endangers life. This, however, is only one of many anomalies which may be pointed out in this branch of the law.[31] Though the point does not appear to have been articulated in any judgment, it is submitted that this principle of liability without *mens rea* for a crime of "basic intent" is applicable only where the defendant's act is such that any reasonable and sober person would foresee the consequences in question. In effect, an objective test is applicable.

A Statutory Exception

In an exceptional case, Parliament has gone back on the subjective principle. Of course it is and must be open under our constitution to Parliament to depart from even the most basic principle of law if it thinks it necessary to do so. The Race Relations Act 1965 created an offence of incitement to racial hatred and required an "intent to stir up hatred against any section of the public in Great Britain distinguished by colour, race or ethnic or national origins". The Race Relations Act 1976 replaced this provision by a new s. 5A of the Public Order Act 1936. The new offence consists in publishing written matter, or using in a public place words which were threatening, abusive and insulting where, "having regard to all the circumstances, hatred is likely to be stirred up against any racial group". We have here moved from a subjective to an objective test, Parliament's judgment being that this is necessary to cope with a particular—and, it is to be hoped, temporary—threat to the harmony of British society.

Reckless Conduct

Stephenson[32] and *Flack* v. *Hunt*[33] may be taken to have settled the law as to the meaning of the word "reckless" when it is used in the definition of a crime with reference to a particular result, such as damage to property or wounding. That principle cannot be applied in precisely the same way where the definition of the offence proscribes conduct but does not require that the conduct should have any particular result or any result whatever. The outstanding example of this in English law is reckless driving. A driver may commit this offence without causing any damage or injury of any kind. It is an offence which has existed in our law since 1930 but has been little used until very recent times. The reason is that the related offence of dangerous driving in the same section of the Road Traffic Acts was punishable with the same maximum of two years imprisonment and apparently easier to prove so that prosecutors naturally relied almost invariably on dangerous rather than reckless driving. Now the offence of dangerous driving has been abolished by the Criminal Law Act 1977 and the prosecutor must choose between driving without due care and attention (a relatively minor offence punishable on summary conviction with a maximum fine of £500 or, in the case of second or subsequent conviction, by imprisonment for a maximum of three months or a fine of £500 or both) and reckless driving.

It is clear that driving without due care is an offence of negligence in a strict sense requiring the defendant not merely to do his best but to achieve the standard of a competent and prudent driver. The nature of the fault, if any, required by reckless driving has not until recently been considered by the courts. The same statute applies in England and Scotland but, in the sphere of criminal law, the two legal systems are quite distinct. There is no appeal to the House of Lords from the Scottish courts in criminal matters. Unfortunately the two jurisdictions have taken divergent views about reckless driving. The matter came first before the Scottish High Court of Justiciary which in *Allan* v. *Patterson*[34] on October 24, 1979 applied, as it said, "a totally objective" test.

> Inquiry into the state of knowledge of a particular driver accused of the offence created by the section as amended and into his intention at the time is not required at all. The statute directs attention to the quality of the driving in fact, but not the state of mind or intention of the driver. . . . All that is in issue and all that Parliament requires the court or the jury to consider is the degree to which the driver in question falls below the standard to be expected of a careful and competent driver in all the circumstances of the particular case and whether the degree is such as properly to attach in the judgment of court or jury the epithet or label of "reckless".

In the English case, *Murphy*,[35] the trial judge told the jury that recklessly was an English word which he would not explain as the jury knew what it meant. When they returned for further guidance and asked whether driving in excess of the speed limit was the same thing as reckless driving he told them that it was not but that speed could be an element and repeated that recklessly was a perfectly standard English word. There was authority at the level of the Court of Appeal for this approach:[36] but it is easy to demonstrate that the word is capable of bearing more than one distinct meaning and different juries and benches of magistrates, if left without direction, would certainly put different meanings upon it. The Court of Appeal, though on looking at the direction as a whole they dismissed the appeal, held that it was not enough to leave it to the jury to give to the word recklessly whatever meaning they thought fit. The appellant argued that the jury ought to have been directed that it must be proved that he foresaw the risk of an accident and deliberately took that risk. The court would not go so far but it held that the test to be applied was subjective.

> A driver is guilty of driving recklessly if he deliberately disregards the obligation to drive with due care and attention or is indifferent as to whether or not he does so and thereby creates a risk of accident which driving with due care and attention would not create.

The court made no reference to *Allan* v. *Patterson* which had not been reported at the time of the decision. The English court clearly requires the jury or magistrates to attempt to look into the mind of the driver, recognising that this will usually be a matter of inference from the evidence as to the manner in which the vehicle was actually driven and as to road conditions—"but it will not always be so. There may be some other explanation, for example, a mechanical defect or an inadvertent failure to observe a traffic sign and so on". *Murphy* continues the trend to subjectivism in English law.

Recklessness and Knowledge

The judgment in *Murphy* raises a fundamental question about the nature of recklessness. ". . . when one speaks of something which a person knows, is one referring to knowledge which is stored in the brain and available if called upon or to knowledge which is actually present because it is called upon?" The court went on to prefer the former meaning. "We do not think that Parliament in using the word [recklessly] in a straight-forward way intended a meaning that would encourage such philosophical quibbles especially as everybody knows that there is a risk of an accident if a vehicle is not driven with due care and attention on the highway, whether he thinks about it or not." This is a matter on which academic lawyers differ and it is certainly not clear that the view preferred by the court in the context of reckless driving is true for other offences requiring recklessness. If, as in *Parker*,[37] a man is alleged to have recklessly damaged a telephone when he slammed it down in a temper should he have a defence where he says truthfully that at the time of incident it never crossed his mind that he might break the telephone but, in the detached atmosphere of the courtroom, he admits that he knows, and always knew, that a telephone is liable to break if it is forcefully slammed down? *Parker* clearly would answer this question in the negative but in the light of *Stephenson*[38] and *Flack* v. *Hunt*[39] it is no longer clear that this is the right answer. The Court of Appeal in *D.P.P.* v. *Smith*, it will be recalled,[40] asked whether the defendant, during the relevant ten seconds, realised that there was a risk of causing serious injury to the policeman. The man breaking the telephone is certainly guilty of negligence, even on the test most favourable to him, for he failed to observe the standards of care of which he himself was well capable; but he is being judged for what he did at that moment and he was not then taking a deliberate risk and thus did not incur that higher degree of culpability which is signified by recklessness. *Murphy* applies a peculiar meaning of recklessness for the purpose of the offence of reckless driving and has no necessary application in other crimes, particularly crimes which require that some specified result, such as damage or injury, be caused[41].

Knowledge of Circumstances

So far I have directed attention to the question of foresight of consequences. There is another, equally important aspect of *mens rea* and that is the defendant's knowledge of the circumstances in the definition of the offence. *D.P.P.* v. *Smith*[42] imposed strict liability for the consequences of an act and s. 8 of the Criminal Justice Act 1967 is confined to the results of an act; it says nothing about mistakes of fact. There is, of course, a necessary connection between certain circumstances and consequences.[43] It is because he is aware of the circumstance that a gun is loaded that a man who pulls the trigger knows that the person at whom the gun is pointed will be killed. It would make no sense to attempt to apply a different kind of test to this sort of circumstance from that applicable to foresight of consequences. If the test of foresight is subjective, so too must be the test for this sort of circumstance. Section 8 implicitly requires that a subjective test be applied to such circumstances. There are, however, other circumstances which have no bearing on the occurrence of the relevant consequences but are relevant to the legal effect of those consequences. The fact that the man at whom the gun is pointed is about to make a deadly and unlawful attack on the holder of the gun is an example. A killing occurs whether this fact exists or not; but its presence or absence alters the legal quality of the killing—it makes the difference between murder and justifiable homicide. Section 8 does not apply to circumstances of this kind.

In cases of mistake of fact the English courts have, even in serious offences, occasionally imposed strict liability, not requiring proof of even negligence. In *R.* v. *Wheat*; *R.* v. *Stocks*[44] in 1921 the Court of Criminal Appeal held that the defendant might be convicted of bigamy even if he believed on reasonable grounds that he had been divorced at the time of the second marriage ceremony. In 1968 that case was overruled by the Court of

Appeal in *R.* v. *Gould*[45] and, applying *R.* v. *Tolson*,[46] strict liability was replaced by liability for negligence; such a belief was defence only if held on reasonable grounds. As Cave J. put it, in a much-cited passage in his judgment in *R.* v. *Tolson*:[47]

> At common law an honest and reasonable belief in the existence of circumstances, which, if true, would make the act for which a prisoner is indicted an innocent act, has always been held to be a good defence.

Morgan's Case

The use of the word "reasonable" of course indicates an objective test. The rule that a mistake to be a defence must be reasonable has been commonly re-asserted in modern times by high authority; but it must now be looked at in the light of the decision in *R.* v. *Morgan*[48] which exposed its illogicality and demonstrated its limits. The defendant invited three younger men to his house and suggested to them that they should all have intercourse with his wife. The three were at first incredulous but were persuaded by the defendant's stories of his wife's sexual aberrations. He told them to expect some show of resistance but to ignore this since it was a mere pretence which stimulated her sexual excitement. All four men had intercourse with her. The three younger men were charged with rape and Morgan with aiding and abetting rape. There was a conflict of evidence. The wife testified that she strenuously resisted throughout in such a way that no one could have been in any doubt that she did not in fact consent to the three men having intercourse with her. They, on the other hand, described her co-operation and expressions of pleasure. If they were believed there was no doubt she consented to what took place; and their defence at the trial was that she consented. The trial judge[49] directed the jury as to the *actus reus* of rape and went on:

> Further the prosecution have to prove that each defendant intended to have sexual intercourse with this woman without her consent. Not merely that he intended to have intercourse with her but that he intended to have intercourse without her consent. Therefore if the defendant believed or may have believed that Mrs. Morgan consented to him having sexual intercourse with her, then there would be no such intent in his mind and he would not be guilty of the offence of rape, but such a belief must be honestly held by the defendant in the first place. He must really believe that.

Here then is an emphatically subjective direction. The defendant's intention must extend to the absence of consent so that, if he believed the woman was consenting, he was not guilty of rape. Immediately, however, the judge went on:

> And, secondly, his belief must be a reasonable belief; such a belief as a reasonable man would entertain if he applied his mind and thought about the matter. It is not enough for a defendant to rely upon a belief, even though he

honestly held it, if it was completely fanciful; contrary to every indication which could be given which would carry some weight with a reasonable man.

There is an obvious contradiction here of what has gone before. A man who believes, however unreasonably, that a woman consents to his having sexual intercourse with her does not intend to have sexual intercourse with her without her consent. Nevertheless the Court of Appeal held that the jury had not been misdirected and dismissed the appeals. By a majority of three to two the House of Lords held that the jury had been misdirected but they upheld the conviction under the proviso. The jury had clearly preferred Mrs. Morgan's evidence to that of the appellants and, in the light of that evidence, there could be no doubt that the appellants knew very well that Mrs. Morgan did not consent. In holding that the jury had been misdirected Lord Cross said:[50]

> . . . to include an intention to have intercourse whether or not the woman consents in the definition of rape and to say that a reasonable mistake with regard to consent is an available defence to a charge of rape are two incompatible alternatives which cannot be combined in a single direction to a jury—as incidentally, the judge combined them in one passage in his summing up in this case.

Lord Hailsham said[51]:

> Once one has accepted, what seems to me abundantly clear, that the prohibited act in rape is non-consensual sexual intercourse, and that the guilty state of mind is an intention to commit it, it seems to me to follow as a matter of inexorable logic that there is no room either for a 'defence' of honest belief or mistake, or of a defence of honest and reasonable belief and mistake. Either the prosecution proves that the accused had the requisite intent or it does not. In the former case it succeeds in the latter it fails. Since honest belief clearly negatives intent, the reasonableness or otherwise of that belief can only be evidence for or against the view that the belief and therefore the intent was actually held. . . .

Other passages in the speeches make it clear that it was enough that the defendant was indifferent whether the woman consented or not.

The decision provoked something of an outcry largely because it was imperfectly understood. The matter was referred to an Advisory Group by the Home Secretary under the chairmanship of Mrs. Justice Heilbron which reported[52] that the principle of the case was correct and it was then embodied in the Sexual Offences Amendment Act 1976, subs. 1(1):

> . . . a man commits rape if
>
> (a) he has unlawful sexual intercourse with a woman who at the time of the intercourse does not consent to it; and
>
> (b) at that time he knows that she does not consent to the intercourse or he is reckless as to whether she consents to it. . . .

So far as the law of rape is concerned then, the decision in *Morgan* is of no further significance in the law of England. In the criminal law of

England generally it is of the greatest importance for it does for *mens rea* with respect to the material circumstances of an offence precisely what s. 8 of the Criminal Justice Act 1967 does for consequences or results in the definition of the offence. Section 8 and *Morgan* together establish that a failure to foresee consequences, whether reasonable or not (s. 8) or a failure to know of circumstances, whether reasonable or not *(Morgan)* which negatives the *mens rea* of the offence charged requires acquittal. The decision is subject to the same limitation as s. 8: it does not affect the *mens rea* required for any offence (except, of course, rape). Its general importance relates to *how mens rea* must be proved, not *when* it must be proved. In order to determine what *mens rea* must be proved we must always first turn to the definition of the offence whether it is contained in a statute or is a common law offence to be derived from judicial decisions. So the decision does not affect offences of strict liability; the law does not require proof of any *mens rea* with respect to one or more circumstances in such cases. Nor does it necessarily affect cases such as *Tolson*[53] which decided that, on a charge of bigamy, the defendant's honest *and reasonable* belief in the death of her first husband was a defence. None of their Lordships was prepared to say that the law of bigamy was not correctly stated in *Tolson* and, from the point of view of the majority, this must be on the basis that bigamy is a crime of negligence so far as the element, "being married", is concerned. Lord Fraser was quite prepared to accept the logical result, that "bigamy does not involve any intention except the intention to go through a marriage ceremony"[54]. If the defendant is in fact married and he ought to know this, then he is guilty. Lord Hailsham saw *Tolson* (previously long regarded as a seminal case on *mens rea*) as "a narrow decision based on the construction of a statute which prima facie seemed to make an absolute statutory offence, with a proviso, related to the seven year period of absence, which created a statutory offence".[55]

Coupled with *Morgan* is the decision in *R.* v. *Smith (D.R.)*[56] that the ordinary principles of *mens rea* require that intention or recklessness must be proved as to all the elements of the offence. The defendant, a tenant, removed certain fixtures which he had installed in the demised premises, thereby damaging property which belonged to his landlord. Being ignorant of the civil law relating to fixtures, he said that he believed that the property which he damaged was his. The judge directed the jury that this belief was no defence to a charge under s. 1 of the Criminal Damage Act 1971. The conviction was quashed. James L.J. said:

> Construing the language of s. 1(1) we have no doubt that the actus reus is 'destroying or damaging any property belonging to another'. It is not possible to exclude the words 'belonging to another' which describe the 'property'. Applying the ordinary principles of mens rea, the intention and recklessness and absence of lawful excuse required to constitute the offence have reference to property belonging to another. It follows that in our judgment no offence is committed under this section if a person destroys or causes damage to prop-

erty belonging to another if he does so in the honest though mistaken belief that the property is his own, and provided that the belief is honestly held it is irrelevant to consider whether it is a justifiable belief.

The application of these "ordinary principles of mens rea" to bigamy would of course require the reversal of *Tolson*; and that case stands as a decision that, in this respect, bigamy is a crime requiring not *mens rea* but negligence.

A Case of Strict Liability?

There is one serious common law offence in which, arguably, strict liability survives. This is the crime of blasphemy. In *R.* v. *Lemon*[57] the first blasphemy prosecution for 75 years was brought against the editor and publishers of a magazine, the readership of which consisted mainly of homosexuals. They published a poem which purported to describe in explicit detail acts of fellatio and sodomy with the body of Christ immediately after his death and ascribing to Christ during his lifetime promiscuous homosexual practices with the Apostles and other men. The defendants were convicted and their conviction upheld by the Court of Appeal and by a majority of three to two in the House of Lords. The view taken by the trial judge in his direction to the jury, by the Court of Appeal and by the majority of the House of Lords is that the law of blasphemy requires proof that the defendant intended to publish the words which he in fact published and no other mental element is necessary. The only remaining question is whether those words constitute a blasphemous libel. The dissenting judges, Lords Diplock and Edmund-Davies, held that the prosecution must also prove that the defendant knew that the publication would, or would probably, shock and insult those holding Christian beliefs. Their view was that the effect of the decision of the majority is that blasphemy becomes an offence of strict liability. The majority were insistent that this was not so.

There is no universally accepted criterion of what amounts to strict liability. The offence committed in what is, in England, regarded as the leading case on strict liability, *R.* v. *Prince*[58], requires proof of a substantial mental element and is "strict" as to one element only, namely the age of a girl (in fact under 16) who is taken out of the possession of her parent without his consent. It may be misleading to say—as is often loosely said—that offences of strict liability "require no *means rea*" for they do require a limited degree of *mens rea.* It is necessary to resort to first principles. The *actus reus* of an offence is the legal definition of the evil which it is the object of the law to prevent. It is proof of *mens rea* which makes the defendant responsible in law for causing that *actus reus*. The principle, it is submitted, on which a man is held responsible for serious crime is that, when he acted, he knew that the evil in question would or might follow from his act; that is, he intended the evil or was at least reckless whether it should occur. If he did not foresee it but ought as a reasonable man to have done so, he may, in exceptional cases, be liable for negligence. It was this general principle that the minority were applying in *Lemon.* The evil to be prevented by the crime of blasphemy is the offence and insult to believers. If the publication has no tendency to shock, insult or outrage it is a lawful publication and not a blasphemous libel. This tendency, then, is the gist of the offence. If a man who is unaware of it is liable to be convicted of blasphemy then he is held no less strictly liable than a butcher who sells meat which, though he neither knows nor has reason to know it, is unfit for human consumption. No one doubts that the latter case is one of strict liability. In both cases there is an intention to deal with the particular thing. In neither case is there awareness of that tendency which alone makes the dealing with the thing criminal. Only by the same fallacious reasoning can it be held that there is an intention to do something forbidden by law[59].

(1) D intends to sell this meat (or to publish this writing).
(2) This meat is unfit for human consumption (or this writing is blasphemous).
(3) Therefore D intends to sell meat unfit for human consumption (or to publish a blasphemous libel).

If the case of the butcher is one of strict liability, so is that of the publisher. Of course, the unfitness of the meat may be undiscoverable by anyone but an analyst, whereas it may be that anyone who could read and understand the words would realise instantly that they would shock and outrage Christians. This, however, merely shows that, in the circumstances posed, it would be easier to prove the *mens rea* on the blasphemy charge than in the case of the sale of the tainted meat. Far from being a ground for not requiring *mens rea,* it demonstrates that there is none of that necessity which is sometimes urged as the justification for strict liability.

It should be noted that the view of the minority did not go so far as to require that the alleged libel be an "attack" on Christianity nor would they have allowed the defendant's alleged worthy motives as such to be a defence. A publisher might have wholly admirable motives of giving comfort to homosexuals and yet still be guilty under the test laid down by the minority, if he knew that the publication would, or was likely to, give offence to Christians generally. It is submitted therefore that the majority did indeed impose strict liability, that the opinion of the minority is to be preferred, and that the decision is something of a setback in our progress towards a rational and consistent theory of *mens rea.*

Subjective Standards

Standards Fixed by Parliament

So far I have been concerned with foresight of consequences or knowledge of facts; and I have argued that the trend to applying subjective tests is right. I now turn to a different matter where I have grave doubts about the desirability of the trend. There is a number of instances in which it has been decided, sometimes by Parliament and sometimes by the courts, that the defendant's liability should turn on whether he has complied, not with some objective standard fixed by law, but with his own standards in the matter. At first sight, at least, the new offence of blackmail created by the Theft Act 1968 is an example of this. Subsection 21(1) provides:

> A person is guilty of blackmail if, with a view to gain for himself or another or with intent to cause loss to another, he makes any unwarranted demand with menaces; and for this purpose a demand with menaces is unwarranted unless the person making it does so in the belief—
> (a) that he has reasonable grounds for making the demand; and
> (b) that the use of the menaces is a proper means of reinforcing the demand.

It will be noted that the test is not whether the defendant has in fact reasonable grounds, but whether he believes he has; not whether the use of the menaces is proper but whether he believes it is. The peculiarity of this provision is that the defendant's belief relates not to matters of fact (which is common enough) but to his belief in standards. The provision, while still in the form of draft bill, was forcefully criticised by a distinguished judge, Sir Bernard Mackenna.[60]

> If a defendant has acted disgracefully by making a certain demand reinforced by threats of a particular kind, I see no injustice in holding him responsible in a criminal court, even though he may have acted according to his own standard in these matters. On the other hand I see some danger to our general standards of right and wrong, if each man can claim to act according to his own, however low that standard may be. That is one objection. Another is the difficulty of the jury's ascertaining the defendant's standard, so that it may be decided whether in the case before them he acted in accordance with it. A man whose standard is below the general may fail in a particular case to observe even his own standard in which event he would, I suppose, be punishable under clause 17 [now section 21]. But are questions of this kind triable?

A case can be made for the introduction of an element of objectivity into this section[61] but no case has yet decided that it should be done and the opinion that it is the defendant's own standards which provide the criterion for his guilt or innocence is not merely tenable but is the most obvious interpretation. If that is right, the provision would justify a terrorist who holds another to ransom and who says truthfully that, according to his lights, the demand was reasonable and the use of the menaces proper. In most cases no doubt there would be other offences available, such as kidnapping, but it would not seem right that the law of blackmail should be governed by the standards of the fanatic making the demand with menaces.

The second legislative example is under the Criminal Damage Act 1971 para. 5(2)(b) which provides that a person who has damaged property belonging to another has a lawful excuse if he did so in order to protect other property and

he believed
(i) that the property, right or interest was in immediate need of protection; and
(ii) that the means of protection adopted or proposed to be adopted were or would be reasonable having regard to all the circumstances.

Subsection (3) states that

> For the purposes of this section it is immaterial whether a belief is justified or not if it is honestly held.

Thus the defendant must be acquitted of criminal damage if he thought the measures taken to protect property were reasonable, even if this was not in fact the case. If, instead of protecting property, the defendant were protecting the person, whether his own or another's, then the standard of reasonableness applied under the existing law would be an objective one; so that if D were, by the use of unreasonable force, to kill P's dog which was attacking him, it would not be an answer to a charge of criminal damage that he thought the force used was reasonable to save himself from being bitten in the leg but it would be a defence that he thought it was reasonable to save his trousers from being torn. This is impossible to justify. If the principle in the Criminal Damage Act is a sound one it ought to be extended to defence of the person.

The principle is, however, open to the same kind of objection as that discussed in connection with blackmail. It allows the standards of the fanatic to decide whether he is subject to the criminal law. If he honestly believes that it is reasonable to blow up an oil refinery because the fumes it emits are damaging his prize geraniums he is immune from liability for criminal damage. If the same principles were applied to offences against the person it would exempt the crank who thought it was reasonable to kill to keep trespassers off his premises.

Standards fixed by the courts

The contribution of the courts to extension of subjectivity to standards has come through their interpretation of the word "dishonestly," a key word in much of the criminal law relating to theft and related offences. An important development took place in *R. v. Feely*[62] in 1968. The Court of Appeal there held, in effect, that the meaning to be attributed to the word "dishonestly" in s. 1 of the Theft Act 1968 was not a question of law to be decided by the judge but one for the jury, applying the "current standards of ordinary decent people".

This decision has been forcefully criticised but it did at least lay down an objective standard to be fixed by the jury in the particular case. The court went further in the case of *R. v. Gilks*[63] where the defendant was overpaid by a bookmaker and took and kept the money knowing that it was more than he was entitled to under the terms of the wager. Gilks agreed in evidence that if his grocer overpaid him it would be dishonest to keep the money but, he said, bookmakers are "a race apart" and he thought there was nothing dishonest about keeping the money in this case. The judge invited the jury to "try and place yourselves in Gilks's position at that time and answer the question whether in your view he thought he was acting dishonestly." The jury either disbelieved Gilks's evidence that he thought there was nothing dishonest about what he did or they took no notice of this direction because they convicted him. The Court of Appeal said that in their view the judge's direction was proper and sufficient. They did not say, as they might have done in upholding the conviction, that it was too favourable. It was not a direction to apply the "current standards of ordinary decent people" but the defendant's own standards and it is possible that the jury might have thought the defendant's standards below those which ordinary decent people apply. It might be thought that this was merely an oversight on the part of the court but, subsequently, the Divisional Court in *Boggeln* v. *Williams*[64] expressly rejected an argument that the defendant's belief in his own honesty was irrelevant and held that, on the contrary, it was crucial. The defendant whose electricity supply had been cut off reconnected the supply through the meter so that the electricity he used was still recorded. He knew that the supplier of the electricity and owner of the meter did not consent to his doing so but he notified them and believed, not unreasonably, that he would be able to pay at the due time. It was held that the crucial question was whether the defendant believed that his conduct was honest.

It may be that on any test Boggeln would have been found by the jury not to be dishonest but it is easy to envisage cases in which the defendant's standards of honesty fall far below those of the community generally. If such a person is to be acquitted of dishonesty it is indeed a case of "everyman his own legislator". It would justify a modern Robin Hood if he were to tell the court that he took Peter's money to pay Paul because Peter is very rich and Paul is very poor and he, Robin, does not consider it dishonest to redress the economic balance in this way. If a belief that bookmakers are "a race apart" is to be allowed as a defence it will not be long before bookmakers are a race apart and are denied the protection of this part of the criminal law. Where do we go from there? There are those who believe that Jews are a race apart. Experience in the armed services will reveal that there are those who think there is nothing wrong with taking small—and sometimes not so small—items of government property; and the same attitude is thought to be not uncommon in large commercial and industrial organisations. These misguided beliefs do not necessarily amount to a defence under the principle of *Feely* for the magistrates or jury may be expected to find that they fall short of the current standards of ordinary decent people; but if *Boggeln* v. *Williams* is followed the defendant must be acquitted unless the court or jury is satisfied that the defendant did not really hold the belief.

It is submitted that in these instances parliament and the courts have carried the subjective principle too far. It is the business of the law to lay down standards and to require the community to observe those standards. It is right to apply a subjective test to ascertain the defendant's knowledge of material facts and foresight of consequences but once these have been ascertained they should be judged by an objective standard applicable to all persons alike except of course in cases such as infancy and insanity.

The Future

There are hopeful signs for the future. In 1978 the Law Commission published its "Report on the Mental Element in Crime"[65] to which is appended the "Draft Criminal Liability (Mental Element) Bill". This Bill provides precise definitions of intention, knowledge and recklessness in subjective terms. It would establish a presumption that offences established after a date to be laid down require intention, knowledge or recklessness as to all the elements in the definition of the crime. Unlike s. 8 of the Criminal Justice Act 1967 and unlike *Morgan* it would go not merely to how intention, knowledge and recklessness must be proved but when they must be proved. The Bill would, of course, leave it open to Parliament to provide for strict liability (as in the case of race relations) or negligence liability in cases in which it considered that the public interest required it; but Parliament would have to direct its mind to the point and specifically so provide. This is as yet only a draft bill. There is still much conservatism to be overcome and many battles to be fought before it becomes law. The definitions of intention and recklessness may well prove controversial, but they have now received support from the Criminal Law Revision Committee in their Fourteenth Report on Offences against the Person[66]. In paragraph 9 the Committee states:

> 9. The term 'intention' is used in so wide a variety of circumstances and has so variable a meaning in the criminal law that we can understand (though we do not necessarily share) the disquiet which some may feel at the introduction of a single definition of that term and of 'recklessness' to be applicable throughout the law. Even if there are good grounds for this disquiet, they do not in our opinion apply to the proposal we make for the definition of these terms for the purposes of the relatively narrow area of offences against the person. We have carefully scrutinised their application in each of the proposed offences and Ministers and Parliament would no doubt do the same before they were passed into law. Once enacted for offences against the person, the workability and the advantages of the definitions would in the course of time, we believe, encourage their adoption in other legislation and indeed in the construction of other statutes in which the definitions were not expressly incorporated.

Flack v. *Hunt,*[67] decided after the committee signed the Report, adopted a view of recklessness substantially in accord with that in the Report and this seems a good omen for the acceptability of the part of the Report.

NOTES

1. [1961] A.C. 290, at p. 303.

2. *Hyam* v. *D.P.P.,* [1975] A.C. 55, at p. 71.

3. [1961] A.C. 290, at p. 297.

4. [1961] A.C., at p. 327.

5. *Ibid.*, at p. 331.

6. See, especially, Williams, "Constructive Malice Revived" (1962), 23 M.L.R. 605; Salmon J. "The Criminal Law Relating to Intent" (1961), 14 C.L.P. 1; Cross, "The Need for a Re-Definition of Murder", [1960] Crim. L.R. 728; Lord MacDermott "Murder in 1963", *Presidential Address to the Holdsworth Club* (University of Birmingham, 1963).See also, Denning "Responsibility before the Law" (1961), Hebrew University Press; Prevezer, "Recent Developments in the Law of Murder" (1961), 14 C.L.P. 16; Smith, [1960] Crim. L.R. 765; Travers and Morris, "Imputed Intent to Murder or *Smith* v. *Smyth*" (1961), 35 A.L.J. 154.

7. *Parker* v. *The Queen* (1963), 111 C.L.R. 610, 632-3; revd on another ground (1964), 111 C.L.R. 665. See [1963] Crim. L.R. 675.

8. "The Retreat from Smith", [1966] Crim. L.R. 195.

9. See Criminal Justice Act 1972, s. 36.

10. See the discussion by the writer in "Intention in the Criminal Law," (1974), 27 Current Legal Problems 93.

11. *R.* v. *Grimwood*, [1962] 3 All E.R. 285.

12. *Wilkins* v. *An Infant*, [1965] Crim. L.R. 730.

13. *Supra*, note 4.

14. See The Law Commission, "Imputed Criminal Intent (Director of Public Prosecutions v. Smith"), HMSO, 1967.

15. *D.P.P.* v. *Majewski*, [1976] 2 All E.R. 142, at pp. 151, 170.

16. 283 H. of L. Official Report 248-253.

17. [1968] 2 Q.B. 367.

18. [1975] A.C. 55.

19. *Ibid.*, at p. 65. Ackner J. explained that he put brackets round the words "kill" and "death or" because he advised the jury to concentrate on the intent to do serious harm rather than the intent to kill.

20. *Ibid.*, at pp. 69-71.

21. "I see no reason to review [the House's] decision in *D.P.P.* v. *Smith* on the questions raised in this case. No question here arises of any objective or subjective test, for the jury must be taken to have found that the appellant knew it was highly probable that serious bodily harm would be caused."

22. [1977] 1 All E.R. 475.

23. [1977] 2 All E.R. 37. See commentary at [1977] Crim. L.R. 103.

24. See Edwards, *Mens Rea in Statutory Offences*, pp. 194-205.

25. [1979] 3 W.L.R. 193.

26. "Provided that the Court may, notwithstanding that they are of opinion that the point raised in the appeal might be decided in favour of the appellant, dismiss the appeal if they consider that no miscarriage of justice has actually occurred."

27. (1980), 70 Cr. App. R. 51.

28. [1976] 2 All E.R. 142.

29. *R.* v. *O'Driscoll* (1977), 65 Cr. App. R. 50.

30. *Orpin*, [1980] Crim. L.R. 304.

31. See Smith and Hogan, *Criminal Law* (4th ed.), pp. 185 *et seq.* and authorities and articles there cited.

32. *Supra*, note 25.

33. *Supra*, note 27.

34. [1980] R.T.R. 97, especially at p. 101 and see [1980] Crim. L.R., at p. 312.

35. [1980] Crim. L.R. 309.

36. *R.* v. *Cato*, [1976] 1 All E.R. 260, where the Court of Appeal held that a judge correctly refrained from explaining the meaning of the word reckless in the definition of manslaughter at common law: "After all, recklessness is a perfectly simple English word. Its meaning is well known and in common use. There is a limit to which the judge in summing up is expected to teach the jury the use of ordinary English words." There is indeed a limit, but it is by no means easy to define where it should be drawn.

37. *Supra*, note 23.

38. *Supra*, note 25.

39. *Supra*, note 27.

40. *Supra*, note 3.

41. On the question discussed in this paragraph generally, see *Bello*, [1978] Crim. L.R. 551 and commentary with authorities referred to.

42. *Supra*, note 1.

43. For the writer's earlier discussion of this distinction see "Two Problems in Criminal Attempts" (1957), 70 Harv. L. Rev. 422 and "Intention in Criminal Law" (1974), 27 Current Legal Problems, at pp. 103-106.

44. [1921] 2 K.B. 119.

45. [1968] 2 Q.B. 65.

46. (1889), 23 Q.B.D. 168.

47. *Ibid.*, at p. 181.

48. [1976] A.C. 182.

49. *Ibid.*, at p. 187.

50. *Ibid.*, at p. 203.
51. *Ibid.*, at p. 214.
52. Cmnd. 6352, 1975.
53. *Supra*, note 46.
54. [1976] A.C., at p. 215.
55. *Ibid.*
56. [1974] Q.B. 354.
57. [1979] 1 All E.R. 898.
58. (1875), L.R. 2 C.C.R. 154.
59. See Devlin, "Statutory Offences" 4 J.S.P.T.L. (N.S.) 206, at p. 212.
60. "Blackmail: a Criticism", [1966] Crim. L.R. 467, at p. 472.
61. See Smith, *Law of Theft* (4th ed.), paras. 323-330.
62. [1973] Q.B. 530.
63. [1972] 3 All E.R. 280.
64. [1978] 2 All E.R. 1061.
65. Law Com. No. 89.
66. Cmnd. 7844.
67. *Supra*, note 27.

16

Policy Factors and the Law of Tort

B. S. Markesinis

Introduction

American scholars have, for some time now, been arguing that "the courts cannot and should not escape taking into consideration in the determination of tort or other cases the interests of 'we the people' at large, or important groups whose interests are identified within the interests of the social order".[1] This "third phase" of the judicial process, which goes far beyond the interests of the immediate parties to the litigation, is dominated by wider considerations of policy which, until recently, were deliberately obscured behind such elusive concepts as duty, unlawfulness, *faute*, foreseeability, remoteness and the like.

In England, ideas not dissimilar to these have, from time to time, been echoed by a number of academics.[2] Dennis Lloyd, for example, in his monograph on *Public Policy* argued that it is "difficult to resist the conclusion that the law of tort has been developed by the English judges very largely on the basis of their feelings as to what the public interest demands".[3] Yet, he excluded from the scope of his comparative monograph the law of torts on the ground that it was only in the law of contract that judges (both in England and France) were prepared to admit *openly* that their decisions were based on public policy.[4] His reasons for this omission, valid some 25 years ago, seem to have lost some of their force since, in recent years, certain members of the judiciary have become increasingly willing to refer to various reasons of "policy", the "public interest", the "demands of society" etc. when formulating their judgements.

This "judicial legislation or interpretation founded on the current needs of the community"[5] is, undoubtedly, helping develop both the civil law and the common law and bring it in tune with the economic and social demands of our times. However, differences in judicial styles,[6] as much as anything else, make it difficult to find in civil law *judgements* the type of explicit and, it is submitted helpful, pronouncements that one can find in many modern common law decisions (though in France the annual reports of the Cour de Cassation, submitted to the Garde des Sceaux since 1968, throw a great deal of light on the importance the supreme court attaches to these wider policy factors in its attempts of adapt the law to the demands of modern society). But, whether admitted or not, considerations of wider policy and social advantage play a decisive role in the determination of a quantitatively small but qualitatively crucial number of cases. Discovering and evaluating these policy factors involves an inquiry into, amongst other things, the whole method of judicial thinking and style. It is thus a topic which does not lend itself to facile generalisations; nor is it within the scope of this work. Yet, it is desirable to look, however briefly, at some of these policy factors which appear to have played an unusually important role in the determination of negligence litigation. Three reasons can be advanced for this.

One reason for wishing to bring into the open some of the policy reasons which lie behind these judgements is the belief that this can lead to a more intelligent discussion of the real issues involved. A second reason is purely didactic since a policy-orientated approach can help students realise that the various concepts they encounter in their books and in judgements are often little more than verbal devices, "means of formulating conclusions"[7] but not the reasons that dictate them. This in turn can help students appreciate the considerable equivocation that exists between many of these concepts; and it can also minimise their use—especially in circumstances where it is clear that they have become little more than judicial fictions. (The term "foreseeability" immediately springs to mind as a most apposite illustration of such use.) For present purposes, however, the most important reason for emphasizing this policy-orientated approach is the belief that it can facilitate the comparison of the various legal systems. For it can prevent the student from adopting a barren comparison of different abstract concepts and encourage him, instead, towards a functionally-orientated method of examination of the different legal systems.

Two additional observations must be made at this stage. The first is that it would appear that nowadays lawyers seem to have recourse to these policy factors whenever their aim is to *limit* rather than *expand* delictual liability. Since in the law of torts in general and the law of negligence in particular the crucial problem is that of limitation of liability, the study of policy reasons that help achieve this goal thus acquires an added dimension. The above is increasingly true of the common law and, in many instances, of German law as well. French law, on the other hand, already broader in its conception of delictual liability than the other two systems, appears to be utilising broader policy arguments in order to extend its law of delict even further. The decisions of the Chambre mixte of the late 1960's and early 1970's bear witness to this tendency and, as the court itself put it in its annual report to the Garde des Sceaux of 1975, ". . . la Cour marque aujourd'hui moins d'hésitation et prend moins de temps que par le passé, à revenir sur telle ou telle décision de principe, dès lors qu'il lui apparaît que cette décision n'est plus adaptée à l'évolution générale des moeurs, de l'ordonnancement social ou des institutions". Secondly, to return to the common law, policy may intervene to prevent the imposition of *all liability* or, it may affect the right of a *particular plaintiff* to recover, or to recover a *particular item of loss*. Different concepts are, more often than not, used to give effect to these different aims but here, for reasons of space, we shall concentrate on the first aspect of this problem.

A Closer look at Some of These Policy Factors

It could be argued that amongst the most frequently encountered policy factors are the following: the "administrative factor"; the "superior value" factor; the "environmental" factor and the "insurance" factor. None of them are mutually exclusive and, more often than not, there is considerable overlap.

The "Administrative Factor"[8]

Courts, especially though not exclusively in countries with uncodified systems, are notoriously fearful of the risk of being flooded by large numbers of claims—some of them, no doubt, fictitious—which the legal and economic system would not be able to support. This is what MacCormick[9] calls a "consequentialist" type of argument and it is not limited to negligence actions only. It could, for example, be argued that the gradual erosion of the imaginative rule in *Rylands* v. *Fletcher*[10] is, surely, as much due to the traditional dislike of the idea of no liability without fault as it is to the fear that the new right of action might, if not carefully circumscribed, get out of control.[11] The courts' treatment of nervous shock and economic loss, however, offers better and more appropriate examples of how such fears can help defeat claims.

The number of persons who can suffer some form or other of mental distress through seeing or hearing an accident can be clearly greater than the number who can be injured in the accident itself hence the anxiety of the courts both in common law and civil law jurisdictions to find effective means of keeping potential liability under control. "As a policy decision this may be intelligible. In a small crowded island (like England), on whose 200,000 miles of road some seven or eight thousand people are killed every year, and another 100,000 are seriously injured, it is obvious that many people must witness some very distressing scenes on the roads. . . . It would probably be undesirable to attempt to compensate all those who suffer some small degree of distress, even if some slight pecuniary loss were suffered as a result—for instance if a person witnessing an accident had to go home and lie down for the afternoon instead of going to work. Certainly the claims of such a person must have a low priority when it is remembered that thousands of victims with physical injury go uncompensated every year because they are injured in accidents not caused by negligence."[12] To this problem the "impact theory,"[13] widely accepted by common law systems, originally provided a crude but effective solution. But, as the social pressures to increase the number of persons entitled to claim damages grew, and the "impact theory" was progressively questioned, the search for new means of control intensified. For English lawyers, the answer seemed to lie in the use of the concept of duty and foreseeability.[14] The advantage of such an approach is that it involves the use of known concepts which are flexible enough to yield the desired results; and it also confers an *appearance* of consistency since it gives the *impression* that whenever a person can foresee damage to another (be it physical injury or mental distress) he is under a duty to take care. These advantages, however, are bought at the price of using these notions in an extremely artificial manner which prevents the intelligent discussion of the true policy issues that lie behind these cases. So, for example, our courts appear to have been more concerned to prevent such actions in general getting out of hand—and in the process imposing arbitrary limitations—than to try to distinguish between the more serious consequences of shock (such as were experienced in *Bourhill* v. *Young*)[15] which deserve compensation, from the more trivial forms of distress which are commonly experienced by the witnessing or hearing of tragic accidents. One wonders, however, if the time has not come to say that if the plaintiff, as a result of the defendant's conduct, has suffered some kind of serious and "recognizable psychiatric illness"[16] he should be allowed to recover damages irrespective of his relationship with the victim, his physical position at the time of the accidents, or even his personal propensities towards such type of injury.[17] Indeed, the law may be slowly moving in that direction.

The fear that a chain reaction of claims may follow an isolated negligent act has been voiced even more strongly in cases of pure economic loss. This anxiety lay behind the rule in *Winterbottom* v. *Wright*[18] and was echoed in *Donoghue* v. *Stevenson* by Lord Buckmaster when he said; "If one step, why not fifty?"[19] Perhaps, too much has been made of this consequentialist' argument since it is, after all, the function of the courts to draw the line and distinguish the deserving from the undeserving case. But however over-emphasized this fear may be, it has, nevertheless, been voiced with some measure of frequency during the last 15 years in important "economic loss" cases both in England and in Germany. In *Weller & Co.* v. *Foot and Mouth Disease Research Institute*,[20] for example, Lord Widgery stressed the fact that in an agricultural community (such as the one involved in this case) the escape of foot and mouth virus could be a tragedy which could foreseeably affect *almost every* business in that area. Yet how decisively this fear weighed in his mind and led him to decide the case in favour of the defendants can be only a matter of conjecture since he cautiously added that such fears "should not be allowed to deprive the plaintiffs of their rights".[21] In *Spartan Steel and Alloys, Ltd.* v. *Martin & Co. (Contractors), Ltd.*[22], on the other hand, Lord Denning M.R. was more forthright. ". . . if claims for economic loss were permitted for this particular hazard, there would be no end of claims. Some might be genuine, but many might be inflated, or even false. A machine might not have been in use anyway, but it would be easy to put it down to the cut in supply. It would be wellnigh impossible to check the claims. . . . Rather than expose claimants to such temptation and defendants to such hard labour . . . it is better to disallow economic loss altogether, at any rate when it stands alone, independent of any physical damage."[23]

Whatever the value of such fears, the fact is that they are voiced not in this country alone. So, for example, in one of the leading "cable cases" in Germany, the courts had to decide whether Art. 18 III of the Baden-Wurttemberg Building code (a local by-law) was a *Schutznorm*, *i.e.*, a rule intended to protect an individual against the infliction of pure economic loss. This was necessary since the claim was based, *inter alia*, on para. 823 II BGB. The Court of Appeal held that the by-law was not a *Schutznorm*. In the absence of a clear legislative indication to the contrary, the Federal Supreme Court refused to assume that 'Art. 18 III entitles individual electricity consumers to compensation claims for which no provision is made by the general stipulations, *particularly in view of the fact that this would be bound to result in a considerable and unreasonable extension of liability*'.[24] A year later the BGH,[25] once again, relied on this type of "consequentialist" argument. The facts were very similar to those of the earlier case though this time the argument proceeded on a different basis. The negligent worker was here employed by a local body and had been warned against the risk of damaging submerged electricity cables. Since all earlier attempts to found a claim in tort (based on either para. 823 I or 823 II BGB) had been, for a variety of reasons, repeatedly rejected by the Federal Supreme Court,[26] the plaintiff, in this case, tried to put his claim on a contractual basis. His argument was that the worker had, by ignoring the warning given him, breached his contract with his employer. It was further contended that this contract should be treated as one with "protective effects with regard to third parties," including the plaintiff. The court rejected this argument adding that if the plaintiff's contention was correct then not only he but a further 1300 plus electricity consumers, who had been affected by the same incident, should be allowed to recover. However, to ascribe protective effects to a contract *vis à vis* so many persons was clearly absurd, not only because it would be overstretching the notion of contract to intolerable limits; but also because it would be indirectly undermining the broad policy of the Code not to recognise (outside the normal boundaries of contract) the compensability of pure financial harm.

In *Rondel* v. *Worsley*,[27] one finds yet another and, for present purposes, the last illustration of this policy factor though formulated in an interesting variation. The "opening of the floodgates" argument is to be found emphasized in varying degrees in some judgements[28] but policy appeared to militate against the plaintiff in another, and stronger way. For the judges were not only anxious to spare the courts from other, *similar*, actions but also eager to shield them from the otiose task of having to re-try the *same* case. As Lawton J. put it at first instance: "many who have been convicted of criminal offences and who had unsuccessfully exhausted all their rights to appeal would seek, maybe years later, to get a retrial by means of action for negligence against the advocate who had defended them. There would be no end to litigation."[29] This argument must have carried a great deal of weight in the Court of Appeal for its members opted for a more radical solution to the problem before them by holding that this was a situation where policy prevented the rise of *any* duty of care. The alternative approach, proposed by the plaintiff's solicitor,[30] that a duty should in principle be recognised to exist and the control of the court limited to an investigation in each case whether it had been breached, was thus rejected, presumably on the ground that it was a less efficient measure for giving effect to the courts' decision of policy. The case is therefore interesting not only because it illustrates how policy (and the administrative factor in particular) can be openly invoked to decide a particular claim; but also because it shows how (and why) the courts decide through which abstract concept they will exercise their controlling function.

The "Superior Value" Factor

A prime concern of any legal system is the protection of certain things (tangible or not) which are of value to human beings. Not all these things can have the same value; nor can they always be given efficient protection against all invasions. A hierarchy is thus dictated by moral, economic and other considerations with the result that the law affords better protection to the better things in life. We can, in fact, "see how highly the legal system rates a thing by checking how much protection the law gives to it relatively to other good things. We know, for example, that liberty is more highly rated than property because habeas corpus is a better remedy than detinue. We know that the integrity of a person is more important than the integrity of property because the victim of assault can claim from the Criminal Injuries Compensation Board whereas the victim of theft cannot, and because you must have insurance against liability for causing personal injury with your car but need not have insurance against liability for causing property damage. The carrier by air must pay more for killing or injuring a passenger than he need pay for losing or damaging his property; and since he need pay nothing at all for mere financial loss, as by delaying the passenger or his property, we can infere that wealth is in fact rated lower than property or person. This last point is evident also from the fact that taxation, or the imposition of financial loss, is more acceptable than expropriation, or the taking away of property. It is clear also from the relative strength of the remedies which protect tangible property, namely conversion and detinue, as compared with the remedies for unjustified enrichment.''[31] This kind of hierarchy, which is not necessarily immutable, not only determines the degree of protection afforded to the various interests; it also resolves potential clashes between them. A few examples can show how this kind of reasoning, concealed behind abstract legal terminology, has often dictated the outcome of negligence litigation.

This first example comes from France and it involves a clash between the idea of ''sanctity of marriage,'' which every civilised society accepts as one of its cornerstones, and the right to be indemnified for loss suffered as a result of another person's harmful conduct (Art. 1382 C.C.). In France this clash reached quite considerable proportions and, perhaps, one could even say that no other system has felt so strongly in its law the effects of fluctuations in ideas about marriage and extra-marital relationships. The reasons for this last-mentioned phenomenon, quite widespread in practice, are far too complex to relate here but may, paradoxically, be partly due to the simultaneous idealisation and repression of women during the peak of the romantic movement in the nineteenth century. For, in practice the flowering of the romantic ideal separated rather than brought closer together man and wife, while the Catholic Church preaching an austere conception of marriage with the procreation of children as its main if not sole aim, unwittingly contributed to adultery becoming what a distinguished scholar has described as an ''almost inevitable'' institution.[32] Such adulterous relations had some bearing on the criminal law and some parts of the civil law (mainly family law, legitimisation and, to a lesser extent, the law of succession) but, on the whole, left the law of civil responsibility untouched. The position, however, was very different in the case of more permanent relationships with ''kept women'' *(concubinage)*, for here serious financial loss could be proved by such women when deprived through accidents of the financial support of their paramours. Initially, such claims were tolerated (so long as the relationship was long and the damage ''certain'')[33] but by the early 1930's fears were expressed that such extra-marital cohabitations were on the increase and that compensation of mistresses only helped undermine the sanctity of marriage.[34] This ''hommage posthume au concubinat'' as Josserand branded it in 1932 was, to him at any rate, legally indefensible and represented ''la victoire du fait sur le droit, de l'union libre sur l'union lêgitime''.[35] Five years later Josserand, who by then had joined the Cour de cassation, was able to give effect to these ideas by prompting the Supreme

Court to adopt his views and to deny a mistress' claim for compensation on the grounds that she did *not* possess and "intérêt légitime juridiquement protégé".[36] This requirement that the plaintiff's claim be "juridiquement protégé" was clearly a gloss on the basic text (Art. 1382 C.C.) introduced solely in order to frustrate the mistress' claim and it was not until 1970 that this extraneous requirement was excised, no doubt under the pressure of altered social and economic conditions.[37]

The clash between property and its free enjoyment on the one hand and the right to be indemnified for damage caused by such uninhibited use of land offers a different and equally interesting setting for potential clash of values. Nowadays such a competition has a frightening ring about it though more and more people would, almost certainly, be inclined to favour the latter value rather than the former. But in days gone by, and certainly during the eighteenth and nineteenth centuries the balance was often tipped in favour of property and its free exploitation. For it was felt that any other solution would, above all, place a heavy burden on business by obliging land owners to incur great expense in order to take preventive action. Though not without force, especially in its day, this argument is nevertheless, unsatisfactory in so far as it implies that the courts would expect landowners to ensure the safety of entrants rather than take reasonable precautions to protect them against injury. No doubt, control through the concept of reasonable care would have meant a more flexible standard, lower perhaps in the nineteenth century, higher in the twentieth. But, as in *Rondel* v. *Worsley,*[38] the courts obviously felt that the concepts of reasonableness or careless breach of duty were not as effective a way of bolstering the prevailing policy as was the complete denial of any duty in the first place. It was thus not until the early 1970's when as a result of a considerable change in the environment, the harsh rule towards trespassers was finally overruled. Lord Reid frankly acknowledges this when he declared that "legal principles cannot solve the problem (of child trespassers). How far occupiers are to be required by law to take steps to safeguard such children, must be a matter of public policy;[39] and Lord Pearson openly referred to the changes in the social environment which, in his opinion, dictated the abandonment of the old, harsh, rule.[40]

A not dissimilar clash of competing values can be found in the development of the doctrine of abuse of rights in French law—particularly in the area of the so-called "troubles de voisinage".[41] In France this term covers the ground which the common lawyers include in their law of nuisance. For the common lawyer, with his forms of action abolished only the other day, the emphasis is, understandably, on the wrong rather than the right; and it also reflects his suspicion of hollow declarations of rights unaccompanied by effective remedies. But to the French (and, indeed, the civilian) eyes what is in issue in these cases is the proper ambit of *ownership* and not the personal duty of a neighbour not to commit a delict of encroachment. The subject is thus treated in the section of property where one finds in Art. 544 C.C. a definition of ownership[42] which is modelled on the lines of the Roman law concept of *dominium* and which in its absolute character reflects the aspirations of an era which treated private selfishness as a public virtue. So conceived, the right of ownership inevitably predominated over the other important right—the right to be indemnified for harm culpably caused—enshrined in Art. 1382 C.C.

This situation could not, in fact, last for ever and, surprisingly, the break with the past came earlier than one might have expected.[43] The way the change was affected was also, to some extent, predestined. For if a system (for example, the English) avoids conferring rights in broad terms, the need for controlling their limits is not felt so strongly. But if rights are conferred in sweeping terms, the control of their excessive and antisocial use becomes imperative. A notion of abuse of rights becomes almost inevitable and the first way of fixing the limits of the permissible use of rights was by making their malicious exercise actionable. The decision of the Court of Colmar in 1856[44] marked this turning point and the idea was subsequently enshrined in the famous *Schikanverbot* of the German Civil Code.[45] But it did not go far enough since it is rare that a man will act out of sheer spite or malice in order to hurt his neighbour; more often than not he may be trying, like the defendant in *Mayor of Bradford* v. *Pickles*,[46] to put pressure on the plaintiff which, though it may not bring the defendant immediate benefits, is clearly calculated to benefit him in the long run. A further step had thus to be taken and when it was, the emphasis was switched further towards Art. 1382 C.C. This was, in fact, quite easy to achieve once attention was concentrated on the abnormal character of the defendant's exercise of his right. Of course, one still had to find a suitable test for determining what was normal and what was abnormal, but academics were quick to come up with suggestions. The most elaborate of those proposed came from Josserand[47] and, though no longer widely accepted,[48] it earned itself a quite unique reputation. According to it, every right has its own spirit and every act which is consistent with this spirit is normal; all other acts are abnormal. Rights, in other words are not absolute but relative or, to use a more English terminology, they are more in the nature of powers of which the repository is a trustee. Of course, some rights are in, Josserand's terminology egotistical, established in the interest of those persons on whom they are conferred; and property rights should be classed in this group. To exercise them without malice was, of course, essential; but was this "minimum" requirement sufficient? With the passage of time it was felt that it was not. But the further search of a solution within the context of the social aims or objectives of the right of property was unpalatable, especially since its socialistic flavour had quickly earned it some influential enemies.[49] The answer was finally to be found in the standard of behaviour of the hypothetical *bon père de famille*; if he would not have exercised his right in this way neither should the defendant do so with impunity.[50] The integration with the fault system of Art. 1382 C.C. was now complete. Indeed, in the context of the "troubles de voisinage" the courts moved even beyond liability based on fault to stricter forms of liability determined by what can be reasonably tolerated in neighbourly relations.[51] The final outcome of the cases is thus nine times out of ten quite similar to that reached by common law courts in similar circumstances and, indeed, as the number of dicta that are prepared to take into account bad motives increase in the English law,[52] the similarity of *results* may spread from "neighbour disputes" to other areas of the law of torts. But in terms of technique the two systems are poles apart and will remain so for as long as English law (unlike French law) chooses to place the emphasis on the commission of a "wrong" rather than the existence of a "right". That the techniques are diametrically opposed can be shown clearly by two cases which cry out for comparison. In *Christie* v. *Davey*[53] the defendant, annoyed by his neighbour's piano lessons, started to produce loud noises with the intention of making life intolerable for the neighbour (plaintiff). The defendant's malice was decisive in characterising the disturbance to the plaintiff as unreasonable. In a parallel French case[54] the defendant hired an orchestra to play loudly near his neighbour's boundary whenever the latter organised a hunting party on his own land. His bad motive was used to characterise the exercise of his right as abusive and he was then held liable. The comparison of these two cases is interesting not only because the same results were achieved in what were substantially similar factual situations but also because they demonstrate that whenever nuisance is linked to fault fault plays a different role in each system: in France it characterises the defendant's conduct as "abusive"; in England, in view of the fact that in nuisance one looks at the effect on the plaintiff and not the defendant's conduct, fault is an element which, taken with others, may render unreasonable what might otherwise be regarded as reasonable.

The "Environmental" Factor

Though there is clearly a considerable overlap between this and the previous policy factors, in this present type the emphasis is not so much on "moral" or "value" considerations but on the exigencies of the economic environment. Once again, lawyers and judges have, on the whole, avoided mentioning these factors in public and, instead, have chosen to conduct their argument on the basis of abstract concepts and legal doctrine. But unexpressed though these considerations may be they are there nevertheless. Indeed, few are the cases which, once stripped of their legal technicalities, do not reveal the environmental forces that dictated their outcome. Leon Green, for example, has analysed *Rylands* v. *Fletcher*[55] as a case having to decide which of two industrial users of land (the milling or the mining industry) should bear the loss of the type of hazard encountered in that case.[56] Analysed in such a way the case can only produce the result actually reached by Blackburn (and the House of Lords) not only because the surface industrialist alone could provide protection for the mine beneath; but also because to decide otherwise would be tantamount to striking a severe blow to the mining industry and, in the nineteenth century, to harm the mining industry would be to harm England. Such an analysis is attractive but, displaying as it does concern for loss-spreading ability and accident preventive procedures it could be accused of telescoping into the nineteenth century ideas and methods of reasoning more appropriate to the twentieth. On the other hand, there is no evidence to suggest that judges did not think in this way even though they did not openly express it in judgements which were more anxious to appear to be relying on analogies. And comparison with the eastern United States at that time would lend *some* indirect support for this for, as Green, once again, has observed, ". . . in a new country like Atlantic seabord, where industrial enterprise was just getting on its legs and where water storage was so important for its uses, it is quite understandable that American courts should reject the doctrine (of *Rylands* v. *Fletcher*) as unsuitable to our economic situation".[57] It was thus only after the economic and industrial environment changed that the *Rylands* v. *Fletcher* doctrine came to be accepted and, in some instances, even to be extended.

It could be argued that a similar concern for the land-owning classes encouraged the common law to adopt the varying and confusing standards of care owed by occupiers of land towards lawful entrants.[58] The emphasis on the plaintiff's status rather than on the nature of the defendant's land, the risks attendant to it, and his ability to prevent them, was clearly in tune with the economic demands of the time and the desire not to hinder or burden the free exploitation of one's property. But it also gave judges the extra bonus of being able to control the findings of juries on the issue of carelessness by enabling them, through the "proper" characterisation of the plaintiff, to raise or lower the standard of care due to him. With the passage of time, however, the vagueness if not outright artificiality of these distinctions became an asset which judges were prepared to utilise in response to the exigencies of a changed economic and social environment. The use of the "implied licence" concept thus became the "most palpable fiction ever employed in order to impose legal responsibility"[59] and recently Lord Denning openly admitted the utility of such fictions as a means of avoiding the rigidity of the old law.[60]

The law related to industrial accidents and workers' compensation can provide us with our last example of environmental factors influencing the development of the law of torts. In the rise and fall of the doctrine of "common employment" we can find a neat illustration of these forces at work.[61]

Priestley v. *Fowler*[62] is commonly regarded as the *fons et origo* of this doctrine[63] though this must be qualified before being accepted. For, first, there is nothing in the plaintiff's declaration about an act of another servant; instead the attempt is to make the employer liable for breaking his own duty to provide a safe conveyance. Secondly, since at this period of time the tort of negligence has not yet acquired a foothold in English law, the case could not really have been decided in tort. Certainly, counsel for the plaintiff argued his case on the basis of an implied term in the contract of employment; Chief Justice Shaw, in the almost contemporaneous decision in *Farwell* v. *Boston & Worcester Railroad Corp.*,[64] spoke the language of contract; and subsequent decisions rationalised the immunity on the basis of an implied term in the contract of employment.[65]

At this juncture, the comparative lawyer can pause for thought. A moment's reflection will remind him that about this time French lawyers, too, started to experience similar problems. In those days actions against employers had to be brought under Art. 1382 C.C. and this requires the plaintiff (employee) to prove his employer's (defendant's) fault which was (and is) more often than not, impossible. For practical purposes, therefore, French law was very close to English law; for, though it recognised the existence of a "duty" in tort (if we may use the English terminology) it did not accept easily its careless breach. Progressive lawyers tried to avoid this result—iniquitous as far as the workmen were concerned—by trying (unsuccessfully) to expand the contents of the contract of employment by implying in it a term of "security" and "safety" for the benefit of the worker.[66] The point at issue is not identical to that considered in the above-mentioned cases of the common law; but the cases do show how, in the absence of an "amenable" law of tort, civilian lawyers are tempted to expand their law of contract in order to afford a remedy to "deserving" plaintiffs.

But let us return to *Priestley* v. *Fowler*.[67] In his judgement Lord Abinger had no doubt that the plaintiff's claim should fail; the consequences of deciding the case otherwise were too horrible even to contemplate. In fact he gave a series of hypothetical instances to illustrate the multiplicity of actions that might ensue from the adoption of a different rule. These examples have been selected from an "engagingly domestic"[68] scene and the author of the standard monograph on "Employer's Liability" wonders whether Lord Abinger's mind was not dwelling at that moment on his own immense household as master of Inverlochy Castle near Ben Nevis![69] Of course, one should not carry this kind of thinking too far. Roscoe Pound,[70] for example, has warned against the danger of explaining such decisions *solely* by reference to the conscious or unconscious desires of the economically dominant class of the time. But there seems little doubt that the immunity, once accepted, could be transplanted into the industrial context and there become a potent shield for employers against all legal consequences of industrial accidents. In *Hutchinson* v. *York, Newcastle & Berwick Ry.*,[71] Alderson B. did precisely this and it is hard to believe that this and the other cases that followed do not reflect a conscious decision *to allocate the risk* in such cases in the *economically* most suitable manner.

The result was harsh on poor workers; and some judgements reveal this preference for strong economic logic to any feelings of compassion.[72] But the decision was harsh not because it refused to hold the employer liable but because the welfare system was pitifully inadequate. For, if the social welfare system works properly, it can even today be argued that "broader social responsibility" is preferable to one which taxes a particular industry for the claims of its workers.[73] Of course, which of these two possibilities is preferable, in economic and political terms, is not relevant for present purposes.

Industrial accidents posed similar problems for the civil law. In France, attempts to improve the lot of workers through the law of contract met with little success with the courts and for the better part of the nineteenth century the possibilities offered by Art. 1384 C.C. remained unused. In a decision delivered in 1870,[74] for example, the Chambre civile of the Cour de cassation refused to apply Art. 1384 C.C. to a case involving the explosion of a boiler installed in a laundry and, instead, insisted that recovery in such cases depend upon the plaintiff producing evidence of the defendant's fault. Commenting on this decision in Sirey in 1871,[75] Labbé let the cat out of the bag by admitting that the case simply could not have been decided otherwise. Industry, he argued, had its dangers, but it also benefited the community at large which should therefore carry such risks. The implication is, once again, that one should not hamper unduly the gradual industrialisation of the country. Those who favoured greater protection for the working classes were still very much in the minority and the pressure for legislative reform remained weak throughout the first two decades of the life of the Third Republic. But by the end of the century increased mechanisation and a steady growth of industrial accidents demanded some modification in the approach and, through the medium of more efficient insurance, industry was becoming increasingly able to shoulder such risks. Equally important, perhaps, is the fact that this is the era of the growing strength of the socialist movements which began to generate strong pressures on the Parliaments of the day to intervene. In actual fact, the change came first from the courts[76] and some 30 years later M. le Conseiller le Marc'Hadour, in the celebrated *Jand'heur* case, admitted that this was the result of the "nécessité chaque jour plus impérieuse de protéger l'ouvrier contre les consequences des accidents survenues au cours du travail".[77] And, lest France should be regarded as being backward with other European countries, he added: "Déjà, à l'étranger des lois speciales avaient réglé la matière des accidents du travail; la jurisprudence française ne pouvait d'être impressionnée par des tendances qui correspondaient à un souci évident de justice sociale. . . ." Incidentally, the admiring reference to foreign legislation (the English Compensation Act of 1897 and the German laws of the 1870's and 1880's) is partly misconceived, for Professor Kahn-Freund amongst others has shown that the prime purpose of this legislation—which was based on inquiries which the German Consulate in London made in voluntary schemes established by the trade unions in this country—was not meant to assist the German workers but to "take the wind out of the sails of the Social Democracy" by satisfying in advance some of its more pressing demands.[78]

The "Internal Balance of the Code" Factor

Lon Fuller has pointed out that judges are "confronted by a problem of system. The rules applied to the decision of individual controversies cannot simply be isolated exercises of judicial wisdom. They must be brought into, and maintained in, some systematic interrelationship; they must display some coherent internal structure."[79] This need to interrelate results is both strong and obvious in codified systems, where the outcome of a particular case may often be determined or justified by the structure of the Code. In such cases to sanction a result other than that actually reached would disturb the internal balance of the Code and run counter to the wider policy decisions embodied in it. The various rules on cumulation of contractual and delictual actions, invariably worked out by courts and jurists rather than by legislatures, offer a very good illustration. The German rule allowing cumulation of actions is, for example, very largely the result of paras. 253 and 847 BGB and the German attitude towards damages for pain and suffering *(Schmerzensgeld)* which are only available in tort actions.[80] To prohibit cumulation would, for example, be tantamount to holding that a negligent driver would be liable to pay such damages to an injured pedestrian (suing him in tort) but not to his injured passenger (who would normally sue him in contract). Yet the driver's conduct amounts to a breach of contract as well as tort and to allow the passenger to sue in tort means allowing him to recover for pain and suffering which he would not be allowed to claim if he were suing in contract. Such a solution is, in practice, just and perfectly acceptable in a system such as the German which provides only for impossibility for performance and delay but not for positive breaches of contracts and thus clearly envisages the possibility of contractors suing each other in tort.

The opposite solution obtains in French law where most authors accept the principle on *non cumul des actions*. Once again,the internal structure of the Code makes this solution desirable if not, indeed, inevitable. The reason for this is that Art. 1382 C.C. is extremely wide and Art. 1384 C.C. is extremely strict. To allow cumulation in such circumstances would sap the law of contract of all its contents since every breach of contract could be treated as a tort. "The same risk does not arise in West Germany or the Common law where economic harm, the typical consequence of the typical breach of contract, gives rise to no liability in tort if it is caused by mere negligence. Thus in Germany admission of concurrence still leaves much to the exclusive regulation of the law of contract." "In France on the other hand, the admission of concurrence would have a very different and much more serious effect, for it would mean the effective abolition of the special rules of contractual liability except in so far as they benefited the victim only."[81] Secondly, the admission of concurrence would, in effect, make such persons as doctors and bailees liable to the patients and their bailors respectively under Art. 1384 C.C. and this would be clearly contrary to the kind of duty imposed on such persons by the law which is invariably an *obligation de moyens* rather than an *obligation de résultat.* It is, therefore, necessary for French law to prevent recourse to the articles on delict by reserving those articles to the exclusive use of strangers or third parties.

The internal structure of the code argument can also be found in some of the economic loss cases in Germany. Thus in the leading "cable case" mentioned earlier[82] the Supreme Court did not allow compensation for pure economic loss under para. 823 II BGB by refusing to hold that the violation of an article of a building statute of Baden-Wurttemberg gave a right of action to factory owners affected by a power cut which was the result of damage to a near-by electricity cable. To do so, reasoned the court, would be tantamount to allowing a *state legislator* to sanction the recovery of pure economic loss despite the contrary provision of the basic, Federal, enactment (para. 823 I BGB). This could clearly not have been in the mind (or the competence) of the state legislator and this was therefore an additional argument in favour of the view that the violated rule (Art. 18 III of the Baden-Wurttemberg Building Code) was not a *Schutznorm.*

To a common lawyer the above-mentioned policy factor may sound unduly restrictive—in so far at any rate as it ties down developments in the law to the pre-arranged structure of the Code. To some extent this is correct though, on the other hand, one should not take the civil codes too seriously since often those who have to live under them do not. Thus, for example, 'the French courts have so disturbed the balance between Arts. 1119 and 1120 of the Code as to make the recognition of third party rights in contract normal instead of exceptional, as was assuredly the intention of the compilers. The German Code, too, has received some mauling at the hands of the courts, and that too before the two world crises had placed an exceptional strain on it. Thus, the courts allow a debtor to charge his stock-in-trade in favour of a creditor without actual delivery, and without the registration which English Law would require for a bill of sale. This is certainly *contra legem.* The old practice, permitted by Roman law, of alienating a thing by *constitutum possessorium, i.e.,* by attorning to the alienee, has maintained itself in defiance of para. 1205 BGB, which insists that a pledge be accompanied by a transfer of physical possession to the pledgee. This may not worry common lawyers unduly, but the Germans are certain that the Code is being at least evaded. However, the principal way of evading inconvenient provisions of the Code is to have recourse to other provisions which establish what Professor Gutteridge once called super-eminent principles, such as para. 242 BGB, which provides that the performance of an obligation must be in accordance with the requirements of good faith, having regard to business usage. Obviously such a provision enables the courts to cut through many difficulties by operating on the conscience of contracting parties as the old Chancellors would have done in similar circumstances. And the courts have taken advantage of it especially in relation to the repayment of mortgage debts in inflated currency and in the handling of frustration cases.'[83]

The Insurance Factor

It is a well known fact that insurance companies nowadays meet the vast majority of claims for damages for personal injury and death.[84] It is not surprising, therefore, that liability insurance has had a great impact on the law of tort which, at the very least, is now obliged to reconsider familiar problems in a new perspective. So much we can say without any hesitation. But it is less easy to be precise as to the exact way in which this influence is manifested given a certain reluctance on the part of judges to make public what they may well be thinking in private. Certainly English, and for that matter French and German, legal theory has it that the presence or absence of insurance should have no bearing on the imposition of liability in the case actually before the judge. Viscount Simmonds, for example, has expressed himself clearly in this respect in two leading tort cases[85] and legal orthodoxy would, undoubtedly, be on his side. It would be idle, however, to deny that judges are not aware of the fact that defendants are insured, particularly against third party traffic risks and just as futile to pretend that the law has not altered to take into account the spreading of insurance practice. But in the United States they have gone even beyond such simple "awareness" and many courts and authors would agree that "if loss administration rather than deterrence is the principle aim (of the law of torts) . . . then lack of insurability should be considered an important factor in *its own right* and also a reflection of the difficulties that face enterprises forced to become self-insurers by the unavailability of insurance on the market".[86]

Professor Tunc has spoken in the same vein: "Les problèmes de responsabilité civile" he wrote a few years ago,[87] "ne doivent . . . plus être envisagés comme s'ils se posaient entre deux individus. La plupart du temps, aujourd'hui, l'assurance en transforme les donné. Et si la solution d'un procès ne peut guère dépendre du fait que l'une ou l'autre des parties soit assurée . . . ce serait condamner le droit à un contenu singulièrement artificiel que ne pas en élaborer les règles en tenant compte, selon les circonstances, de ce qu'une catégorie de personnes a la possibilité de s'assurer, ou est couramment assurée ou même est obligatoirement assurée." The same is now true in some of the Scandinavian systems where a distinguished member of the Danish Supreme Court has said extra-judicially that in his country judges while expressing themselves in terms of fault, are actually thinking in terms of who is in a better position to bear the risk.[88]

This *open* approach has yet to acquire respectability in this country[89] even though many of the controversial cases lend themselves very easily to such an analysis. The "cable cases", for example, can be approached either in the conventional, abstract, way (presence or absence of duty; remoteness etc.) or they can be seen as deciding who is in the better position to bear the risk they involve. To put it differently, the answer to these cases can be made to turn "on the practicability of insurance against various types of risk, whether of loss or liability, which can only be described in the policy in general terms. If, for example, it is a practical proposition for a business to insure against 'loss of production, however, caused', there would be more to be said for a general rule of non-liability for such losses than if it is in practice necessary to specify the causes of any loss of production covered by the policy."[90] In fact, consequential losses of the kind suffered by the plaintiffs in these "cable cases" have come to be regarded as usual insurable risks, and loss insurance rather than liability insurance seems to be more practicable and economical.[91] It is, therefore, not surprising that the courts have so far resisted the temptation to extend tort liability to this type of situation. Whether insurance was the dominant consideration when they reached these conclusions is, however, difficult to say since they have given little away in their judgements.[92] But, as Professor Atiyah has pointed out, "whatever motives have actuated the courts, there seems no doubt that their instincts have been sound".[93]

There are other instances which show that a particular plaintiff may, for reasons of insurance, be regarded as a better loss distributor. Though not openly acknowledged, this factor may, nevertheless, have influenced the courts to decide against liability for water companies who failed to keep their water pressures up and thus contributed to the spreading of fires.[94] Similar reasons lie behind the so-called "New York fire rule" "which exempts tortfeasors (usually railroad companies) from liability for all but the first building set alight"[95] though, once again, open acknowledgement of this is more than lacking.[96] Finally, to give one last example, this time from France. The more modern tendency of the Court de cassation to make, where possible, each and every member of a group liable *in solidum* for the damage caused by one of them who cannot be discovered, can also be attributed to modern insurance practice. Originally, none of the members of the group were held liable and this was explained by reference to the theory of *conditio sine qua non* which was the theory of causation which prevailed at that time. Then the courts changed their policy and had recourse to a multitude of causal and non-causal concepts to justify this change. It is only rarely however that one finds an open allusion to the insurance factor which must have played a dominant role in this judicial *volte face*.[97]

By contrast we find some acknowledgement of the insurance factor in some recent road accident cases, probably because here insurance is compulsory. In *Launchbury* v. *Morgans*,[98] the majority of the Court of Appeal were prepared to incorporate insurance arguments in their attempt to expand the area of responsibility in total disregard to the traditional reticence on the subject though the House of Lords in that same case was much more cautious. In *Nettleship* v. *Weston*[99] Lord Denning was, once again, clearly of the opinion that in these cases the question to be asked was not whose fault had caused the damage but who was in a better position to carry the risk. "Morally the learner driver is not at fault", he said, "but legally she is liable to be because she is insured and the risk should fall on her."[100]

Nettleship v. *Weston*[101] presents an additional interest in so far as it reveals yet another influence of insurance on traditional tort thinking: the willingness of modern courts to objectivize the standard of care to near strict liability standards. For since the damages are not going to be met by the defendant but by his insurer, one can afford to ignore the defendant's personal shortcoming and, instead, focus attention on the plaintiff and the consequences of his not being adequately compensated. The same is true of the tendency to approach contributory negligence in a more subjective way and anyone reasonably familiar with the law reports will notice how judges often describe conduct as negligent but are most reluctant to describe the very same conduct as contributory negligence.

One could go on listing examples of tort rules which bear strongly the marks of insurance thinking but it would serve no further purpose. It should be noted, however, that insurance has affected rules of procedure as well as substance and of course, the overall preventive function of the tort rules. And it has almost certainly affected the size of awards. To what extent this has actually occurred is difficult to say though such empirical evidence as exists in the United States would support the view that juries tend to award higher damages in cases of insured defendants.[102] The value of such surveys is, of course, small as far as our system is concerned though, on the other hand, it cannot be entirely ruled out that even judges are not influenced by this factor. And yet, despite all the above, the influence of insurance on the law of tort still tends to be "invisible"[103] in the sense that it is not, as a general rule, openly discussed or admitted by the common law and civil law courts. True, the insistence of judges to formulate their judgements in abstract and rather conventional terms has not prevented liability insurance from having the kind of effect on torts rules which we have described above; but, it is submitted, it has, on occasion, hindered the intelligent discussion of the policy issues that lie behind all these cases. The prevailing view must, therefore, be regretted for, if the law of tort is, as most would nowadays accept, concerned with the allocation of risks and the best way to absorb them, one should be prepared to discuss in public the bearing of liability insurance and the ways in which it can help achieve these aims.[104] And it has been argued, it is submitted correctly, that this would, among other things, bring a greater degree of certainty in the law "for once the allocation of the most frequently recurring kinds of risk had been determined there would be little litigation. Disputes on fact would be very rare and the remaining litigation would be concerned with the question of law—on which of the parties did the risk in question lie.''[105]

Some Tentative Suggestions

The prime aim of this paper was to discuss some of the real policy factors that seem to determine the outcome of some important tort cases. One could follow this up with a discussion of the wider implications that this method of approach can have not only for the purposes of the comparative exposition of different legal rules, but also for the teaching and development of one's own legal system. At this stage, however, some tentative suggestions are all that one can offer in the hope that they may lead others to develop them even further.

That the comparative exposition of the law can be facilitated by this kind of approach has, I hope, been made reasonably clear. For how else can a common lawyer explain to his German counterpart the notions of, say, ''duty'' or ''duty owed to the plaintiff''? Certainly, the fact that he, himself, had, until recently at least, doubts about these concepts hardly makes his task any easier. Conversely, how can you direct the common law mind towards an approach based on a list of enumerated interests (such as has been adopted by para. 823 I BGB) rather than a number of legal relationships? And how can you compare ''unlawfulness'' *(Rechtswidrigkeit)* with ''faute'' and ''duty'' without becoming involved in a nightmarish dialogue on abstract concepts? On the other hand, belief in the idea that all these notions are simply verbal formulae which enable judges to express their value judgements in particular situations can lead to a proper understanding of their *common* basis. For the real issues that lie behind many of these cases are remarkably similar—at any rate in countries with similar socio-economic structures and comparable levels of industrial development.

This manner of approach will also lead the student to realise that in most cases it matters little which concept one chooses to rely upon in order to produce a particular result for there is, truly, a remarkable possibility of equivocation between all of them.[106] Does it matter, for example, if you deny an owner of a silver fox farm the right to claim damages for harm caused to his foxes by overflying airplanes by saying that there is ''no duty'' (as a Canadian court has done)[107] rather than by saying that his damage is not ''adequately caused'' (which is the reason given by a German court)?[108] Does it matter if you deny the plaintiff in *Bourhill* v. *Young*[109] her right by saying that no duty was ''owed to her'' rather than by saying (as the French courts have come close to doing) that her damage is ''indirect''?[110] Does it matter if you say that a rescuer should be allowed to recover for his hurt because his intervention is causally ''adequate'' (which is what German courts do)[111] rather than by reaching the same result through the medium of duty?[112] Does it, finally, matter if you say that a particular plaintiff cannot claim damages for her nervous shock because the harm was not foreseeable[113] or because no duty was owed to her,[114] personally, or finally, because it was not adequately caused?[115] The answer to all these questions must be "no". However, what does matter is the realization that in all these instances the common results were dictated by similar considerations of policy. Similar, and similarly concealed behind abstract concepts. If this is correct, however, is it not desirable and useful to discover these policies? To bring them out into the open and discuss them rationally rather than fudge the issues behind terminology which is misleading and can only lead to inconsistencies?

Finally, this kind of analysis will help the comparative lawyer in yet another way. For it will help him understand *why* the common results sometimes have to be achieved by reliance on different concepts. It is clear, for example, that in the common law systems, where the notion of damage was in the province of the jury, judicial control had to be exercised through some other concept. Causation proved intially a suitable vehicle and, in fact, the first nervous shock cases and pure economic loss cases were decided on causal grounds.[116] Causation, here was, in fact, understood in a strongly normative sense. And where this is so, the logical progression seems to be towards something like the notion of "duty". This is especially true for systems like the common law which tend to fix the limits of extra-contractual liability for negligence by reference to defined relationships. Yet the same trend can be found even in German law. There, the list of enumerated interests made, and to some extent still makes, the notion of duty redundant. But when we move to omissions (which can only be made actionable if a pre-existing duty to act can be discovered) the picture changes. The *Verkehrssicherungspflichten*[117] prove this, and they have brought German law closer to the English duty-based approach. All these, however, are issues which are too complicated to be discussed at the end of this paper, so they had better wait for its sequel.

NOTES

1. Notable amongst them is Leon Green, in "Tort Law Public Law in Disguise" (1959), 38 Texas L.R. 1, 2 (from which the quote in the text is taken); *idem.* "Duties, Risks, Causation Doctrines" (1962), 41 Texas L.R. 42, 45. For a similar approach see: J. G. Fleming, "Remoteness and Duty: The Control Devices in Liability for Negligence" (1953), 31 Can. Bar Rev. 471; A. M. Linden, "Down with Foreseeability! Of Thin Skulls and Rescuers" (1969), 47 Can. Bar Rev. 545; *cf.* M. A. Millner's more cautious approach in "Growth and Obsolescence in Negligence" (1973), 26 Current Leg. Prob. 260, 280.

2. Most recently by C. R. Symmons in his useful discussion of a number of leading cases decided in the 1960's and early 70's in, "The Duty of Care in Negligence" (1971), 34 M.L.R. 394, 528. See, also, M. D. A. Freeman, "Standards of Adjudication, Judicial Law-Making and Prospective Overruling" (1973), 26 Current Leg. Prob. 166 and, more broadly, Neil MacCormick, *Legal Reasoning and Legal Theory* (1978) *passim.* and B. Rudden's comments in *The Juridical Review* (1979), 193-201.

3. *Public Policy* (1953), xi-xii.

4. *Ibid.*

5. This is how Winfield, rather hesitantly, defined public policy in, "Public Policy in the English Common Law" (1928), 42 Harv. L. Rev. 76, 92.

6. The literature on this subject is immense. The following may be particularly useful for what follows: Lord Devlin, "Judges and Lawmakers" (1976), 39 M.L.R. 1; A. Tunc, "Methodology of the Civil Law" (1976), 50 Tul. L. Rev. 459; J. L. Goutal, "Characteristics of Judicial Style in France, Britain and the U.S.A." (1976), 24 Am. J. of Comp. L. 43; F. H. Lawson, "Comparative Judicial Style" (1977); 25 Am. J. of Comp. L. 364; B. Rudden, "Courts and Codes in England, France and Soviet Russia" (1974), 48 Tul. L.R. 1010; A. Touffait and A. Tunc, "Pour une motivation plus explicite des décisions de justice notamment de celles de la Cour de cassation," *Rev.trim.dr.civ.* (1974), 487 (an article of seminal importance); P. Perrot, "Le rôle du juge dans la société moderne", *GP* 1977, I. 91; J. Déprez, "A propos du rapport annuel de la Cour de cassation", *Rev.trim.dr.civ.* (1978), 504.

7. J. G. Fleming, *supra* note 1, at 497-498. This was acknowledged by M. Bellet, the first President of the Cour de cassation in a speech delivered on December 19, 1979 to the Société de Legislation Comparé published in 1980 *Rev.int.dr.comp.,* p. 293.

8. The "administrative factor", as explained and illustrated in the text above, appears to have played a very limited role in the French law of *responsabilité civile,* its most obvious applications to be found in the decisions of the Chambre criminelle of the Cour de cassation when deciding on the "recevabilité de constitution de partie civile" in a criminal action. Further illustrations can be found in decisions limiting the circle of persons who can claim "dommage moral par ricochet", especially whenever this appears a *priori* to be negligible. For another illustration, see the revealing comments of M. le Conseiller Ponsard in his Rapport in the decision of the Assemblée Plénière of 12 Janv. 1979, *JCP* 1980, II, 19335.

9. *Op. cit. supra* note 2, at 129 *et seq.* In brief, MacCormick's thesis is that in complicated cases "the adduction of the principle . . . although necessary to is not sufficient for a complete justification of the decision. The ruling which directly governs the case must be tested by *consequen-*

tialist argument as well as by the argument from 'coherence'. . . ." *Ibid.* at 250 (italics supplied).

10. (1865), 3 H. and C. 774 (Court of Exchequer); (1866), L.R. 1 Ex. 265 (Court of Exchequer Chamber); (1868), L.R. 3 H.L. 330 (House of Lords).

11. See, for example, Lindley L.J. in *Green* v. *Chelsea Waterworks Co.* (1894), 70 L.T. 547, at 549 and *cf.* G. H. L. Fridman, "The Rise and Fall of *Rylands* v. *Fletcher*" (1956), 34 Can. Bar Rev. 810.

12. P. S. Atiyah, *Accidents, Compensation and the Law* (3rd ed., 1980), 80. *Cf.* J. Harvard, "Reasonable foresight of nervous shock" (1956), 19 M.L.R., 478.

13. Exemplified in this country by *Dulieu* v. *White and Sons,* [1901] 2 K.B. 669 and other authorities given in Clerk and Lindsell, § 872. For American authorities see Prosser, 327 *et seq.* See, also, F. Stone in (1974), 48 Tul. L.Rev. 782.

14. The Germans, fully conscious of the nature of the problem, have opted for an *apparently* mechanical application of the adequate cause theory. There is little doubt, however, that it is applied in a normative and not factual manner. On this, see E. von Hippel, Haftung, für Schokschaden Dritte, NJW 1965, 1890, 1891-2; U. Huber, "Verschulden, Gefährdung und Adäquanz", *Festschrift E. Wahl* (1973), 301, 318.

15. [1943] A.C. 92.

16. *Hinz* v. *Berry,* [1970] 2 Q.B. 40, 42 (*per* Lord Denning M.R.).

17. For a strong criticism of the English law see P. Atiyah, *op. cit. supra* note 12, at 77 *et seq.*

18. (1842), 10 M. & W. 109, and in *Cattle* v. *Stockton Waterworks* (1875), L.R. 10 Q.B. 453, the first modern case of pure economic loss.

19. [1932] A.C. 562, 577.

20. [1966] 1 Q.B. 569, 577.

21. *Ibid.*

22. [1973] Q.B. 27. The same fears were voiced by Lord Kissen in the factually similar Scottish case of *Dynamo Ltd.* v. *Holland and Hannen and Cubitts (Scotland) Ltd.,* [1971] S.C. 257, at 263.

23. *Ibid.,* at 38-39. Lawton L.J., on the other hand, while admitting that policy accounted for the different treatment of economic loss, was unwilling to elaborate further on the subject. *Ibid.,* at 49. See, also Geoffrey Lane J. in *Electrochrome Ltd.* v. *Welsh Plastics Ltd.,* [1968] 2 All E.R. 205, at 208. In *Hedley Byrne and Co. Ltd.* v. *Heller and Partners Ltd.,* [1964] A.C. 465, some of the Law Lords attributed the different treatment accorded to negligent acts and negligent words to the greater propensity of the latter to provoke unlimited litigation. Thus, Lord Pearce, at 534 and Lord Reid, at 482-483. Others, however, could see no logic in the distinction. So, for example, Lord Devlin, at 517.

24. BGH NJW 1976, 1740, and Emmerich, *JuS* 1977, 120. Similarly, NJW 1975, 221.

25. BGH NJW 1977, 2208.

26. OLG München NJW 1956, 1719; BGHZ 29, 65; BGH NJW 1976, 1740.

27. [1969] 1 A.C. 191.

28. [1965] 2 W.L.R. 300, 317 (*per* Lawton J.); [1967] 1 Q.B. 443, 504 (*per* Lord Denning M.R.); [1969] 1 A.C. 191, 251 (*per* Lord Morris).

29. [1965] 2 W.L.R. 300, 317; [1967] 1 Q.B. 443, 503, (*per* Lord Denning M.R.); 519 (*per* Salmon L.J.); [1969] 1 A.C. 191, 230 (*per* Lord Reid); 248 (*per* Lord Morris).

30. The plaintiff was unrepresented on the appeal but his solicitor (instructed before the appeal came on for hearing) tendered to the court a written brief setting out the arguments against barristers' immunity.

31. J. A. Weir, "Abstraction in the Law of Torts", City of London L. Rev., Oct. 1974, 15, 20.

32. Th. Zeldin, *France 1848-1945,* I. (1973), 307. (This erudite work contains at pp. 285-314 a brief but most interesting description of the social and economic background of the time.) Adultery even became the subject of "serious" monographs, *e.g.*, P. Vernon, *Paris vicieux: le guide de l'adultère* (1883); E. Cademartori, *L'Adultère à Marseille* (1886)!

33. Crim. 28 févr. 1930, *D.P.* 1930.1.49 and note Voirin; Paris, 5 juin 1923, *GP* 1923.2.417; Montpellier, 24 juin 1924, *D.P.* 1924.2.145 note Savatier; Paris, 2 juin 1928, motifs, *S.* 1928.2.125 etc.

34. Thus, L. Josserand, "L'avènement du concubinat", D.H. 1932.1.45; M. Nast, "Vers l'union libre, ou le crépuscule du marriage légal", D.H. 1938.1.37. As these dramatic titles suggest for many the phenomenon had reached cataclismic proportions. The alarmists put the figure of "faux ménages" at 40 percent of the population whereas a study conducted by the Church put the figure at 16-29 percent. (Le Bras, *Revue d'histoire de l'Eglise de France,* 1945, 328 *et seq.).* The most recent sociological study by R. Thery, "Le Concubinage en France", *Rev. trim.dr.civ.* 1960, 33 *et seq.,* puts the figure at a much more modest 3 percent. Yet its author admits that since his figure is based on information supplied at the population census of 1954 it may err on the optimistic side.

35. *Ibid.,* at 48.

36. Civ. 27 juil 1937, *S.* 1938.1.321 and note Marty; *D.* 1938.1.5 and note Savatier. The view that the words "juridiquement protégé" were really another way of saying that the intérêt must be légitime (Civ. 26 janv. 1954, *D.* 1954, 217 and note Levasseur) was never widely accepted.

37. Cass. 27 févr. 1970, *D* 1970, 201. The English Fatal Accidents Act 1976, still refuses to recognise a mistress as a "dependent in law". But the woman's children with the deceased may have a claim for the loss of dependency.

38. [1969] 1 A.C. 191.

39. *British Railways Board* v. *Herrington,* [1972] A.C. 877, 897.

40. *Ibid.* at 929.

41. A selection from the vast literature on the subject can be found in Mazeaud and Tunc, *Responsabilité civile,* 6th ed. nos. 547 *et seq.,* especially notes 547(1) and 593(2). The pioneering French work is L. Josserand's *De l'ésprit des droits et de leur relativité (théorie dite de l'abus des droits)* (2nd ed., 1939) and *Cours de droit civil positif français* (1933). For an eloquent opposition see, G. Ripert, *La règle morale dans les obligations civile* (1949), esp. 157 *et seq.* For a stimulating comparative study see, Catala and Weir, 38 Tul. L.R., 221 *et seq.* See, also, Gutteridge, 5, *CLJ* 22-45; Scholtens, "Abuse of Rights" (1958), 75 S.A.L.J., 39; M. Rolondi, *Inchieste di Diritto Comparato* vol. 7 (1979) (a collection of essays on abuse of right), and, generally, C. K. Allen, *Legal Duties* (1931), 95-118.

42. "La propriété est le droit de jouire et disposer des choses de la manière la plus absolue. . . ."

43. The change came with the decision of the court of Colmar in 1855 (see note 44). On the other hand, one must remember that the older French jurists, probably under the influence of cannon law, had come to regard as actionable any purely malicious exercise of rights. Thus, in 1577 the Parlement of Aix condemned a wool-carder for singing continuously solely in order to annoy his neighbour. Mazeaud and Tunc, I, no. 556. This break with the Roman law tradition can also be found in Scots law which, from about the seventeenth century onwards, apparently accepted the doctrine of abuse of rights within its law of real property. See B. W. Napier, "Abuse of Rights in British Law", in M. Rotondi, *Inchieste di Diritto Comparato*, 267 *et seq.* But this came to an abrupt end when Lord Watson agreed (it is submitted erroneously) with the English Law Lords in *Mayor of Bradford v. Pickles,* [1895] A.C. 587, 598, that Scots law was the same as English law.

44. *D.P.* 1856.2.9.

45. Paragraph 226 BGB: "The exercise of a right is inadmissible if it can only have the purpose of causing damage to another." In practice, better results have been achieved by relying on para. 826 BGB which requires of malicious damage not that it be against the law but merely *contra bonos mores*—a formulation which sidetracks the defence that the damage was done in the exercise of a right.

46. [1895] A.C. 587. French courts have penalised conduct identical to that of Mr. Pickles. See: *D.P.* 1902.1.454; *S.* 1903.1.11.

47. *Cours de droit civil positif français* (2nd ed., 1933), nos 428-37; *De l'esprit des droits et de leur relativité,* passim.

48. For an up-to-date account of the doctrine in France see, Antoine

Pirovano, "L'abus de droit dans la doctrine et la jurisprudence françaises", in M. Rotondi, *Inchieste di Diritto Comparato,* vol. 7, 313 *et seq.*

49. Notably by Ripert in *La règle morale dans les obligations civile* (1949) esp. 157 *et seq.*

50. Mazeaud and Tunc, I, nos 568 *et seq.*

51. Cass 29 mai 1937, *D.H.* 1937.393; *S.* 1937.1.244. Cass. civ. 4 fév. 1971, *JCP* 1971, 16781 and note Lindon; cass. civ. 18 juil. 1972, *JCP* 1972, 17203 and rapport Fabre.

52. Lord Denning M.R. has been one of the most persistent exponents. See, for example, his dissenting judgement in *Chapman* v. *Honig,* [1963] 2 Q.B. 502; *Morgan* v. *Fry,* [1968] 2 Q.B. 710, 729; *Secretary of State for Employment* v. *ASLEF (No 2),* [1972] 2 All E.R. 949, 967; *Re Brocklehurst,* [1978] 1 All E.R. 767, 775.

53. [1893] 1 Ch. 316.

54. Amiens 7 fevr. 1912, 1913 D.2.177, at 179. For what is probably the leading case see Req. 3 aout 1915, D.P. 1917. I. 79.

55. (1866), L.R. 1 Ex. 265; (1868), L.R. 3 H.L. 330.

56. "Tort Law Public Law in Disguise" (1959), 38 Texas L. Rev. 1, 5. Harper and James, *The Law of Torts,* II (1956), 14.3, though putting forward a slightly different view, also explain the case by reference to its economic and political environment. Similarly, F. H. Bohlen, in *Studies in the Law of Torts* (1926), 359. This kind of interpretation, however, is rejected by Roscoe Pound in (1940), 53 Harv. L. Rev. 365, 383-384. *Cf.,* Fridman, 34 Can. Bar Rev. 810, 812.

57. *Ibid.,* at 5. The early milldam cases in the United States could, arguably, be used to support this. *Shrewsbury* v. *Smith* (1853), 12 Cush 177 (Mass.); *Livingston* v. *Adams* (1828), 8 Cow. 175 (N.Y.). This attitude remained unaltered even after *Rylands* v. *Fletcher.* Thus, *Losee* v. *Buchanan* (1873), 51 N.Y. 476, 10 Ann. Rep. 623; *Marshall* v. *Welwood* (1876), 38 N.J.L. 339, 20 Am. Rep. 394; *Brown* v. *Collins* (1873), 53 N.H. 442, 16 Am. Rep. 372. With some exceptions (*e.g., Sanderson* v. *Pennsylvania Coal Co.* (1878), 86 Pa. 401, 27 Am. Rep. 711; *Ball* v. *Nye* (1868), 99 Mass. 582) the new doctrine was thus avoided by many courts and liability was made to rest on nuisance or negligence. The principle, however, is nowadays accepted by a majority of jurisdictions. For details see Prosser, 508 *et seq.*

58. Fleming, 432 *et seq.* Leon Green, *"Landowner* v. *Intruder; Intruder* v. *Landowner. Basis of Responsibility in Tort"* (1923), 21 Mich. L.R. 495.

59. Green, *ibid.,* 508.

60. *Pannett* v. *P. McGuinness & Co. Ltd.,* [1972] 2 Q.B. 599, 606.

61. L. M. Friedman and J. Ladinsky, "Social Change and the Law of Industrial Accidents" (1967), 67 Colum. L. Rev., 50.

62. (1837), 3 M. & W. 1, 7 L.J. Ex. 42.

63. Thus, Windfield and Jolowicz, on *Tort* (11th ed.), 169; J. Muncman, *Employer's Liability at Common Law* (7th ed., 1971), 7. *Contra,* F. H. Newark, "Bad Law" (1966), 17 N.I.L.Q. 469, 477.

64. (1842), 45 Mass (4 Met.) 49. For a fuller discussion of this important case see Friedman and Ladinsky, 67 Colum. L. Rev., 54 *et seq.*

65. *Bartonshill Coal Co.* v. *Reid* (1858), 3 Macq. 266 (H.L.).

66. For example, Marx Sauzet, De la responsabilité des patrons vis à vis des ouvriers dans les accidents industriels, *Rev. crit. leg. et jur.* 1883, 596 *et seq.* and 677 *et seq.*

67. *Supra,* note 62.

68. B. Rudden, *The Juridical Review* (1979), 198.

69. Muncman, *op. cit. supra* note 63, at 6. "These instances seem to show personal apprehension rather than any principle." *Per* Lord Wright in *Radcliffe* v. *Ribble Motor Services Ltd.,* [1939] A.C. 215, at 239.

70. "The Economic Interpretations and the Law of Torts" (1940), 53 Harv. L. Rev. 365.

71. (1850), 5 Exch. 343. This was a tort case under Lord Campbell's Act, 1846. It was later said that "Lord Abinger planted the doctrine of common employment. Baron Alderson watered it and the Devil gave it increase."

72. For example, Bramwell B. in *Dynen* v. *Leach* (1857), 26 L.J. (N.S.) Ex. 221.

73. Friedman and Ladinsky (1967), 67 Colum L. Rev. 50, 56.

74. *D.P.* 70.1.361.

75. *S.* 1871.1.9. It must be said that it is not clear from the "arrêt" whether the plaintiff was an employee of the defendant's or not. The headnote to the *Sirey* report talks of injury "à un tiers" but the facts of the case are quite similar to some of the "boiler-explosion" cases decided a few years later and indisputably dealing with injured employees. In any event, Labbé's case-note is couched in sufficiently wide terms to be able to cover both kinds of situation.

76. First from the Conseil d'Etat, 21 juin 1895, *D.P.* 1896.3.65 and then the Cour de cassation 16 juin 1896, *D.P.* 1897.1.433 and note Saleilles; *S.* 1897.1.17 and note Esmein. A year later the legislator intervened in a manner similar to our 1897 Workmen's Compensation Act. The relevant law can now be found in the Social Security Code.

77. *D.P.* 1930.1.57.

78. K. Renner's *The Institutions of Private Law and their Social Functions* (1949), 238. (English ed. with an introduction by O. Kahn-Freund.)

79. *Anatomy of the Law* (1971), 134.

80. T. Weir, *International Encyclopedia of Comparative Law,* XI, ch. 12 §§ 24, 63; RGZ 88, 317.

81. *Ibid.,* at § 54.

82. BGH NJW 1976, 1740.

83. F. H. Lawson, *A Common Lawyer Looks at the Civil Law* (1955), 56.

84. According to the Pearson Report, vol. II no. 509 "It is estimated that claims on insurers represent about 88 per cent of the total number and about 94 per cent of the total value of all personal injury claims in tort."

85. In *Davie* v. *New Merton Board Mills,* [1959] A.C. 604, 627; *Lister* v. *Romford Ice and Cold Storage Co. Ltd.,* [1957] A.C. 555, 572.

86. Fleming James Jr., "Limitations on Liability for economic loss caused by negligence: a pragmatic appraisal (1972-73), 10 JSPTL 104, 113. See also, *Rowland* v. *Christian* (1968), 69 Cal. 2d 89, 94, 443 P. 2d 561, 564, 70 Cal. Rept. 97, 100. Among the scholars who have for many years advocated the substitution of the fault principle by the risk insurance approach is A. Ehrenzweig, "Assurance oblige—A Comparative Study" (1950), 15 Law & Contemp. Prob., 445. See, also, his "Negligence without Fault" (1966), 54 Cal. L.R. 1422. In this country the case for the risk approach has been made by, amongst others, J. A. Jolowicz, "Liability for Accidents", (1968) *CLJ,* 50.

87. In *Dalloz Chr.* 1975, 83, 86 and *Archiv. de Philosophie du droit,* vol. 22, 31.

88. Trolle, *Risiko og Skyld* (1960) (quoted by S. Jorgensen, *Scandinavian Studies in Law,* 1963, ed. F. Schmidt at pp. 47-48). For the Swedish Law of 1972 see J. Hellner, "The New Swedish Tort Liability Act" (1974), 22 Am. J. Comp. L. 1, at 6-7.

89. The same is true of French law even though, once again, much of the development of the law can only be understood against the background of insurance. Thus, see, Cass. civ. 2 mai 1968, *GP.* 1968.2.109 and, more generally, A. Tunc, *International Encyclopedia of Comparative Law,* vol. XI, Chap. 1, note 304 and in JCP 1966.1.1983.

90. J. A. Jolowicz, "The Law of Tort and Non-Physical Loss" (1972-73), 10 JSPTL 91, 98.

91. D. Riley, *Consequential Loss Insurance and Claims,* (4th ed., 1977) §306. A. V. Alexander, "The Law of Tort and Non-Physical Loss: Insurance Aspects" (1972-73), 10 JSPTL 119.

92. But see Lord Denning M.R.'s judgement in *Spartan Steel* v. *Martin,* [1973] Q.B. 27, 38, and Lawton L.J.'s remarks at p. 48.

93. *Accidents, Compensation and the Law* (2nd ed., 1975), 87 Prof. M. A. Millner, however, in "Growth and Obsolescence in Negligence" (1973), 26 Current Leg. Prob. 260, at 272, is not so sure of the result nor happy with "the pure policy approach adopted by Lord Denning".

94. *Atkinson* v. *Newcastle and Gateshead Waterworks Co.* (1877), 2 Ex. D. 441; *Moch Co.* v. *Rensselaer Water Co.* (1928), 159 N.E. 896 (N.Y. Ct. of Appeals).

95. *Ryan* v. *New York Central Ry. Co.* (1866), 35 N.Y. 210.

96. J. G. Fleming, "More Thoughts on Loss Distribution" (1966), 4 O.H.L.J. 161, 166. See, also, Fleming James Jr., "Accident Liability Reconsidered: The impact of liability insurance" (1947-48), 57 Yale L.J. 549, reprinted in Harper and James, *The Law of Torts,* vol II, §§13.2 *et seq.*

97. Since 1966 the *Fonds de garantie* will idemnify victims of hunting accidents where it is impossible to discover which of the hunters involved caused the damage or where they are not covered by private insurance. The problem discussed in the text will thus no longer arise in the context of *hunting* accidents. On this and its consequences see Durry, *Rev.trim.dr.civ.* (1971), 377. A decision of the Court of Grenoble of 16 May 1962 (*D.* 1963, 137 and note Azard; *Rev.trim.dr.civ.,* 1963, 555, note Tunc) offers, however, an excellent example of how the insurance factor operated before the *Fonds de garantie* were brought into the picture. In that case, two hunters, insured with the same insurance company, negligently discharged their guns but only one pellet hit the victim. Since it was impossible to discover from which gun it had come, the court (ignoring the tendency prevailing at the time to hold both defendants responsible) refused to hold either of them liable to the plaintiff. Nevertheless, it obliged their *common insurer* to indemnify the victim in the amount specified by the terms of the insurance contract most favourable to the insurer. The plaintiff was thus compensated even though *neither* of the defendants was held liable for his hurt.

98. [1971] 2 Q.B. 245; [1973] A.C. 127.

99. [1971] 2 Q.B. 691. The implications of insurance were also taken into account in *Ministry of Housing* v. *Sharp,* [1970] 1 All E.R. 1009, 1019 and *White* v. *Blackmore,* [1972] 2 Q.B. 651, 667.

100. *Ibid.,* at p. 700.

101. [1971] 2 Q.B. 691.

102. Kalven, "The Jury, the Law and the Personal Injury Damage Award" (1958), 19 Ohio St. L.J., 158. The position in France may not be different. See, for example, A. Tunc, "Logique et politique dans l'élaboration du droit, spécialment en matière de responsabilité civile", *Mélanges Jean Dabin* (1963), 317, 324.

103. The expression comes from G. Williams and B. Hepple's *Foundations of the Law of Torts* (1976), 141 *et seq.*

104. See A. Tunc, Le droit en miettes, 22 *Archives de Philosophie du Droit* (1977), 31, 34 and references given in notes 101 and 102, *supra.*

105. J. A. Jolowicz, *op. cit.,* note 86, at 63.

106. According to Leon Green, *Judge and Jury* (1930), 19, which concept is selected is often "a matter of taste and finesse". *Cf.,* J. A. Weir in Catala and Weir, "Delict and Tort: A Study in Parallel", 39 Tul. L. Rev. 705. ("It is a question of aesthetics as much as anything else whether one feels that the acceptable solution is better produced by emphasizing causation or duty or damage.")

107. *Nova Mink Ltd.* v. *T.C.A.,* [1951] 2 D.L.R. 241.

108. RGZ 158, 38.

109. [1943] A.C. 92.

110. Cass. 17 mai 1973, *GP* 1974.1.71 and note H.M.; Cour de Lyon, 26 juin 1973, *GP* 1974.1.4; Durry, 1974 *Rev. trim.dr.civ.,* 409.

111. *E.g.,* RGZ 50, 219, 223.

112. *Wagner* v. *International Railway Co.* (1921), 232 N.Y. 176, 13? N.E. 437; *Haynes* v. *Harwood,* [1935] 1 K.B. 146.

113. *King* v. *Phillips,* [1953] 1 Q.B. 429, 442, *per* Lord Denning.

114. *King* v. *Phillips,* [1953] 1 Q.B. 429, *per* Singleton and Hodson L.JJ.

115. This is, invariably, the German approach. Thus, RGZ 133, 270; RGZ 157, 111; OLG Freiburg, *VersR* 1953, 322; OLG München, *NJW* 1959, 819; LG Frankfurt, *NJW* 1969, 2286 (with an interesting note by Berg, *NJW* 1970, 515); L.G. Tübingen, *NJW* 1968, 1187. But many authors stress that this apparently causal approach really conceals policy decisions. See, E. von Hippel, Haftung für Schokschaden Dritte, *NJW* 1965, 1890, 1891-2; U. Huber, Verschulden, Gefährdung und Adäquanz, *Festschrift für E. Wahl,* (1973), 301, 318.

116. *Victoria Rly. Commrs.* v. *Coultas* (1888), 13 App. Cas. 222; *Cattle* v. *Stockton Waterworks* (1875), L.R. 10 Q.B. 453.

117. For a short but excellent account see D. Medicus, *Bürgerliches Recht* (9th ed., 1979), nos 641 *et seq.* For a more detailed consideration of some of these problems, E. von Gaemmerer, Wandlungen des Deliktsrechts (1960), reprinted in his *Gesammelte Schriften,* I, 452 *et seq.* and, most recently, Christian v. Bar, *Verkehrspflichten* (1980) (the most exhaustive monograph on the subject). For an English summary, B. S. Markesinis, "The not so dissimilar tort and delict" (1977), L.Q. Rev., 78, 120-122.

17

The Right to Know the Case Against You in Administrative Law

The Honourable W. Z. Estey

Introduction

The City of Barrie applied to the Ontario Municipal Board to annex the adjoining townships. One of the issues was the need for space for future growth, and hence the importance of population estimates. After some of the evidence was in, the Board read a letter into the record from the Minister of Treasury, Economics and Intergovernmental Affairs of Ontario. The letter announced that the Government of Ontario had determined that the population of the City of Barrie in the year 2011 would be 125,000. The Board had already heard evidence that the population would be 76,752. The Board then deferred a request by objectors for cross-examination of the Minister or his representative on the contents of the letter. It announced that it was bound by the Minister's letter and that the assumption of a population of 125,000 would be the basis of the Board's decision on the outstanding issues. The Board then rejected the application to advance evidence contradicting the letter. The objectors immediately brought an application for judicial review.

In Re Township of Innisfil et al. and City of Barrie et al.[1] the Divisional Court held that the Board was not bound to accept the figure given in the Minister's letter but had committed no jurisdictional error in deciding to proceed on the basis of an expected population of 125,000. The Court of Appeal refused leave to appeal from that decision.

The Board then resumed hearings. On a subsequent application by landowners to examine the departmental representative who delivered the letter for the Minister, the Board refused the applicants both an opportunity to file contrary evidence and an opportunity to cross-examine on the letter. It reiterated its conclusion that the assumed population would be 125,000 in 2011.

Once again the matter came before the Divisional Court.[2] It held that the Board must have interpreted the earlier court decision incorrectly. The Board was entitled to give government policy preponderant weight, yet that weight must be determined on *all* the evidence, including cross-examination and contrary evidence. Craig J. dissented.

A majority of the Court of Appeal decided that the Board was correct in denying the owners an opportunity to cross-examine the government representative.[3] Blair J.A., in dissent, found that the Board had erred in denying a chance to cross-examine. All members of the court agreed that the Board had committed an error in denying the landowners an opportunity to call evidence to challenge the accuracy of the Minister's assumption of population growth.

The case is now pending before the Supreme Court of Canada, and so I must refrain from making comments on its particular merits. It is no secret, however, that the circumstances in the *Barrie* case suggest several important issues regarding the respective positions of the members of the modern triumvirate of administrative law—the government department; the administrative tribunal; and the party appearing before the tribunal. For example, how should a tribunal treat instructions from the government setting out policy decisions that will affect the interests of parties before it? What is the nature of a tribunal's duty to announce to the contending parties any policies which it may have formulated in advance, so as to alert the litigant or suppliant to the standards it will apply? Does it depend on what tribunal we are talking about?

Words like "fairness" and "natural justice", Latin maxims like *"audi alteram partem"*, and its English cousin "the right to know the case against you" all abound in the discussion of these issues. Perhaps that last phrase, "the right to know the case against you," is the most useful. It tells us we are talking about a "right", in the context of an adverse case. Yet we must go behind these words, to ask where the right comes from, what it is, and most importantly, where it stops and why. A brief overview of these questions is the task of this paper.

The Sources of the Right

If there be such a right it finds its root in the ancient rules concerning what we now call, in an omnibus way, the right to a fair hearing. This right has many aspects. It is obvious that without knowledge of the case being brought against the citizen by the state or another citizen, he cannot fully defend himself and consequently he has lost his right to a fair hearing. The English texts take us back a long way in tracing the origins of this rule. It would appear that this concept was known in Roman times (Seneca's *Medea* cited in *Boswell's* case).[4] By 1723 the courts of England had gone one better and drawn upon the Scriptures so as to trace this right back to the Garden of Eden.[5]

> I remember to have heard it observed by a very learned man upon such an occasion, that even God himself did not pass sentence upon Adam, before he was called upon to make his defence. ''Adam, says God, where art thou? Hast thou not eaten of the tree, whereof I commanded thee that thou shouldst not eat?''

There are many side alleys to be explored in filling out the modern version of this rule. For example, its expansion may well have been fed by the reaction to the procedures and practices of the Court of Star Chamber and other arbitrary forums and institutions adopted in the Middle Ages for the disposition of contests in the community. By the early 19th century the courts in England had revived the concept in the form of the *audi alteram partem* rule. It was a convenient source of authority, allowing the law to meet the needs of the 19th century, which had seen the revival of fundamental freedoms in connection with the right to membership in trade unions and voluntary associations generally as well as the right to freedom from harassment by the state in criminal law and in civil law concerning licensing and the precursor of modern community zoning rules. Probably an even greater source of the need recognized in the courts was the evolution of the modern statute and the birth of the hyperactive legislature. It was to fill in the holes in these rough and ready statutory patterns that the courts reached back through the canons of statutory construction to insert by implication doctrines such as the right to be heard, no doubt on the theory that in its haste the legislature had simply omitted mention of the citizen's right. Anyway we now have the rule, whatever its origin. The question is, how far has it been extended in its application to present day administrative tribunals?

The Ambit of the Right

One can find no better starting point in our century for the exploration of the limitations of this right than in the judgment of Lord Loreburn L.C. in *Board of Education* v. *Rice*;[6]

> In the present instance, as in many others, what comes for determination is sometimes a matter to be settled by discretion, involving no law. It will, I suppose, usually be of an administrative kind; but sometimes it will involve matter of law as well as matter of fact, or even depend upon matter of law alone. In such cases the Board of Education will have to ascertain the law and also to ascertain the facts. I need not add that in doing either they must act in good faith and fairly listen to both sides, for that is a duty lying upon every one who decides anything. But I do not think they are bound to treat such a question as though it were a trial. . . . They can obtain information in any way they think best, always giving a fair opportunity to those who are parties in the con-

> troversy for correcting or contradicting any relevant statement prejudicial to their view. Provided this is done, there is no appeal from the determination of the Board. . . . But if the Court is satisfied either that the Board have not acted judicially in the way I have described, or have not determined the question which they are required by the Act to determine, then there is a remedy by mandamus and certiorari.

The idea is carried forward a shade further in *Local Government Board v. Arlidge,* where Viscount Haldane L.C. stated:[7]

> My Lords, when the duty of deciding an appeal is imposed, those whose duty it is to decide it must act judicially. They must deal with the question referred to them without bias, and they must give to each of the parties the opportunity of adequately presenting the case made. The decision must be come to in the spirit and with the sense of responsibility of a tribunal whose duty it is to mete out justice. . . . Such a body as the Local Government Board has the duty of enforcing obligations on the individual which are imposed in the interests of the community. Its character is that of an organization with executive functions. In this it resembles other great departments of the State. When, therefore, Parliament entrusts it with judicial duties, Parliament must be taken, in the absence of any declaration to the contrary, to have intended it to follow the procedure which is its own, and is necessary if it is to be capable of doing its work efficiently.

When the *Arlidge* case was before the Court of Appeal, Buckley L.J., in dealing with this subject, had occasion to remark:[8]

> Natural justice requires that the mind of the deciding officer shall not be affected by original statements of fact not communicated to the person to be affected by the decision and upon which he has never been heard. In my opinion the reports of the inspector ought to be disclosed to the appellant, and he ought to have an opportunity if he thinks fit to deal with them. It is not consistent with natural justice that the mind of the tribunal should be swayed by statements which are not communicated to the appellant, and with which he is given no opportunity to deal, and which are either (a) a summary of, or an expression of, the result of the evidence given before the inspector, or (b) statements of fact made by the inspector as the result of his inspection. An order cannot justly be made against any man upon evidence not disclosed to him so that he may rebut it if he can.

In our country we find these sentiments reflected by the court in *Re The Imperial Tobacco Co. Ltd. et al. and McGregor,*[9] wherein all members of the Court of Appeal approached the question as to whether or not the accused had received a proper notice of certain prior investigations and reports of the commissioner. As a matter of fact, Gillanders J.A. assumed the right in the defendants to know the contents of the reports issued concerning their conduct and then stated:[10] "Nor can I think that the manner in which the investigation was conducted in the circumstances deprived the appellants of natural or substantial justice." This general theme has been picked up in the Supreme Court in *St. John* v. *Fraser,*[11] where Davis J., having set aside for the moment the rather arbitrary distinction between judicial and administrative functions, stated:[12]

> The investigator was not a court of law nor was he a court in law, but to say that he was an administrative body, as distinct from a judicial tribunal, does not mean that persons appearing before him were not entitled to any rights. An administrative tribunal must act to a certain extent in a judicial manner, but that does not mean that it must act in every detail in its procedure the same as a court of law adjudicating upon a *lis inter partes.* It means that the tribunal, while exercising administrative functions, must act "judicially" in the sense that it must act fairly and impartially.

The court in that instance did not carry the principle so far as to require that an administrative officer in investigating the conduct of a citizen must afford the citizen's counsel an opportunity of cross-examining every witness brought before the investigating officer. The court took the view that, since the investigation was a preliminary administrative proceeding in the overall functioning of the executive branch of government, the limits of the principle were the requirement that:[13]

> . . . while the investigator was bound to act judicially in the sense of being fair and impartial, that, it seems to me, is something quite different from the right asserted by the appellants of freedom of cross-examination of all the witnesses.

The same sort of limitation was encountered in *Arlidge,* where the court, having pronounced the principles governing the conduct of a hearing by a tribunal, stopped short of ordering that tribunal to disclose to the citizen-adversary the contents of a report prepared under the direction of the Board by a member of its staff on the very issue being determined. Viscount Haldane stated:[14]

> It is said that the report of the inspector should have been disclosed. It might or might not have been useful to disclose this report, but I do not think that the Board was bound to do so, any more than it would have been bound to disclose all the minutes made on the papers in the office before a decision was come to. . . .

Lord Shaw[15] continued with the same principle in this way:

> I incline to hold that the disadvantage in very many cases would exceed the advantage of such disclosure. And I feel certain that if it were laid down in Courts of law that such disclosure could be compelled, a serious impediment might be placed upon that frankness which ought to obtain among a staff accustomed to elaborately detailed and often most delicate and difficult tasks. The very same argument would lead to the disclosure of the whole file. It may contain, and frequently does contain, the views of inspectors, secretaries, assistants, and consultants of various degrees of experience, many of whose opinions may differ but all of which form the material for the ultimate decision. To set up any rule that that decision must on demand, and as matter of right, be accompanied by a disclosure of what went before, so that it may be

weakened or strengthened or judged thereby, would be inconsistent, as I say, with efficiency, with practice, and with the true theory of complete parliamentary responsibility for departmental action. This is, in my opinion, implied as the legitimate and proper consequence of any department being vested by statute with authority to make determinations.

Before leaving this general statement of the rules concerning the right to know the details of the case being advanced against the citizen, one should refer but briefly to the enforcement or application of these rules in our courts. This, by reason of the nature of our judicial remedies, has been brought about largely by the writ of *certiorari* or an order in lieu thereof. Sometimes the importance of the principle requiring a fair hearing has been submerged by the battle over the limits of the jurisdictional reach of the court through *certiorari*. For example, in *Nakkuda Ali* v. *Jayaratne,*[16] the court declined to apply the principle to an elected authority, who was a member of the executive branch of government, in the conduct of his statutory licensing function—not because the principles of natural justice would or would not be applicable, but because it was determined that the writ of *certiorari* did not run in such a circumstance. This contest was finally resolved in *Ridge* v. *Baldwin*[17] by Lord Reid when he determined that *certiorari* did indeed apply to instances where a tribunal affected "rights", although it was not under a super-added duty to act "judicially". Hence, he applied the general principle of a right to a fair hearing to "administrative" proceedings, where what was ultimately at stake was the right of a police chief to a pension—a permissive, as contrasted with an absolute right.

In reaching this conclusion, Lord Reid stated:[18]

If Lord Hewart [in *R.* v. *Legislative Committee of the Church Assembly,* [1928] 1 K.B. 411] meant that it is never enough that a body simply has a duty to determine what the rights of an individual should be, but that there must always be something more to impose on it a duty to act judicially before it can be found to observe the principles of natural justice, then that appears to me impossible to reconcile with the earlier authorities.

Lord Reid then applied those "earlier authorities".

To complete this side alley discussion on the subject of rights which will attract the procedural right to fairness and the right to a fair hearing (that distinction, if it exists, I will return to), it should be noted that in *R.* v. *Liverpool Corporation, Ex parte Taxi Drivers,*[19] Lord Denning applied *Ridge* v. *Baldwin* in replacement of the doctrine established in *Nakkuda Ali,* and found that a public authority, in discharging its licensing responsibilities, must "act fairly", whether fulfilling a judicial or an administrative function.

For many years the courts and the legal writers found it convenient in determining the application of the rules of natural justice to resort to an analysis of the function of the public body to whom the writ of *certiorari* was proposed to be directed. Thus we find a century of discussion in the courts of the distinctions between the legislative function, the executive function and the administrative function. These political science distinctions were overlayed by the concept of the judicial function in contrast to the administrative function, and perhaps also in contrast to the so-called ministerial function. Given our parliamentary form of government, with cabinet responsibility, the separation of functions is largely mythical, although we continue to contend, probably successfully, that the judicial function is indeed an independent activity in fact and in law isolated from the legislative and executive activities. But these distinctions proved in the end to be of no importance in determining the application of the principle that the citizen is entitled to natural justice which, for the purposes of this discussion, centers upon the right to know the charge brought against him. Thus we see a blurring, if not obliteration, of these distinctions in *Nicholson* v. *Haldiman-Norfolk Regional Board of Commissioners of Police.*[20] This departure from the ancient technicality of allegedly distinctive functions is also well illustrated in the judgment of Laskin C.J. in *Association of Radio and Television Employees of Canada* v. *C.B.C.*[21]

In the end the problem comes back, using one set of terminology or another, to the two basic functions either or both of which are performed by administrative tribunals.

(a) The board or agency may determine issues arising between contending parties on an adversarial basis analogous to the judicial procedure. In doing so, it may draw upon a familiarity with the subject matter sometimes called "expertise". "Tribunals are normally employed where decisions can be decided according to rules and there is no reason for the Minister to be responsible."[22] Lord Denning, in his *Freedom Under the Law*[23] put it this way: "The tribunals have to decide between the individual and the state and if the scales are to be kept even it is vital that the law they apply should be laid down by a superior court and not by a government department." This comment by the Master of the Rolls is not likely relevant today unless it is read as requiring such tribunal to apply the rules of law as laid down by Parliament as to substantive law and by the courts as to the essential procedures, applicable jurisdictional limitations and natural justice where it applies.

(b) The board may be designed to extend the policy of Parliament as embodied in general terms in the statute, and in more particular terms by the issue or denial of licences, the approval or rejection of prospectuses, the application of rules relating to the conduct of a business or trade, for example working conditions, collective bargaining rules, etc.

We are not here directly concerned with the side of the problem sometimes referred to as the clash between the thesis of responsible government and judicial independence. It may be, for example, that a core element of the executive branch of government such as the Cabinet, will, in its prime executive function, be free from judicial interference. This is not part of the subject at hand for we are assuming that the agency exercising a particular function is within the reach of the court, the issue with which we are concerned being the principle to be applied by the court in measuring the conduct of such an agency. See *The Attorney General of Canada* v. *Inuit Tapirisat of Canada et al.*[24]

This leads one to a discussion of another element sometimes determinative of the application of the administrative rules under discussion, namely the nature of the case or the subject matter before the administrative unit. What portion of the "adverse case" must be revealed, when, for example, part of that "case" is predetermined board policy, or staff studies, or a business competitor's confidential records?

Administrative tribunals have, of course, a mandate or directive from the legislature to implement defined or described policy. The Court of Appeal of Ontario discusses this matter in *Hopedale Developments Ltd.* v. *Town of Oakville*[25] where McGillvray J.A. stated:[26] "The right of an administrative tribunal to formulate general principles by which it is to be guided is undoubted." S. A. de Smith[27] put it this way:[28] "It is obviously desirable that a tribunal should openly state any general principle by which it intends to be guided in the exercise of its discretion."

This principle was the subject of decision in the Supreme Court of Canada in *Capital Cities Communications Inc.* v. *Canadian Radio-Television Commission*,[29] where the court found it proper for the CRTC to announce it was no longer following the prior policy of the Department of Transport concerning the alteration of signals received off-air by a Cable Television system. This policy was adopted after public hearings but there is no suggestion that this was necessary. Of course the CRTC could have achieved the same result by regulation without any hearing and probably could have done so without regulation but presumably the better plan would be to "telegraph" the change of policy to the community before determining rights on the basis of the new policy. That is not to say that a Board may not alter its policy direction as the public interest requires; the question is, however, may it do so on the advice of the executive branch without notice to the parties before the Board. This is the essence of the issue here under discussion.

There is, of course, a collision between the theory that an administrative tribunal will be staffed by people who bring expert knowledge of the subject to their work and the right of persons appearing before that Board to meet evidence or submissions advanced against them from whatever source prior to the determination of the issue or policy by the Board. Speight J. discusses this problem in *Denton* v. *Auckland City*:[30]

> Knowledge and experience of the field in which decisions are made are highly desirable but this must be general knowledge and the distillation of a mass of experience and it is proper that these matters should be taken into account, but to do so is far removed from receiving and acting on confidential information

> in relation to the matter in issue given by a person whose face is not seen and whose voice is not heard by the parties whose rights are being affected.

The court was there relying upon a statement by Lord du Parcq in *R.* v. *City of Westminster Assessment Committee*:[31]

> It is said that as the committee is entitled to use its own knowledge and experience and is not obliged to state the result of those to the contestants it must follow that it can enlarge its knowledge by calling in an independent expert without coming under the necessity of revealing his evidence. One answer to this contention, and we think a sufficient answer, is that the experience of an expert tribunal such as this, is part of its equipment for determining the case. Litigants must take that experience as they find it and because the tribunal is assumed to be impartial they have no grievance if they cannot test it by cross-examination. An expert witness or adviser, however eminent, is in a very different position. He must not be substituted for the tribunal. Those whose claim is being considered have a right to question and to test every statement he makes, and any opinion he expresses. If that opportunity is denied them, justice is not done. On the ground, therefore, that the committee improperly (though no doubt with the best intentions) considered and gave weight to evidence, and it may be, argument, which was never communicated to the parties most interested, we are of opinion that the respondents are entitled to have the determination of the committee quashed.

This general clash of function is brought home in Canadian terms by Professor H. N. Janisch in his study entitled *The Regulatory Process of the Canadian Transport Commission*:[32]

> Not disclosing the bases of a decision can raise doubts, whether justified or not, about the decision as well as about the usefulness of the Commission's public procedures. On the other hand, CTC commissioners consider the confidential relationship with the Commission's staff to be an essential ingredient of their capacity for information and expert decision making.

Here the learned author has gone beyond the general information background brought to the Transport Commission by commissioners appointed from the transportation industry. The next step in the process, of course, is the enlargement of the general background knowledge brought to the Commission by the commissioner, by staff studies on specific transportation problems received by the commissioners prior to either the hearing or the determination of the issue raised in the hearing. The author goes on to state:[33]

> How the information of a confidential nature is used internally by the CTC and its relationship to staff studies are the understandable concern of intervenants, such as the CAC. If the information forms part of a general study prepared to give commissioners background knowledge of a broad area or topic then the information is used as a "legislative fact" and ought not offend against procedural fairness. If, on the other hand, the information is used in a staff study dealing with a specific issue and particular parties, then the infor-

mation is used as an "adjudicative fact" and non-disclosure would be perceived as offending procedural fairness. Disclosure of both types of facts and studies, as a matter of policy, if not law, would clearly make the hearing process more meaningful. Disclosure of neither reduces the effectiveness of the hearing, the perceived accuracy of the decisions, and raises concern about the application of the legal rules of fairness, and natural justice.

This clash between the need for knowledge, general and special, in the Board and the need for the applicant or respondent before the Board to know the issues and the facts being brought against his interests comes up in many other ways. One way is illustrated in *Sarco Canada Ltd.* v. *Anti-Dumping Tribunal.*[34] The statute there required that information obtained from a business may not be disclosed so as to be available to its competitors. The tribunal had gathered information by an investigator prior to the hearing and did not reveal the information to the applicant. The Federal Court of Appeal decided that such non-disclosure resulted in a violation of the right of the appellant to a fair hearing, particularly where it is evident that the Board acted in part in reliance on such information. In the result, the applicant secured the opportunity to meet such information. This, of course, raises the opposite question, namely, did such a court order not in turn violate the competitor's right to keep such material out of the public eye.

A similar contest of public versus private rights is found in *Lazarov* v. *Secretary of State of Canada,*[35] where the Federal Court of Appeal referred an immigration issue back to the Secretary of State because that public officer had reached a decision concerning the issuance of a citizenship certificate on the basis of a confidential police report not disclosed to the applicant. Thurlow J., as he then was, discussed the application of the *audi alteram partem* rule in these circumstances in the following way:[36]

> In my opinion therefore the rule *audi alteram partem* applies whenever the minister proposes to exercise his discretion to refuse an application on the basis of facts pertaining to the particular applicant or his application and where he has not already had an opportunity in the course of the proceedings before the Citizenship Court he must be afforded a fair opportunity in one way or another of stating his position with respect to any matters which in the absence of refutation or explanation would lead to the rejection of his application. That is not to say that a confidential report or its contents need be disclosed to him but the pertinent allegations which if undenied or unresolved would lead to rejection of his application must, as I see it, be made known to him to an extent sufficient to enable him to respond to them and he must have a fair opportunity to dispute or explain them.

In the general common law of course we have to ask when does a privilege recognized in the law of evidence conflict with the *audi alteram partem* rule in administrative proceedings. This subject is, of course, so large as to put it beyond the purview of this discussion, and I simply note in passing that the reconciliation between exclusionary rules of evidence and the administrative right to know will doubtless, in the future, follow the same principles as we have seen and will see applicable to the reconciliation between conflicting demands in public law. Obviously the creation of a right in the citizen to know within reasonable, practical limits all the information under consideration by the administrative tribunal so as to enable the citizen to respond cuts across the common law rules of evidence, and the statutory provisions requiring the preparation of reports in essence confidential, as well as what may be classified under our constitutional system as the executive branch "right to secrecy" in the determination and implementation of public policy when acting as the executive branch of government. I attempt no more here than the cataloguing of these conflicts. We find further illustration of what really is a difficulty in political science as much as in jurisprudence in *B. Johnson & Co.* v. *Minister of Health.*[37] The Minister confirmed an expropriation order issued by a local authority without disclosing to the property owners certain reports, including some prepared for the public authority prior to the expropriation and some prepared during the expropriation process. The court found no obligation in the Minister to decide anything before the objection of the owners to confirmation, which is the birth of the *lis* so far as the Minister is concerned, and therefore no obligation to disclose reports prepared for the public authority or the Minister prior thereto. Material arising thereafter, however, the court found must be made available to the objecting owners, and in this the court applied the doctrine of *Arlidge.*[38] Lord Greene, in describing the general function of a Minister of the Crown in confirming a recommendation from a public agency, stated:[39]

> It may well be that, on considering the objections [of the owners], the Minister may find that they are reasonable and that the facts alleged in them are true, but, nevertheless, he may decide that he will overrule them. His action in so deciding is a purely administrative action, based on his conceptions as to what public policy demands. His views on that matter he must, if necessary, defend in Parliament, but he cannot be called on to defend them in the courts. . . .
>
> . . . [E]very Minister of the Crown is under a duty, constitutionally, to the King to perform his functions honestly and fairly and to the best of his ability, but his failure to do so, speaking generally, is not a matter with which the courts are concerned.

It will be noted that in this 1947 judgment the Court of Appeal were still engaged in the process of determining the outcome of a claim of wrongful non-disclosure on the basis of the classification of a function being performed by the public authority. Consequently, the court found the watershed between non-disclosure and disclosure according to when the Minister assumes "the quasi-judicial role".[40] Nevertheless the judgment would appear to have at least strong persuasive value today because elsewhere in his judgment Lord Greene found that where a quasi-*lis* is pending, then different rules apply than where the state of affairs is otherwise. This takes us back to what was earlier referred to as a political science consideration and about which Lord Green said:[41]

> It is not unfair to say that, generally speaking, the idea that a Minister can be compelled to disclose to anybody information of that kind [that is obtained by him prior to the commencement of the action in question], which he has obtained as a purely administrative person, is alien to our whole conception of government in this country.

In the result, the Court of Appeal concluded that the only obligation which arises in a Minister of the Crown in such circumstances is to disclose material to both sides where it has come into existence for the purpose of this administrative quasi-*lis*.

This vein of administrative litigation extended into Australia in *R.* v. *Anderson, Ex parte Ipec Air Pty. Ltd.*,[42] where the Director General of Aviation denied both an import licence to import DC 4's for freight operations and a licence to operate a freight service, the applications being made under two separate statutes. He denied the freight service licence because the appellant could not get the import certificate for the aircraft from the Director General under the first application. The court of five judges divided on all issues. The majority directed the issuance of a *mandamus* to compel the official to issue the air freight licence. The two dissenting judges said that there was no purpose in granting the *mandamus* as the applicant could not import the necessary aircraft.

The majority, differently constituted, refused the *mandamus* on the question of the import licence acknowledging that the official must take into account announced government policy which here was to the effect that the economics of the country could not support two airlines.

Kitto J., for the majority on the first issue, found that the only reason for refusing the licence was that the same official had refused the import permit for the necessary aircraft:[43]

> The refusal was based entirely on government policy of limiting the air freight business to those already in it. Therefore, because the refusal was contrary to regulation 192, being a mandate to the Director General, the mandamus issued.

On the second issue Kitto J. and Menzies J. dissented stating that the officials should not blandly implement government policy, but Kitto J. did concede:[44] "Where the law confers a discretionary decision upon an officer of the civil service in his official capacity, government policy is not in any case an extraneous matter which he must put out of consideration." and:[45] ". . . but what he did was seek from his Minister and then automatically obey an *ad hoc* pronouncement from the government as to the direction in which he ought to decide the matter."

Similar considerations arose in *Stringer* v. *Minister of Housing*.[46] This is the Jodrell Bank case. Here the Minister rejected an appeal from a municipal authority which refused a permit to build houses within six miles of the Jodrell Bank radio telescope. The court found that the Minister had not, by slavish observance of an earlier agreement between the University of Manchester and the regional authority, denied the applicant a right to a fair hearing, but had merely formulated his policy with the recognition of several factors, including the need to protect the efficiency of the university telescope. Cooke J. found that the general policy adopted by the Minister of protecting the telescope did not preclude consideration of all relevant factors and did not cut off the applicant's right to a fair hearing.

Cooke J., in finding that the ministerial decision should not be interfered with by the courts, cited with approval this statement by Lord Greene in *B. Johnson & Co.* v. *Minister of Health*:[47]

> The decision whether to confirm or not must be made in relation to questions of policy, and the Minister, in deciding whether to confirm or not, will, like every Minister entrusted with administrative duties, weigh up the considerations which are to affect his mind, the preponderating factor in many, if not all, cases being that of public policy, having regard to all the facts of the case.

What would be the position of the parties had the applicant not been aware of the 1952 agreement purportedly binding the regional authority until the year 1990? Has the applicant the opportunity to advise the Minister of the proper protection to be given to the telescope including the effect of precautionary measures which could be taken to allow his development to go forward?

A comparison of the situation prevailing in the administrative law of this country to that in the United States may be of some interest. There, the independence of the administrative tribunal springs from the American Constitution. Federal boards are creatures of the legislative branch and are paid by that branch though appointed by the executive branch. The mandate to such an agency is usually broad. For example, in the case of the Federal Communications Commission, the statute directs that it "regulate in the public interest" the utilization of radio frequencies. As K. C. Davis has said, Congress usually states the equivalent of "Here is the problem. Deal with it." *Humphreys* v. *U.S.*[48] illustrates the United States political science of administrative law. President Roosevelt fired the Chairman of the Federal Trade Commission because the President disagreed with the Chairman's view of the role of the commission. The U.S. Supreme Court held that the President could not discharge him because the statute limited his action in discharge to "inefficiency or malfeasance". The result is that administrative boards are independent of executive surveillance on policy issues.

Perhaps out of this morass of decided cases and political science discussions one can safely extract certain conclusions.

1. We do not have the American concept of independence as between the executive branch of government and the legislative branch of government as, in any case, the executive in fact controls the legislative branch.
2. So long as the executive controls the legislature, the form of direction from government to board is either by legislation, as in the National Energy Act or the Broadcasting Act, or by delegated legislation authorized by such statutes.
3. Within its statutory limits the board is generally held out as independent of executive control but accountable to the community through the courts for its performance of the statutory mandate. Look at, for example, labour relations boards, whose susceptibility to judicial intervention is, for all practical purposes, limited to jurisdiction issues.
4. As to the precise relationship of the board and the executive branch on issues of procedure to be adopted by the board to ensure a fair hearing, we must await the development of these administrative law doctrines in our courts.
5. There have been some classic deadlocks in Canada between the Minister and the agency. For example, the "pay TV" policy of the Minister of Communications has been rejected by the CRTC. In the case of commercial deletions by community antenna operators the Supreme Court of Canada found that the CRTC had the power to issue the order. However, the Minister had persuaded the CRTC to back off and observe the effect of the loss of tax deductibility threatened by the U.S. Congress with respect to certain expenditures in Canada. The result was a meshing of gears between the executive branch of government concerned with American relations on other matters and the CRTC, concerned with the administration of broadcasting policies in Canada but subject always to the overriding directions or policies of the executive branch.

The same problem of interface occurs in other areas of government. Consider the relationship of the Minister of Transport on the one hand and the Canadian Transportation Commission on the other. We find in the proceedings of the standing committee of the House of Commons on transportation the following interesting exchange (reported in Janisch):[49]

> Mr. Stewart: Mr. Minister, have there been any consultations between yourself and the CTC on this application of Transair?
> Mr. Marchand: No, there was no consultation with me. I do not know if there was inside the department, but not with me. I had discussions with Mr. Schreyer and Mr. Evans on this, but not with the CTC.
> Mr. Stoner (Deputy Minister of Transport): Normally when a case is before the CTC as a court of record, there really is not a discussion while the application is, if you will, *sub judice*.
> Mr. Stewart: Mr. Minister, do you not make recommendations to the CTC on areas of the country where there is no air service? Where there has been a formal application made, do you make recommendations to the CTC?

Mr. Marchand: I usually do not. If there is an application to drop a service, there is an appeal to the Cabinet. Of course, I have to discuss that and we can reverse the decision of the CTC.

6. On the other hand the Ontario Municipal Board has adopted a number of government policy announcements and recently has stated that the Board is applying such statements more frequently as the government comes to play a larger and larger role in land use and planning throughout the province. In this developing role the province is apparently promulgating specific land use policies affecting all parts of the province and these policies the OMB apparently consider binding upon them although the statute is silent.
7. The issue will arise even more sharply if and when some owner loses a valuable zoning status by reason of a directive not disclosed to the owner or the public at the time of the OMB confirmation of the zoning by-law and which directive is challenged on the basis that either
   (a) a fair hearing had not been accorded the owner; or,
   (b) the policy in any case was based on wrong information; or,
   (c) it is not a policy statement in the legislative sense but a bill of attainder in the American sense directed at an individual by means of sub-delegated legislation by the executive branch.
8. There is at present a serious lack of procedural regularity in political appeals from such boards as the CTC and the OMB to the federal and provincial cabinets respectively and any agreement on the effect of the resulting isolated or unconnected decisions on future operations of the administrative tribunal concerned. Consider, for example, the position of the CTC in the future, having regard to the fate of its decisions with respect to Transair-P.W.A. ownership issues, the Nordair-Air Canada ownership issue, and the grant of licence to CP Air subsequently reversed and awarded by Cabinet to Eastern Provincial Airlines. There is no conclusion, of course, to the dynamics of the common law, but something in the nature of a conclusion is found in another article by Janisch, "Policy making in Regulation: Towards a New Definition of the Status of Independent Regulatory Agencies in Canada".[50]

There are no quick imported solutions available. It is not a matter of simply choosing to subscribe to political accountability through ministerial responsibility on the one hand or the integrity of impartial, independent decision making on the other. Of course, we must seek to learn from American or English experience (to do otherwise would be to adopt an ostrich-like posture)—but what we have to create is a fully indigenous status for our independent regulatory agencies.

These judicial and political discussions around the free world provide many general answers to the problem of the interlock in administrative law of the right to know and the right of the executive branch to keep its own counsel. Sometimes the courts have found, as we have seen in the *Johnson* case, a convenient watershed for disclosure as against non-disclosure in the arisal of a *lis*. Sometimes the courts, as for example in *H. Lavender and Son Ltd.* v. *Minister of Housing and Local Government*,[51] have found that, where the Minister of the Crown has determined the rights of the citizen by basing his decision on a decision reached elsewhere by another officer of the Crown, such procedure is tantamount to the abdication of responsibility mandated by the legislature and a violation of the right in the applicant citizen to discuss the material adverse to his interest upon which the determining authority is about to rely or has relied. From such instances as *Lavender* we draw no general conclusion or principle because it seems, as in the case of *Johnson*, a ready and convenient expedient by which a line can be drawn between the right in administrative law to know the case being brought before the tribunal and the right in the executive function to remain aloof from the courts and their procedures. More helpful in the search for an operative principle in this field are those decisions conveniently illustrated by *In re Canadian Radio-Television Commission and in re London Cable TV Limited,*[52] where the courts have found that an administrative tribunal, where it is acting upon information furnished to that tribunal by persons other than the applicant, must, in order to afford in the words of Jacket C.J. "a meaningful hearing," give the applicant before the Board the opportunity to examine and meet the operative information in the possession of the tribunal.

The impact of this decision is limited by the fact that the court was there discussing material which did not originate within the staff or facilities of the tribunal but was required to be filed with the tribunal by the company whose business was under Commission regulation. The other parties to the hearing were denied access to the applicant company's financial statements and other information, and therefore the other parties, whatever may have been the status of the applicant company, were not parties to a "public hearing" within the meaning of that term in the context of the parent statute. The loss of opportunity for cross-examination on such material was not found by the court to be determinative of the issue of natural justice but rather it was the condition created by depriving the contending parties of information known only to the tribunal and the applicant company.

The Federal Court founded its judgment not so much upon the nature of the Commission's function but on the requirement of the statute that the Commission must hold "a public hearing". The court found the public hearing to be a condition precedent to the exercise of the Commission's powers and, as an unexpressed condition precedent to the hearing, the contending parties must be on the same footing as regards access to the information upon which the Commission was proceeding to dispose of the issue.

Turning now from the judicial arena to the political arena one finds a developing legislative technique of providing a mechanism whereby public policy formulated by the executive branch of government from time to time is communicated to the administrative tribunal seized with the burden of implementing the public policy. These statutorily authorized "directives" are at the same time made known to the public at large. This technique obviously has the benefit of meeting the right to know before the precise issue arises in the administrative conflict. This technique also has the advantage of placing all parties before a tribunal and the members of the tribunal itself in the same position as though the public policy assigned to the board for implementation had been announced in the parent statute. The genius of the administrative tribunal has long been considered to be the flexibility which it has introduced into democratic government and it would appear that the use of orders in council and other public directives from the executive branch to the administrative unit is a further refinement of the flexibility of the administrative tribunal. Reference in this connection might be had to the Atomic Energy Control Act, s. 7:[53] "The Board shall comply with any general or special direction given by the Minister with reference to the carrying out of its purposes." This presumably relates to government policy with reference to uranium export permits. See also the Broadcasting Act, s. 17(3):[54] "The CBC may require the Minister to consider any licence condition attached by the CRTC to a licence of the Corporation and the Minister (after consultation with the CRTC and the CBC) may give a direction with respect to the condition."

A discussion on the general position of the administrative tribunal and the courts would not be complete without some reference to the increasingly important function of the modern administrative tribunal in the field of delegated or sub-legislation. Many of the federal and provincial boards now have varied, diverse and perhaps even conflicting responsibilities. Some boards must, for example, determine issues between members of the regulated sector of the community and at the same time establish regulations tantamount to orders in council flowing from the executive branch of government itself. This appears to be a peculiarly Canadian development. There are many examples, including the National Energy Board, the CRTC and the CTC. In the provincial field we see regulations promulgated by highway transport boards, workmen's compensation boards, the Alberta Energy Conservation Board and various planning boards.

Sometimes these roles become entwined or confused. For example, a licensing tribunal frequently might in essence create a regulation by the insertion of conditions in licences issued on an individual basis but repeatedly and across the industry in question. Obvious difficulties arise where the condition is not universally included in issued licences. Other difficulties flow from the fact that sometimes the regulations adopted by the board require for their legal effectiveness confirmation by order in council. Where other techniques are adopted by the administrative board to create regulations binding upon the regulated industry, the safeguard of executive confirmation is avoided. Further difficulties arise where the administrative tribunal is a licensing agency as well as an agency seized with the duty of determining issues between licence holders and between the licence holder and the administrative board itself. Finally, there is the adminisrative confusion which arises where the administrative tribunal holds hearings prior to the adoption of industry-wide regulations. The adoption of regulations by such a technique may, in some instances, be the basis for a challenge of succeeding regulations adopted after some other procedure wherein the right of the industry member to participate is disregarded. Into these many problems this study does not delve. We are here concerned with a much narrower issue arising in those administrative proceedings which constitute, in the legal sense, a *lis*. In that circumstance we have witnessed the evolution of some kind of a public right to know, prior to or during the disposition of the *lis*, the potentially decisive or controlling material or information upon which the tribunal proposes to or does ultimately rely. This is, at the moment, something more than an embryonic right and something less than a clearly defined, broadly applicable principle of law. The evolution of these principles will no doubt be the subject of much administrative litigation in the 1980's.

NOTES

1. (1978), 80 D.L.R. (3d) 85.
2. (1978), 7 O.M.B.R. 233.
3. (1979), 95 D.L.R. (3d) 298.
4. (1606), 6 Co. Rep. 48b.
5. *R.* v. *University of Cambridge* (1723), 1 Str. 557, *per* Fortescue J.
6. [1911] A.C. 179, at p. 182.
7. [1915] A.C. 120, at p. 132.
8. [1914] 1 K.B. 160, at p. 188.
9. [1939] O.R. 627.
10. *Ibid.*, at p. 645.
11. [1935] S.C.R. 441.
12. *Ibid.*, at p. 452.
13. *Ibid.*, at pp. 453-454.
14. [1915] A.C. 120, at p. 134.
15. *Ibid.*, at p. 137.
16. [1951] A.C. 66.
17. [1964] A.C. 40.
18. *Ibid.*, at p. 75.
19. [1972] 2 Q.B. 299.
20. [1979] 1 S.C.R. 311.
21. [1975] 1 S.C.R. 118, at p. 137.
22. Wade, *Administrative Law* (4th ed. 1977), pp. 744-745.

23. (1949, Hamlyn Lecture), p. 83.
24. Judgment of the Supreme Court of Canada rendered Oct. 7, 1980.
25. (1965), 47 D.L.R. (2d) 482.
26. *Ibid.*, at p. 486.
27. *Judicial Review of Administrative Action* (4th ed. 1980).
28. *Ibid.*, at p. 313.
29. [1978] 2 S.C.R. 141.
30. [1969] N.Z.L.R. 256, at p. 263.
31. [1941] 1 K.B. 53, at p. 69.
32. Law Reform Commission of Canada study paper, 1978, at p. 72.
33. *Ibid.*, at p. 73.
34. (1978), 22 N.R. 225.
35. [1973] F.C. 927.
36. *Ibid.*, at p. 940.
37. [1947] 2 All E.R. 395.
38. [1915] A.C. 120.
39. *Supra*, ftn. 37, at pp. 399-400.
40. *Supra*, ftn. 37, at p. 401.
41. *Ibid.*
42. (1965), 118 C.L.R. 177 (H.C. of Aust.).
43. *Ibid.*, at p. 188.
44. *Ibid.*, at p. 192.
45. *Ibid.*, at p. 193.
46. [1971] 1 All E.R. 65.
47. *Ibid.*, at p. 80.
48. (1934), 295 U.S. 602.
49. *Op. cit.*, ftn. 32, at p. 115.
50. (1979), 17 Osgoode Hall L.J. 46, at p. 62.
51. [1970] 3 All E.R. 871.
52. [1976] 2 F.C. 621.
53. R.S.C. 1970, c. A-19, as amended.
54. R.S.C. 1970, c. B-11, as amended.

18

Judicial Review under Common Law Remedies and the Statutory Code of Section 28 of the "Federal Court Act"

D. Michael M. Goldie

Introduction

Since June 1, 1971 the Federal Court of Canada has exercised virtually exclusive jurisdiction over the administrative agencies of the Government of Canada.

This superintending jurisdiction was split between the Trial Division and the Court of Appeal: the former, by virtue of s. 18, having the exclusive power to grant injunctive or declaratory relief or to issue any of the prerogative writs (except habeas corpus) and the latter, under s. 28, having the power to review decisions of federal administrative agencies upon complaints of failure to observe principles of natural justice, of exceeding or declining jurisdiction, for error in law or because the decision was based on an erroneous finding of fact made in a perverse or capricious manner or without regard to the material before it.

It will be seen that s. 28 describes the reasons commonly given when granting relief under the principal prerogative writs identified by name in s. 18.

Thus the Trial Court grants relief in the traditional form. The Court of Appeal works with a statutory code. Both are directed to the same end—the superintending of inferior tribunals.

The Court of Appeal early limited its jurisdiction by saying that s. 28 was available only in respect of a final decision. Apart from this, it was for many years accepted that what could be done under the prerogative writs in the Trial Division could be done by the Court of Appeal and since the former's jurisdiction was ousted whenever the latter's was available the business of the one soon far outstripped that of the other. In the first six and one half years of the Federal Court's existence some 2,187 applications were made to the Court of Appeal under s. 28 while in the same period only 438 applications were made to the Trial Division under s. 18.

All of this appeared to support the conclusion of the Law Reform Commission of Canada, as stated in Working Paper No. 18 of 1977 (p. 16) that:

> ". . . there is some reason to suppose that the sole purpose of Section 18 was to remove from the provincial courts the power of review of federal administrative authorities. . . .

and that the real instrument of judicial review was to be the Court of Appeal acting under s. 28.

The legislative scheme, perceived in this light, was to blot out the common law remedies exercised by the provincial superior courts by vesting this jurisdiction in the Trial Division of the Federal Court while, at the same time, superseding it with a statutory code of review applied by the Court of Appeal.

So much was said by Mr. Turner, when, as Minister of Justice speaking on second reading of the "Federal Court Act" on March 25, 1970, he said:

> There is a growing feeling among those who practise law and those who observe the judgments of the courts that these ancient common law remedies are no longer adequate for present-day purposes. We as legislators must surely be certain that when we set up a statutory body to administer the fine legal principles in accordance with defined procedures, or in accordance with the rule of law and natural justice as interpreted by the courts, the jurisdiction we have created and conferred will be exercised properly and for the proper benefit of those for whom it was established. There is only one mechanism that can afford us that satisfaction, and that mechanism is the duly constituted and independent courts of this country.
>
> I believe that our courts must be properly empowered to make certain that the jurisdiction which Parliament has created and given to boards and tribunals is exercised in the way that Parliament intended the jurisdiction to be exercised. For this reason, the bill provides that the new court of appeal will have jurisdiction to review the decisions and orders of the federal boards, commissions and tribunals stripped of the archaic legalisms that have traditionally applied to the old remedies.

The result of this desire to cast off the shackles of these ancient remedies was s. 28(1) which reads as follows:

> 28.(1) Notwithstanding section 18 or the provisions of any other Act, the Court of Appeal has jurisdiction to hear and determine an application to review and set aside a decision or order, other than a decision or order of an administrative nature not required by law to be made on a judicial or quasi-judicial basis, made by or in the course of proceedings before a federal board,

commission or other tribunal, upon the ground that the board, commission or tribunal

(a) failed to observe a principle of natural justice or otherwise acted beyond or refused to exercise its jurisdiction;
(b) erred in law in making its decision or order, whether or not the error appears on the face of the record; or
(c) based its decision or order on an erroneous finding of fact that it made in a perverse or capricious manner or without regard for the material before it.

If you are with me so far, you will appreciate that the Trial Division was handed the tortoise—the archaic legalisms of the prerogative writs, while the Court of Appeal was handed the hare—a shiny new statutory code of review from which these archaic legalisms had been stripped. And just to make sure, the Trial Division was handicapped by the opening words of s. 28.

The purpose of this paper is to examine briefly recent case law dealing with these two sections and to put the question: which has come closest to attaining the objective stated by Mr. Turner some nine years ago?

The Advantages of Section 28

The positive aspects of s. 28 are obvious. Some are:

(a) Questions of standing are resolved liberally by virtue of the provisions in subs. (2): "any party directly affected by the decision or order in question";
(b) The direction in subs. (5) to deal with applications summarily and without delay has been faithfully followed by the court;
(c) The removal of the privative clauses obtained by virtue of the words in subs. (1) "Notwithstanding Section 18 or the provisions of any other Act. . . ." has been beneficial but I should note, notwithstanding this clause, the re-appearance of privative clauses aimed at s. 28: a recent amendment to the "Canada Labour Code: (S.C. 1978, c. 27 as amended) provides:

> 122.(1) Subject to this Part, every order or decision of the Board is final and shall not be questioned or reviewed in any court, except in accordance with paragraph 28(1)(a) of the *Federal Court Act*.

I refer also to s. 156(1) (1978 amendment).

(d) Further, the broad definition of "federal board, commission or other tribunal" in conjunction with the availability of review under s. 28 has opened a number of doors that would be otherwise difficult to enter.
(e) There was an advance over the old forms which governed applications for the prerogative writs. The procedural law governing the old writs was complex. The cure represented by the judicial review statutes in some of the common law provinces shows what can be done at this

level. Certainly the means of seeking the common law remedies now available in Ontario and British Columbia are simple and straightforward and as to these, s. 28 now offers no great advantage to the litigant. It did when enacted.

(f) The question of the discretionary nature of the remedies under the prerogative writs became academic.

(g) For the litigant the process was relatively inexpensive. The court registry prepares the equivalent of the case on appeal—often a costly part of any proceedings before an appellate court.

(h) Finally, starting at the Court of Appeal level was seen as eliminating one level in the judicial level.

Disadvantages of Section 28

For our purposes the basic disadvantage of s. 28 must be seen in the exclusionary clause:

> . . . other than a decision or order of an administrative nature not required by law to be made on a judicial or quasi-judicial basis, ...

Professor Wade noted that these words are more than faintly reminiscent of the famous passage in the judgment of Atkin L.J., in *R.* v. *Electricity Commrs.*[1] where he said:

> Wherever any body of persons having legal authority to determine questions affecting the rights of subjects, *and having the duty to act judicially,* act in excess of their legal authority. . . .[2]

they would be subject to *certiorari.* This was said by Lord Hewart some four years later to superadd a characteristic: that the body has to act judicially. All this was criticized by Lord Reid in *Ridge* v. *Baldwin,*[3] where he sought to show that the judicial element is to be inferred from the nature of the power exercised. Finally, it should be noted that the draftsman of the 1970 "Federal Court Act" would have or should have had before him the criticism contained in S. A. de Smith's book *Judicial Review of Administrative Action* published in 1968 on the debilitation of the *audi alterem partem* rule by the division between judicial and administrative decisions.

It is easy to criticize the Canadian courts for not being sufficiently innovative in the field of administrative law but it is not a valid ground of criticism to bring this charge against those who have to work with these words. Look at what is required:

First: one might well ask what is the purpose of the word "administrative" in the phrase ". . . a decision or order of an administrative nature . . ."? It describes the end result and implies a test based on the function of the order. It is far from precise. The succeeding clause "required by law to be made on a judicial or quasi-judicial basis" suggests a second exclusionary test directed to the manner in which the decision was arrived at and in itself surely provides enough problems. The most recent struggle with this language is found in *M.N.R.* v. *Coopers and Lybrand,*[4] where Dickson J., for the court, said:[5]

> Government ministries and agencies carry out a different form of work than that done by the Courts. They do not simply take on closely analogous functions. Their primary concern is with policy objectives, rather than adjudication *inter partes,* in regulating relations between individuals and Government in the distribution of benefits. The dichotomy between judicial and administrative is still reasonably easy to discern but the great growth of Government at all levels, the proliferation of Government agencies, and increased Government involvement in social and economic affairs have all tended to render classification more difficult. There is much overlap. Administrative decisions and orders frequently subsume the judicial and *quasi*-judicial. Section 28 of the *Federal Court Act* expressly recognizes that some decisions or orders of an administrative nature are required by law to be made on a judicial or *quasi*-judicial basis; superimposed upon the administrative and institutional decision-making process of an official may be the duty to act judicially.

Having said this, he deals at length with the second of the two exclusionary requirements of s. 28. His reason is fairly plain: if the decision making body is clearly required to act in a judicial or quasi-judicial manner, then it matters not how you classify the result. The difficulty lies in the phrase ". . . not required by law to be made on a judicial or quasi-judicial basis . . ." and since this describes a process, that is what you must look to.

In itself this represents an advance. In 1977 the Supreme Court decided in *Howarth* v. *National Parole Board,*[6] that the action of the National Parole Board in revoking a parole fell outside the scope of s. 28. The majority treated s. 28 as an exception to the general jurisdiction in s. 18 and based its decision on the *nature* of the decision. The dissent, written by Mr. Justice Dickson, after calling in aid the "fairness" doctrine of *Ridge* v. *Baldwin,* focused upon the process of adjudication and not upon the classification of the result. And now, for practical purposes, the Supreme Court has told us, when dealing with s. 28, to look primarily at the process. This direction in *Coopers and Lybrand* must also be taken to modify the reasoning of the majority in *Martineau* v. *Matsqui Institution Inmate Disciplinary Bd.,*[7] where Mr. Justice Dickson joined in the dissenting judgment written by the Chief Justice. There the question turned on whether the internal directive describing the procedure followed by a discipline board was "law" sufficient to bring the result within the words "required by law". Some of the majority held that the result was still an administrative act and that the procedural rules were not "law" as that word was used in s. 28.

I will refer to the *Martineau* saga again, the last chapter of which was heard by the Supreme Court this spring.

My point here is that it has taken eight years from the passage of the Federal Court Act to get us to where we can say that the exception to the jurisdiction under s. 28 is to be determined primarily by looking at the process and not the result. Not a very impressive track record for Mr. Turner's vehicle stripped of archaic legalisms!

Having directed our attention to the proper test Mr. Justice Dickson in *Coopers and Lybrand* then seeks to provide us with a road map on how to distinguish what matters are reviewable and what are not.

He sets up four criteria and measures the decisions in question against them. At first blush these criteria appear to provide some objectively defined means of letting us know when a decision is by law required to be made on a judicial or quasi-judicial basis. But in truth they do not. He implicitly acknowledges this when he quotes Professor Mullan's article because Professor Mullan was arguing against the very use of such classifications. Indeed, this is a curious reference for Mr. Justice Dickson to use with respect to s. 28. In *Howarth* Pigeon J. said of s. 28:[8]

> Practically all the argument addressed to us by Counsel for the Appellant merely tended to show that a case could possibly be made for some common law remedy, that the Parole Board must have a duty to act fairly, not that it has to decide on a judicial or quasi-judicial basis.

Be that as it may, Mr. Justice Dickson concludes by acknowledging that the problem defies classification when he says:[9]

> Viewed from the broader perspectives of power, issue, and sanctions, it is difficult to conceive that the conclusion could be otherwise.

But the practitioner is left with his problem! He can expect no better guide than Mr. Justice Dickson's four points. But as we shall see, the common law has done much better in this area in simplifying this problem.

What can be done when the courts are not bound by statute was, of course, demonstrated some 16 years ago by the House of Lords in *Ridge* v. *Baldwin*.[10] During this time it was the most often cited, least followed case in Canada.

That it has triumphed, at least in the Provincial Courts is to be assumed from the 5-4 judgment of the Supreme Court of Canada delivered last fall in the case of *Nicholson* v. *Haldimand-Norfolk Regional Bd. of Commrs. of Police.*[11] Judgment was pronounced on October 3, 1978—some seven weeks before *Coopers and Lybrand.*

Nicholson was a constable with less than 18 months' service when he was discharged. His employer was entitled to do this without regard to the formalities attendant upon the discharge of one whose service exceeded this period. He was given no reason and he applied for judicial review on the ground that he had not been treated fairly. Mr. Justice Hughes of the Ontario Divisional Court made the order sought.

The Court of Appeal reversed. The Supreme Court of Canada allowed the appeal with four of the nine judges dissenting. Here we come to an important aspect of the case: relief was sought under the Judicial Review Procedure Act of Ontario where an applicant is entitled to relief as he would be entitled to in proceedings by way of an application for *certiorari*. It was acknowledged that *certiorari* for failure *to observe the rules of natural justice* was unavailable.

The result may be said to obliterate the distinction between "administrative" and "judicial" for courts called upon to apply the common law—both kinds of decisions are subject to judicial review. The distinction appears to be preserved with respect to the procedural steps the courts will require be observed—the Chief Justice, speaking for the majority, adopted the statement of Megarry J. in *Bates* v. *Lord Hailsham of St. Marylebone*:[12]

> . . . that in the sphere of the so-called quasi-judicial, the rules of natural justice run, and that in the administrative or executive field there is a general duty of fairness. . . .

What the common law courts can do is to examine the substance of the decision-making process and the effect of the decision and to fit to that process the requisite procedure. But what the Federal Court of Appeal is left with is the "black or white" problem of jurisdiction.

There is a further problem. The words of s. 28(1)(a) ". . . failed to observe a principle of natural justice . . ." are related to jurisdictional excess and leave no room for the application of the "fairness" rule where, in the circumstances, the procedural requirement calls for something short of the rules of natural justice.

The full effect of this was demonstrated in a judgment of the Federal Court of Appeal heard before *Nicholson* but pronounced some six weeks after the *Nicholson* judgment was handed down. The plaintiffs in *Inuit Tapirisat of Canada* v. *The Governor-in-Council*[13] sought from the Trial Division a writ of *certiorari* and a declaration that they had been denied a fair hearing.

The issue arose when the Governor in Council declined to vary a decision of the Canadian Radio-Television and Telecommunications Commission (CRTC). The Commission's decision was made on a rate application by Bell Canada. The plaintiffs opposed the application and had requested the Governor in Council, pursuant to s. 64(1) of the National Transportation Act to set aside the decision in part and to substitute its own order therefor. The Governor in Council's "hearing" consisted of a review of papers prepared by various government departments. The plaintiffs neither saw these papers nor were they informed of the substance. The Trial Division struck out the Statement of Claim, characterizing the process I have described as political and not one requiring adherence to any procedural requirements. On appeal the plaintiffs sought restoration only of the claim for declaration.

The Court of Appeal reversed, squarely resting its decision on *Nicholson*. Le Dain J.A. said:[14]

> In view of this decision it is not sufficient, . . . when a question is raised as to a duty to act fairly in a procedural sense, to find that the function or power in issue is neither judicial nor quasi-judicial.

Thus, s. 18 is now seen to be free of the characterization imposed on the Court of Appeal by virtue of the exclusionary clause in s. 28.

And it has achieved this freedom because the language of s. 18 allows the Trial Division to respond to the flexibility accorded the common law remedies.

Section 18 appears to have escaped from the blot of s. 28 but the final word on this awaits the decision of the Supreme Court of Canada in *Martineau* to which I will return.

Conclusion

We come now to the latest decision: *Harelkin* v. *The University of Regina*[15] pronounced on March 30, argued June, 1978. The Supreme Court of Canada, by a 4-3 decision, dismissed an appeal from the Saskatchewan Court of Appeal which denied to an expelled student *certiorari*, primarily on the ground that he failed to exercise a right of appeal. Dickson J. wrote the dissenting judgment.

The majority judgment reintroduces the notion that *certiorari* is a discretionary remedy even where there has been a breach of the rules of natural justice and requires exhaustion of remedies even where there has been a breach of a statutory direction.

The statutory code under s. 28 is free of this vice and on this one ground is superior to judicial review in the Provincial Courts.

The answer lies perhaps in the judicial review statutes which typically include the power to grant any relief in the nature of *mandamus*, prohibition or *certiorari*, declaration or injunction in relation to the exercise, refusal to exercise or proposed or purported exercise of a statutory power. A recent Trial Division judgment in British Columbia, *Islands Protection Society* v. *The Queen*,[16] said, *obiter*, the court could make a declaration that the Minister of Forests was under a duty to act fairly in exercising his power of decision in respect of renewing a Tree Farm Licence in advance of the actual decision. This dictum was based on *Nicholson* and *Inuit Tapirisat* and was decided before *Harelkin*.

Declarations, to which Canadian lawyers are accustomed may, however, answer in part the problem revived by *Harelkin*.

Whether the Trial Division of the Federal Court possesses this flexibility by virtue of s. 18 remains to be seen from *Martineau*. The *Inuit Tapirisat* case suggests this is so.

I have spoken of *Martineau*. The facts are simple. He and a fellow inmate were disciplined. His attempts to seek relief under s. 28 were to no avail. He started over again in the Trial Division seeking relief under s. 18. An application to strike out his Statement of Claim succeeded in the Federal Court of Appeal—that court holding that the decision of the Supreme Court on the s. 28 application applied—the Chief Justice saying that every method of obtaining *certiorari* under s. 18 was covered off under s. 28. The appeal in the Supreme Court of Canada was heard in the spring and judgment may be pronounced any day.

Whatever it says, the time has clearly come to overhaul the Federal Court Act. The rigidity and obsolescence of the statutory code in s. 28 has been demonstrated.

Canadian courts have shown that they can be as astute as their English counterparts when dealing with judicial review statutes which rely upon relief in the nature of the prerogative writs and provide for declaratory relief.

The Canadian Bar's Committee on the Federal Court recommended that all proceedings for judicial review of federal agencies commence, but for statutorily stated exceptions, in the Trial Division.

If this is done, and the trap of s. 28 is avoided, the prospects for adequate judicial review of federal agencies in Canada will be as good as anything we have heard described in the United Kingdom.

NOTES

1. [1924] 1 K.B. 171.
2. *Ibid.*, at p. 205.
3. [1964] A.C. 40, at p. 74.
4. (1978), 92 D.L.R. (3d) 1 (S.C.C.).
5. *Ibid.*, at p. 4.
6. [1976] 1 S.C.R. 453.
7. [1978] 1 S.C.R. 118.
8. *Supra*, ftn. 6, at p. 474.
9. *Supra*, ftn. 4, at p. 9.
10. [1964] A.C. 40.
11. [1979] 1 S.C.R. 311.
12. [1972] 1 W.L.R. 1373, at p. 1378. See also the quotation from de Smith, at p. 680 in the Chief Justice's judgment.
13. (1978), 24 N.R. 361.
14. *Ibid.*, at p. 368.
15. (1979), 26 N.R. 364.
16. [1979] 4 W.W.R. 1 (B.C.).

19

The Royal Commission and the Courts

Gordon F. Henderson

Introduction

Judicial supervision of the proceedings, orders and decisions of Royal Commissions in Canada is intensely controversial because of the unique position of Royal Commissions in our system of government. The controversy has intensified in recent years because of the inclination of Royal Commissions to affect the rights of individuals with almost numbing contempt when they exercise their mandate. It is natural that the courts are invited to afford the protection that individuals require from the abuse of power of Royal Commissions.

To put the topic in perspective, a brief discussion of the place of these commissions in our system of government is necessary.

The Position of the Royal Commission in Canada

Like most major institutions of government, Royal Commissions in Canada have a British origin. In the course of history, however, the Canadian concept of Royal Commission has substantially changed and is today very unlike a British Royal Commission.

The first general statute that conferred upon the government the authority to establish Royal Commissions was enacted in Canada on June 9, 1846 by the Assembly of the United Provinces of Canada. This statute marked the first step toward a distinct course of Royal Commissions in Canada. Although the statute was intended as temporary, it was re-enacted repeatedly until Confederation in 1867, thus institutionalizing Royal Commissions in various enactments often called "Public Inquiries Act". The enactment of the general inquiry statute transformed Royal Commissions into a machinery of government unlike its British counterpart. Whereas a British Royal Commission is generally an extension of the executive and dependent upon the royal warrant which confers the powers of the commission, the Canadian Royal Commission is a statutory body. Its members are appointed by a commission from the Governor-in-Council, but its powers are articulated in the statute. Yet they are different from the British "statutory commissions", which are commissions established under a specific statute to review a given specific situation. The significance of this distinction is that the British Royal Commission yields to a mechanism of control in the political arena in each individual instance since its powers are limited to those conferred upon it by the royal warrant or specifically by statute. In Canada, on the other hand, the general inquiries statute, drafted in broad terms, has enabled the government, virtually without restraint, to establish a commission on any subject it wishes, and such commission may exercise powers that are conferred by the general statute.

The Canadian Royal Commission has broad powers under the general inquiries statute. These powers are generally beyond the ambit of power conferred upon the British Royal Commission, either by royal warrant or statute. As early as the 1846 Act, for instance, a Royal Commission in Canada had coercive powers in conducting its proceedings. This statute provided:

> Whereas the power of procuring evidence under oath in such cases would greatly tend to be to the public advantage as well as to afford protection to Her Majesty's subjects from false and malicious testimony on representations,

The commission was given the power to compel a witness to appear and give evidence. These broad and pervasive coercive powers are more far-reaching than the coercive jurisdiction provided in the British statute, The Tribunal of Inquiry (Evidence) Act, 1921. The coercive jurisdiction under British statute is subject to stringent and well-defined limitations. They are less frequently invoked since such tribunal can only be created by resolution of both Houses of Parliament and only for the purpose of inquiring into matters of "urgent public importance". The Salmon Commission in England in its report on Tribunals of Inquiry states that in 1966 there were only 16 such tribunals created since the Act was enacted in 1921.

In comparison, a Royal Commission in Canada may be established to inquire into "any matter connected with the good government of Canada in the conduct of any part of the public business thereof". They have been established to inquire into such significant problems as taxation, dominion-provincial relations, bilingualism, and Canadian unity, but they have also considered matters as mundane as the causes of the floods in the St. Lawrence, the living conditions of the musk-ox, the collapse of a bridge and the sex life of the oyster. The Federal Law Reform Commission has estimated that in 1977 approximately 1,900 federal commissions have been established since Confederation.

The most fundamental difference between the Canadian Royal Commission and its British counterpart can be found in the conduct of their proceedings. The institutionalization of the Royal Commission in Canada brought with it the introduction of a formalized and adversarial procedure. This "judicialization" of Royal Commissions in Canada has clouded their social and political functions and underlined their inquisitorial and adversarial proceedings.

The procedure in Canada is characterized by the use of subpoena and search powers, the requirement of counsel, and the various mechanisms for review of their action, decision or orders. It proceeds from the assumption, valid for judicial proceedings, that facts will better emerge from adversarial contest, by counsel and their witnesses, than from the diligence and imagination of the commission. Aside from creating problems of cost, such assumption creates problems of power. More importantly, it has created a barrier between the commissioners and the people from whom it expects to collect its facts, data, information and opinions.[1]

Royal Commissions in Canada today are thus unique, almost anomalous institutions. Pursuant to the general statutes of inquiry, the public, and more importantly, the politicians, consider Royal Commissions to be an essential device of government in Canada. The Federal Law Reform Commission believes that they bring "objectivity and expertise, free from constraints of a legislative timetable to the solution of problems. They provide an additional vehicle for the expression of public opinion."[2] I share the view that Royal Commissions are useful tools in the efficient and open operation of parliamentary democracy.[3]

The challenge to the rights of individuals that invites judicial review of their actions stems, not exclusively from their position in our system of government, but mainly from the manner in which they discharge their mandate. The increasing "judicialization" of their proceedings, especially the exercise of their coercive jurisdiction, argues for the need of judicial review. Unfortunately, we have not yet reached that degree of sophistication to establish as an undisputed proposition of law that Royal Commissions, although not judicial or quasi-judicial bodies, exercise some judicial or quasi-judicial powers that should yield to judicial review. The reason for this stems from the apparent inability of some courts to recognize that in resolving the conflict between individual rights and the power of the commission, the relevant issue is not whether the commission, as an entity is judicial or quasi-judicial but whether the particular action it has taken can be characterized as judicial or quasi-judicial.

The Nature of the Commission or The Nature of the Action of the Commission

In the absence of a clear statutory direction that particular actions of a Royal Commission are subject to judicial review, judicial review can only arise if the general principles of judicial review of administrative action apply to the Royal Commissions. The major issue for determination in these cases is whether the commission is exercising a judicial or quasi-judicial function that it becomes amenable to judicial supervisory jurisdiction.

Before discussing this problem, it is useful to review some aspects of the general inquiries statute. I have chosen for this purpose the federal statute and the Ontario statute. In respect of the Federal Inquiries Act,[4] a distinction is made between Public Inquiries which are governed by Part I of the Act, and Departmental Investigations which are regulated in Part II. Public Inquiries can only be initiated by the Governor-in-Council and the subject of inquiry may be any matter connected with the good government of Canada or the conduct of any part of the public business. The powers of the commission include the summoning of any witnesses, requiring them to give evidence on oath or solemn affirmation, and the power to require production of such *documents* and *things* as the commission may deem necessary to carry on a full investigation. As a corollary, the commission is given the power to enforce the attendance of witnesses and to compel them to give evidence in a manner analogous to a civil court of record.

A departmental investigation in initiated by a Minister of a department, and the subject matter refers simply to the "state and management of the business, or any part of the business, of such department". Sections 7 and 8 of the Act confer wide powers on the commission conducting a departmental investigation. The commission may enter any public office or institution, and has the authority to examine records, books and documents in such office. The commission may also require the attendance of witnesses and give evidence on oath or affirmation, and to issue subpoena or summons. It is also given the power to delegate to others the taking of evidence. Under s. 10 of the Act, a violation of the various orders, subpoena or summons of the commission constitutes a summary conviction offence.

Both types of commission are given general powers to employ counsel, advisers and experts, and some of these experts may be deputed to inquire into certain aspects of the commission's mandate. Those persons may be given, by order-in-council, the same powers possessed by the commission.

The Ontario Public Inquiries Act, 1971,[5] enacted after the Royal Commission on the Inquiry into Civil Rights published its Report in 1968, has a better system. It transferred certain powers of the commission to the courts, or limited them accordingly, to ensure protection of individual rights. Like its federal counterpart, however, a commission may require, by summons, any person to give evidence on oath or affirmation and to produce documents and things relevant and admissible as evidence at the inquiry. The governor-in-council may authorize the application of Part III of the Act in respect of a particular commission. This Part creates various enforcement methods through the courts that would not otherwise be available. Further, by s. 17, the commission is permitted to appoint a person to make an investigation relevant to the subject matter of the inquiry which the commission is conducting.

The courts have considered, on the basis of the statutes, the status of the commissions of inquiry and the nature of the proceedings conducted by them. It has never been disputed that they are not courts and that accordingly they do not decide substantive law issues, or issues concerning rights and duties of individuals. Attempts have been made to characterize commissions as administrative tribunals, acting in judicial or quasi-judicial roles and thus make them subject to review by the courts. The courts, however, have been adamant in insisting that commissions of inquiry are not to be classed as judicial tribunals and are thus not subject to the same rules that govern a judicial tribunal. The most recent expression of this position is that of Mr. Justice Cattanach in *Re Copeland and MacDonald*,[6] which considered the nature of the McDonald Inquiry into R.C.M.P. wrong-doing. The McDonald Commission of Inquiry was established under the Inquiries Act to investigate and report on certain alleged illegal activities of the R.C.M.P. Mr. Copeland, alleged to have been a victim of the R.C.M.P. activities, sought a prohibition order under s. 18 of the Federal Court Act. He contended that he could not expect a fair hearing from the McDonald Commission on the ground that each of the three commissioners were biased. He argued that the function of the commission is to determine the extent to which the members of the government, the Cabinet and the Liberal Party were aware of, authorized, or were in any way involved in the illegal activities of the R.C.M.P. Since, in his view, Mr. Justice McDonald and Commissioners Rickert and Gilbert were close personal friends and supporters of the Solicitor-General and of the Prime Minister, they were biased.

Mr. Justice Cattanach first considered whether the commission was obliged to determine an issue or *lis inter partes*. The existence of such an issue before a tribunal characterizes a judicial or quasi-judicial function. This question was central to the case as it is only if the commission is exercising a judicial or quasi-judicial function that it would be subject to the bias prohibition. Examining the Order-in-Council, Mr. Justice Cattanach found that the commission, as constituted under the Federal Inquiries Act, was merely authorized to "conduct an investigation," "to report the facts" and "to advise and make reports" on the R.C.M.P. activities.

> Thus at its very highest the commission is but a fact-finding, reporting and advisory body.
>
> Paraphrasing and applying the words of Lord Denning, M.R., to the Commissioners herein, they are not even *quasi*-judicial, for they decide nothing, they determine nothing.
>
> The commission reports to the Governor-in-Council and it is for him to decide what shall be done. He may implement the advice given in the report in

> whole or in part or he may consign the report to oblivion. The action to be taken thereon is exclusively his decision.
>
> In contrasting the position of a Judge in Court and that of a fact-finding and advisory body which can only be classed as administrative, notwithstanding that both hold hearings, the gulf is so wide between them that the common law standards of bias are not applicable to the latter.

In my judgment, the Supreme Court decision in *Martineau* v. *Matsqui Institution Inmate Disciplinary Bd.*[7] has cast very serious doubt on exclusion of judicial review of the proceedings and decisions of Royal Commissions on this traditional ground. In *Martineau*, the Supreme Court has shown willingness to allow review of ministerial action by *certiorari* on the ground of fairness. In my view, any demonstrable unfairness in the proceedings or decision of a Royal Commission or bias by a member of the commission invites judicial review by the appropriate prerogative writ.

Judicial Review of Specific Actions

In the background of the general conception of Royal Commissions, there have been instances in which the courts have, for various reasons, asserted their supervisory jurisdiction. I wish to examine some of these cases.

The Constitutional Competence of the Appointing authority

The federal system in Canada creates some constraints on the ability of the various levels of government to appoint a commission to inquire into certain matters. The major allocation of legislative powers between Parliament and the provinces in ss. 91 and 92 of the B.N.A. Act also marks the boundaries upon which a Royal Commission appointed by them may inquire into subject matters. The courts, in their role as arbiters of power under our Constitution, may exercise supervisory jurisdiction over Royal Commissions although they are not, in the traditional sense, judicial tribunals. They may examine whether a commission appointed by one level of government can validly inquire into a subject matter in that it does not fall within the competence of that level of government.

An example of this judicial supervision occurred in inquiries into criminal activities in Canada. Section 91(27) of the British North America Act confers upon Parliament legislative competence in matters of criminal law including procedure. Section 92(14), on the other hand, grants to the provinces the power to legislate in matters relating to the "Administration of Justice in the Province". In *Di Iorio* v. *Warden of the Montreal Jail*[8] the authority of a provincially constituted commission to inquire into criminal activities was challenged on the ground that the inquiry into these matters falls within the competence of Parliament. The appellants were summoned as witnesses before the Quebec Police Commission, but they refused to testify. On a finding of contempt by the Commission, they petitioned the courts for writs of habeas corpus with *certiorari* in aid. The Supreme Court held that the provinces have the power to confer upon the commission to inquire into criminal activities within the province pursuant to their authority under s. 92(14). Mr. Justice Dickson, in a concurring judgment, held that the inquiry does not act as a criminal court or exercise criminal jurisdiction. The function of the inquiry is merely to investigate and report; no person is accused; those who appear do so as witnesses; there is no *lis*; the proceedings of the commission are not criminal proceedings in the sense that punishment is their aim. Accordingly, the commission is not seeking to encroach upon the authority of Parliament to legislate on criminal law or procedure.

In a subsequent case, *The Attorney-General of Quebec* v. *The Attorney General of Canada*,[9] otherwise known as the *Keable Inquiry* case, the Supreme Court had occasion to refine its reasons in *D'Iorio*. The Keable Inquiry was established by the Province of Quebec to investigate into certain criminal activities, including the alleged involvement of the Royal Canadian Mounted Police. On a claim of a coercive power under s. 7 of the Quebec Police Inquiry Commission Act[10] that confers upon the commission all powers of a judge of a Superior court in respect to the hearing, the commission issued a subpoena to the Solicitor General of Canada and subsequently issued orders requiring him to produce a number of documents respecting the administration of the R.C.M.P. The Supreme Court qualified its broad pronouncement in *Di Iorio* and stated that the power of the provinces cannot be construed to allow an inquiry into the management and operation of a federal institution such as the R.C.M.P. or to compel the Crown, through the Solicitor General, to appear as witness.

Judicial Review of The Exercise of Coercive Jurisdiction of the Royal Commission

The common-law rule articulated by Viscount Haldane in *Attorney-General for Australia* v. *Colonial Sugar Refining Co. Ltd.*[11] is that a Royal Commission has no power to compel answers from witnesses, and that such power is not incidental to the execution of its powers under common law. This rule was applied in Canada in the *Keable Inquiry* case when the Supreme Court rejected the contention that the Keable Commission should be recognized to have this power since it was not necessarily conferred by the relevant provincial legislation. Mr. Justice Pigeon stated that

> Such powers are not available to a commission set up by virtue of the royal prerogative, they depend on statutory authority, in the present case, on the *Inquiries Act* under which this Commission was established.[12]

In Canada, since the first general inquiries legislation was enacted, Royal Commissions have been granted the power to summon witnesses, to compel them to testify, to produce documents and to disclose information within their control. Section 4 of the Federal Inquiries Act and s. 7 of the

Ontario Act create these exceptional powers that traditionally only courts possess. A Federal Royal Commission is, accordingly, given the power to punish for contempt by s. 5 of the Federal Act. The Ontario Act, under s. 8, authorizes the courts to whom the commission may refer the non-compliance, to punish or to take steps for the punishment of the person for contempt.

The Ontario position, novel in Canada, clearly contemplates the power of the courts to review the basis of the exercise of the coercive powers of the commission. The introduction of this procedure has gone far in neutralizing the thought that in matters of the exercise of coercive powers, the commission appears to be a judge and prosecutor of its own case. Mr. Justice Estey, then with the Ontario Court of Appeal, observed in *Re Yanover and Kiroff and The Queen*[13] the significance of this change in procedure:

> It is my view that, in the light of the variations in the powers of a commission brought about by the enactment of the Act and the repeal thereby of the *Public Inquiries Act*, R.S.O. 1960, c. 323, the powers of a commission now are essentially, if not exclusively, investigatory and are not judicial. When the authority of a commission to do any act or thing is called into question the power vested in the commission is limited to stating or refusing to state a case for the opinion of the Divisional Court. Nor has a commission the power it enjoyed under the former Act, now repealed, to enforce the attendance of witnesses and to compel them to give evidence and produce documents and things 'as is vested in any court in civil cases'. Specifically a commission no longer has the power to adjudge the conduct of a witness before it to be punishable contempt and to impose punishment for such conduct.
>
> Notwithstanding the removal from a commission of the power of punishing for contempt of it, it continues to be recognized that for the proper discharge of its duties under a commission issued under the Act, it is essential that the disobedience to or defiance of the lawful requirements of the commission attract punishment of the nature that Courts have traditionally meted out to those in contempt of Court. Nevertheless the legislation has denied to a commission any punitive power.

Mr. Justice Estey concluded that the function of the Divisional Court is that of a trial court, hence to judge, and that a stated case is in "the nature of information but one which constitutes *prima facie* but not conclusive evidence of the impropriety alleged". The court stated that the question whether the witness acted here "without lawful excuse" within the meaning of s. 8 of the Act is for the Divisional Court to find and the commission is precluded from making such finding. This finding is a "legal finding" that the court, not the commission, is entitled to make.

Where the commission may exercise a direct contempt power, however, the issue of coercive jurisdiction has been somewhat clouded. In some cases, the courts have found the position that Royal Commissions, as such, are not judicial or quasi-judicial bodies compelling enough that they hesitate asserting their supervisory jurisdiction. For instance, in *Stevens* v. *Restric-*

tive Trade Practices Commission,[14] the applicants urged the court to lift the order issued against them requiring them to appear and testify since they could not be compelled to testify against themselves. The trial division of the Federal Court stated:

> On the question of whether the well established Common Law Principle of 'nem tenetur se ipsum accusare' would be available to the Applicants, in order to exempt them from being compellable witnesses at the enquiry, it is clear that this principle applies only to proceedings where the person invoking it is in fact and in law an accused person.
>
> The Applicants do not presently stand accused of any criminal offence. There exists only allegations by certain persons that in their belief, the Applicants committed offences and that the evidence which they presented to the Director justifies that belief. The very purpose of the enquiry which resulted is to have the Commission examine whatever evidence which might be available, in order to enquire into what breaches of the Act might appear to have occurred, the nature of these breaches and what persons might be suspected of having committed them and finally to report its findings to the Minister. Should the Minister then, decide that charges should be laid it is only at that moment that the Applicants might become accused persons and no longer be compellable to testify in the resulting proceedings.

The courts have been less hesitant in exercising powers of judicial review if the issue is already beyond the mere issuance of coercive orders and has reached the point of enforcing such orders by contempt. They assert very simply that the punishment for contempt must be exercised with circumspection and that the action of the commission must be scrutinized under the same criteria as an inferior court's power to commit a person to prison or fine for contempt.

More recently, the Supreme Court of Canada has taken the position that no distinction between the power to compel witnesses to testify and to produce documents, on the one hand, and the power to punish for contempt, on the other, can be made. In *Cotroni* v. *The Quebec Police Commission*,[15] the Supreme Court stated that the validity of the conviction of a witness for contempt by a commission is a matter subject to judicial review. In the *Keable Inquiry* case, the court went further and held that because a commission of inquiry is not, in conducting the investigation and preparing a report, acting in a judicial or quasi-judicial capacity, the courts are not precluded from reviewing the exercise of the power to punish for contempt. The power to compel witnesses to testify, to produce documents, and to punish for contempt is "strictly a judicial act", hence amenable to judicial review.

Judicial Review of the Conduct of the Inquiry

The manner in which a Royal Commission conducts its inquiry has not been standardized by the general inquiries statute. This matter is generally left to the Commission for determination. The Royal Commission may hold a public hearing or an *in camera* hearing; it can adopt any manner of investigation it wishes; it may carry out the investigation directly or delegate the investigation to some commission personnel. The commission can appoint an expert, such as an accountant, engineer or scientist, to prepare and submit a research report and on the basis of such research report make its recommendations. In respect to witnesses, it can deal with the witness in a manner that courts or traditional tribunals customarily adopt. The evidentiary standard that it applies does need to be as high as the generally accepted standard of courts and traditional tribunals. The issue that arises during the conduct of the inquiry is to what extent these techniques of investigation may be reviewed by the courts at the instance of a person who is affected by the investigation. The ways in which the rights of individuals may be adversely affected by the conduct of the inquiry are legion. For purposes of this paper, I would like to examine the more usual and controversial instances: the right not to be exposed to prejudicial publicity generated by the inquiry, the right to be heard and to confront adverse witnesses, and the privilege against disclosure.

Modern society, characterized by instant and universal communication, suffers less from secrecy than from excessive publicity in the conduct of the inquiry by Royal Commissions. A person involved in the subject matter of the inquiry, whether as witness or otherwise, may be a prospective defendant in a civil or criminal case. Prejudicial publicity may influence the outcome of such future action. Even if no potential action is involved, the reputation of persons may be harmed by the publicity generated by the inquiry. In most cases, the major objective in establishing an inquiry is to generate publicity, to involve the public in a pedagogical exercise or to express opinion in a public forum. The Federal Law Reform Commission supported this objective in the following words:

> It should, however always be remembered that since one function of a public inquiry is often to allay public concern of some sort, and since it is desirable that a commission be seen to be operating fairly, whenever possible a commission to investigation should operate publicly.[16]

In contrast, the Balfour Committee in the United Kingdom found that the British Royal Commissions it had consulted had shown a high concern for the confidentiality of the proceedings.[17]

The courts, understandably, have not been willing to intervene in the conduct of the inquiry proceedings on a showing of prejudicial publicity. In *Re Ontario Crime Commission, Ex parte Feeley and McDermott*[18] Mr. Justice Schroeder, in fact found that in respect to organized crime the "inquiry and publicity are both powerful weapons in coping with this and other characteristic modern social evil".

In respect to the right to be heard and to confront adverse witnesses, the broad powers of the commission may permit it to exclude the person being investigated and their witnesses from appearing and participating in the proceedings before the commission. The Supreme Court of Canada, as early as 1935, has rejected the right to be heard and the right to confront during the course of an investigative process. In *St. John* v. *Fraser*,[19] the Attorney-General of British Columbia was conducting, through a delegate, an investigation into certain fraudulent acts pursuant to a provincial legislation. The appellants, among others, contended that they were not given notice of the examination of certain witnesses and were not accorded the opportunity of cross-examining such witnesses. The court was unanimous in reaching the decision that the investigation provided by the statute was not a judicial proceeding and that the statute intended the investigation to be private. Accordingly, no person shall have the right of cross-examining any witness whether the evidence or that witness affects the reputation of such person or not. Mr. Justice Davis considered the argument that the investigator was acting judicially and thus it was a denial of natural justice when the appellants were denied the right of cross-examination. The investigator was, in Mr. Justice Davis' view, an administrative officer, and the machinery set up by the statute was administrative, established solely for the purpose of inquiring into whether or not fraudulent practices had been committed. The investigator must act judicially, but "judicially" only in the sense that he acts fairly and impartially. This rule has not changed substantially in recent years in Canada.

In contrast, the Ontario Act recognized the right to be heard and to confront. In two Ontario cases, *Re The Ontario Crime Commission, Ex parte Feeley and McDermott*[20] and *Re Public Inquiries Act and Shulman*,[21] the Ontario Court of Appeal has recognized the right to appear and cross-examine specifically on the language of the statute rather than on general principles of right to be heard and to be confronted. In *Ex parte Feeley and McDermott*, the counsel for a witness who was examined *in camera* and two other prospective witnesses appeared before the commission to ask for an opportunity to call witnesses and to cross-examine witnesses called by the counsel of the commission. The commission refused to recognize the right claimed by counsel. The Court of Appeal recognized that the inquiry was purely investigative in character, and that it was a search for facts and the truth. Accordingly, Mr. Justice Schroeder, writing for the majority, accepted that as a general rule there is no absolute right vested in anyone to appear before a Royal Commission. Counsel representing persons who claim to have an interest in proceedings may not appear as of right, but only by leave of the commissioner. Section 5 of the Ontario Public Inquiries Act, 1971 is, however, a unique provision and the right of a "person affected" to question the validity of the commission, jurisdiction of the commissioner or validity of the decision, order, direction or other act of the commissioner must be recognized. Mr. Justice Schroeder argued:[22]

> In the present inquiry, allegations of a very grave character have been made against the applicants, imputing to them the commission of very serious

> crimes. It is true that they are not being tried by the Commissioner, but their alleged misconduct has come under the full glare of publicity, and it is only fair and just that they should be afforded an opportunity to call evidence, to elicit facts by examination and cross-examination of witnesses and thus be enabled to place before the commission of inquiry a complete picture rather than incur the risk of its obtaining only a partial or distorted one. This is a right to which they are, in my view, fairly and reasonably entitled and it should not be denied them. Moreover it is no less important in the public interest that the whole truth rather than half-truths or partial truths should be revealed to the Commissioner.
>
> Any suggestion that the examination and cross-examination of witnesses by counsel for the Commission, and more particularly by counsel for the two political parties, is adequate to elicit all relevant facts concerning the applicants, against whom so much incriminating evidence is being accumulated and widely circulated, fails to carry conviction. It is no improper reflection upon counsel for the two political parties to observe that they may well be more concerned with doing what they deem best calculated to serve their own clients' ends and in so doing with promoting interests perhaps violently opposed to those of the applicants. To impose a dual burden upon these latter counsel might make their position not only embarrassing but intolerable.

In *Re Public Inquiries Act and Shulman*, the Court of Appeal sought to explain the wide scope of the right to be heard and to confront witnesses under s. 5 of the Ontario Act. The right to cross-examination is not to be a limited cross-examination but is to be a cross-examination upon all matters relevant to eliciting truth or accuracy of the allegations or statements made. Similarly, the Court of Appeal stated that any person affected by allegations made before the commission should be accorded the privilege of examination as a witness by his own counsel and should be subject to a right of cross-examination, not only by counsel for the commission but by any person affected by the evidence of that witness. The court emphasized that "counsel for the Commission has a heavy responsibility in these matters and will be the proper person to call witnesses and to examine them in chief where these witnesses are not represented before the Commission by their own counsel".[23]

In this regard, the Ontario Inquiries Act, 1971 is superior to the Federal Inquiries Act in permitting judicial supervision to confine the abuse of power that intrudes into a person's right to be heard and to confront witnesses against him. The amendments to the present Ontario statute, enacted after the two Ontario cases, has further extended this right. Section 5 now reads as follows.

> 5(1) A commission shall accord to any person who satisfies it that he has a substantial and direct interest in the subject matter of its inquiry and opportunity during the inquiry to give evidence and to call and examine or to cross-examine witnesses personally or by his counsel on evidence relevant to his interest.

The Court of Appeal of Ontario in *Re Ontario Crime Commission*[24] had before it an instance of private investigation. In that case, the Commissioner interviewed a prospective witness to the inquiry for the purpose of determining the relevance of the evidence of the witness before being formally called to give evidence at the hearing. It appeared, as well, that any evidence secured on the investigation would not be used at the inquiry and there would be full opportunity for cross-examination of the witness. Counsel for the person affected sought to disqualify the Commissioner, arguing that the practice is analogous to the interview by a judge of a witness. The court stated:

> Counsel for the applicant laid much stress on the statement of the Commissioner that he intentionally kept the examination of Clarke from counsel for an obvious reason. If that purpose was to prevent interference with the prospective witness the concern of the Commissioner was justified by subsequent events when the applicant interviewed or said he interviewed Clarke at night in a car in a deserted parking lot.
>
> Counsel for the applicant compared what occurred with Clarke to a trial Judge interviewing a witness during the course of a trial with counsel for only one party present. This analogy is completely unsound. It has been said time and again, and recently in the decision already mentioned, that the function of a commissioner under the *Public Inquiries Act* is fundamentally different in its essential nature from that of a Judge, an arbitrator or an administrative tribunal which deals with rights between parties. Here there are no parties. The Commissioner's duty is to inquire and to report.

In reaching this conclusion the court affirmed the traditional concept of broad discretion of the commission:

> A Commissioner under the *Public Inquiries Act* is not governed by any specific rules as to the manner in which the inquiry is conducted and must necessarily have the widest discretion in the way in which he conducts the inquiry. While ordinarily we would think it unnecessary and perhaps undesirable to put witnesses under oath when interviewed in a preliminary way to determine the relevancy of their evidence, nevertheless in some types of inquiry, such as this one, there may be considerations which make it desirable in some instances that such witnesses be requested to give their statement under oath. This is a matter entirely in the discretion of the Commissioner conducting the inquiry. It is perhaps unnecessary to add that the Commissioner has no power to compel a witness to answer questions or be sworn on such a preliminary investigation.

The law on evidentiary privilege against disclosure is not now regulated in the federal statute. The Federal Law Reform Commission has, in support of the protection of these interests, argued:

> We think a witness who gives evidence under oath before a commission should have the same safeguards as a witness in a judicial proceeding. The underlying reasons for the evidentiary privilege against disclosure are not restricted to judicial proceedings. If state secrets, the marital relationship, trade secrets and

so on constitute valid reasons for refusing to give testimony in court, we see no reason why this is not equally true of commissions.[25]

Section 11 of the Ontario Act now provides recognition of this privilege. This section directs that an evidence that is inadmissible by reason of privilege under the law of evidence is inadmissible in an inquiry.

The conduct of the inquiry by the Krever Commission provides an interesting occasion for the courts to consider the scope of the Ontario provision. The Krever Commission was established to inquire into various aspects of the delivery of health services in Ontario, and among its mandate was the power to investigate any misconduct by any person coming within or arising from the various health legislations in Ontario. During the inquiry, the Commission has ruled that R.C.M.P. witnesses testifying at the inquiry were required to disclose the names of physicians and hospital employees from whom information had been received without the knowledge and consent of their respective patients. At the time the disclosure to the R.C.M.P. officers was made, the police officers were acting in the course of their duty in the investigation of crime on national security. The issue in this case is whether the privilege against the disclosure of the identity of the informer can be invoked. This question was somewhat complicated by the fact that under the Health Disciplines Act of Ontario and the regulation issued thereunder it is professional misconduct for a physician to give information concerning a patient's condition or any professional services for a patient to any person without the consent of the patient. Further, the Public Hospitals Act of Ontario prohibits, and accordingly, penalizes as offence, any permission being given to any person by the hospital board to remove, inspect or receive information from a medical record.

The Commissioner ruled that the informer privilege does not apply and accordingly required the R.C.M.P. witnesses to disclose the identity of the physicians and hospital employees. The Ontario Court of Appeal, in a 2-1 decision,[26] held that the *policy* behind the Health Discipline Act and the Public Hospital Act is against disclosure of medical information. Since the informer was in breach of a duty embodied in this policy, even where no penal consequence arose, the majority stated that it would be contrary to public policy to recognize the informer privilege asserted in this case. This decision is subject to further consideration by the Supreme Court of Canada which is now holding the matter under advisement.

Judicial Review of the Commission's Report

Section 13 of the Federal Inquiries Act provides as follows:

> No report shall be made against any person until reasonable notice has been given to him of the charge of misconduct alleged against him and he has been allowed full opportunity to be heard in person or by counsel.

Section 5(2) of the Ontario Act states:

> No finding of misconduct on the part of any person shall be made against him in any report of a commission after an inquiry unless that person had reasonable notice of the substance of the misconduct alleged against him and was allowed full opportunity during the inquiry to be heard in person or by counsel.

These two sections give an opportunity to a person to be informed of the charge of misconduct and an opportunity for the person concerned to appear in the proceeding and confront or refute the evidence against him. It is, therefore, an approximation of the right of the accused in a criminal case to be informed of the charge against him and to establish his defence.

Section 13 has not been the subject of much comment, and it is still unclear today what the word "charge" of misconduct means. Mr. Justice Davis, then of the Supreme Court of Canada, commented on s. 13 when he was the commissioner inquiring into the "Bren Machine Gun Contract" in 1939. He stated:

> That a report upon the Inquiry is contemplated by the statute is not open to doubt. But that a finding of misconduct cannot be made against any person, until reasonable notice shall have been given to him of the charge of misconduct alleged against him and he shall have been allowed full opportunity to be heard in person or by counsel, is expressly enacted by sec. 13 of the statute. No charges of misconduct, however, were formulated against any particular person.
>
> Having fully weighed the objections advanced on this ground, as well as the weighty consideration brought to my attention by counsel that the rights of the individuals interested in the contract might become the subject of legal controversy elsewhere, I have come to the conclusion that it is inexpedient to comment upon the evidence in respect to its bearing on the conduct of the individuals concerned.

Mr. Justice Collier, in *Landreville* v. *The Queen (No. 2),*[27] relied on s. 13 of the Act to strike down the Royal Commission report. In that case, counsel for Landreville contended that when the commission reached his decision to assert or allege that Landreville's conduct in giving his evidence before other tribunals amounted to a misconduct or misbehaviour in office, notice of the "charge" of misconduct should have been given and Landreville should have been allowed to call witnesses, if he wished, to answer the so-called charges and to make his defence. The first notice that Landreville received was the publication of the commissioner's report. Mr. Justice Collier stated:[28]

> I agree with the plaintiff that the assertion of gross contempt was a very serious one. The Commissioner said at pp. 94-5:
>
> > The unpleasantness of the matter investigated cannot be allowed to minimize its derogatory character. There was conscious contempt

> before all three tribunals; it may or may not have passed the borders of criminality; but to confuse, to raise doubts by the juxtaposition of contrived and emphatic assertion and nullifying qualifications and reservations, is not to be distinguished in effect from deliberate falsity.

I translate that as a finding of perjury.

Counsel for the defendant maintains the allegations or charges are set out in the Order in Council and letters patent; they are the notice of the charges of misconduct alleged; the impugned conclusions obviously and reasonably arose out of charges set out in the terms of reference.

I do not agree that the matters of gross contempt of the other tribunals can be said to be included, by implication or necessary intendment, in terms of reference.

This was a somewhat unusual Royal Commission. The majority of Royal Commissions seem to be constituted to investigate a particular subject, thing or state of affairs. Rarely do they relate to one person. This Commission was, however, directed to the investigation of one particular person and his dealings with a certain company, its officers, or its shares. The Commissioner was requested to inquire into those dealings and to express an opinion whether, in the course of them, there had been misbehaviour by the plaintiff as a Judge, or whether the plaintiff, by the dealings, had proved himself unfit. I am unable to see how those general terms indicated to the plaintiff there would, or might be, an allegation of gross contempt of certain tribunals amounting to misconduct.

Conclusion

The nature of the function of the Commission of Inquiry, as an investigative and advisory body, deprived of the power to decide a substantive law controversy, has shielded commissions from the supervisory jurisdiction of the courts. The commission is not a judicial or quasi-judicial body; it is, therefore, not amenable to the traditional methods of judicial review. Further, it does not have the personality required to sue or be sued. In *Re B and Commission of Inquiry,*[29] Mr. Justice Addy analyzed various barriers faced by an individual to obtain judicial review of the action or decision of the Commission of Inquiry:

> Apart from special statutory provisions, a board, commission or tribunal, which is not performing a judicial or *quasi*-judicial function, is not itself liable to direct control by the Courts in any way; it is not subject to prohibition or *certiorari* because it is not an inferior board or tribunal over which the superior common law Courts could exercise powers of supervision, and it is not subject to any of the above-mentioned equitable processes because it is not liable to be sued as a party and is therefore not itself amenable before the Courts.
>
> Although there are some isolated decisions to the contrary, the great weight of Canadian jurisprudence follows the long-established view that *certiorari* and prohibition are not alternative remedies to an action for injunction or a declaration. In any event, since a judicial tribunal or board is not a suable

> entity, prohibition or *certiorari* must be used and not a declaratory action (see *Hollinger Bus, supra* and *Credit Foncier Franco-Canadien* v. *Board of Review et al.,* [1940] 1 D.L.R. 182, [1939] 3 W.W.R. 632, 21 C.B.R. 166) unless, of course, there is a special statutory provision to the contrary.
>
> In a case of alleged misuse of power where a public board or commission, such as a labour relations board, is about to exercise or has exercised *quasi*-judicial functions, prohibition or *certiorari* will lie, but where it does not, then, the remedy, if there be one, should be by action. In the latter case, the difficulty, of course, arises immediately as to whether the board is an entity amenable before the Courts in an action. Besides individuals and corporations, which could be always sued at common law, legislation now permits the Crown either directly or represented by the Attorney-General to be sued as of right. It also permits partnerships to be sued and certain boards, commissions and officers where a special statute makes them answerable before the Courts as party defendants. There are, therefore, five different types of entities which may be sued.

This position is consistent with the position taken by Mr. Justice Pratte in *Landreville (No. 1)* v. *The Queen.*[30]

The Supreme Court has impliedly recognized this position. There is, however, an encouraging development in recent years. In *Nicholson* v. *Haldimand-Norfolk Regional Board of Commissioners of Police,*[31] the Supreme Court generalized the duty to act fairly and has made it apply even in cases where the commission is not acting in a judicial or quasi-judicial capacity. The Federal Court of Appeal has followed the lead of the Supreme Court in *Inuit Tapirisat of Canada* v. *The Governor-in-Council.*[32] It can be confidently stated today that in Canada the duty to act fairly does not only flow from the limited concept of the rule of natural justice. In *Martineau No. 2,* the Supreme Court has also recognized that a breach of the duty to act fairly can attract a challenge in the courts by way of *certiorari* although *certiorari* has been traditionally confined to the review of judicial and quasi-judicial actions of tribunals. The Supreme Court has also made a small concession insofar as the commission's coercive powers are concerned. In the *Keable Inquiry* case, Mr. Justice Pigeon stated that although the commission's report will not amount to any judicial or quasi-judicial decision, the coercive powers such as the compulsion of witnesses to testify and produce documents, are strictly judicial acts. Relying on the case of *Cotroni* v. *The Quebec Police Commission,* he affirmed that the validity of a witness' conviction of contempt by the commission is subject to judicial review. Further, the court has held that the interpretation of the mandate, especially where the mandate clashes with constitutional limitations, is subject to judicial review.

In Ontario, the statute clearly recognizes the court's supervisory powers over actions of the Commission of Inquiry. The procedure is by way of stated case. This procedure refers firstly to the notice required to be given to any person against whom a finding of misconduct may be made as provided under s. 5(2) of that Act. A further opportunity for a stated case is recognized under s. 6(1) of the Act which provides as follows:

> 6(1) Where the authority to appoint a commission under this Act or the authority of a commission to do any act or thing proposed to be done or done by the commission in the course of its inquiry is called into question by a person affected, the commission may of its own motion or upon the request of such person state a case in writing to the Divisional Court setting forth the material facts and the grounds upon which the authority to appoint the commission or the authority of the commission to do the act or thing are questioned.

In *Evans* v. *Milton,*[33] the Ontario Court of Appeal considered the scope of judicial review in relation to a coroner's inquest. Mr. Justice Dubin stated:

> Subject to one minor exception which does not arise in this case, it was the view of the majority of the Divisional Court that a coroner's inquest is immune from the supervisory jurisdiction of a superior Court, and, indeed, that the applicants had no status to bring the application. Reid, J. took the opposite view and appears to have held that every step taken and every ruling made in the convening of the inquest are subject to be quashed by judicial review.
>
> With respect, I do not agree with either of those opposite views. In my opinion proceedings before a coroner's inquest are not entirely immune from the supervisory jurisdiction of a superior court. On the other hand, I do not agree that every step taken in the convening of the inquest, or every ruling made during its preliminary stages, or at the inquest itself, are subject to review. What first must be determined is the nature of the complaint made.

The Royal Commission is perhaps a classical example of a non-judicial or quasi-judicial tribunal; it exercises purely administrative and advisory functions. It does not make any decision or order that determines rights and obligations although the decisions or orders it makes may affect the rights and obligations of persons. In the context of the criteria discussed by Mr. Justice Dickson in *The Minister of Natural Revenue* v. *Coopers and Lybrand,*[34] a Royal Commission is not a tribunal whose decision is reviewable under s. 28 of the Federal Court Act. As a purely administrative tribunal, however, the courts have found it necessary to review its actions in other respects. Particularly, the standard of fairness is applied by the court, and statutory limitations, such as s. 13 of the Federal Inquiries Act and s. 5 of the Ontario Inquiries Act, are rigorously enforced.

NOTES

1. J. E. Hodgetts, "Should Canada be de-commissioned? A commoner's view of Royal Commissions" (1964), 70 Queen's Q., at 477-8.

2. Law Reform Commission of Canada; Commissions of Inquiry: a new Act. Working Paper No. 17 (hereafter Working Paper).

3. Courtney, J.C., Canadian Royal Commissions of Inquiry, 1946 to 1962: An investigation of an Executive Instrument of Inquiry (Ann Arbor; University Microfilms, 1964).

4. Inquiries Act, R.S.C. 1970, c. I-13.

5. Public Inquiries Act, 1971, S.O. 1971, c. 49.

6. (1979), 88 D.L.R. (3d) 724 (F.C.T.D.).

7. [1978] 1 S.C.R. 118.

8. [1978] 1 S.C.R. 152.

9. [1979] 1 S.C.R. 218.

10. Public Inquiry Commission Act, R.S.Q. 1964, c. 11.

11. [1914] A.C. 237.

12. See note 4, *supra.*

13. (1974), 6 O.R. (2d) 478.

14. [1979] 2 F.C.R. 159.

15. [1978] 1 S.C.R. 1048.

16. Working Paper, at 35.

17. Gt. Brit: Departmental Committee to Consider the Procedures of Royal Commissions Report, 1910. Cmnd. 5325.

18. [1962] O.R. 872.

19. [1935] S.C.R. 441.

20. See note 18, *supra.*

21. [1967] 2 O.R. 375.

22. *Supra,* note 18, at p. 896.

23. *Supra,* note 21.

24. [1963] 1 O.R. 391.

25. Working Paper at p. 35.

26. *Re Inquiry into Confidentiality of Health Records in Ontario* (1979), 24 O.R. (2d) 545.

27. (1977), 75 D.L.R. (3d) 380.

28. *Ibid.,* at p. 403.

29. (1975), 60 D.L.R. (3d) 339 (F.C.T.D.).

30. [1973] F.C. 1223.

31. [1979] 1 S.C.R. 311.

32. [1979] 1 F.C. 710.

33. (1979), 9 C.P.C. 83 (C.A.).

34. [1979] 1 S.C.R. 495.

20

Recent Developments in the Criminal Law

Glanville Williams

The Criminal Law Act 1977 comes to mind as one of the most important recent statutes for English lawyers, but I fear it holds little instruction for Canadian lawyers. One of the matters it tackled was trespass, about which our criminal law has always been singularly pusillanimous. The Canadian Criminal Code makes it an offence to loiter at night upon the property of another near a dwelling-house (s. 173), and one of the forms of criminal mischief is obstructing the lawful enjoyment of property, whether real or personal (s. 387). These are salutary provisions, and unfortunately they are lacking in English law.

The Law Commission attempted to do something in this area, but a major stumbling-block was the fact that it is now common for workpeople to "sit in" or "work in" by way of protest against closure of the factory or an announcement of redundancies; and it was not thought to be politically possible to do anything about this. In fact, workpeople are rarely prosecuted even for ordinary offences committed in the course of strikes and demonstrations, and it seems extraordinary that the theoretical possibility that a new general law of criminal trespass might be used against discontented workers was enough to foreclose the possibility of it. Even squatters who commit the outrage of moving into another person's house during his temporary absence had to be treated tenderly. So all that the Criminal Law Act 1977 gives us are (1) an offence of using or threatening violence to gain entry to a building that is actually occupied at the time (an offence that does little more than duplicate the law of assault), (2) an offence by a person who is trespassing on residential premises in failing to leave on request, and (3) an offence of trespass on a foreign embassy.

The Act does not apply if squatters enter a dwelling when it is vacant because it is for sale or to let; they commit no offence, even in failing to leave upon request, apart of course from an offence of criminal damage if they damage the building. On the other hand the offence of using violence to gain entry is applied to a displaced owner who tries to reoccupy his factory, warehouse, University office or other premises; there is an exception for the displaced residential occupier, but not for the owner of a house that is illegally occupied after he has put it up for sale. If the owner uses force to re-enter in the latter type of case, he commits an offence under the Act. All in all, this part of the Act is of more interest as a social document evidencing the nervelessness of government in the face of social unrest and political sympathy for illegal action than as a rational piece of legislation.

Another part of the Act relates to conspiracy. The Law Commission is engaged on the entirely creditable but uphill task of producing a criminal code. The first part of its programme involves the abolition of common law offences, and the most difficult to deal with is conspiracy having non-criminal objects. The Canadian Code, if you will allow me to say so, showed less than full valour on this point, because while its general object is to supersede the common law offences, it preserves conspiracies to effect an unlawful purpose or a lawful purpose by unlawful means (s. 423(2)). The Law Commission rightly decided to do a proper job, so the Criminal Law Act 1977 sweeps away all non-criminal objects of conspiracy. This is excellent, even though two exceptions had to be made for the time being. The first exception is conspiracy to defraud, which is left standing pending the enactment of such new offences of fraud as may be necessary to enable conspiracy to defraud to be abolished. Secondly, the Act saves conspiracies to corrupt public morals or outrage public decency; but this saving was probably unnecessary, since these acts are probably offences for individuals. Anyway, the law of obscenity is under review and will, one hopes, shortly be put on a statutory footing.

In other respects, the conspiracy sections of the Act are for the most part unfortunate. The Bill drafted by the Law Commission was not well done, and the House of Lords in trying to improve part of it during its passage through Parliament did some further damage. In consequence, serious problems are now capable of arising in the law of conspiracy.

Another major confusion has been caused in the law of inchoate offences by the notion that one cannot in law attempt or conspire to do the impossible. Before 1975 this notion was given a fairly limited application: at any rate, no one doubted that one could attempt to steal from an empty pocket. But in that year, in *R.* v. *Roger Smith* (otherwise called *Haughton* v. *Smith*),[1] the House of Lords gave its approval to a wider interpretation of the rule. The facts of the case were that the defendant thought he was receiving stolen goods, but unknown to him the goods had been recovered by the police, who were merely setting a trap for him, so that in law the goods were no longer stolen. The House held that the defendant was not guilty of attempting to handle stolen goods, since, in their lordships' view, what the defendant was aiming to do was not a crime. The case stands for the principle that there can be no attempt when an essential circumstance of the crime is lacking.

Two reasons were advanced. One was that to hold the defendant guilty "would be for the courts to manufacture a new criminal offence not authorised by the legislature". This remark is certainly true where the defendant attempts an imaginary crime, that is to say where what he thinks to be a crime is not a crime on the books.[2] But their lordships applied the proposition even to cases of circumstantial impossibility, where there is such a crime on the books (here, handling stolen goods), and the defendant would have committed it had the facts been as he believed them to be, but an ingredient of the crime is missing in the particular case. It does not seem apt in these circumstances to say that the punishment of an attempt to commit the crime would be to manufacture a new criminal offence: the problem relates simply to the proper limits of the law of attempt.

The second reason for the decision was that the argument for the prosecution was "really an attempt to punish people for their guilty intention," without an *actus reus.* This misunderstands the notion of an *actus reus* in the law of attempt, which does not require an intrinsically unlawful act but requires only a proximate act of attempt. A man who offers his wife a glass of sherry laced with rat poison commits an attempt to murder, but he is not guilty of any other illegality, whether criminal or civil. In adjudicating upon an attempt there is absolutely no occasion to enquire whether the act is unlawful apart from the law of attempt.

Despite the unpersuasiveness of the reasons advanced, *Roger Smith* must be accepted as an authoritative pronouncement in England, and the House of Lords has shown no disposition to reconsider it. In consequence of that decision, a Divisional Court has now held that there can be no attempt to steal from an empty pocket, or from any other place that lacks the thing that the defendant was attempting to steal.[3]

In *Nock,*[4] the House of Lords extended the same rule to conspiracy at common law. One can no more conspire to do the impossible than attempt to do it. The case arose under the Misuse of Drugs Act, which makes it an offence to produce a controlled drug (that is, a drug of addiction). The defendants were charged with conspiring to produce a controlled drug of Class A, namely cocaine. In fact, all that they had agreed to do was to obtain cocaine by separating it from other substances contained in a certain powder, and they were mistaken in thinking that they could obtain cocaine in this way. The House therefore held that the charge of conspiracy failed. Apart from other objections to this remarkable decision, it might have been thought that the only impossibility in *Nock* was one of the means used, and the House of Lords had recognised in *Roger Smith* that an attempt was punishable notwithstanding that it was impossible by the particular means chosen. The same should have been true for conspiracy.

There is a modern proverb: today we climb out of the hole we made yesterday. The trouble is that one is not always so immaculate on climbing out as one was in the first place. Lord Scarman in *Nock* offered us a messy escape tunnel. He expressed the opinion that the practical effect of the decision in *Nock* in relation to conspiracy (and also in relation to attempt) can be avoided if the charge is drawn with suitable width and if it can be inferred from the evidence that the defendants had a general intent to commit the crime in question which was not confined to some specific and inapt means that were intended to be used in the first place. We have to distinguish between men who agree to produce cocaine by means that are in fact inapt, and men who agree to go into business of producing cocaine and who begin by using means that are in fact inapt. It is a very fine distinction, so fine that it would seem to be undesirable as the basis of the law; but English law is now saddled with it. Lord Scarman's well-meaning effort to improve matters has the regrettable effect of putting the law of attempt into still more doubt, because it had previously been regarded as perfectly clear that impossibility of means was no defence to a charge of attempt. In *Roger Smith,* Lords Hailsham and Reid put the case of a burglar attempting to force a window with a jemmy that was not good enough for the job: they expressed the opinion that he would be guilty of attempted burglary. But suppose that such a burglar, finding the impossibility of his task, gives up and is arrested on the way home. If Lord Scarman's opinion is accepted, it would seem that the would-be burglar is not guilty of an attempt, because by going home he has demonstrated that he had no intention to burgle beyond his intention to tackle a specific window with insufficient means.[5]

The Canadian Code, in its definition of attempt (s. 4), wisely avoids the problem by providing that one can attempt the impossible, and accordingly it is held that there can be a conviction of attempting to steal "a sum of money" from a place where there was no money.[6] Presumably the courts will have no difficulty in applying the same rule to conspiracy and incitement. A siren voice has recently been heard urging the courts to disregard the express provision in s. 4, and to introduce an impossibility rule into the law of attempt by supposed deduction from the proximity rule: if the crime in view is impossible, the alleged act of attempt cannot be proximate.[7] I regard this argument as fallacious, and its conclusion as pernicious.[8]

On the construction of statutes in general I must mention (again, I am sorry to say, with disapprobation) the decision of the House of Lords in *Cozens* v. *Brutus.*[9] It was there held that the meaning of ordinary words in a statute is a question of fact for the jury or magistrates as triers of fact. *Cozens* v. *Brutus* was a decision on appeal from a magistrates' court (via the Divisional Court). In this application the decision has taken virtually no effect, because the appellate courts habitually exercise tight control over magistrates, and the Divisional Court has continued to do so notwithstanding *Cozens* v. *Brutus.* The decision has also been very much a *brutum fulmen* in relation to jury trials. For example, the Court of Appeal has held that it is part of the judicial function to rule upon the meaning of the words "reckless,"[10] "retention",[11] "assist"[12] and "produce"[13] in a statute. These are certainly important words in legal matters, but they are not exclusively legal words; yet the jury were not given a free hand to interpret them, as *Cozens* v. *Brutus* would seem to require.

There is sound historical tradition to support these defiant decisions. In the nineteenth century the judges peremptorily told juries how they were to understand words in statutes. The interpretation of statutory words often involves questions of policy, as well as a knowledge of the framework of the statute, of previous legislation and the common law, and of rulings upon the meaning of similar words in other statutes. It should be obvious that the interpretation of the law is properly a function of the judge, except within narrow limits when a question of degree is involved and the facts are borderline. Putting the decision in the hands of the judge not only makes it more likely that the intention of the legislature will be carried out but is the only way to ensure that the law is applied consistently. Besides, if judges go wrong their decisions can be criticised, and they can perhaps be persuaded to change their minds in future, or aberrant decisions can be set right by statute. These corrective mechanisms do not apply to jury verdicts, which settle nothing beyond the issue between the parties. The opinions delivered in *Cozens* v. *Brutus* show no awareness of these important considerations.

The Theft Act 1968 can hardly be called recent, but some of the decisions under it are worth recording. The Act was substantially the product of the Criminal Law Revision Committee (CLRC). It follows your Code in shifting the basis of theft from a taking of property, as at common law, to what you call a conversion. Our Act prefers the term "appropriation," on the ground that this is more likely to be intelligible to the layman than the word "conversion". (The commonest form of appropriation is a taking, but we did not feel a need to refer to this expressly.)

There is one considerable difference between our two approaches. Whereas you have wisely introduced the notion of a temporary conversion as theft, our Act follows the common law in generally requiring an intent to deprive the owner permanently. I am bound to add, however, *à propos* Canadian law, that at one time your courts seemed to be construing the notion of temporary conversion out of existence. In a series of cases the courts clutched at every argument suggested by the defence in order to hold that it was not theft to make off with a vehicle, or to remove an article of furniture from a hotel or beer parlour, where the defendant assured the police, after being found out, that he was on the point of coming back with the property.[14] In 1969 the tide turned, and there are now at least three reported cases in which convictions have been upheld on appeal for takings alleged by the defendant to have been with temporary intent;[15] but there is still a judicial tendency to stress that people who carry off hotel furniture commit mere peccadillos for which they ought not to be prosecuted.

I have made particular mention of this matter because it bears on my next topic. In England, the problem on impossible attempts has been compounded by a mess that the courts have now made of the notion of intention in relation to theft and attempted theft. I am sorry that this lecture appears to be so largely a cautionary tale, but it will have done good if it persuades you to avoid following in the footsteps of the English judges in some of these areas.

The trouble originated with *Easom.*[16] There had been thefts in a cinema, and in order to catch the offender, or offenders, a policewoman occupied a seat with her handbag on the floor but attached to her wrist by a thread. History does not record how many performances she witnessed without success, but on the occasion in question she happened to cast her line in the right place and caught a fish. The defendant, sitting behind her, took up her handbag, looked through it, decided that there was nothing inside worth stealing, and replaced it. He was convicted of theft of the handbag and its contents; but the conviction was quashed on appeal, on the ground that the defendant had no fixed intention to steal any of the articles specified in the indictment. Fingering articles to see if they were worth stealing was not theft. Nor was the defendant guilty of an attempt to steal, for the same reason—that he lacked a present intent to steal. The Court of Appeal reaffirmed this rule in the later case of *R.* v. *Husseyn,*[17] Lord Scarman making a remark of which he must have repented many times since, that "it cannot be said that one who has it in mind to steal only if what he finds is worth stealing has a present intention to steal".

Canadian courts would not be bound to reach the same result on facts like *R.* v. *Easom,* if only because it would be open to them to hold, if they are so inclined, that theft is committed on such facts by temporary conversion. The thief who takes up an article to see if it is worth stealing can well be said to have converted or appropriated it, just as a person who goes off with a chair from a beer parlour does, because it will be only by his own grace that he will give it back. But slightly altered facts would debar this line of approach. Suppose that a would-be thief is groping in a bureau. He does not touch any article that is attractive to him. It would be difficult to say that he has converted anything to his own use. However, the problem on attempted theft would remain.

The rot was not long in spreading to the law of burglary, which requires one of certain intents to be present, including an intent to steal. Bill Sikes is discovered leaving a house, having found nothing inside worth stealing, but he entered it hoping to find money or something else worth his attention. Or he is actually found in the house, but it cannot be proved that there is anything there that he would have taken. On two occasions Crown Court judges ruled that such a person could not be convicted of burglary: an intent to steal cannot be proved in the absence of proof that articles were inside the building that the defendant would have stolen. These rulings came to be known as "the burglar's charter". Fortunately, the particular point was largely corrected by subsequent decisions of the Court of Appeal, *R.* v. *Walkington*[18] and *Re Attorney-General's References, Nos. 1 and 2 of 1979.*[19] These cases make it clear that the dictum in *Husseyn* was wrong. As it was put in *Walkington,* "if the jury . . . are satisfied that at the moment of entering he intended to steal anything in the building . . . the fact that there was nothing in the building worth his while to steal seems to us to be immaterial. He nevertheless had an intent to steal." This not only clarifies the notion of intent to steal in burglary but also shows that the impossibility rule (the empty pocket rule) does not apply to burglary; it applies only to inchoate offences in the usual sense of that expression. Nevertheless, we are left with our problem on attempted theft. If a thief looks into a receptacle (such as a pocket or bureau) hoping to find a valuable like money, then if there is such a valuable there the courts have now settled that the thief can be convicted of attempting to steal "some or all of the contents of the pocket/bureau" (or whatever it may be).[20] But if the receptacle contained nothing that the thief wanted, the two cases of *Easom* and *Roger Smith* impale the prosecutor on a two-pronged fork. If the charge is of an attempt to steal things that the thief wanted but were not there, the charge can be met by the "empty pocket" principle of *Roger Smith* as subsequently interpreted by the courts, the reason being the rule of law that one cannot attempt an impossible end. Then if the prosecutor charges an attempt to steal things that were there, which the thief did not want, he can be met by the principle of *Easom*, that theft is not committed by fingering articles that the would-be thief immediately decides he does not want, because in such case there is no intent to deprive the owner permanently.[21] Canadian lawyers can be thankful that the percipience of the framers of their Criminal Code have saved them from both prongs of the fork.

Further problems have arisen with regard to the requirement of the law of theft that is worded in the Canadian Code as "fraudulently and without colour of right". This was the common law, and we made what we thought was little more than a verbal change in the Theft Act 1968 by substituting the adverb "dishonestly" for the whole phrase, again on the ground that this would be more intelligible to a jury and lay magistrates. The word "fraudulently" is certainly inapt, since your courts hold, as ours did before the Theft Act, that a robbery involves a fraudulent taking, even though the robber makes a brusque demand and does not employ fraud in the ordinary sense. We copied the word "dishonestly" from the ALI Model Penal Code.

Trouble started when the Court of Appeal, for once applying the rule in *Cozens* v. *Brutus,* held that the jury were to be left at large in deciding what was honest and what was not. Leaving the whole question to the jury might not matter if our society were culturally homogenous, with known and shared values, as it once very largely was. But the object of the law of theft is to protect property rights, and disrespect for these rights is now widespread. One contributory factor is the replacement of the small shop, with its known proprietor, by an anonymous department store or supermarket. Other causes that are frequently pointed to are the anonymity of town life, the materialism of our outlook, the boredom of repetitive jobs, the breakdown of family controls, and so on. Whatever the reasons, all observers agree upon the very large scale of stealing from shops, stealing from employers by employees, and fraud perpetrated upon customers by employees. "Fiddling" is tolerated by many employers, provided that it does not exceed some ill-defined limit; and employers may even encourage fiddles when they are at the expense of customers, since this is a way of increasing employees' remuneration without cost to the employers. For the employee, illicit remuneration has the advantage of being untaxed. Fiddling also brings non-material rewards: it is a pleasant departure from routine, a game of chance against the risk of detection, all the better since the consequences of detection are now rarely serious. So highly do some workers value the practice that a change in the system of work threatening to interfere with it, or an attempt by employers to prosecute offenders, is met by strikes. Notable examples were the strike at Heathrow Airport when baggage loaders were arrested for pilferage in 1973, and the strike of warehousemen at Ipswich docks when the police enquired into the theft of goods in 1974. Strikes have also followed dismissals for pilfering. London Transport have been prevented by union resistance from making ticket collectors account honestly for excess fares; the collectors' defalcations amount to £2½ million a year.

In this social atmosphere one views with foreboding the decision of the Court of Appeal in *Feely* that the question of dishonesty is entirely one for a jury selected more or less at random. Are the jury allowed to express their own moral system, whatever it may be, or alternatively are they allowed to endorse the defendant's moral system which in his view justifies the taking of other people's property? Can the jury say that it is all right to "rip off" banks, insurance companies, multinationals, betting shops, and anyone who is regarded as "filthy rich"? The courts may put some limit on *Feely,* but they are not at present showing any inclination to do so.

Even Canadian courts seem to be not entirely free from peril in this part of the law. In *R.* v. *Hemmerly*[22] the defendant, claiming payment for drugs illegally supplied, held up the other party at gunpoint in order to get the money. On his trial for robbery, he conceded that he knew he had no legal right to the money, but said he had a moral right. The trial judge charged the jury that if Hemmerly honestly believed that he had an honest claim to the money and that he had the right to enforce payment in the way he did, he should be acquitted. The jury convicted. An appeal to the Ontario Court of Appeal was dismissed, and Martin J.A. said that the defendant was acting fraudulently in the sense of dishonestly in the circumstances there disclosed. The court did not consider the question whether the trial judge acted properly in leaving the question to the jury in such wide terms. It seems regrettable that no reference was made to the earlier pronouncement of the Quebec Court of Appeal in *Bogner,*[23] where Belanger J.A., after quoting the English case of *R.* v. *Williams,*[24] concluded that "it seems that the term 'fraudulently' refers to the deliberate taking of the thing by the accused, knowing that it does not belong to him, with full knowledge of a state of facts that does not give him the right to take it." This may be slightly too narrow: for example, a person who takes an article believing that the owner would give his consent if asked should not be held to take it fraudulently and without colour of right. But it seems to me that the detailed definition of what is meant by this phrase in particular circumstances should be the function of the judge, not of the jury. The defendant should bear an evidential burden of showing honesty, and if the facts of the case do not indicate anything that a reasonable jury could find as honest conduct, the judge should be allowed to withdraw the issue of honesty from the jury, leaving the jury to decide the case on other issues. In adjudicating the issue of honesty (or of acting "fraudulently") the judge should proceed primarily on the basis that honesty involves a belief in legal right, with belief in non-legal right allowed only in narrowly defined circumstances, where an honest person in the traditional sense would have acted as the defendant did.

In providing the definition of theft that is now in the Theft Act, the Criminal Law Revision Committee decided by a majority not to incorporate a requirement that the appropriation should be wrongful or illegal. I notice that there is no express requirement to this effect in the Canadian Code either, but it is perhaps implied there by virtue of the word "fraudulently". The reason why the CLRC was against the inclusion of "wrongfully" was that the committee did not want to incorporate the complexities of the civil law into the definition of theft. I was a member of the committee, but I thought, and still think, that the decision was wrong. Theft being an offence against property, and property being a concept of the civil law, it is inevitable that questions of civil law should to some extent arise in connection with theft. Moreover, it would be highly unsatisfactory if an act adjudged perfectly legal by the civil courts were held to amount to theft by the criminal courts. However, this is the way the cases are going. In *R.* v. *Gilks,*[25] the defendant backed a horse called "Fighting Scot," and won a small amount; in paying out, the bookmaker thought that Gilks had won a much larger sum on another horse, "Fighting Taffy." Gilks realised the mistake when he received the money, but nevertheless kept it. By our law, bookmakers cannot recover back sums paid by mistake, so if Gilks had been a lawyer he could have said to the bookmaker: "I see you have paid me too much, but in law you cannot get it back and I propose to stand on my civil rights." In fact he did not know the law, but he kept the money all the same because, he said, he regarded bookmakers as fair game. On a prosecution for theft, the deputy chairman in effect left it to the jury to decide whether Gilks thought he was acting honestly, which on its face would allow the defendant to construct an idiosyncratic moral system. The jury convicted, and the conviction was upheld on appeal. Putting aside the social objections to leaving the question to the jury in the terms used by the judge (which were not disapproved by the Court of Appeal), no one seemed to notice that Gilks was being convicted for doing something that he had a legal right to do, purely on the basis of subjective dishonesty. Can one be guilty of a consummated crime merely because one thinks one is committing a crime, when in fact what one does is legal? English courts hold that not even an inchoate crime can be committed in these circumstances; I believe that their opinion is unfortunate, but certainly there is good reason for saying that a charge of consummated crime should not lie merely because the defendant believes that he is committing it.

We have experienced both technical and political difficulties in respect of obtaining services by false pretences—or, as we now say in England, by deception. The Canadian Code lacks any general provision on the subject, though s. 320(1) is wide enough to cover the hiring of a car by fraud, and additionally it contains an offence of obtaining the execution of a valuable security by fraud and obtaining food and lodging by fraud. Our chief difficulty in England is that neither theft nor obtaining by deception covers a temporary obtaining. The cases I have just mentioned are the major ones needing to be dealt with, but certain lesser frauds are perpetrated from time to time: for example, fraud used to obtain the repair of an article, the hire of a lecture hall or taxi, entry to a theatre or a ride on a public conveyance. Some of these you presumably cover by provincial legislation.

After a bad start in the Theft Act 1968, and a good deal of subsequent debate, we now have a fairly comprehensive statute on the subject: the Theft Act 1978. This makes it an offence to use deception whereby another person is induced to do an act or to cause an act to be done, on the understanding that the benefit has been or will be paid for. The offence covers the hiring of a car or lecture hall, signing in to a hotel, getting a meal at a restaurant, and even obtaining a sexual service from a prostitute, provided that deception is used.

Another useful section of the Act makes it an offence for a person who obtains goods or services, knowing that payment on the spot is expected, to make off without paying. This takes care of the motorist who makes off with a tankful of petrol and the diner who slips out of the restaurant, where it cannot be proved that the offender had a fraudulent intent before obtaining the goods or service. Section 322 of the Canadian Code does not adequately deal with this behaviour.

Since this survey has been largely critical of the English courts and legislation, I have set myself to find some useful advance we have made that I can commend to you. One relates to the occasions when a judge can withdraw a charge from the jury. I notice that Canadian judges still act on the principle that the judge must leave the case to the jury if the charge is supported by some of the prosecution witnesses whom a reasonable jury, properly instructed, might believe. The judge is supposed to leave out of account the fact that the prosecution witnesses are not agreed among themselves and that the evidence as a whole is insufficient to convince a reasonable jury. Lately, the English courts have been applying a better principle derived from the statutory powers of the Court of Appeal. That court may allow an appeal if the conviction is unsafe or unsatisfactory,[26] and in general it is now accepted that the judge may anticipate matters by withdrawing the case from the jury if the evidence is such that a conviction would be unsafe or unsatisfactory. This is an excellent change, but unfortunately there are still some doubts and possible qualifications in respect of the new rule.

As I say, I am sorry that this report on what has been happening in the old country offers more by way of warning than by way of example: but even warnings, if duly attended to, can be of value.

NOTES

1. [1975] A.C. 476.

2. Or where the defendant is charged with attempting to commit a specified crime and the achievement of his object could not have amounted to that crime (as distinct from some other crime) even on the facts as he believed them to be. An interesting illustration is *R.* v. *Burgess* (1976), 33 C.C.C. (2d) 126. This, like the imaginary crime cases, is not properly called a case of impossibility; it relates simply to the limitations of the substantive offences.

3. *Partington* v. *Williams* (1975), 62 Cr. App. R. 220.

4. [1978] A.C. 979.

5. For a further discussion of methods suggested by English judges for escaping from the difficulty that they have created see (1979), 129 New Law Journal 1167.

6. *R.* v. *Gagnon* (1975), 24 C.C.C. (2d) 339.

7. Alan D. Gold, "To Dream the Impossible Dream" (1979), 21 Crim. L.Q. 218.

8. I have written a reply to Mr. Gold's article, which is due to appear shortly in the same Quarterly.

9. [1973] A.C. 854.

10. *R.* v. *Briggs,* [1977] 1 W.L.R. 605, [1977] 1 All E.R. 475.

11. *R.* v. *Pitchley* (1972), 57 Cr. App. R. 30.

12. *R.* v. *Vickers,* [1975] 1 W.L.R. 811, [1975] 2 All E.R. 945.

13. *D.P.P.* v. *Nock,* [1978] A.C., at 984E.

14. *R.* v. *Wilkins,* [1964] 2 O.R. 365, 44 C.R. 375, [1965] 2 C.C.C. 189; *R.* v. *Kerr* (1965), 47 C.R. 268, 52 W.W.R. 176, [1965] 4 C.C.C. 37; *McCormick* v. *The Queen* (1968), 3 C.R.N.S. 150, [1969] 4 C.C.C. 154.

15. *R.* v. *Heminger and Hornigold,* [1969] 3 C.C.C. 201; *Paris* (1971), 15 C.R.N.S. 111; *Bogner* (1975), 33 C.R.N.S. 348.

16. [1971] 2 Q.B. 315.

17. (1977), 67 Cr. App. R. 131.

18. [1979] 1 W.L.R. 1169, [1979] 2 All E.R. 716.

19. [1979] 3 W.L.R. 577, [1979] 3 All E.R. 143.

20. *Ibid.*

21. There is reason to suppose that judges do not appreciate the strength of this dilemma. See (1979), 129 New Law Journal 1167.

22. (1976), 30 C.C.C. (2d) 141 (Ont. C.A.).

23. (1975), 33 C.R.N.S. 348.

24. [1953] 1 Q.B. 660.

25. [1972] 1 W.L.R. 1341, [1972] 3 All E.R. 280.

26. The analogous principle in the Canadian Code s. 613(1)(a) is that an appeal against conviction may be allowed if ". . . on any other ground there was a miscarriage of justice".

Appendix

CANADIAN INSTITUTE FOR ADVANCED LEGAL STUDIES

Honorary Patrons

The Right Honourable Bora Laskin, P.C.
The Honourable Paul Martin, P.C., Q.C.
The Honourable John V. Clyne, C.C.
The Right Honourable Lord Elwyn-Jones C.H.

Governors

Professor Trevor Anderson
Professor Harry Arthurs
* The Honourable Douglas H. Carruthers
Professor Gisèle Côté-Harper
* The Honourable Edward M. Culliton
* The Honourable Jules Deschênes
* The Honourable Willard Z. Estey
* The Honourable Gregory T. Evans
Professor F. Murray Fraser
Donald M. Gillis, Q.C.
D. Michael M. Goldie, Q.C.
Graeme T. Haig, Q.C.
Professor Frank Iacobucci
Kenneth Jarvis, Q.C.
Raynold Langlois, Q.C.
* The Honourable William A. McGillivray
Dr. Derek Mendes da Costa, Q.C.
* The Honourable Nathaniel T. Nemetz
Her Honour Sandra E. Oxner
Richard B. Peterson
The Honourable Lawrence A. Poitras
Joseph H. Potts, Q.C.
The Honourable David C. Prowse
John J. Robinette, Q.C.
William L. M. Somerville, Q.C.
* Jacques Viau, O.C., Q.C.

Officers

The Honourable Douglas H. Carruthers	*President*
The Honourable Willard Z. Estey	*Vice-President*
The Honourable Gregory T. Evans	*Vice-President*
Richard B. Peterson	*Secretary-Treasurer*

Cambridge Committee

The Honourable Douglas H. Carruthers
Professor F. Murray Fraser
Dr. Derek Mendes da Costa, Q.C.
Phyllis H. Ortved
Richard B. Peterson

* *Executive Committee*